# Ethan Allen
*FRONTIER REBEL*

# Ethan Allen

*FRONTIER REBEL*

Charles A. Jellison

SYRACUSE UNIVERSITY PRESS

TO MY MOTHER
*an inspiration then and now*

CHARLES A. JELLISON is Professor of History at the University of New Hampshire. He holds B.A. and M.A. degrees from Stanford University, and a Ph.D. degree from the University of Virginia. Professor Jellison is the author of *Fessenden of Maine: Civil War Senator,* and a contributor to the *Encyclopaedia Britannica* and to various historical journals.

# Preface

SOMEONE whose name I cannot recall once remarked in praise of biography that by reading of greatness in others we tend to inspire greatness in ourselves. It would be nice if this were true, but I doubt that it is. At least, I have never known anyone who was made more virtuous by reading Butler's *Lives of the Saints,* or heroic by Freeman's *Lee.* I do believe, though, that biography does something for us that is almost as important: It reminds us that greatness, so lacking in ourselves, is not totally foreign to our kind, and because this says something for the potential of man, it is in a way very reassuring. Even though few oysters are given the pearl, the lives of all oysters everywhere are exalted because such a thing is possible.

On the turbulent American frontier of the late eighteenth century, where human greatness was certainly no stranger, few men had a fuller share in events than Ethan Allen. Soldier, politician, publicist, land speculator, and aspiring traitor, he was truly a host in himself, who, because he refused to be dispirited or put down, left his indelible mark upon his own time and times to follow. Controversial then and now, a demigod to some and to others an unconscionable thug, he is generally conceded to have played, for fair or for foul, a dominant role in the affairs of early Vermont and the American Republic. It is, in fact, very probable that without him Vermont would never have come into being, or, once under way, could not have survived its early years of crisis. It may also be true that by capturing Fort Ticonderoga and securing control over the Champlain waterways during the early days of the Revolution, he saved the new nation from being stillborn.

Several biographies have been written about this towering, tempestuous man. However, all are highly fanciful and reverential (or in a few cases rancorous) to the point of being unworthy of scholarly notice—with one notable exception: a commendable but brief study done in the late 1920's by John Pell, who through careful research and sound judgment, management to rescue Ethan Allen from the limbo of folklore to which he had been assigned by generations of partisans and popularizers. Now, more than forty years later, it has been my purpose in writing this biography to carry on where John Pell left off, and, by making use of materials that have been uncovered and thinking that has been done since his time, to present a fuller and perhaps more penetrating account of an uncommonly important and colorful figure from the pantheon of early American heroes. If I have succeeded, it is to no small extent due to the help I have received from many people and institutions during the nearly four years this book has been in preparation. To mention but a few: Mrs. Jane Lape of the Fort Ticonderoga Museum; Professor T. D. S. Bassett, Curator of the Wilbur Collection, University of Vermont; Director Charles Morrissey and Curator Walter Hubbard of the Vermont Historical Society in Montpelier; and, for great patience and good humor in typing the manuscript, Miss Gladys Pease and Mrs. Janet Snow of Durham, New Hampshire. Special thanks must go to my good friends and colleagues, Professors Robert Gilmore and Donald Murray of the University of New Hampshire, both of whom read the manuscript and offered helpful suggestions. I am also indebted to the Central University Research Fund of the University of New Hampshire for two separate grants given me to support the research and writing that went into what I hope is a fair and interesting appraisal of a great man. Most of all, I am grateful to my wife Phyllis, my children, Jody, Tom, and Sally, and my faithful dog Trumpet, without whose happy intrusions this book would have been completed two years earlier.

CHARLES A. JELLISON

*Durham, New Hampshire*
*Summer, 1969*

# Contents

Preface   vii

I   Apprenticeship in Litchfield County   1

II   Trouble on the Grants   18

III   Yankees *vs*. Yorkers   39

IV   A Posture of Defiance   61

V   The Enforcer   84

VI   A Fortress Falls   102

VII   On to Canada!   121

VIII   "A Day of Trouble, if Not Rebuke"   143

IX   Captivity!   157

X   Return of the Hero   177

XI   Courtship with Congress   208

XII   Flirting with Treason   230

XIII   The Haldimand Affair   252

XIV   Vermont Stands Alone   275

XV   *The Oracles of Reason*   299

XVI   Emeritus   314

Notes on Sources   335

Index   351

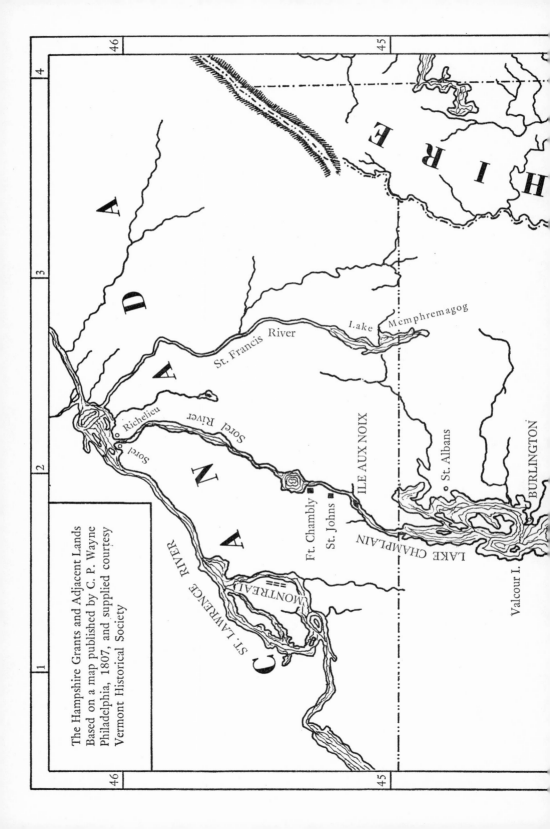

The Hampshire Grants and Adjacent Lands
Based on a map published by C. P. Wayne
Philadelphia, 1807, and supplied courtesy
Vermont Historical Society

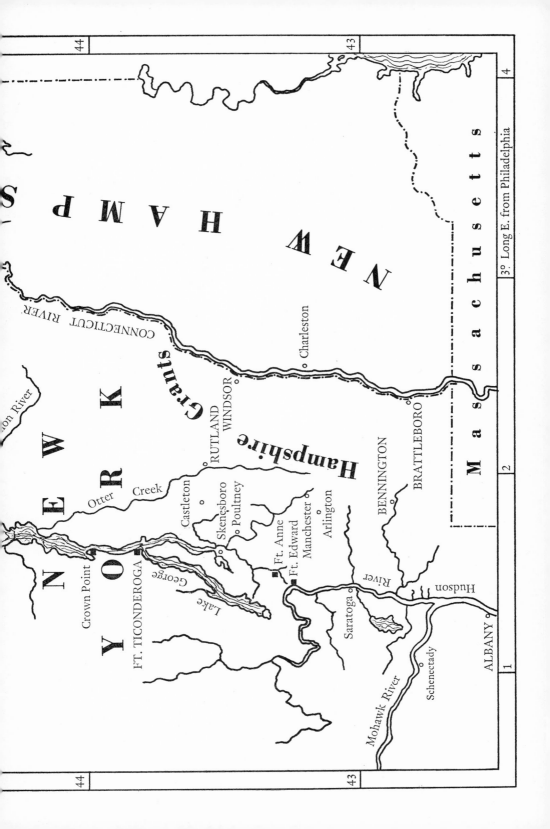

# Ethan Allen
*FRONTIER REBEL*

. . . and the elements
So mixed in him, that Nature might stand up
And say to all the world, "This was a man!"

# I. Apprenticeship
# in Litchfield County

NEW ENGLAND abounds in people named Allen, Allein, Allyn, Alleyn, Alain, and even Ailin. Their numbers are legion, and most of them, if it occurred to them that there might be some reason for doing so, could trace their ancestry back to three brothers, Samuel, Thomas, and Matthew, who as young men set out together from Braintree, England, and arrived in the New World in 1632—"the year of the hunger when many suffered and saw no hope in the Eye of Reason . . . and the Crusts of my Father's Table would have been welcome unto me."

The brothers Allen (or Allyn, for they themselves could never quite agree on a common spelling) settled in Newtowne in the Massachusetts Bay Colony, and there they lived and worked the land for better than three years. In the spring of 1636, however, they chose to follow the lead of their beloved pastor, Thomas Hooker, and, together with a goodly number of their Newtowne neighbors, migrated inland to make a new start in the sparsely settled frontier areas of Connecticut—perhaps because, like Hooker, they had become intolerably chafed by the political narrowness of life in the Bay Colony, or, more likely, because they felt the lure of the land. Already there were mounting population pressures being felt in and around Boston. Land, even of the most marginal sort, was at a premium. Grazing areas especially were becoming critically scarce as the outlying towns continued to crowd in on Boston and one another. But reports had it that a hundred miles or so to the southwest, things were different. There, in the valley of the great Connecticut River, lay endless stretches of virgin land, unsettled and unclaimed—an empire of opportunity to be had virtually for the taking. Land, bountiful and beckoning! In a new world of infinite promise, here was the greatest enticement of all. For generations to come it would stir the souls of American yeomen and keep them on the move, in search of something more and better.

1

It was the first of many such moves for a long and fruitful line of Allens who would spend the next century and a half on the go, moving restlessly from here to there, as if drawn by some secret compulsion to a point just beyond the next horizon where battle might be joined once more with the wilderness. Like the ancient Hebrews, the House of Allen would wander long in the wilderness, searching always for the shores of a new Jordan, and not until at long last the wilderness itself had receded beyond their reach would they come to rest. Through it all many would die in infancy or childhood, sacrificial offerings to the early frontier, lamented and left behind in scattered graves. But many more would live to make their mark upon the land, and not the least of these was the first-born of Joseph and Mary Allen. They called him Ethan, a Hebrew name meaning strong.

By the standards of the day Joseph Allen was reasonably well-to-do. Through inheritance and hard work he had managed while still in his twenties to acquire a large and prosperous farm in the little town of Litchfield, situated near the western frontier of Connecticut. Here in the early spring of 1736, Joseph brought his young bride, the former Mary Baker of nearby Roxbury, and here in a small, gambrel-roof house a mile from the center of town, Ethan Allen was born in January of the following year.*

Virtually nothing is known about Ethan's early years, but they must certainly have been a time of great hardship and danger. When Ethan was barely two, his father sold the farm and moved his family to Cornwall, a brand new township a dozen miles to the northwest of Litchfield. Cornwall was at this time the crudest of frontier communities, a lonely, isolated, desperate little place, overrun with wolves and rattlesnakes, and frequently harassed by marauding Indians. "It was miles distant from any old settled town," one of the original settlers would recall many years later. "The people were scarcely able at first to raise provisions for their own families. . . . So great was the expanse, fatigue, and hardship that I endured for the first three years, that I would not suffer them again for the whole township." Hardly the ideal spot for a youngster, or, for that matter, anyone else.

Nevertheless, the family of Joseph Allen prospered and grew. Almost

---

* Ethan Allen's date of birth is listed in the Litchfield Vital Records as January 10, 1737. The old-style calendar was then in use, however. By present-day reckoning, Ethan was born on January 21, 1738.

yearly during that first arduous decade of settlement in Cornwall, Mary gave birth, until by 1751 the final total of young Allens stood at eight, all of whom, quite uncommon for that day, would live to adulthood. Next after Ethan came Heman, who in many ways was the best of the lot. At least Ethan thought so. Steady, capable, and responsible, Heman was much depended upon by Ethan and the others through the years, and seldom found wanting. From 1765 until the end of his life midway through the Revolution, he kept a general store in Salisbury, Connecticut, but at the same time he managed to participate actively in shaping the early history of Vermont. Closely associated with Ethan and his other brothers in Vermont land speculation and politics, Heman had by the time of his death risen to a position of some importance in the new state. Despite the fact that he never actually settled there, preferring to maintain his residence in Salisbury, his name appears conspicuously on many of the documents pertaining to the establishment of the Republic of Vermont, and when the time came in 1777 for the new state to seek recognition from the American Confederation, Heman was one of those chosen to present Vermont's case to the Continental Congress. Less bizarre than Ethan and less politically adroit than his youngest brother Ira, he was more widely respected than either. Had he lived longer, he would doubtless have achieved a larger measure of fame in the early annals of Vermont. But this was not to be. He died in 1778 at his place in Salisbury, a worn-out man at the age of thirty-eight.

After Heman, in intervals of a year or so, came Lydia, Heber, Levi, Lucy, Zimri, and Ira. Of the brothers, all would figure more or less prominently in the early development of what would one day become Vermont, and with rare exception all could be counted on to close ranks behind Ethan in time of trouble. But it was Ira, the youngest of the lot, whose life was to become most intimately and intricately involved with Ethan's and whose influence upon his attitudes and actions would be by far the greatest. Ira, the brilliant, the imperturbable, and, alas, the sometimes devious. Unlike the extroverted Ethan, he preferred to move in the shadows, making quiet and, if necessary, questionable deals, and in the end getting what he wanted without much fuss or fanfare. Few men were so influential in the affairs of early Vermont. Without Ira, it is unlikely that Ethan's star would have risen so high.

By the mid-1750's life in Cornwall had become less desperate. The Indians, despite an occasional appearance in the outlying areas, had ceased to be a problem, and the wolves and rattlesnakes had been all but wiped out by bounties. Substantial progress had been made in pushing back the forest and clearing the fields of stumps and stones, and by this time most of the settlers had acquired, according to the town records, two cows per family and as many horses and pigs. For the most part Cornwall families continued to live in their rude, roughhewn cabins, but scattered about here and there were a half-dozen or so frame houses to attest to the growing affluence and maturity of the town. The crisis had clearly passed. Life in Cornwall had become reasonably safe and secure —but not easy. For Ethan and the thousands of others like him who spent the greater part of their lives taming the New England frontier, life was seldom easy.

In April of 1755, when Ethan was seventeen, his father died. In many ways Joseph had been a remarkable man, and a successful one. From the earliest days of Cornwall, when he was chosen selectman at the first town-meeting, Joseph Allen had been a respected and influential member of the community. During his decade and a half in the frontier settlement he had become one of the town's two or three largest landholders, and by his own toil had carved out of the forest one of the finest working farms in the area. In matters of politics and religion he had been a consistently free spirit who had dared speak out for what he believed. Never one to underrate the worth and dignity of humanity, he had refused to accept the mean and frosty dogma of conventional Congregationalism, which seemed to him to assign mankind to an inevitable ash-heap. Although formally an Episcopalian, as were all of his children, he was actually an early-day Universalist who believed that within each man there was a redeeming grace that would guarantee his eventual salvation.

It is clear that much of what Joseph Allen was and believed in was passed on in good measure to his children, and none was more profoundly affected by the legacy than Ethan. The father had stood for strength and independence of thought and action; so would the children, most especially Ethan. But above all, Joseph exemplified that striking quality of unstinting vigor so frequently found on the American frontier. A job was a thing to be done, and life a thing to be lived, with all the energy and ability that could be mustered and brought to bear. Anything less than total commitment was foreign to Joseph Allen's nature, as it was to his sons and millions of other American frontiersmen before and after who refused to spare themselves in their agonizing struggles with the wilderness. They lived relentless lives of toil and danger, perhaps because they knew no other way, and as a result many would die before fifty, their bodies but not their spirits ground down by the cruel erosion of the hardships they encountered and, more often than not, overcame. So it was with Joseph Allen, and so it would be with Ethan.

Shortly before the death of his father, Ethan had been sent to the neighboring town of Salisbury to study under the tutelage of the Congregational minister, the Reverend Jonathan Lee, in hopeful preparation for admission to Yale College. From an early age Ethan had, according to his brother Ira's later recollection, shown a marked inclination for learning and a lively interest in matters above and beyond the narrow world of his frontier environment. To Ethan, a boy in his teens guiding a plow on the outer edge of civilization, the universe abounded in wondrous mysteries, and somewhere, he knew, for every question there must be an answer. What Ethan would many years later refer to as "my youthful disposition to contemplation" was recognized and encouraged by his father, and it seemed appropriate and within the bounds of Joseph Allen's frontier affluence that his eldest son be directed toward that highroad to eighteenth century distinction and preferment—a college education.

But the boy who was turned over to Pastor Lee for polishing was a rough article indeed. Since there was no school of any kind in Cornwall prior to 1759, Ethan had received no formal education whatsoever. What he had learned of words and numbers had come to him through his parents and his own efforts. His principal and virtually only textbooks were the family Bible and Plutarch's *Lives,* both of which he read avidly and repeatedly, extracting from each new reading added pleasure and meaning. The Old Testament, with its wonderfully heroic quality, was his special favorite, and he committed to memory many of its more dramatic passages, which later in life he would thunder forth verbatim at the proper time in order to reassure his friends or unnerve his adversaries.

But all this was a long way from Yale, and Ethan had scarcely begun to study under Dr. Lee when he was recalled from Salisbury by the death of his father. At seventeen Ethan, as the eldest son, had suddenly been cast into man's estate, where he found himself at the head of a large family and extensive holdings. Thoughts of college, or anything approaching it, must now be abandoned, but not his fondness for learning. Throughout the remainder of his life he would continue to display a lively spirit of inquiry and a genuine veneration of knowledge that would mark him as something of an oddity on the Vermont frontier.

Although history remembers him mainly as a soldier and frontier strong man who specialized in bluster and violence, Ethan preferred to think of himself as a scholar—a sort of backwoods Aristotle who in writing to friends and relatives often signed his letters, "The Philosopher." He took immense satisfaction from his published writings, and well he might have, for although they were not great, the best of them had considerable merit. Had his father lived longer, Ethan might in time have acquired a polish and discipline that, together with his gift of fluency, would have enabled him to take a prominent place in the world of letters. This was not to be, however, and Ethan, denied the formal education he should have had, would sorely feel the lack. Although he tended to be a braggart and a snob on the subject of his intellectual prowess, he was forever painfully aware of those inadequacies of form that marred his writings, and there is something pathetic in the fact that time and again in his published works this proud and talented man felt compelled to apologize for his grammar and spelling.

Still, perhaps it is better that things turned out as they did. If Ethan had been allowed to continue his studies, he might never have come to the Vermont frontier. And who can deny that his presence there turned out to be a matter of some consequence? In the long sweep of history, it was probably more important that Ethan Allen was able to capture Ticonderoga than spell it.

In the second summer following his father's death, Ethan, then a strapping big boy of nineteen, rode off to war. It had been three years since the British and French had resumed their long duel for control of North America, but up to this time the whole affair had seemed rather remote and irrelevant to the settlers of Litchfield County. Suddenly, however, in July of 1757, their indifference was shattered by the report that the Marquis de Montcalm was moving in strength against the British garrison at Fort William Henry. Here indeed was something to be concerned about. Situated at the southern extremity of Lake George in

New York Province, the fort commanded the main approach routes from the north. Its capture would clear the way for French penetration southward into the Hudson River Valley, with who could say what unspeakable consequences for the nearby frontier settlements of western Connecticut?

When militia muster was sounded throughout Litchfield County that summer, Private Ethan Allen saddled up his favorite horse and reported for duty. Two days later he was moving northward up the Housatonic Valley as part of a sprawling column of several hundred Connecticut farmers bound for the relief of Fort William Henry. Scarcely had they crossed through Berkshire County, Massachusetts, and reached what is now southern Vermont, when word arrived from the west that they were too late. The fort had already fallen to the French, and there was obviously nothing for the expedition to do but head for home and disband. Thus, after only fourteen days, Ethan found himself back home again on the Cornwall farm. All in all, his first military campaign hadn't amounted to much, but at least it had given him a chance to see something of the world beyond Litchfield County, and perhaps had set him to thinking about those immense stretches of unclaimed land he had passed through in the north country.

Happily, the French failed to follow up their victory at Lake George, and Ethan and his neighbors were allowed to cultivate their fields in peace throughout the remainder of the war. During this time, until mid-1763, Ethan remained on the family farm, improving the land and, according to the town records, adding substantially to the Allen holdings through purchase of wild acreage in and about Cornwall. Not much else is known of his activities during this period, save that in January of 1762 he became part-owner of an iron operation in nearby Salisbury, and in June of that same year he made what was probably the biggest mistake of his life.

Some matches, it is said, are made in heaven, but Ethan's marriage to Mary Brownson was not one of them. It would, in fact, prove to be a most unhappy affair from beginning to end. Not that it was Mary's fault. She probably did her best, but she was simply not equipped to cope with the likes of Ethan Allen. Dull, dreary, and far from pretty, she was tailored by nature and training for a life of cheerless mediocrity. As the wife of a middle-aged harness-maker she might have done quite well. But Ethan was no harness-maker, and never, regardless of his years, would he be middle-aged.

Since by all accounts Mary was something less than a treasure, it is difficult to understand what Ethan saw in her. Was he dazzled by the dowry she brought? Her father, a miller in nearby Roxbury, was generally conceded to be a man of some wealth, and it is not at all unlikely that he was willing to bestow a generous sum upon the man who would marry his aging daughter. For Ethan, who was then in the throes of promoting an ambitious iron operation, this new capital, if such it were, was perhaps too much to resist. Or perhaps not. At any rate, his choice of mate was little short of disastrous. For Ethan's twenty-four years, Mary could claim at least a half-dozen more, which meant that by the standards of the day, particularly frontier standards, she was practically an old woman. Furthermore, as if by way of calculated balance, she matched her husband's most outstanding traits and inclinations with opposite ones of her own. In contrast to Ethan's élan, Mary possessed a singularly unimaginative and humorless stolidity that could wither all but the heartiest enthusiasm. To counter Ethan's scholarly interests, she brought to the marriage an inability to write even her own name. And against her husband's easy-going religious attitudes, Mary posed a rigid and unrelenting piety that hung like a pall over the Allen household. Add to all this the fact that Mary was an intolerable scold and Ethan was a husband about whom there was much to be scolded, and it is not difficult to understand why their marriage left something to be desired.

And yet, the partnership, such as it was, held together for more than twenty years until Mary's death in 1783, and during that time five children were born of it, three of whom would die before reaching adulthood. Upon none of the children did Ethan ever lavish much affection or even attention. Like their mother, they were adequately provided with food and shelter—and little else—by a father whose interests obviously lay outside the home, and whose presence at the family table after the first three or four years of marriage was something of a rarity.

After the wedding in Roxbury, Ethan brought his bride home to the Cornwall farm, where he remained for the next year or so. Sometime during the summer of 1763, however, he handed over the running of the farm to his brothers, and with Mary and his infant daughter Loraine, born that spring, moved a dozen miles up the road to the town of Salisbury. There in the Lakeville district of the town he purchased a small farm adjacent to the ironworks he had recently bought into, and proceeded to do what he could to make a success of himself in the world of manufacturing.

An iron operation of sorts had been begun at Lakeville in the mid-1730's when one of the early settlers in the area erected a small forge on the outlet of Lake Wononscopomuc. For the next quarter-century, however, the business managed to do little more than hold its own, and it was probably with small regret that its owner agreed in the winter of 1762 to sell out to Ethan and three other buyers for the modest sum of £430, Connecticut currency, or about 1,200 Spanish dollars. What the new owners received for their money was not much. The property included only the forge itself and water rights on the outlet, but from these meager beginnings Ethan and his partners would manage to establish within a surprisingly short time a vigorous and productive enterprise, generally recognized as Connecticut's first successful, full-fledged ironworks.

Almost immediately after purchase, the operation started to grow. Construction was begun on a giant blast furnace. Large stands of hardwood were purchased for charcoal. Additional water rights were obtained; dams were built, and a tote road was pushed through to the site of a nearby iron mine—all at considerable cost to Ethan and the others. Within three years the business blossomed into a complete and rather sophisticated iron-making process that employed upwards of fifty men. Inside the huge egg-shaped furnace, which measured twenty-four feet high and ten feet across at its greatest diameter, three tons of crude ore reacted with 250 bushels of charcoal and a half-ton of limestone flux to produce at one charge nearly two tons of molten iron. Something of a marvel for its time, the furnace would remain in blast throughout the Revolution, performing valuable service for the American cause long after Ethan had severed his connection with it.

Ethan's expenses at this time proved to be much greater than he had anticipated. In fact, they were quite staggering. His farm alone had cost him well over $1,200, and the demands of his expanding business for more and greater outlays of capital seemed without end. Furthermore, not long after his arrival in Salisbury, he had begun to indulge his passion, which would prove to be life-long, for speculating in land. He was not a poor man, but his resources had limits, and to help make ends meet he was forced to sell off a considerable amount of the extensive Cornwall property he had inherited from his father. It was probably also at least partly because of money pressures that in mid-1764 he sold half of his share in the ironworks, together with half of his farm, to brother Heman. This transaction realized Ethan a badly needed sum of $1,500.

It also brought Heman to Salisbury to live and work with his elder brother.

With the two oldest Allen boys in the same town, there was bound to be trouble. By the mid-1760's Salisbury had become a bustling community of nearly 1,500 inhabitants, something of a metropolis to Ethan and his brother who were more accustomed to living among trees than people. And, of course, bigness had brought congestion, with its inevitable restrictions and encroachments—all of which seems to have roughed the grain of the Allen frontier nature. Modern-day sociologists would call it "an inability to position themselves in a societal attitude"; the Allen boys would have said that they were merely sticking up for their rights. At any rate, the result was that they were almost constantly in one kind of trouble or another, which more often than not ended in their being hauled up before the local justice of the peace. There was, for example, the case of the errant pigs, told in fine detail by the Salisbury court records.

In August of 1764, not long after Heman had moved to Salisbury, eight pigs belonging to neighbor Samuel Tousley wandered onto Ethan's and Heman's land and proceeded to make great nuisances of themselves before being retrieved by their owner. As soon as the Allens learned of this invasion of their property, they went immediately to Tousley's pigsty and seized the eight offenders. Over Tousley's protests, the pigs were carried away by the brothers and deposited in a pen belonging to another of the Allens' neighbors, and there they were held captive despite Tousley's demands that they be returned.

Tousley turned to the law and got his pigs released on a writ of replevin. He also had Ethan and Heman brought before the justice of the peace on charges of trespassing and pig-stealing. In addition, claiming that he had suffered financial loss by being deprived of his pigs' presence, Tousley sued the Allens for damages. Ethan, making his debut as a lawyer, handled the case for the defense. He "averred" that the pigs had not been stolen, but rather taken into custody. He also "averred" that the pen to which they had been assigned met all the physical qualifications of a lawful pound, and that it was every man's right to commit obnoxious animals to a pound. In closing his argument, Ethan reminded the court that if Tousley had taken care of his damned pigs in the first place, none of this trouble would have happened. The court was not overly impressed by Ethan's defense, however. The fact remained that he and his brother had acted outside of the law, and for this they were fined ten shillings. Neighbor Tousley, for his and his pigs' distress, was awarded five shillings in damages.

No sooner had the judgment been given than Ethan countered by swearing out a complaint against Tousley's brother John. Two could play at this game of legal harassment. Back in January of that year John Tousley had borrowed five dollars or so from Ethan, with the understanding that the loan would be repayable with interest on demand. Well, in view of the pig affair, Ethan was now demanding, and when Tousley failed to pay up, Ethan called in the law. Eventually the matter of the debt was settled out of court, but in the process more bad feeling was generated between the Allens and the Tousleys, as is indicated by the fact that not long thereafter Heman punched Samuel Tousley in the face. For this indelicacy, "which is a break of the Peace of our Sovereign Lord the King and a break of the law of the coloney," Heman was fined sixteen shillings and given a stern warning to behave himself in the future. Obviously the warning was meant to apply to his brother as well.

It wasn't long, however, until Ethan was again brought before the Court, this time for brawling with George Caldwell, a fellow townsman who happened to be involved in some sort of business deal with Ethan. What started the fight is not known for certain. Apparently Ethan was convinced that Caldwell was out to cheat him. At any rate, what happened is made clear enough by the Salisbury Court Records. Confronting Caldwell on a public road not far from the center of town, Ethan proceeded to dress him down "in a tumultuous and offensive manner . . . in the presence of and to the disturbance of many of His Majesty's good subjects." He then, according to the Records, stripped off his clothing "even to his naked body" and tore into the hapless Caldwell. For all of this he was fined ten shillings—obviously not enough, for scarcely a month later he attacked Caldwell again. This time Caldwell had a friend with him, but Ethan soon evened the odds by hitting Caldwell over the head with a club.

Throughout his adult life Ethan would frequently find himself at odds with the law, usually for disturbing the peace in one way or another. Only a short time before his death, in fact, when he was approaching fifty and had begun to mellow somewhat, he was hauled before the court at Sunderland, Vermont, for fighting with a neighbor. This is not to say, however, that he held the law in contempt. On the contrary, he had a high regard for it, at least in the abstract. As a philosopher he recognized the need for restrictions in society, and the desirability of rules to insure orderly procedure among people. But when the restrictions impressed him as excessive or otherwise unreasonable, or when the orderly procedure seemed too slow or cumbrous or unlikely to produce equitable results, he was more apt than not to make his own law. Once during his stay in Salisbury, for instance, Ethan deliberately and openly violated a Connecticut statute that forbade the use of smallpox serum, except with the express consent of the selectmen. This law, which bespoke a lingering suspicion that inoculation was the Devil's work, impressed Ethan as being both stupid and oppressive. Consequently, despite repeated warnings from the selectmen, he proceeded to inoculate himself, an act which probably saved his life many times over, for in the days that lay ahead he would, as a soldier and prisoner of war, frequently be exposed to smallpox epidemics.

After the inoculation Ethan celebrated the event by having a few drinks at the local tavern, and while in his cups he unleashed a torrent of hair-curling profanity against the selectmen and threatened to whip the whole lot of them if they dared call him to account for what he had done. Call they did, but not for breaking the law against inoculation. Instead, Ethan was brought before the Litchfield County Court to answer for his outrageous display of blasphemy. What happened then is not recorded, but his escape from punishment by mutilation can be explained only by the fact that by this time Calvinism had lost much of its control over the manners and morals of back-country New England. Had Ethan been born a generation, or perhaps even a decade earlier, he would almost certainly sooner or later have rated a clipped ear or two or been nailed by his tongue to the nearest tree, for he was by all accounts one of the most profane men of his day—or any other day—all of which has caused considerable embarrassment for those Americans who prefer to have their national heroes set a lofty example, or at least avoid setting a bad one.

And so it was too with hard liquor, a commodity that Ethan could and did dispose of in great quantities. Throughout his adult life, and probably for some time before, he drank long, lustily, and often. He was by no means a habitual drunkard. Far from it. But he was an experienced and accomplished tippler who often became roaringly drunk and outraged respectability for miles around. When sober, Ethan generally behaved himself reasonably well. He was never widely acclaimed as a paragon of propriety, but in most of his dealings with others he was as considerate and forbearing as the next man. Indeed, given his independent nature along with his great physical strength, it is rather remarkable that he resisted as well as he did what must have been a strong urge to smash his way through to solutions. Even in his bitter contests with the Yorkers and the British, his actions, if not always his words, were marked by a high degree of restraint. When drunk, however, he was by all accounts an absolute terror who was just as likely as not to knock down anyone or anything that stood in his way. In fact, no small part of Ethan's richly deserved reputation as a troublemaker stemmed from his propensity for getting himself involved in drunken brawls.

These Salisbury days were busy ones for Ethan. As his iron business expanded, it required more and more of his time. Then too, there were fields to be plowed and corn and pumpkins to be cared for on acreage that he and Heman had put under cultivation. Add to all of this Ethan's interest in buying and selling land for speculation, his attention (such as it was) to his family, and the bothersome business of making frequent appearances before the local justice of the peace, and it is clear that there was little room for leisure. And yet, as he always would, he somehow managed to find time for probing into the world of ideas and letters.

Under the spell of a pompous but nevertheless genuine devotion to what he liked to call "matters of the mind," Ethan, boy and man, would frequently put all other things aside and closet himself, often for several days at a time, in some quiet place for the purpose of solitary reflection. On these occasions he would spend hours on end exploring the very essence of reality. Then he would jot down his findings before they escaped or lost their sharpness. Writing—that was the thing! For Ethan, it was almost a compulsion that he put something on paper. To him, writing was more than a means of communication or a vehicle for self-expression, although certainly it was both of these. Mainly, it was a process whereby he could bring order to his thoughts and thus extend the limits of his understanding. "This method of scribbling I practiced for many years," Ethan once remarked in his later years. "From it I experienced great advantages in the progression of learning and knowledge."

But contemplation, even when distilled by writing, is unlikely to amount to much unless provided with something to feed upon. There must, in other words, be grist for the mill. And whence came Ethan's? Certainly not to any great extent from his reading. Although he is known to have held books in high regard, there is no indication that after leaving his boyhood home in Cornwall he spent much time reading them. Perhaps this was because books were in short supply in the frontier areas he traversed, or, more probably, because Ethan lacked the time and patience to become seriously involved with them. At any rate, it is unlikely that during his entire adult life he read more than a half-dozen books from cover to cover. What reading he did do (and it was probably not much) was largely from newspapers, which were usually more readily available than books and much better suited to Ethan's hurried ways. In fact, during the early years in Vermont when he was frequently on the move, his reading was confined almost entirely to occasional back-issues of the *Connecticut Courant*—an excellent newspaper, but hardly the sort of reading apt to excite one to philosophical flight.

It was nature, rather than reading, that taught Ethan most of what he knew or thought he knew about the universe, and the process was at least partly intuitive. He was a child of nature, and although like his frontier contemporaries he spent much of his life despoiling it with his ax and musket, still he felt a reverence toward it that was genuine and at times almost mystical. For him there was constant wonderment in its ordinary and extraordinary miracles. They played upon his curiosity and sensitivity, and from them he extracted sensations and meanings that were often missed by other men. While his frontier neighbors merely lived with nature and used it, Ethan experienced it. In return, it was his abiding teacher—sometimes cruel, sometimes benign, but always forthright and unrigged—and if at times it failed to give him the answers he sought, at least it was seldom at a loss to provide him with awesome questions. Many times throughout his writings, as indeed throughout his life, Ethan's thoughts and decisions were fashioned in accordance with lessons he had learned through communion with the wilderness of western New England, and on the whole the results were not at all bad.

Next to nature, talking men taught him most; not just ordinary men who could speak of nothing beyond the horizon, but men who dealt with subjects of the mind and the soul and talked of great abstractions.

Throughout his adult life Ethan sought out men of this sort. He deferred to them, questioned them, listened attentively to what they had to say, and not infrequently gobbled up indiscriminately whatever he heard. As a brain-picker he was determined and tireless, and not at all reluctant to lift directly from the minds of other men ideas which he would later bring out, unaltered and unadorned, and offer up as his very own.

One such sage, at whose knee Ethan sat for a time during his Salisbury days, was Dr. Thomas Young, a practicing physician who lived just across the line in Amenia, New York. This remarkable man, who like Ethan would later play an important role as a Revolutionary patriot, was five years older than Ethan and infinitely more learned. In fact, by all accounts, including his own, Dr. Young knew just about everything there was to know, and it is understandable that Ethan, given his special hunger, should seek out the scholarly doctor and attach himself to him.

Without question, Ethan's association with Young was an exciting and stimulating adventure for him. In his mid-twenties at the time, Ethan had never before had access to such great erudition, nor would he ever again. Naturally, he made the most of his opportunity. From the time of Ethan's arrival in Salisbury in 1763 until Young's departure for Albany a year later, the two men spent much time together, discussing philosophy, political theory, and other subjects worlds removed from the routine of their workaday lives. Ethan was clearly the pupil, reveling in a new awareness of things, and Young was just as clearly the master, flattered by the younger man's attention and obviously pleased to find a kindred spirit in so unlikely a place. Still, each learned from the other. To the great erudition of Dr. Young, Ethan could respond with observations and revelations that had come to him mainly from sources other than books. Let Young speak of Locke and freedom, and Ethan could introduce his own concept of freedom which had been shaped for him by a quarter-century of life on the outer rim of civilization. To Young's version of Newton, Ethan could add a sensitive appraisal of the wondrous order and balance of nature as he had seen it manifested in the wilds of Litchfield County. All in all, each man was in his own way an authority, or at least considered himself such, and in their frequent dialogues they seemed to complement one another nicely—so much so that they eventually decided to pool their resources and write a book.

The book was to be about religion, or, more accurately, against religion as it was then conceived of by most men. Through his reading

Young had come to reject most of the conventional religious beliefs of the time as sheer fantasy. Like the French "philosophes" and English Deists whose writings he had read, he was willing to accept the concept of an omnipotent deity as the instrument responsible for originating the universe and setting it in motion, but beyond that he would have nothing to do with supernaturalism. As a devotee of Newton he was a firm believer in order and natural law as the great realities of life. God, such as He was, was a benign but neutral bystander, not given to whimsical interference with the orderly and well-oiled process of things which He himself had set up.

It was an easy matter for Ethan to subscribe to Young's religious views. According to Ira Allen's recollection many years later, "After an acquaintance with Dr. Thomas Young, a Deist, my brother embraced the same sentiments." But it is likely that even before his friendship with Young, Ethan had traveled a considerable distance along the same road and that by the time of his meeting with the learned doctor he was ripe for final conversion. Clearly, by the mid-eighteenth century the power of conventional religion had begun to crumble in America, and although few men were willing to go so far as Young, religious libertarianism was everywhere on the rise, especially in the more remote areas. As a young man of free and inquiring spirit, who had inherited his father's aversion to Calvinist orthodoxy, Ethan had doubtless been in the forefront of defection, and only the finely reasoned arguments of Dr. Young were needed to give form and order to his dissent. Young did his job well. For the rest of his days Ethan, although he refused to label himself as such, would remain essentially a Deist and would let pass few opportunities to rail against what he considered the vicious inanities of supernaturalism.

The book that Ethan and Young undertook to write was intended to be a blistering frontal attack upon supernatural religion, followed by arguments in support of Deism. Through long hours of discussion, ideas were sorted out, refined, and finally committed to paper. Especially helpful was Ethan's encyclopedic knowledge of the Bible, particularly the Old Testament, which was singled out for special ridicule by the two authors because of its outrageous fantasy: Now, where in the world did Eve find the thread for stitching her fig leaves together—or, exactly how did the serpent learn to talk?

Everything considered, including the inexperience of the authors and their many other commitments, the project moved along very smoothly, and the book was probably somewhat more than half completed when suddenly, in the autumn of 1764, Dr. Young ended the collaboration by moving away from the area. During the years that followed he traveled far afield, carrying the unfinished manuscript with him. Ethan would never see him again, but he managed to keep track of his whereabouts. Eventually, after nearly two decades had passed and Young himself had long since died, Ethan was able to retrieve the precious manuscript, which he proceeded to rework, expand, and publish under his own name. All in all, it would turn out to be quite a book. Ethan called it *Reason the Only Oracle of Man.*

## II. Trouble on the Grants

His Excellency Benning Wentworth was a man of some elegance. As Royal Governor of the Province of New Hampshire, he set the tone for style and grace in old Portsmouth town during the middle years of the seventeen hundreds. Picture him now as Longfellow would a century later:

> A portly person with three-cornered hat,
> A crimson velvet coat, head high in air,
> Gold-headed cane and nicely powdered hair,
> And diamond buckles sparkling at his knees.

> For this was Governor Wentworth driving down
> To Little Harbor, just beyond the town,
> Where his Great House stood looking out to sea.
> A goodly place where it was good to be.

All things considered, he was a strong governor and perhaps even a good one. During his long tenure, which began at about the time of Ethan Allen's birth and lasted for a quarter-century, he was sincerely devoted to promoting the welfare of the Province. He was also, however, sincerely devoted to becoming as rich as possible as soon as possible, and on occasions when these two interests clashed, the governor's prospects for personal gain were seldom known to suffer. As an early New Hampshire historian remarked of Benning Wentworth and his administration: "During his career New Hampshire advanced rapidly in wealth and prosperity—though not so fast as the Governor did."

The position of Royal Governor paid a salary of only £500 in New Hampshire currency, or about $1,500—hardly enough to bother with. But in New Hampshire, as elsewhere, the perquisites of the office were highly attractive. Not the least of these was the right to grant unclaimed land at a fee. Here was an excellent way for an enterprising governor to supplement his meager salary, and of course Benning Wentworth was not slow to exploit the possibilities. For a time he issued land warrants more or less within the limits of his instructions from the King, which specified that grants should be made in township-size to groups of fifty or more families who intended to settle the land themselves. Under these restrictions, however, grants came slowly and so did governor's fees. Consequently, he soon came to disregard the King's instructions and began granting townships to any group that could meet his modest price and would agree to hold certain areas in reserve for "worthy causes." One of these worthy causes was Governor Wentworth himself, whose cut, all quite illegal, averaged around five hundred acres of well-situated land in every township granted.

As a result of Wentworth's liberal policy, unclaimed lands were taken up rapidly; so rapidly, in fact, that before long the governor began granting townships west of the Connecticut River—a rather brazen step in view of the fact that this area was not generally conceded to be a part of New Hampshire. To give Governor Wentworth his due, however, it must be admitted that a considerable amount of doubt existed over the jurisdictional status of the vast wilderness that lay to the west of the Connecticut in what is now Vermont. Nearly a century before, this area had presumably been included in an extensive grant by Charles II to his brother James, then Duke of York. Consequently, it was usually thought of as belonging to the Province of New York. But the so-called Duke's Charter, based as it was upon an incomplete and faulty knowledge of the geography of the region, was so murky in many of its provisions and so obviously inconsistent with charters granted earlier to other colonies, that confusion soon arose as to the exact extent of its limits. Through the passing decades, as the land remained unsettled in the face of the continuing French and Indian menace, there developed out of this confusion a series of claims and counter-claims by four Colonies to the territory west of the Connecticut—including some rather shadowy pretensions by the Province of New Hampshire.

Fully aware of the fact that he really had no right to do so, but emboldened by the possibilities for profit, Governor Wentworth seized the initiative in December of 1749 and issued the first of his township grants in the disputed area. Obviously this was meant to be a probing action, and it is likely that if New York had made much of a fuss about it, the governor would have beaten a hasty retreat. But New York showed surprisingly little concern over what had happened, and so Governor Wentworth tried again, and then again. During the next fifteen years, while neither New York nor the Crown did much to stop him, the New Hampshire governor issued warrants to an amazing total of one hundred and thirty-eight townships in the region across the river, or nearly 3,000,000 acres. In the process the governor obtained over 65,000 acres as his personal share of the newly granted land, in addition, of course, to his regular fees. He also created a situation out of which would one day be born the State of Vermont.

Despite the King's explicit instructions, the Wentworth grants were for the most part issued to men who had no intention of settling the land. Many of them were relatives, friends, or political henchmen of the governor. For example, the township of Halifax in the disputed area included among its original proprietors three members of Wentworth's family and seven members of his government, along with, of course, the governor himself. From 1749 to 1764 Wentworth's father-in-law received proprietary rights to approximately 350 acres in each of fifty-seven different townships granted across the river, while the members of the Governor's Council received a total of three hundred and twenty-four rights, or about 113,000 acres. But even those who were less near or dear to the Governor seldom encountered much difficulty in getting Wentworth's signature on a land warrant. All that was required was for them to meet the governor's very reasonable terms. Speculators all, friends and strangers, these original grantees were interested primarily in resale rather than settlement or development, and with their investment running to little more than a half-cent an acre, they could hardly fail to make a substantial profit in the long run.

As long as the shadow of the French and their Indian allies continued to hover over the region, the prospects of settling in the wild lands to the west of the Connecticut were anything but appealing, and as a result the Wentworth speculators had a difficult time in disposing of their merchandise during the 1750's. The situation changed radically, however, with the fall of the great French citadel of Quebec in the autumn of 1759. For all practical purposes, this meant the end of French power in North America. It also meant that the Indians of the area, who had for so long sought and received support from the French in Canada, now had little choice but to start behaving themselves. Thus, in the early 1760's the market for Wentworth land titles suddenly grew very brisk indeed, and settlers began pouring into the disputed region in considerable numbers.

It was at this point that the New York authorities finally bestirred themselves. For a dozen years or more they had remained amazingly slothful in the face of Benning Wentworth's great effrontery, but now, as settlers with Wentworth titles started to flock into the area west of the river, the Yorkers began to send up loud cries of protest which in time were heard as far away as London. In fact, so anguished and persistent did their complaints become that His Majesty's Government was eventually forced to make a decision it should have made fifteen years earlier. Accordingly, in the summer of 1764, the King in Council announced in favor of New York's claims to the disputed territory and "doth hereby order and declare the western banks of the river Connecticut from where it enters the province of Massachusetts Bay, as far north as the 45th degree of north latitude, to be the boundary line between the . . . province of New Hampshire and New York."

In his Great House at Little Harbor, Governor Wentworth received the news calmly. He could not, of course, agree that the Crown's decision was a wise one, but he graciously announced that he would go along with it. As for the holders of Wentworth titles to lands in the affected area, there was really no need for them to worry. Let them simply manifest "a spirit of due obedience to the authorities and laws of the colony of New York," and in the end, the governor assured them, things would work out all right. But even though Benning Wentworth was not especially upset by the news from London, others were. By this time, ownership of Wentworth titles had become widely scattered. Divided and subdivided, often broken down into fifty-acre lots, the New Hampshire grants had found their way into the hands of thousands of purchasers, large and small. Some of the owners were speculators living as far away as New Jersey; others were settlers already established on their lands. All were clearly worried, and all had good reason, for the Crown decision of 1764 could very well bode ill for their ventures.

By mid-1765 every reasonably well-informed owner of Wentworth lands must have seen the situation for what it was. In a sense he had, consciously or otherwise, acted as the receiver of stolen goods, and as such his position was hardly a strong one. The proprietors who had not settled their lands, and indeed in many cases had no intention of settling them, stood to lose the least. Even at best, however, they could expect to have their acreage fall under quit-rent, a venerable tax imposed upon all lands by several of the Colonies outside of New England, including New

York. At worst, they could have their titles declared invalid, with the resultant loss of their investments and the ruin of their expectations for profit.

In a considerably more unpromising position were those Wentworth grantees who had actually settled in the disputed region, which, significantly enough, had by this time become more or less commonly known as the New Hampshire Grants, or just "the Grants." Even if New York were to act very generously toward them and recognize their titles, they were faced with the unhappy prospect of having to live under the political jurisdiction of the Yorkers. In the opinion of the settlers, virtually all of them New Englanders, such an arrangement would be less than pleasant. In fact, with its insistence upon quit-rents and its preference for appointive officials and county government over the Yankee's beloved tradition of town democracy, the New York system seemed disturbingly arbitrary and aristocratic. Things would be much worse, however, if New York should decide, now that the King had confirmed its claim to the area, not to honor the settlers' right of soil. Then the settlers would stand to lose everything—including not only the purchase price of lands which most of them had bought in good faith, but (infinitely more important) their homes as well, and the fields they had labored so arduously to wrest from the wilderness.

In an especially vulnerable, if not indeed desperate, position were those settlers, perhaps as many as two hundred families by mid-1765, who had established themselves in the southwesternmost part of the Grants. Even before the King's decision of 1764, the Province of New York had started issuing warrants of its own to acreage in this southwest corner, which lay only a few miles east of the settled areas of New York's Hudson River Valley, and a few of these warrants overlapped lands already peopled by Wentworth claimants. The consequences of all this began to become painfully clear in the summer of 1765 when New York survey teams started showing up in the vicinity of Bennington and Shaftsbury, and were seen stretching their chains across the farms of Wentworth settlers. If, in the wake of the King's decision, the Yorkers should choose to press their advantage, the settlers in this exposed area would doubtless witness much more of the same—and soon.

After the initial shock of the King's ruling had passed, the holders of New Hampshire titles seemed for the most part to be willing to come to an accommodation with the new situation. A few of the larger speculators balked for a time at the prospect of having to pay quit-rent on their holdings, but soon they, like the others, were ready to admit rather reluctantly that their lands now fell within the jurisdiction of New York and that consequently they had no recourse but to submit to the political authority and practices of that Province. As for the right of soil, however, speculators and settlers alike insisted, and with much justification, that the decree of 1764 had no bearing upon the validity of their land titles. After all, the lands that had been granted by Governor Wentworth and subsequently distributed among thousands of purchasers, had been the Crown's land, granted by the Crown's authority through a Crown agent. By the very nature of the situation, these transactions had been based upon and derived from contractual agreements between the King and individual purchasers, and the recent decision regarding political jurisdiction over the New Hampshire Grants neither had nor could have any relevancy to these agreements.

If the Province of New York had acted judiciously in the matter, the problem of the Wentworth grants might have been settled quickly and without much difficulty. A simple declaration confirming the Wentworth titles would almost certainly have been enough to accommodate the great majority of speculators and settlers, and thereby resolve the controversy while it was still of manageable proportions. Instead, however, the New York authorities foolishly refused to recognize the realities of the situation and determined to unscramble the giant omelet that Governor Wentworth had so resolutely prepared over a period of fifteen years.

In the summer of 1765, New York made known that it had no intention of honoring the property rights of the far-flung thousands of Wentworth titleholders. In a move designed to bring the New Hampshire claimants into line, the Yorker governor announced that all Wentworth titles, in order to be recognized as legitimate, would have to be validated by payment of a confirmation fee to the government of New York. This fee was by no means excessive. In no instance did it amount to more than a dozen cents an acre. Still, for most of the New Hampshire claimants the figure represented at least twice the original purchase price of their land, and for many settlers and small-time speculators the additional cash now demanded, at a time when wealth was more frequently measured in cows than currency, was simply not available. Furthermore, there was a great principle involved here, most keenly felt perhaps by those least able to pay: the land had been bought and paid for once, and to demand additional payment was a palpable and illegal assault upon the property rights of free-born Englishmen.

Understandably, then, the response to the Yorker directive was anything but brisk among the Wentworth proprietors. By mid-November of that year only 20 per cent of them had applied for New York confirmation of their titles. Clearly it would be necessary for the Yorker authorities to apply more pressure. Consequently, in June of 1766 all holders of unconfirmed Wentworth titles were ordered to appear in person before the proper New York officials within the next three months to arrange for payment of the fee, or be prepared to relinquish all claim to their lands. As for those Wentworth proprietors unfortunate enough to hold title to overlapped areas, obviously nothing could be done to permit them to retain their land, even though many of them were actually settled on it. They would simply have to make room for the new owners. They could be assured, however, that generous grants of wild land would be provided for them elsewhere by the Province of New York, after, of course, they had met their confirmation obligations.

As their position became more critical, the New Hampshire claimants turned to the Crown for relief. Certainly if the King were made aware of how badly his loyal subjects were being treated, he would take swift measures to right the situation. In a petition which bore the names of over six hundred Wentworth proprietors and was carried personally to London in the spring of 1767 by one of the settlers, the New Hampshire claimants stated their grievances against New York and asked that their titles be confirmed directly by the Crown. What the petitioners received for their effort was more of a truce than a victory, but it was a decidedly lopsided truce that would work to the benefit of the Wentworth proprietors in no small way. In July of that year the King and Council ordered the New York authorities to refrain from issuing any further grants in the area under contention, including confirmatory grants, until the Home Government could make a careful study of the entire problem. At the same time, the Crown warned New York that "until the King's pleasure be known," settlers in the area were to be in no way molested in their right of soil.

The King's Decree of July, 1767, was in no way intended to recognize the validity of the Wentworth grants, but by seeming to question the propriety of New York's policy, it gave a significant boost to the hopes of the New Hampshire claimants. Furthermore, by placing an interdict upon the Yorkers while at the same time permitting the Wentworth proprietors a free hand, the Decree obviously stacked the deck in favor of the latter. The prospects now confronting the New Hampshire claimants appeared to be distinctly more favorable than at any other time since before the King's decision, three years earlier, to place the Grants under New York's jurisdiction. As a result, speculators sold and settlers settled in the Grants area, all at an increasingly rapid pace and in increasingly greater number. Meanwhile, New York, forbidden to interfere, stood helplessly by and watched the deteriorating situation with audible chagrin.

For two years the New York authorities behaved with remarkable restraint while their prospects on the Grants worsened considerably with the arrival in the region of several hundred more Wentworth settlers. But there is an end to all patience, and in the autumn of 1769, as the Home Government continued to bumble along on the problem with no discernible progress toward a solution, New York decided to wait no longer. King or no King, it would mount an offensive against the Wentworth proprietors that would take care of their pretensions once and for all. During the next thirteen months the New York Government issued warrants to more than 600,000 acres on the Grants. Most of the warrants, covering vast tracts of land in the area west of the Green Mountains, were issued (directly or otherwise) to a small handful of wealthy New York speculators who were closely associated with the ruling circle of the Province. Many of these new warrants conflicted with earlier Wentworth titles; some overlapped areas of actual settlement; and all, according to the generally accepted meaning of the Decree of 1767, were granted in open defiance of the King's pleasure. At the same time the New York authorities, despite letter-clear instructions from London not to do so, returned to their earlier practice of harassing the Wentworth settlers in an attempt to bring them into line or force them from their property.

During the autumn of 1769, as tensions between Yankees and Yorkers mounted to a new high, several more of the Wentworth settlers and speculators came to terms with New York by filing for confirmation. The great majority did not, however, and gave no indication that they ever would. Violence was now more than a possibility, especially in the sensitive areas of the southwest, where claim overlapped claim and the giant power of the Province of New York stood poised along the Hudson only a few miles to the west. Here the fuse was growing dangerously short, and farmers worried and waited and carried their muskets with them into the fields. In mid-October of that year, bloodshed was narrowly averted when a Yorker survey team arrived at the farm of James Breakenridge, a Bennington settler whose lands had been overlapped by New York warrants. Backed by more than sixty of his neighbors, some of them armed, Breakenridge demanded that the Yorkers clear out, and clear out they did, but not until after many anxious moments. The New York governor later referred to the episode as a "disorderly riot"; the settlers insisted instead that it had been nothing more than "a peaceful parley" which had broken up in a spirit of good fellowship with each group God-blessing the other. Whatever else it may or may not have been, however, the incident was clearly an indication of the gravity of the situation, and helped bring about a tacit agreement between New York and the Wentworth proprietors to let matters lie until the courts could declare themselves on the question of what to do about the New Hampshire land titles.

The wait would not be a long one. A series of ejectment suits had already been initiated by a group of Yorker grantees against certain Wentworth settlers in the Bennington area, and had been scheduled to be heard before the New York Supreme Court at Albany in June of the following year. Although only nine of their number—all of them settled on overlapped land—were directly involved in the litigation, the New Hampshire proprietors as a whole could hardly fail to recognize the implications of the proceedings. It was obvious that all of their titles were on trial, and consequently, although not at all deluded about their chances for justice before a Yorker court, they determined to close ranks and do what they could to make a real legal fight of it.

In the winter and spring of 1770 a number of non-resident proprietors, most of them from northwest Connecticut, took the lead in organizing a defense for the nine embattled farmers of the Grants. At meetings held in Sharon and Canaan, Connecticut, plans were agreed upon for raising an emergency defense fund, and responsibility for collecting the money was assigned to several area committees, made up of non-resident proprietors and settlers alike, whose job it would be to pass the hat among the New Hampshire claimants. As for other arrangements, such as procuring necessary documents, obtaining the services of top-notch legal counsel, etc., there was much to be done and little time in which to do it. What was really needed was someone to coordinate the defense effort and push it along. He would, of course, have to be a very special kind of person with very special qualifications, including, above all, the ability to get things done. In other words, he would have to be the kind of man who could step forward and take charge. The question was: Where could such a man be found?

Given the way things were, it was almost inevitable that Ethan Allan should sooner or later show up on the New Hampshire Grants. In the mid-eighteenth century, Connecticut was caught up in a population spiral which saw the number of its inhabitants jump from an estimated 32,000 in 1732, to nearly five times that figure thirty years later. This amazing increase, which was officially attributed to "an industrious, temperate life, early marriage, and divine benediction," posed many serious problems at a time when most people worked the soil and measured their wealth and aspirations in acres. Good land became scarce, even at inflated prices; home lots were divided and subdivided to provide for the needs of sons and grandsons; and along the frontier fringes of the western counties the sound of the settler's ax was heard everywhere, attesting to the relentless push of humanity. Numbers alone would have been bad enough, but with numbers came restraints and counter-restraints, laws and regulations, which to the mind of many an independent farmer were simply too much to endure.

With their world crowding in upon them, men began to wonder about the future, and when in the early 1760's Wentworth jobbers came through Connecticut hawking titles to virgin land at a few cents an acre, the response was brisk. Sometimes purchases were made in large tracts by speculators, singly or in groups, most of whom had no intention of becoming settlers themselves. Mainly, however, the land was sold in small lots to individual farmers who, after studying their prospects, decided to deplete their meager savings in order to buy wild acreage in the north country as a likely place for settlement someday for themselves or their sons.

The end of the French and Indian War in the early 1760's served not only to open the land to the north, but also to advertise it. Many a discharged Colonial soldier returned home from service along the Champlain frontier to regale his Connecticut neighbors with vivid tales of a land where the intervales were broad and rich and untouched by man, where the streams and springs were plentiful, and the forests abounded with game and choice timber. And because they believed and liked what they heard, men of Connecticut began to move northward, by trickles at first, but later in waves of such magnitude that when in the mid-1770's the time came to choose a name for the new state that had blossomed out of the wilderness, the settlers of the Grants thought seriously of calling it "New Connecticut."

For more than a generation they would continue to come. Many of them traveled by water, sometimes alone, sometimes in small groups, transporting themselves and their belongings in flat-bottom boats, or during the cold months inching their way over the treacherous ice of half-frozen rivers and streams with their hand-sleds in tow. Others set out along blazed trails through the woods, often on snowshoes, with their dogs alongside and their horses or oxen lumbering behind, loaded down with pork, corn meal, seed corn, and a little rum. But whether by water, ice, or forest, the trek onto the Grants was no easy matter—scarcely a move to be undertaken by the weak or the timid.

Once arrived upon the Grants, they found even greater hardships awaiting them, at least during the early years. For the most part they faced them alone, for nearly all of the early settlers preferred to leave their families at home, entrusting the care of the crops and animals to the oldest boy or a hired man, while they themselves went about the task of taming the northern forest with musket and ax. For months they toiled, from the first light of day until the last, in good weather or bad, straining to clear another half-acre, or to raise their cabin walls another arduous foot or two, or to rut out of the virgin soil a few more grub holes into which to cast their precious kernels of seed corn. Frequently they came down with dysentery or the ague, and accidents not uncommonly befell them from a fallen timber or a glancing blow of the ax. Worst of all was the grinding attrition of loneliness and fatigue. At times they must have been all but overwhelmed by despair, but with rare exception they refused to yield to it, and in the end the forest had no choice but to give way before them, and men, filled with satisfaction and hope, returned home to fetch their families or their brides to a new life on the New Hampshire Grants.

Such a man was Thomas Ashley, who came to the Grants in the

spring of 1771 to make his pitch in the township of Poultney on the outer frontier, some forty miles north of Bennington. One of the earliest settlers in the area, he worked furiously through the spring and well into the summer to ready his land for the arrival of his family. He built a shanty by sticking four forked branches into the ground, joining them by poles through the crotches, and finally filling in the roof and sides with boughs and bark and mud. After that he cleared two or three acres, planted hills of corn amongst the stumps, and then returned to Connecticut to get his family. Well before harvest time the Ashleys were settled in their new home—Thomas, his wife, and their six children—committed now to the abrasive isolation of the wilderness until such a time as civilization would overtake them. The prospects before them would have cowed more ordinary folk, but the Ashleys did not doubt that before long, if fortune favored them, they would have wheat growing alongside their corn, a "sass" garden behind a sturdy cabin of hewn hemlock, and perhaps a pig or two roaming after beechnuts in the woods nearby. Until then they would just have to get along as best they could, and what with fish and game for the taking and a few sacks of dried corn to fall back on, it seemed more than likely to the Ashleys that they would make out all right. And, of course, they did, as did thousands of others like them.

The Connecticut migrants followed two nearly parallel routes onto the Grants. Those from the eastern and central parts of the Colony generally worked their way up the Connecticut River and settled in the area between the river and Green Mountains, while those from the western part moved northward along the Housatonic and Hoosic Valleys into the region west of the mountains. As a rule Connecticut was glad to see them go, for by and large they were a restive lot—the unsuccessful, the frustrated, the bored—often given to playing by their own rules, and playing very roughly at that. Without these malcontents and their progeny, Connecticut would become a much more tranquil and reasonable place. With them, the region that would one day be Vermont would grow and prosper beyond the bounds of all sensible expectation.

Among the multitudes of west-siders were hundreds, and later thousands, from hard-pressed Litchfield County, where the fields were lush but crowded begrudgingly into narrow intervales among hills too steep for anything but grazing. Many of these Litchfield County migrants were men whom Ethan had known in Cornwall and Salisbury. Some were close friends, and not a few, such as Remember Baker, Seth Warner, and Israel Brownson, were related to him by blood or marriage. Northward they went in ever-increasing numbers as the 1760's wore on, and with them, well before the decade had ended, went Ethan himself.

Not much is actually known about how Ethan came to arrive upon the New Hampshire Grants, or why. In late October of 1765, after three very demanding and not very profitable years of it, Ethan sold out his interest in the iron-works at what amounted to not much more than a break-even figure. So did brother Heman, who, with his share of the proceeds, decided to stay in the booming community of Salisbury and open a general store. There he would remain, buying and selling everything from hogs to ribbons, until his death in 1778, although much of his time after 1770 would be spent visiting the Grants. As for Ethan, the course of his movements during the following four years or so is more than a little obscure. With few exceptions, town records that might have revealed much have long since disappeared. So have the early chapters of Ira Allen's autobiography, which doubtless had much to say about Ethan during this time. In fact, only a few scattered fragments of evidence remain to suggest the barest outlines of Ethan's doings from the time he left the ironworks until he emerged as a prominent figure in the Albany ejectment suits in the spring of 1770.

It appears that in the late autumn of 1765, not long after he had severed his connections with the iron business, Ethan moved away from Salisbury. He may have gone south to Roxbury and spent a few months there with relatives while he examined the possibilities of a newly discovered mine, said to be rich in both iron and silver. But by the spring of the following year, soon after the birth of his son Joseph, Ethan and his family were settled in Northampton, Massachusetts. There they remained for more than a year while Ethan, as part-owner and overseer, attempted to breathe life into a lead mine that had been discovered as early as 1679 and subsequently worked by a long succession of owners without much to show for their efforts. Ethan's stay in Northampton ended abruptly in July of 1767, however, when the town fathers, for reasons unknown but not difficult to imagine, ordered him to leave at once and take his family with him.

After his expulsion from Northampton, Ethan returned to Salisbury where he lived for a time with Heman, and toyed with the idea of becoming his brother's partner in the store. But not for long. Sometime late in 1767 he moved to Sheffield, Massachusetts, only a few miles across the line from Salisbury, and took to farming on land acquired from an uncle, either by sale or inheritance. There he made a home for Mary and the children and for his brother Zimri, ten years younger than Ethan and unmarried—perfect hired-man material. For Ethan, though, the Sheffield farm was never to be anything more than a base of operations. All told, his family and Zimri would live there for a decade. Two of Ethan's children, Lucy Caroline and Mary Ann, would be born there, but Ethan was only an infrequent visitor. Leaving the care of his farm and family to Zimri, he would strike out at the slightest provocation or excuse and be gone for months at a time, sometimes driving hogs for Heman and sometimes wandering with his smooth-bore musket through the forests of western New England looking for game and who knows what else.

It was probably in the winter of 1766–67, while still in Northampton, that Ethan made his initial visit to the Grants. According to Ira's later recollection, Ethan went there first to hunt, most likely on invitation from his cousin and good friend Remember Baker, who had settled on the Grants in 1763 and was by this time well established in the little town of Arlington, about a dozen miles north of Bennington. What Ethan found on this first trip to the Grants must have appealed to him, for he returned frequently after that; often to hunt or to gather pelts for Heman's store, but sometimes simply to visit with friends and neighbors from back home in Litchfield County. During the course of his visits, some of which lasted for several weeks, he ordinarily "lived around" here and there, lending a hand with the chores or at times contributing nothing more than his company in return for supper and a night's lodging. In the process he ranged widely over the Grants area west of the mountains and came to know and be known by a goodly share of its two thousand settlers. All of this must certainly have counted for something when in the spring of 1770 the Wentworth proprietors, with their titles about to face judgment before the New York Supreme Court, decided to appoint someone to take charge of things.

The choice of Ethan Allen to organize and direct a defense for the Wentworth titles in the upcoming New York ejectment trials represented an excellent job of casting, much more so than his employers could possibly have realized at the time. It also represented the beginning of Ethan's ascension to fame and greatness of a sort. Finally, at the age of thirty, after not much to show for his efforts with the plow and the blast furnace, he was on his way to becoming what, at least in his own opinion, he was clearly intended to be—a leader of men. And who can deny that his credentials for command were impressive? Magnetic of personality, gifted in the art of self-publicity, and surfeited with confidence in his own powers, he fairly radiated a spontaneous and exciting enthusiasm for any project he thought worthy of his attention. And when the time came to get down to the business at hand, he rarely spared himself. He was not an "almost" or "half-way" sort of man. He seldom, if ever, merely undertook things; he pounced upon them with a vigor, and sometimes a fury, that enheartened his friends and confounded his enemies.

Throughout his life Ethan could usually be found near the center of the scene, available and eager to assume control, and while other men grumbled and groaned and then excused themselves for lack of time, Ethan stepped forward to take charge and start things moving. It probably never occurred to him not to. He had, as one early Vermont historian pointed out, a compulsion for command: "Among his associates . . . he put himself forward and was tacitly acknowledged as leader, a distinction to which he felt himself entitled at all periods of his life. It would appear that personal subordination on his part never once entered his thoughts." Time and again Ethan would break trails for other men to follow, and although these trails were often difficult and somewhat crooked, in the end they generally managed to get the people where they wanted to go.

In May of 1770 Ethan, acting on behalf of the Wentworth proprietors, set out on horseback from Bennington to Portsmouth, New Hampshire. The fact that this involved traveling nearly one hundred and fifty miles through rough and sometimes unsettled country bothered him not at all. Like most of his frontier contemporaries, he gave little thought to distances and was quite capable of coping with the rigors of wilderness travel. The purpose of the trip was to obtain the original Wentworth land certificates and other documents pertaining to those grants soon to be contested in the New York court. He also hoped to persuade Governor John Wentworth, Benning's nephew and successor, to announce his support of the New Hampshire claimants.

As matters turned out, however, Ethan's trip was less than a total success. Getting the documents was easy enough. A cordial and helpful

Governor Wentworth saw to that. But as for the governor's siding openly with the New Hampshire claimants, this was clearly not to be, even though his sympathies were with them 100 per cent. Recently he had been indelicate enough to advise the New Hampshire proprietors, more or less publicly, not to pay the Yorker confirmation fee, and for so doing he had been given a stiff reprimand by the Home Government. Consequently, it behooved the governor to behave with greater propriety. This much he could and did do, though: having had some experience with the ways of the Colonial courts, he advised Ethan to get the best lawyer obtainable, and in the governor's estimation there was none better anywhere than Jared Ingersoll of New Haven.

And so, with the precious documents tucked in his saddlebag, Ethan headed for New Haven, some two hundred miles to the southwest of Portsmouth. There he looked up Jared Ingersoll, and with Governor Wentworth's endorsement was able to persuade him to present the defense of the New Hampshire claimants at the ejectment trials. As one of the ablest and most prominent lawyers in all America, Ingersoll could hardly fail to lend importance and dignity to the proprietors' cause, and the securing of his services was certainly something of a coup for Ethan. So far, so good. By mid-June, two weeks before the trials were set to begin, Ethan was home in Sheffield, paying one of his infrequent visits to Mary and the children and resting up from his recent journey. In less than a month he had covered over four hundred miles on horseback, much of it over rugged terrain.

By the time the ejectment trials opened at Albany, Ethan had himself become a Wentworth proprietor through purchase of three rights to Grants land—two in Poultney and one in Castleton. All told, he had acquired about 1,000 acres of wild land, at a cost of fifty Spanish dollars, not really a very extensive undertaking for a practiced speculator like Ethan who at this time had probably upwards of $1,500 invested in land, most of it in and about Litchfield County. Still, his newly acquired property on the Grants was enough to cause many later historians to conclude that Ethan's determined efforts to provide an effective defense for the New Hampshire claimants before the New York Supreme Court were inspired wholly or in part by his own financial stake in the outcome of the trials.

Such a charge overlooks not only the relatively modest size of his holdings on the Grants, but also the fact that his property there was acquired several weeks after he had agreed to help the Wentworth proprietors. Over a course of several generations, repeated searches through the ancient land records of the Vermont towns have produced not a shred of evidence to indicate that he held title to a single acre of Grants land until he was well along in his arrangements for the Wentworth defense. It might very well be that a few years later, after he had acquired vast holdings on the Grants, his actions were strongly influenced by his property interests—but not at this early stage. It makes more sense to assume that he sided with the Wentworth proprietors in the first place because he knew them and sympathized with their predicament, and that his purchase of three rights on the Grants just prior to the ejectment trials better represented a gesture of confidence in the proprietors' cause than a reason for his attachment to it.

When the trials opened in Albany during the final week of June, 1770, it was apparent from the outset that Ethan and his friends would not have an easy time of it. As Ethan later described the scene in the courtroom:

> The plaintiffs appearing in great state and magnificance, which, together with their junto of land thieves, made a brilliant appearance; but the defendants appearing but in ordinary fashion, having been greatly fatigued by hard labor wrought on the disputed premises, and their cash much exhausted, made a very disproportionate figure at court.

Furthermore, it was too much to expect that the proceedings would be conducted in an entirely disinterested manner. In view of the powerful forces aligned in support of the New York cause, it would indeed have been unusual if the court had not felt some anxiety over the outcome. Most of the New York land issues had been made in the form of extensive tracts to a small, but highly influential, group of Yorker speculators. Some of these grantees, including the lieutenant-governor and the attorney-general of the Province, were men of high office in the New York government. Others were persons of eminent social position in the Colony whose views carried considerable weight. Of the latter group, none was more deeply involved in Grants land and none would figure more prominently in the protracted struggle for title rights in the disputed area than James Duane, who had ridden up from the capital at New York City to serve as counsel for the plaintiffs.

Duane, aptly referred to by one historian as "the life and soul of New York claims to the Grants," was an unusually sober man who by talent and training was admirably equipped to show a profit in his dealings, and by disposition profoundly intent on doing so. Of keen although unimaginative mind, he had made an early reputation and fortune in the law by specializing, appropriately enough, in the collection of debts and in actions of trespass and ejectment. Soon after the King's proclamation of 1764, which appeared to place the Grants solidly within New York's jurisdiction, he had begun to acquire land there for purposes of speculation. Exactly how large his holdings were at the time of the Albany trials is not known, but they were certainly extensive—probably more so than those of any other New York claimant. In his late thirties at the time of his appearance as plaintiff's counsel at Albany, Duane was a person of considerable power in New York Province. Important people deferred to him, and then perhaps felt ashamed of themselves for having done so, for he was by all accounts a most unlovely person. There was, in fact, something about him that suggested evil. Perhaps it was his shifty glances, which had earned him the nickname "swivel eye" among his colleagues of the New York Bar, or perhaps it was the realization that his reputation as an oppressor of the poor was not entirely unmerited.

In the years that followed the ejectment trials, Duane would continue to acquire title to land on the Grants until his holdings there encompassed more than one hundred and ten square miles. And the more land he acquired, the more loudly he would demand that the New York authorities force the Wentworth claimants into compliance, one way or another. Even as late as 1791, at a time when Vermont was preparing to enter the Union as a sovereign state, he would still be demanding. Of all the Yorkers, none was more persistently obnoxious to Ethan and his friends than James Duane, and none of greater help to the Wentworth cause. In fact, by being what he was, or seemed to be—a money-grubbing, shifty-eyed, New York land-jobber—and by acting as he did, he contributed in no small way to the ruination of Yorker prospects on the Grants, for he provided the Wentworth proprietors with a symbol of all that was hateful and menacing to them. In a very dramatic way he personified the forces of oppression, and this was no small matter, for as any hero knows, a bona-fide, flesh-and-blood villain can do a great deal to lend cohesion and vehemence to a popular cause. Ethan understood all this very clearly, and throughout the long struggle over land titles on the Grants he was able to exploit Duane's sinister image with considerable success.

In late June of 1770, the ejectment suits came up before the New York Supreme Court, presided over by Judge Robert Livingston, who, it later turned out, was himself a holder of New York titles to Grants land. In all, there were nine of these suits scheduled to be heard, but attention centered on the case of *Small* v. *Carpenter,* not only because it was first on the docket, but, more important, because it most clearly and simply involved the fundamental question of land ownership on the Grants. Isaiah Carpenter occupied a farm in Shaftsbury, about a half-dozen miles north of Bennington. He had acquired this property through purchase of a Wentworth title in 1765 and had subsequently settled on it and improved it. In 1769 Lieutenant-Governor Colden of New York granted the same land as part of a 3,000-acre tract to Major John Small, a retired British army officer, who upon attempting to take possession of his property found part of it already occupied by a stubborn Yankee farmer who showed no intention of moving. The case now before the Court technically concerned only the ownership of the contested Shaftsbury land, but what was really at stake was the validity of all Wentworth titles.

The case of *Small* v. *Carpenter* did not pose much of a strain upon the resources or patience of Judge Livingston's court. It was, in fact, decided (for all practical purposes) during the early moments of the trial when the Judge upheld an objection by plaintiffs' counsel, James Duane, against the introduction of Wentworth titles as admissible evidence. These so-called titles, declared Judge Livingston, were generally known to be fraudulent and consequently could not be recognized by the court in any form or manner. And so that was that. If there had been doubt before about the quality of Yorker justice, there was no doubt now. Jared Ingersoll gathered up his papers, declared the case "already prejudiced," and left the courtroom with Ethan in tow. "Interest, conviction, and grandeur being all on one side, easily turned the scale against the honest defendant," Ethan noted later in reflecting on the trial. "Judgment without mercy."

Since their outcome was now a foregone conclusion, the remaining eight ejectment suits went uncontested by the defense. In fact, within a few hours after the court's decision in the Carpenter case, Jared Ingersoll was on his way back to New Haven and Ethan was making ready to carry the bad, but by no means unexpected, news to Bennington. Shortly before leaving Albany, however, he received important visitors at the tavern where he was staying. James Duane, fresh from his triumph in court, had seen fit to approach Ethan on a matter of some delicacy, and he had brought with him two of his influential friends and co-speculators, one of whom was John Tabor Kempe, attorney-general of the Province.

The three visitors got right to the point. Now that the legality of the Grants situation had been firmly established in favor of New York, it would be a good thing, Duane and the others suggested, if the Wentworth proprietors, one and all, were to fall in line and "make the best terms possible." Of course, they might need a little prodding from the right quarter, and since Ethan was obviously a man of some standing among them, he was a fitting person to put in an effective word of persuasion here and there. By doing so he would be performing a great service to his friends, who might otherwise be foolish enough to resist the authority of the Province of New York and thereby do themselves great injury. He would also be doing himself a favor, because James Duane and associates hardly expected him to contribute his services for nothing. Did he want land? He could have it. Money? That too.

As to what happened next, who can say? In Duane's journal there appears an entry apparently made not long after the meeting: "Paid Ethan Allen for going among the people to quiet them," and until the end of his days Duane would insist that Ethan had accepted a cash payment in return for his promise to exercise his persuasion among the men of the Grants. Naturally, Ethan denied all this, but when the occasion seemed to him to merit it, Ethan was not above lying. Neither, for that matter, was Duane. In this instance, however, it is more than likely that Duane's account is essentially true and Ethan actually did take the money, although he almost certainly had no intention of earning it. In view of the desperate situation into which his friends had been forced by Duane and others like him, it probably did not seem at all inappropriate to Ethan to skin the New York sharpsters in any way he could. In fact, the transaction may even have appealed to his sense of justice. Later, perhaps, he would boast about it to his friends over a cup or two of flip.

Still, this was obviously not the sort of behavior that one would want to go on the record. Far better for appearance's sake that he be cast in a more virtuous role—as indeed he was in his own account of the meeting. According to Ethan, he recoiled with outrage before the wretched attempt to bribe him into betraying his friends, and he loudly proclaimed his belief in the righteousness of their cause. Attorney-General Kempe then pointed out that the matter of righteousness might well be completely irrelevant. After all, Kempe declared, "we have might on our side, and you know that might often prevails against right." But Ethan was unimpressed. "The gods of the hills are not the gods of the valley," he cautioned his visitors, and when Kempe asked what was meant by that strange remark, Ethan replied: "If you will accompany me to the hills of Bennington, the sense will be made clear." This was one way of putting Duane and his friends on notice that, might or no might, the Yorkers could expect trouble if they attempted to separate the Wentworth proprietors from their land. These were bold words of defiance, and if, as is probable, Ethan did not actually say them—no matter. It would soon be clear to everyone that the men of the Grants meant to defend their right of soil. It was the settler Thomas Rowley, later to become known as the Green Mountain Bard, who perhaps said it best:

> We value not New York with all their powers,
> For here we'll stay and work.
> This land is ours.

# III. Yankees *vs.* Yorkers

SOON AFTER the Albany ejectment trials, a group of settlers met at Stephen Fay's tavern in Bennington to ponder the situation confronting them. The principal result of the convention was a resolution formally affirming the title rights of the Wentworth proprietors and announcing a fixed determination to uphold these rights by force if necessary. "It was," as Ira Allen later remarked, "a bold stroke by a hundred men who wanted to oppose the most favored colony under the Crown."

Out of the convention's resolution was born a minuteman type of military organization made up of volunteers from among the settlers living on the western part of the Grants. It is said that when Governor Colden of New York heard the news, he threatened to drive this rag-tail mob back into the Green Mountains, and thereby prompted the new militiamen of the Grants to call themselves "The Green Mountain Boys." Considered by themselves and their neighbors as "a band of rough but kindly and honest backwoods yeomen," but by their Yorker adversaries as a rowdy bunch of bullies and outlaws, the Green Mountain Boys were from the moment of their inception a highly controversial outfit, and even today historians differ bitterly in their appraisals of them. One point is clear, however: For better or for worse, they would prove to be the instrument principally responsible for frustrating New York's designs upon the Grants. Had it not been for them, the area that is now Vermont would today almost certainly be a part of New York State.

By the autumn of 1770 the Green Mountain Boys had been organized into a regiment of several local companies, each commanded by a captain chosen by the people of the various towns. Of the company commanders, at least two, Seth Warner and Remember Baker, would play conspicuous roles in the defense of the Grants, first against the Yorkers and later the British, and both would in time become deservedly enshrined in Vermont's pantheon of heroes. Baker, first cousin to both

Ethan and Warner, had grown up in Roxbury, Connecticut, as had Warner, but while still in his teens he had left home to take part in the French and Indian War. Unlike Ethan he participated in several engagements over a period of four years, including General Abercrombie's disastrous assault against Fort Ticonderoga in which Baker distinguished himself for bravery and, incidentally, ferocity. It was during the course of his military meanderings that he first became acquainted with the Grants, and not long after the treaty with France in 1763, Remember moved with his wife Desire and young son Ozzie to the new town of Arlington, not far north of Bennington.

In time of trouble Remember was a good man to have around. Ethan certainly found him so. Good-natured, somewhat irresponsible, and abundantly endowed with freckles and an unruly mop of sandy hair, he seemed more boy than man, but those who knew him were not deluded. He was not very big, "about five foot nine or ten inches high, pretty well set," but he had the strength and courage of a catamount, and he was durable almost beyond belief. His good friend Ira liked to say that Remember could be cut in two and grow back together again. But Ira was wrong. Not long after the outbreak of the Revolution, Baker, while scouting for the Colonials near British-held territory, was set upon by a band of marauding Indians who cut off his head. He did not grow back together again. Until then, however, he would do more than his share in protecting the Grants from would-be intruders.

A far different sort of man was Seth Warner. Although a half-dozen years younger than Remember and Ethan, he had been in the forefront of the great migration to the Grants. Arriving there at the age of twenty in 1763, only a few months before Cousin Remember, he made a pitch with his father in the just-opened town of Bennington, at a time when the entire white population west of the mountains probably did not exceed one hundred. Two years later he rode back to Roxbury to marry his childhood sweetheart and bring her to the new home he had built for her in the rapidly growing little community he had helped establish. There in a simple frame house perched not far from the crest of the hill, Warner lived with his family for more than twenty years, during which time he repeatedly distinguished himself in defending the lives and property of his neighbors on the New Hampshire Grants.

Like Remember Baker, but unlike Ethan, Seth Warner was an innocent victim of the controversy with New York, having joined with his father in purchasing a Wentworth title to the Bennington land, and, indeed, having actually settled there, well before the King's Decree of 1764. Once the King's decision had become known, Warner stepped resolutely forward to rally the settlers against the Yorker menace and to help organize a paramilitary protective association among the Bennington farmers—all of this long before Ethan had made his first appearance on the Grants. From that time onward, pitted in turn against Yorkers and British, he was never far from the firing line until late in the Revolution when the long strain of combat finally culminated in his physical ruin.

He was a big man of great bodily strength and majestic appearance, "six foot two inches, straight as a hickory tree and strongly built." He was also a pleasant, unassuming person of quiet ways who, although well educated by the standards of his day, was notably lacking in gifts of tongue and pen. Never given to display or self-acclaim, he was content to do what had to be done and let others take the credit if they cared. Consequently, he received far less fame than he deserved. Today his name is scarcely known outside of Vermont, but let there be no mistake about it: in Seth Warner the men of the New Hampshire Grants had a champion who towered head and shoulders above all others, including Ethan Allen himself.

Headquarters for the Green Mountain Boys was the Catamount Tavern in Bennington. Owned and operated by Stephen Fay and his sons Jonas and Joseph, the tavern was a square, unpainted building of two and a half stories which was situated on the top of the hill from where it could keep a watchful eye on the surrounding countryside. In front of the tavern on a raised platform atop a twenty-foot pole stood a large and rather shabby-looking stuffed catamount, snarling in the direction of New York Province a few miles to the west. Inside the building in what was usually called the big room, the officers of the Green Mountain Boys would meet from time to time in military council to take stock of things over a bowl of flip. Here they would celebrate their victories over the hated Yorkers and lay out their strategy for future harassment. Presiding over the proceedings from his place at the head of the long table could be found the high chieftain of the Grants' resistance movement, Ethan Allen, Colonel Commandant of the Green Mountain Boys.

Here again, as so often before and after, it was Ethan's towering confidence in himself that most suited him for the job at hand. In his new position he would have to act as soldier and showman, propagandist and con-man, blusterer, psychologist, diplomat, and gambler—and he would have to play all of these roles with surpassing skill. Just the thought of having to hold together and exercise control over the fiercely independent Green Mountain Boys would have shaken a person of less monumental self-assurance, while the idea that this miniature rag-bag outfit could conceivably ward off the encroachments of the powerful Yorkers for an indefinite period of time would have seemed sheer madness. With legal right and physical might arrayed powerfully on the side of the Yorkers, and with little or no support seen forthcoming from any outside quarter, the outlook for the Wentworth proprietors was grim indeed. Who in all honesty could have entertained serious doubts about the eventual outcome of so uneven a match? And yet, in the end Ethan would win out. He usually did, perhaps because it never occurred to him that he might lose. Throughout his tempestuous life he would parade boldly forward with magnificent aplomb, secure in his instinctive awareness that regardless of the odds against him it would be only a matter of time before he would be able to set things straight.

Certainly the principal source of Ethan's mighty self-confidence was his awesome physical power, which would be a considerable asset in his new assignment. On the American frontier of the eighteenth century, individual strength and stamina were staple commodities. Survival often depended upon them in the relentless contest of man against the wilderness and the always possible, if not probable, encroachments of other men. But even at such a time and place Ethan was widely marveled at and admired for his great feats of physical might and endurance. By the time of the Albany ejectment trials he had already become something of a living legend among the men of the Grants, and although many of the stories told about him were obviously untrue, the important thing was that most people believed them. Here was a man, it was said, who had strangled a bear with his giant hands and emerged with scarcely a scratch, who could run a deer to death without getting his wind up, and fell an ox with a single blow of his massive fist:

> And when they tell you [wrote the nineteenth-century romancer, Daniel Pierce Thompson], and they truly may, that they have seen him bite off the heads of broad nails by dozens—seize by his teeth and throw over his head bags containing each a bushel of salt, as fast as two men could bring them round to him—grasp two oppo-

nents who had beset him, one in each hand, and lifting them clear of the ground, hold them out at arm's length and beat them together until they cried for mercy—engage alone with a York sheriff and his posse of six common men, rout the whole, and leave them sprawling on the ground . . . [etc., etc.].

To have been truly deserving of such an impressive reputation, Ethan would indeed have had to have been something more than human, but the very fact that such mighty stories were told of him and widely believed indicates that his physical powers were those of no ordinary man. By all accounts, including his own, Ethan was a host in himself.

In view of his fondness for display, it is unlikely that Ethan settled for any common sort of uniform. For the regular, run-of-the-mill Green Mountain Boy an evergreen spring stuck in the hat would be uniform enough, but for the Colonel Commandant something of a very splendid and distinctive nature was called for—an outfit that befitted the majesty of his high position. Actually, however, aside from the fact that he carried a huge sword and wore "fancy, gold-braid epaulettes," nothing is known about his professional dress.

Even less is known about the appearance of the man himself. No description of him exists, except a few scattered references to the fact that he was "a large frame man," "a man powerful of build," and "robust." Nor is any authentic likeness of Ethan available. Presumably, at least one portrait and a miniature were done of him during the late years of his life, but if there ever were such paintings, they have long since disappeared, and exhaustive searches by dozens of scholars and collectors during the past century and a half have failed to turn up a single trace of their whereabouts.

In attempts to overcome this awkward deficiency, several painters and sculptors through the years have created "idealistic likenesses" of Vermont's most famous figure. Some of these works have been of impressive quality, and at least two of them, including the statue that now stands in front of the State Capitol in Montpelier, have achieved wide acceptance as true representations. The fact of the matter is, however, that these so-called likenesses have been created almost entirely out of hearsay and the artists' powers of imagination, and there is little reason to suppose that any of them bears much resemblance to the real Ethan.

Despite all that has been done or can be done to alter the situation, Ethan Allen remains, for better or for worse, a faceless hero, and he probably always will.

Under Ethan's direction the campaign of the New Hampshire proprietors against the Yorkers would be conducted simultaneously on two fronts. First, and foremost from the viewpoint of long-range strategy, was what might be called the diplomatic front. Since the power of the Yorkers was so obviously superior to that of the men of the Grants, it seemed likely that outside help of some sort would be needed if the controversy were to end happily. Consequently, Ethan and his friends missed few opportunities to present their case to the world at large in the best possible light and to expose their Yorker adversaries as a bunch of rapacious and heartless land-jobbers.

Of special concern to the New Hampshire proprietors was the attitude of the Home Government. A strong word from that direction could bring a quick end to their difficulties, and it was widely believed on the Grants that the King, who had come to their relief once before with his cease-and-desist decree against New York in 1767, would certainly help them again if he only knew how badly they were being treated. Thus, from 1770 to 1775, no fewer than five petitions were drawn up by the Wentworth proprietors and sent to London. The Home Government seemed generally sympathetic, but, as usual, it was slow to act—in this case too slow. Before London could or would get around to reaching a decision, the American colonists, including those on both sides of the Grants controversy, would be in open rebellion against the King, and Great Britain would be in no position to do much one way or the other about matters on the New Hampshire Grants. It can be argued, therefore, that during those critical years of the early 1770's when the future of the Grants was being decided, the Home Government played virtually no role in determining the course of the controversy. On the other hand, however, by failing to resolve the problem, London made it possible for the men of the Grants to go on to win, at a later time, a complete and unqualified victory over the Yorkers that would result not only in the validation of their land titles, but also in the emergence of a free and sovereign state of their own.

Along with the Home Government, the neighboring Colonies were kept mindful of the fact that great injustice threatened the men of the Grants. Pamphlets written in support of the proprietors' position were taken down to Hartford for printing and from there were given wide distribution throughout New England, together with Albany County and other parts of New York where, it was supposed, there was some sympathy for the Wentworth cause. Newspaper articles, some of them tediously long, were also published, many of them in the pages of the friendly *Connecticut Courant* of Hartford, which served as the more or less official organ of the Grants' resistance movement. Some of the pamphlets and several of the articles were authored by Ethan, who clearly derived great satisfaction from seeing his work in print. Seldom signing them with his own name, but rather with "A Lover of Reason and Truth," "A Lover of Liberty and Property," etc., Ethan pulled no punches. Although his style may have lacked something in literary grace, it was invariably highspirited and there was no mistaking the meaning of his message: The Wentworth proprietors were good, honest, innocent farmers who were plainly in the right, while their New York tormentors were money-grubbing land-jobbers who would stop at nothing to separate the men of the Grants from their property. It was like Ethan to come up with such a neat polarization of the situation. To put the enemy so entirely and so simply in the wrong was excellent psychology, of course, and Ethan was a psychologist of the first order. Besides, he probably honestly believed in the total depravity of his adversaries. Like so many other men of great intensity and commitment, Ethan thought and lived pretty much in a world of black and white, and he had little understanding of or patience with the uncertain area in between.

While continuing attempts were being made to gain the support of outsiders, another kind of battle had to be fought—this one on the home front—and it was here that Ethan had to be, and was, at his most effective best. This home-front campaign would be a two-pronged affair. First, the Yorkers had to be prevented from making encroachments upon the Grants, and at the same time, in order to present as solid a resistance as possible, the proprietors themselves had to be kept from paying confirmation fees or otherwise coming to terms with the New York authorities. In other words, Ethan's performance would be essentially a holding operation aimed at both his enemies and his less determined friends, and more often than not the weapons were the same— friendly persuasion, threats, and, all else failing, violent coercion.

It is worth noting, however, that with Ethan the use of violence was relatively rare, and when violence did occur it was with fists, whips, and clubs, rather than with more lethal weapons. Ethan Allen has been called a bully and a hoodlum, and not without reason. It is true that he was less than delicate in many of his actions, but given the conditions of his life and times, it is greatly to his credit that he was no worse than he was. When the final appraisal of him is made, the fact should loom large that during his long years of conflict with the hated Yorkers he neither killed nor seriously injured anyone, nor did he permit his Boys to do so. It has been said that he imposed these restraints upon himself and his men as a matter of policy, lest by spilling blood he give offense to the Crown or alienate his supporters nearer home. Perhaps so, but whatever the reason, it is no mean tribute to his leadership that for several years when tempers ran high Ethan and his small contingent of farmer-soldiers managed to frustrate the Yorkers' designs upon the Grants without firing a shot at anyone. For the most part he relied upon sheer bluster, and he blustered exceedingly well.

As it became increasingly apparent during the months immediately following the Albany ejectment trials that the great majority of the Wentworth proprietors were determined not to yield their right of soil, three logical and almost surefire courses might have been followed by New York to resolve the Grants problem before it could get out of hand. First, the Province of New York could have brought a quick end to the controversy by validating all Wentworth titles. This, of course, would have meant backing down on what some Yorkers considered a matter of principle. More important, an acknowledgement of the property rights of the New Hampshire proprietors would have involved the forfeiture of some 3,000,000 acres of Grants land and consequently a sizable loss of potential revenue for the New York governor, the attorney-general, and other officials who customarily shared in land-issue fees, including those charged for confirmation. It would also have meant that compensatory grants would have had to have been issued to a number of Yorker proprietors, like James Duane, whose New York patents conflicted with Wentworth titles. Still, despite its expensive and somewhat mortifying features, such a generous gesture would doubtless have paid handsome long-range dividends to New York by winning from the grateful New Hampshire claimants recognition of New York's political jurisdiction over the area, and thereby bringing the Grants controversy to a reasonable close. There is no indication, however, that the New York authorities even contemplated such a solution.

A second course of action, which would have proved far less expensive for the Yorkers, more acceptable on grounds of principle, and probably just as effective, was actually considered for a time by the New York Governor and Council, but for reasons unknown was never attempted. This would have involved the validation of titles for those lands actually settled, along with non-recognition of all other Wentworth claims. Such a move would hardly have pleased the absentee Wentworth proprietors, but it would most likely have had the effect of satisfying the settlers and splitting them off from the non-resident claimants. Without the settlers to do their front-line fighting for them, the non-residents would have been in no position to cause much trouble, and their titles to over a million acres of unsettled Grants land could have been ignored by New York. In other words, by accommodating the actual settlers in this manner, the Yorkers would probably have at least neutralized the more troublesome and dangerous segment of the opposition and thus emerged from the Grants controversy without excessive damage. But because of avarice, insensitivity, or just plain stubbornness, they chose not to do so, and as a result they eventually lost everything, including political jurisdiction over the area.

Another very apparent and very feasible approach might have been attempted by the Yorkers to bring about an early end to the troubles on the Grants. This was the use of force. In the year or so following the ejectment trials the settlers of the Grants were few in number and widely scattered. Furthermore, most of them were desperately poor, hard put to make it through to the next harvest, and certainly ill-equipped with the materials of war. Many of them lacked even sufficient powder and ball for hunting and were forced to go out after game with bow and arrow. Surely they were in no position to offer effective resistance to a determined show of force by the mighty Province of New York with its great wealth and numbers. Had a constabulary of a thousand well-armed men entered the Grants at this time with a cannon or two in tow, put the torch to a few cabins and fields, and otherwise made its presence felt, it is unlikely that the settlers would have delayed long in coming to terms with the New York authorities.

Against a force such as this, the recently organized Green Mountain Boys would have proved little more than a nuisance. Most of them, confronted with the prospect of burned-out farms or worse, would have soon made their peace with the Yorkers and returned home to work their fields and attempt to figure out ways of raising enough money to pay for confirmation. Others, probably no more than a scattering of die-hards, would have been easily driven into the hills, from where, outlaws even among their own people, they might have caused sporadic distur-bances but could have offered no real threat. Perhaps a month or so of token occupation by Yorker troops would have been necessary in order to make sure the dust had settled, but at no time could there have been any real doubt about the eventual success of the operation. The entire controversy could have been brought to a quick and easy solution if New York had chosen to apply force of arms. Here again, however, save for a single abortive attempt in the summer of 1771, the Yorkers did nothing.

The failure of New York to take positive action at a time when such action would have been relatively simple and probably successful, re-sulted mainly from a lack of decision on the part of the political leader-ship of the Province, attributable, in part at least, to much coming and going at the top. Had doughty old Cadwallader Colden remained in con-trol of New York affairs, the Grants problem would most likely have been resolved within a matter of months after the ejectment trials. But soon after the trials, at precisely the moment when a decision of some sort should have been made and acted upon, Colden was forced to step down in favor of the new royal governor just arrived from London, John Murray, Earl of Dunmore.

Dunmore, a Scottish noble of high lineage that could be traced back through the Stuarts, had been given his new position in early 1770 be-cause he was an important person who wanted to be a colonial gover-nor. These were his principal qualifications for the job, although, as it later turned out, he was actually a man of some ability and a variety of interests. Fortunately for the men of the Grants, none of these interests concerned the welfare of the Province of New York. He had preferred a colony farther south, but had agreed to be satisfied with New York until a more suitable opening arose. Therefore, as little more than a visitor on the New York scene he saw no need to bother with decisions of policy, and contented himself with entertaining lavishly at his Battery castle in New York City and adding to his personal fortune by granting lands with something approaching reckless abandon. During his brief term as governor, he completely ignored the King's restraining decree of 1767, still very much in effect, and issued patents to nearly a half-million acres of Grants land, mainly in areas already held under Wentworth titles. When Lord Dunmore left for a warmer climate in mid-1771 after a scant eleven months in office, he was a considerably richer man, and the situation on the New Hampshire Grants was considerably more entangled.

In June of 1771 there arrived in New York Harbor, to the accompaniment of booming cannons and much huzzaing, a person who for the next three years would play a conspicuous, although not always brilliant, role in the Grants controversy. This was His Excellency William Tryon, a man in his early forties whose more or less successful military career had some time earlier led to his appointment as royal governor of North Carolina. There he reigned for a time, living in considerable splendor at "Tryon's Palace" and doing a better-than-average job of governing the Colony. Only a month before his arrival in New York, however, he had been confronted with a situation of growing unrest among settlers of the North Carolina back-country who called themselves Regulators and made no secret of the fact that they considered the western counties badly discriminated against by the government of the Colony. When in mid-May the Regulators announced that they would no longer feel bound by North Carolina law, Governor Tryon concluded that this was treason and that something had better be done to reaffirm the King's authority.

Actually, a few reasonable concessions to the unhappy western farmers would almost certainly have been enough to quiet the disturbance, but Tryon preferred to use force. The result was the Battle of Alamance in which the Colonial militia, led by the governor himself, brutally mauled a large, but undisciplined and poorly armed, body of Regulators. So ruthless, in fact, was Tryon's handling of the affair that he appears to have been rather chastened by the experience. Perhaps it was for this reason that when, only a few weeks after the Battle of Alamance, he took over as Governor of New York, he showed a noticeable disposition to "get along." Later, upon reflection, he would wonder why he had not been given a baronetcy for his outstanding service against the Regulators, but for the time being at least, Governor William Tryon, former soldier of the King, seemed somewhat cautious and hardly of a mind to initiate an Alamance against the Green Mountain Boys.

Tryon was not an evil man, although generations of Vermont historians have done their best to make him seem so. Nor was he stupid.

There was, in fact, much to recommend him. He was well-intentioned, conscientious, and fairly capable and just. Compared with the other royal governors of his time and before, he rated rather high. But he was remarkably vain—"vain to an extreme degree," noted one of his contemporaries, "the quintessence of vanity. You should keep such people at home; they are excellent for a Court parade." And in view of his great vanity, it is not surprising that he should be stubborn, self-righteous, and intolerant of dissent. Seldom did he have serious doubts about his own infallibility, and he was never more steadfast than when in error. For better than three years this pompous, determined man did his best to resolve the increasingly exasperating Grants controversy to New York's advantage, but his best was not good enough, for his efforts were frustrated time and again by the outrageous antics of Ethan and his friends. It was a humiliating experience for a man of William Tryon's mighty self-esteem. On more than one occasion he must have wished that he was still in North Carolina—or that Ethan Allen was roasting painfully away in the lower recesses of Hell.

By the time Governor Tryon was comfortably settled in office, the men of the Grants had góne a long way toward organizing their defenses. During the year or so following the ejectment trials, delegates from most of the towns west of the mountains met several times in convention to determine how best to deal with the Yorker menace. In addition to providing for the formation of the Green Mountain Boys, these conventions authorized the establishment of committees of safety for the various towns, plus a super-committee, located in Bennington, to coordinate defense activity and planning throughout the Grants. All this was quite illegal under New York law, of course, but then, as far as the Wentworth proprietors were concerned, what wasn't?

Out of the conventions there also came a number of important resolutions designed to lay down guidelines for the contest with the Yorkers. Among other things, it was declared that under no circumstances were New York surveyors to be permitted to run their lines across any land, settled or otherwise, within the limits of the New Hampshire Grants. By specifying all lands, not just those held under Wentworth title, the

Yankee settlers were engaging in a rather brazen bit of presumption, but it was understandable presumption and perhaps necessary. Since there was often no way of determining on short notice what was Wentworth property and what was not, the safest way to prevent Yorker land-grabbers from encroaching was to keep them off the Grants altogether.

It was further decided by the settlers in convention that Yorker officials should not be allowed to remove any person from the Grants without having first obtained permission from the Committee of Safety in Bennington, or from the leaders of the Green Mountain Boys—a ruling that would later figure prominently in the adventures of Remember Baker. In all other matters, except those challenging the validity or security of the Wentworth land titles of course, the men of the Grants were supposed to recognize New York's jurisdiction over the area, abide by New York laws, and in no way hinder Yorker judges, sheriffs, or other officials in the performance of their duties. After all, the Wentworth proprietors were (and let the world so note) loyal, peace-loving subjects of the King, and were not determined upon revolution or any other nefarious business, but only upon the defense of their property. In order to provide more effectively for this defense, the convention delegates sent out an appeal to Wentworth proprietors far and near, calling upon them to stand firm in defense of their titles. At the same time a resolution was passed which prohibited all holders of Wentworth lands from accepting confirmation from New York. He who might choose in a moment of fear or weakness to defy this resolution would, in the words of the convention, "risk the great displeasure of the Green Mountain Boys."

As leader of the Green Mountain Boys it was mainly up to Ethan to see to it that these rules (and later rules of a more severe nature) were adhered to, and he was as equal to the task as any man could be. In the long run, however, the job of keeping the Yorkers at bay would prove too much, even for him. By 1775, despite all that Ethan and his Boys could do, the Wentworth proprietors were clearly losing the Battle of the Grants, and had not the Revolution come along when it did, it is likely that the Wentworth defenses would have completely crumbled before the decade had grown much older. But the Revolution *did* come along and in so doing saved the day for the men of the Grants. Ethan was not surprised. With his boundless confidence he had always supposed that something would turn up sooner or later, and from the first he had known that he need only hold the line until that something could occur.

Ethan's main contribution to the Grants fight, then, was his successful holding action, which, by slowing down the Yorker advance, made it possible for the Revolutionary crisis to come to the relief of the Wentworth proprietors. For four years just prior to the outbreak of the Revolution, dozens of small skirmishes between Yankees and Yorkers took place on the New Hampshire Grants, and although Ethan himself was directly involved in only a few of these, more often than not members of one or more of his Green Mountain companies could be found not far from the center of action. Sometimes the Boys appeared in small bands, with their faces blackened with soot, or disguised as Indians or women. Sometimes they presented themselves two hundred strong in military array. At other times they were not seen at all. "They assemble themselves together in the night time," wrote a hapless Yorker peace officer in the Bennington area, "and throw down all the Yorker fences, etc., and drive the Cattle into the fields and meadows and destroy both Grass and Corn, and do every mischief they can think of." Always, however, their doings were in line with standing orders from their Colonel Commandant that bloodshed be avoided, and that harassment, humiliation, and perhaps a little mauling be the principal instruments of persuasion.

Consider, for example, the manner in which Ethan and his Boys handled the ornery Dr. Samuel Adams of Arlington. Adams was one of a fair number of Yorkers who had acquired New York title to Grants land and had settled there prior to the time of the Albany ejectment suits and the ensuing crisis. Most of these Yorkers, fully aware that their position was at best a risky one, were careful not to rough the grain of their Yankee neighbors. Even so, they were frequently abused. Dr. Adams didn't even try to get along with the Yankees. Time and again he publicly argued against the validity of their land titles, and more than once he was heard to denounce the Green Mountain Boys as a bunch of ignorant roughnecks. Worse yet, he was continually attempting to persuade his neighbors to obtain New York confirmation. In fact, the portly doctor of Arlington proved so successful in making a loud nuisance of himself, that in time his behavior came to the attention of Ethan and his friends, who decided that, in a very friendly way, Adams should be warned to conduct himself in a more seemly fashion. And warned he was—but to no avail. Dr. Samuel Adams was not a man to pale before the threats of ruffians. He armed himself with a brace of pistols and proclaimed, for all to hear, that he would blow a hole clear through the first person to lay a finger on him.

Not long thereafter Adams was set upon and taken by surprise by a small band of Green Mountain Boys, who carted him away to Stephen Fay's tavern. There in the long room, with Ethan presiding, his case was heard by the Bennington Committee of Safety, which wasted little time in finding him guilty of being a public nuisance. His punishment, at Ethan's suggestion, was to be public humiliation. Tied securely into an armchair, the doctor was hoisted by ropes to the top of the tavern sign-post. There, twenty feet off the ground and on eye-level with the Fays' stuffed catamount, he dangled in his armchair for two hours while the assembled inhabitants of Bennington looked on with wonder and amusement. At the end of his sentence the doctor, noticeably chastened, was lowered, warned to mend his ways, and dismissed by the committee. "This mild and exemplary disgrace," according to Ira, "had a salutary effect upon the Doctor, and many others."

It was in the spring of 1771, nearly a year after the ejectment trials, that Ethan's war with the Yorkers began in earnest, and from that time until the outbreak of the Revolution hardly a month went by without a skirmish of some sort. In late May of 1771, word reached Bennington that William Cockburn, a New York surveyor, had recently arrived on the Grants and was already working with his linesmen in the woods near Pittsford, about sixty miles to the north. Ethan had spent the early part of the month in Litchfield County selling off some of his holdings there, and he had just arrived back on the Grants, with a considerable sum of money in hand and doubtless some choice land purchases in mind, when he heard the news about Cockburn. He immediately assembled a small group of his Boys and set out on horseback for the north country. Arriving in the vicinity of Pittsford on the afternoon of the second day, he reined up and sent word ahead to Cockburn that the Green Mountain Boys were coming, and that if he and his crew wanted to go on living, they had better pack up their chains and take the shortest route off the Grants. Cockburn was a brave man and a determined one, but he was no fool. He did as he was told and later took the matter up with his employer, James Duane. He had tried to do his job, Cockburn explained without apologizing for anything, but working conditions had been far from favorable. The few scattered settlers he had encountered in the area had been hostile and obstructive, but, far worse, "approaching through the woods was your acquaintance Nathan Allen [*sic*] . . . with a party blacked and dressed like Indians," threatening to fall upon him and murder him at any minute. Enough was enough. Let the lands go unsurveyed, at least until a more auspicious time.

No sooner had Cockburn been routed than reports reached Ethan that a small group of Yorkers had made a pitch a few miles south of Poultney and were clearing the land under a New York title. Ethan turned the matter over to his cocky and vicious little lieutenant Robert Cochran, who with around a dozen Boys pounced upon the Yorkers, roughed them up a bit, and then drove them off the Grants. The news of this affair reached William Tryon in New York City just as he was stepping off the boat to assume his new position as governor of the Province. It was, he stated, an inexcusable act of lawlessness. "The dangerous Tendency of such Disorders calls loudly for the Exertion of Civil Authorities." Then he did nothing.

An exertion of sorts was made soon after, however; not by Tryon but by Henry Ten Eyck, Esq., High Sheriff of Albany County, who in the summer of 1771 gathered together a sizable posse of Yorkers and set out to evict James Breakenridge from his farm on the overlapped Walloomsac tract in the Bennington area. Breakenridge had been in danger before. It may be remembered that as early as 1769, several months before the ejectment trials, a Yorker survey team had come onto his property but had been dissuaded from its business by an armed gathering of Breakenridge's neighbors. In the following year, not long after Breakenridge had been officially ordered off his land by the government of New York, a small posse of Yorkers had tried to take possession, only to meet with the same sort of reception as before. Now, on this third attempt, the Yorkers were descending in considerable numbers in order to get rid of Breakenridge once and for all, and in so doing perhaps deliver a persuasive object lesson to his friends and neighbors. It was the Yorkers' first substantial show of force against the men of the Grants, and, oddly enough, it would also be their last.

At first things went well enough for Sheriff Ten Eyck and his posse of about one hundred and fifty men as they set out from Albany in early July bound for Bennington, about thirty miles to the northeast. When they arrived within a mile or two of their destination, however, they learned from an emissary who had been sent ahead to confer with

Breakenridge, that once again a body of armed men had assembled with a view to protecting Breakenridge and his property. This much had been expected, but what had not been expected was that they would gather in such great number. From what the emissary had seen and heard, he judged that there were perhaps as many as three hundred men in the vicinity of Breakenridge's house, all bearing firearms and strategically positioned in groups of forty or more. Obviously the Yorkers would not have an easy time of it.

The effect of this news as it spread among the members of the posse was unsettling, to say the least. If the truth were known, most of them had never had much stomach for the expedition anyway. Farmers themselves, they were not anxious to run Breakenridge or any other settler—Yankee or Yorker—off his land, and now that it appeared they might die in the attempt, the entire business suddenly seemed worse than senseless. Consequently, when the sheriff ordered them to advance, all but forty of them refused to budge. "They had become at once backward," noted one of the sheriff's assistants, and despite Ten Eyck's threats, cajolery, and initial determination to carry on without them, in the end this backwardness left the Yorker sheriff with no reasonable choice but to abandon his mission without having fired a shot.

The defense force at Breakenridge's farm was made up largely of Ethan's Green Mountain Boys. This affair provided them with their first real opportunity to assemble in significant strength for the purpose of flexing their muscles in defense of the Wentworth land titles, and they flexed them well. How many companies were actually represented, and which ones, is not known, but almost certainly Seth Warner's Bennington Company was there, and it is likely that both Remember Baker and Robert Cochran had been notified early enough to hurry down from the Arlington area with most of their men.

Ethan himself was not on hand. At the time he was many miles to the north in the vicinity of Poultney and did not receive the news until the danger had passed. He arrived in Bennington soon after, however, and reviewed with his chiefs the events of the recent victory. From what he could learn, he concluded that the Green Mountain Boys had done themselves proud. They had acted with efficiency and restraint, and there was no doubt that the news of their performance would give a decided boost to the morale and determination of the Wentworth proprietors. He also concluded, probably correctly, that by and large the plain people of New York had no argument with the settlers of the Grants, and that they could not be counted on for much help by the Yorker officials and land-jobbers. In a pamphlet written sometime later, Ethan claimed that the victory at Breakenridge's farm was attributable in great part to the refusal of the members of Ten Eyck's force to abuse a fellow farmer in possession of his land. This was probably not an entirely accurate appraisal. Even if they had fought like lions, the Yorkers could have been driven off without much difficulty, and Ethan knew it. Still, it was excellent psychology on his part to highlight their compassion rather than their cowardice. The future of the Wentworth cause might very well be determined by the attitude of the thousands of Yorker plain folk living right next door in Albany County.

Not long after the Breakenridge victory had been discussed, analyzed, and duly celebrated at the Catamount Tavern, Ethan headed back to Poultney, a little frontier town some forty miles due north of Bennington. It appears that during the early years of the 1770's Ethan spent much of his time in Poultney and the wilds to the north, although he returned frequently to Bennington to renew his ties with civilization and landlord Fay, who sold the best liquor west of the mountains. In Poultney the Allens were well represented. Although many of the ancient records of the town were destroyed by fire in the mid-nineteenth century, there is evidence to suggest that Ethan and his brothers, Heman, Heber, and Ira, along with Cousin Ebenezer, owned considerable property there —perhaps as much as one-third of the town. Of them all, though, only Heber and Ebenezer were actual residents, and it was with one of these, probably Heber, that Ethan bedded down when in the area.

For Ethan the lure of the north was land. By early 1771 he had become extensively engaged in land speculation on the Grants, and nowhere were the prospects for cheap purchase more promising than in the area north of Poultney. Setting out from Poultney, sometimes alone and sometimes with Ira, who arrived on the Grants in the autumn of 1770, Ethan would frequently be gone for weeks at a time, exploring the area as far north as present-day Burlington with an eye always open for rich intervales and attractive water sites. His experiences were at best gruelling and more often than not hazardous. On one occasion, Ira would recall many years later, Ethan lost his bearings and found himself in the deep woods far from camp when darkness began to overtake him. It was late in the autumn, and a heavy rain had been falling all day, leaving Ethan drenched to the skin "so that he had not a dry thread about him":

> The weather cleared off extremely cold—it was out of his power to make any fire—his clothes began to freeze on him—he knew not what course to take—an extensive wilderness on one side—in this situation he thought it most prudent to mark out a path in a circle in which he could keep himself awake by going 'round, not daring to sit down lest he should fall asleep and perish—this I have often heard him say was among the greatest hazards of his life and required the greatest exertion of body and mind to preserve life till day—being much fatigued by travelling all day without victuals, benumbed with the cold, become sleepy . . . of every exertion. He repeatedly fell. This would so far bring him to his senses that he would spring on his feet, in a few minutes fall again; when daylight came he came more to himself and after travelling a short time came fully to his senses. His clothes were froze except shirt to his skin—before noon he reached a house where he got some refreshment.

But although his wanderings were dangerous and difficult, they were also profitable, for from them came a knowledge of the northern wilds that during the early 1770's was surpassed by that of only a few other men, among them Ira and probably Remember Baker. This knowledge Ethan put to good use by acquiring, sometimes in association with one or more of his brothers, much of the choicest land in the north country. It was a good time and place for buying. Land prices were soaring in the more accessible areas to the south, so much so that in the spring of 1771 Ethan was able to sell unimproved land he had purchased only a few months before in Castleton, just north of Poultney, for four times what he had paid for it. Better things were obviously still to come as more and more settlers poured onto the Grants. Small wonder that Ethan was anxious to buy up large tracts of virgin land in the north country while they could still be had for as little as a few pennies an acre.

By disposing of most of his remaining holdings in Cornwall and Salisbury, by borrowing up to the hilt, and by otherwise scraping together every shilling he could lay his hands on, he was able to accumulate thousands of acres of land during the year or so following the Albany ejectment trials. There is no way of determining exactly how extensive his holdings were, but they were certainly very sizable. For instance, a single purchase, bought in partnership with Ira, involved upwards of 12,000 acres. Although he had owned no property on the Grants when he took up the Wentworth cause in the spring of 1770, there is no doubt that by early 1772 Ethan had become one of the major proprietors of west-side land, all of which, of course, was held under New Hampshire titles. If the Yorkers could have succeeded in their attempts to eliminate these titles he would have been ruined financially, and could conceivably have spent the remainder of his life working his way out of debt or languishing in a debtors' prison.

In other words, Ethan's fortunes had become dependent upon the triumph of the Wentworth land titles, and certainly his deep financial involvement did not lessen his enthusiasm for fighting off the Yorkers. Yet it is not inconceivable that he would have fought just as hard and run just as many risks if he had owned not a single acre of Grants land. Basically, he was what his neighbors called "notional," which meant that he could not always be counted on to behave in a predictable manner. He did pretty much what he wanted to do when he wanted to do it, sometimes, it appears, without really knowing or caring why. Despite his outspoken devotion to reason, Ethan's actions frequently stemmed more from emotion, intuition, and impulse than from calculation. At times during his stormy career he would even lash out against his own self-interest in order to satisfy a whim, settle a grudge, or defend an abstraction which he could neither articulate nor fully understand. It may well be that he fought to protect the Wentworth titles because he owned a great many of them himself. Or it may be that he did so for some quite unrelated reason which made sense, if at all, only to Ethan himself.

Whatever his reasons, Ethan was always ready to give immediate priority to the business of defending the Grants. Before, during, and after the Revolution he was never known to be slow or half-hearted in responding to Yorker encroachments, real or imagined. Let the bugle sound and he would invariably drop what he was doing and rush to the scene of trouble. Thus, in late October of 1771 when Ethan learned that a small cluster of Yorkers had begun pitching in the vicinity of Rupert, some twenty miles south of Heber's place in Poultney, Ethan, with his lieutenants Remember Baker and Robert Cochran and a half-dozen of the Boys, descended suddenly upon the little settlement, where he found

a dozen or so families of Scotch Highlanders clearing the land and building homes under New York titles.

Within a matter of a few hours Ethan and his men had cleared the
area of its intruders and sent them fleeing back to New York for safety
—save for two of them, John Reid and Charles Hutcheson, who, perhaps because they had offered more resistance than the others, were singled out for special treatment. According to a deposition made shortly
thereafter by Hutcheson before the New York authorities, he and Reid
were forced to stand by and watch while their nearly completed cabins
were put to the torch. "A burnt sacrifice to the Gods of the World," proclaimed Ethan. After that, they were ordered to leave the Grants and
warned that if they should ever return, they would be "barbarously
used." "Go your way now," Ethan commanded, "and complain to that
damned Scoundrel your Governor. God damn your Governor, Laws,
King, Council, and Assembly."

Hutcheson was shocked by so much profanity and was injudicious
enough to say so, whereupon Ethan made menacing gestures at him and
shouted: "God damn your soul! Are you trying to preach to us?" Ethan
then unleashed an awful tirade of abuse against Yorker land-jobbers and
their lackeys in government. Let them beware! The Green Mountain
Boys were in earnest, and they would kill anybody sent out to stop
them. Why, in no time at all, Ethan declared, he could raise several
hundred men, if need be, to fight off the Yorkers. And as for any troops
that might be dispatched against him, he would send them all to Hell.
Hutcheson was then released, and he lost no time in making his way to
the safety of New York Province. He, for one, was convinced that these
men meant business, especially their leader, "of whom it is said that he
denys the Being of a God and Denys that there is an Infernal spirit exist-
ing."

Warrants were immediately issued by New York for the arrest of the
"abominable wretches, rioters, and traitors," responsible for the outrage
at Rupert. Seizing them would not be an easy matter, however. John
Munro, New York justice of the peace in the Bennington area and a
man who glowed with hatred of all things Yankee, would have liked
nothing better than to have Ethan Allen and the others cast into Albany
Gaol and kept their for the rest of their lives. But he doubted that they
could be taken, except by surprise or ruse, and even then it would be
virtually impossible to get them off the Grants. Munro knew these

Yankee settlers. He had lived among them for some time now, and he did not delude himself into believing that they would permit any of their number to be seized and carried away to Albany to stand trial before a Yorker court. "A Factious Spirit prevails throughout the Country," Munro wrote to Governor Tryon:

> Its got so that no man durst Speake one word in favor of New York Government without being in danger of both life and property—for they declare themselves not afraid of all the Force that the Government can send against them and they will hold the land in defyance of his Majesty should he go contrary to what they think is right. . . . The conduct of these people will undoubtedly Ruin the Settlement in this part of the Country; for no man Durst settle but a new England man.

As a dedicated official charged with the responsibility of upholding Yorker authority, Justice Munro would do his best to apprehend Allen and the others and deliver them to Albany, but he was not very sanguine about his chances.

And then a suggestion from one of Munro's fellow justices on the Grants: Why not offer a reward? Most of the settlers were desperately poor, and a sufficiently attractive reward might induce "some person of their own sort to artfully betray" Allen and his friends. A good idea, thought Tryon. It was worth a try at least. And so on November 27, 1771, Ethan, Remember, Cochran, and the six others who had ousted the Scots from Rupert a month before, were declared outlaws by the Governor and Council of New York, and a price of twenty New York pounds offered for the apprehension of each.

# IV. A Posture of Defiance

JANUARY 1, 1772, was a big day in Bennington. The new year was ushered in by an impressive military muster staged by Captain Seth Warner's Bennington Company of Green Mountain Boys. There was much wrestling, huzzaing, and firing at marks, and as a high point in the proceedings the troops passed in review through the town, dragging a couple of cannons recently hauled over from the old deserted fort at Williamstown. The cannons were rusty and dilapidated, and it probably would have been fatal to attempt to fire them, but since powder and ball were unavailable anyway, they posed no immediate threat to either friend or foe. Nevertheless, they had a certain morale value. Now the Green Mountain Boys could boast of an artillary of sorts.

In the afternoon a group of the Boys, including Ethan and Robert Cochran, retired to the long room of the Catamount Tavern to discuss the general situation on the Grants. There was much talk, of course, about the rewards that Tryon had recently posted. Most of the conversation, however, centered about a subsequent proclamation, issued by the New York governor in mid-December and just received in Bennington, which forcefully and at great length reaffirmed New York's exclusive rights to the area west of the Connecticut River. It was generally agreed by Ethan and his friends that this proclamation was a damned lie from beginning to end and that Tryon should "stick it in his ars."

As the afternoon wore on and landlord Fay's liquor continued to flow, expressions of outrage and defiance reverberated through the long room, and a crescendo appeared to be nearing when there entered the tavern a hapless Yorker traveler, Benjamin Buck, seeking nothing more than a bite to eat and a few minutes' rest before continuing on his journey. Although he tried not to become involved in what seemed to be "a kind of business meeting," and volunteered to take his meal in another room, Buck was assured by Ethan and the others that his presence would be most welcome, and so he joined the friendly gathering. At

61

once he found himself the center of attention. Governor Tryon's proclamation was read aloud and Buck was asked what he thought of it. He
answered only that he supposed it would hold up, whereupon Ethan hit
him three times and shouted: "You are a damned bastard of old Munro;
we shall make a hell of his house and burn him in it, and every son of a
bitch that will take his part." When Buck mumbled something to the
effect that regardless of who was right, New York had the power to get
its way, Ethan thundered: "How can you be such a damned fool? Have
we not always overcome them . . . ? And if they come again we shall
drive them two hundred miles and send them to Hell." And as for that
lying bastard Tryon, let him "tri on and be damned. He shall have a
match if he comes here."

Buck lost little time in reporting the affair to Justice Munro in nearby
Shaftsbury, and Munro in turn passed on the news to Tryon. Obviously
Ethan had not been cowed by the price placed upon his head. This fact
was made even more apparent a few weeks later when in early February,
Ethan and his friends countered with a reward-offering of their own:

> £25 REWARD—Whereas James Duane and John Kempe, of
> New York, have by their menaces and threats greatly disturbed the
> public peace and repose of the honest peasants of Bennington and
> the settlements to the northward, which are now and ever have
> been in the peace of God and the King, and are patriotic and liege
> subjects of Geo. the 3rd. Any person that will apprehend these
> common disturbers, viz: James Duane and John Kempe, and bring
> them to Landlord Fay's at Bennington shall have £15 reward for
> James Duane and £10 reward for John Kempe, paid by
>
> > Ethan Allen
> > Remember Baker
> > Robert Cochran

Of course, it was never really expected that anything would come of
this, and Ethan and the others would probably have been hard put to
raise the reward money. But it was good sport anyway, and as a propaganda stunt it might have some value. It was one way of announcing
publicly that Ethan Allen and his lieutenants did not take Governor
Tryon's reward offer very seriously, and that they intended to continue
doing what had to be done in order to protect the Grants. After all,
Ethan remarked to a friend, "By Virtue of a late Law in the Province
they are Not Allowed to hang any man before they have ketched him."
A month or so later Ethan journeyed down to Hartford and had several

dozen copies of the counter-reward printed up at his own expense, and then saw to it that they were posted throughout the west side of the Grants and in adjacent areas of New York for friend and foe alike to see.

Although Ethan and his fellow outlaws tended to look upon the Yorker reward offer as something of a joke, there were those who took it more seriously. One of these was the redoubtable Justice Munro, who constantly did his loyal best to uphold New York authority in the turbulent Bennington area. His was an awesome task, but he was an awesome man. Living in hostile surroundings where he was frequently harassed and put upon, he persevered doggedly in his job, refusing to be deterred by the cajolery or threats of his Yankee neighbors. Had Munro's courage and dedication been properly backed by the Province whose interests he served so diligently, Ethan and his friends would soon have been put safely under wraps, and the Grants controversy would probably have been resolved in New York's favor at an early date. As it was, however, he received nothing more substantial from the Province of New York than an occasional letter of encouragement from Governor Tryon, while in the actual business of performing the duties of his office he was left to his own devices to carry on against well-nigh impossible odds at no little danger to himself and his family. "Upon the whole my present situation is very disagreeable," he wrote with considerable understatement to James Duane in the spring of 1772. But Justice Munro would continue to do his best for New York Province, and "one day I shall be preferred to some office of great honor and profit in government—when all others are dead."

In late March of 1772, only a few weeks after Ethan and his friends had issued their counter-reward proclamation, and at a time when Ethan was away from the Grants, Justice Munro and a small posse of Yorkers from the Shaftsbury area descended upon Remember Baker's place in nearby Arlington. In launching what was later described by Ethan as "a wicked, inhuman, most barbarous, infamous, cruel, villainous, and thievish attack," Munro and his men waited until well after dark and then rushed the house and smashed in the door. The surprise was almost complete—almost, but not quite. The Bakers had been sleeping, but at the first sound of danger all of them—Remember, his wife, and young son—had sprung out of bed, prepared to do battle as best they could against their unknown assailants.

While his wife and son were being roughly overcome and pushed aside by Munro's men, Remember made a move for his rifle, but by the dim glow of the fireplace embers he could see that it was not in its accustomed place. The assailants had already seized it. He did manage to reach his ax, however, and this he immediately put to good use. Waving it wildly about his head, he was able to stand his ground for a time while he sized up the situation. Well, whatever else these uninvited visitors were, they certainly weren't Indians, and that in itself was something to be thankful for. At least, his wife and boy would probably not be harmed, and Remember could concentrate on looking out for himself. Taking advantage of the confusion and the semi-darkness, he somehow managed to reach the loft ladder and climb up into the attic. There he quickly chopped a hole in the roof boards, pulled himself through, and jumped into the snow below. In the end his mighty efforts gained him nothing, for no sooner had he landed than he was spotted, and after a brief scuffle was overpowered by several members of the posse, one of whom cut off Remember's thumb with a slash of his sword.

Bleeding badly and clothed only in his winter underwear, Remember was securely tied and loaded onto a sleigh which took off immediately in the direction of Albany, with Munro and his men riding guard. But it was not to be that easy for the Yorkers. Even before they were fully out of sight, Remember's wife had gone to rouse a neighbor, and within an hour a dozen or more men from the Arlington–Bennington area were galloping over the Albany road in pursuit of Munro and their adbucted neighbor. After a furious chase which lasted well into the early morning hours, the pursuers overtook the sleigh nearly halfway to Albany. As they swooped down upon Munro and his Yorkers, all but two of the posse fled, leaving Munro with no choice but to surrender himself and his captive to the angry Yankees. "Had I but ten men that would stand by me when the Bennington mob met me," Munro later complained, "I should have Mr. Baker in Albany gaol."

Baker, dangerously weak from loss of blood, was hurried off to the Catamount Tavern, where he was patched up and nursed back to health. Munro and the two remaining members of his posse were also taken along, supposedly to answer to the Bennington Committee of Safety for their outrageous act. After being held for a time, however, they were unaccountably released without trial, and Justice Munro returned to Shaftsbury, somewhat wiser but not at all chastened by the experience. "You always flatter yourself with the New England men's turning good and faithful subjects," he wrote to Duane a week after the Baker affair, "but believe me that it is my solid opinion if you was to bestow all your land upon them without any fee or reward they never will be faithful to the govt for they are possessed with a spirit of contradiction." To Munro's way of thinking, these people were "so full of venom and spite" that they were well beyond the reach of reason and friendly persuasion. "Oh, they'll talk so smooth and handsome yet the devil lies at the bottom." Eventually they would have to be brought to obedience by sheer force, and Justice Munro only hoped that he could be on hand when the time came to lop off a few of their heads.

Squire Munro's attempted capture of Remember Baker in the early spring of 1772 was certainly not the most serious incident in the long battle of attrition between Yankees and Yorkers for control of the New Hampshire Grants. It was the bloodiest, however. While whippings and maulings were common enough during the contest, only in this one instance was blood actually spilled in any great amount, and Remember's severed thumb would prove to be the greatest casualty of the Grants conflict. For this crime against Baker, Justice Munro would not long go unpunished. Never a great favorite of the men of the Grants, after the Baker episode Munro was clearly a marked man, a special subject of interest to his Yankee neighbors who proceeded to torment him in ways that would have daunted the spirit of a less resolute person and driven him from the Grants. "Since my last to you," he wrote dejectedly to Duane a few weeks after the Baker incident, "the rascally Yankees spoiled my best hat and sword coat with their Pumpkin sticks. . . ." Worse than that, Squire Munro narrowly missed having his head slashed open.

Seth Warner was a mild man, not easily aroused, but once his blood was up he was not to be trifled with. Munro's treatment of Cousin Remember had not set at all well with Warner, and soon after the incident he rode up to Shaftsbury to recover his cousin's rifle from the Squire. He was not spoiling for a fight with Munro or anybody else, but given the way he felt, he surely did not intend to back away from one if he were pressed. As Warner approached the Squire's house, Munro came out to meet him and demanded to know what business had brought him there. When Warner demanded the rifle, Munro grabbed the horse's bridle and declared his visitor under arrest for giving aid and comfort to an outlaw. This turned out to be a mistake. Still mounted, Warner struck Munro a wicked blow on the head with the flat of his sword and, while the Squire lay sprawled on the ground, retrieved the rifle and rode off toward Arlington to return it to Remember. Knocked senseless for a time but not seriously injured, Justice Munro recovered soon enough and went about his business, undaunted by the fact that he had escaped death by only a slight angle of Captain Warner's sword. As for Warner, his run-in with Munro earned him a place on Tryon's reward list along with Ethan and the others. It also gained him the gratitude of many of the New Hampshire proprietors, including the town fathers of Poultney who early in the following year voted to present him with 100 acres of land "for the vallor in cutting Esquire Munroe, the Yorkite."

While all this was going on, Ethan was many miles to the south, spending a few weeks with his family in Sheffield and helping out now and then at Heman's store in nearby Salisbury. Either out of boredom or his abiding compulsion to write something, he spent much of his visit shut off in the front room of the Sheffield farmhouse composing angry tracts against Tryon and all of his "mercenary, intriguing, monopolizing men—an infamous fraternity of diabolical plotters." Many of these writings were taken down to Hartford and eventually printed in the *Connecticut Courant:* "Women sobbing and lamenting, children crying and Men pierced to the heart with sorrow and indignation at the approaching tyranny of New York." There is not much doubt that Ethan was out to make the Yorker authorities appear as evil and depraved as possible, and if in the process he occasionally stretched the truth a little, what did that matter? The important thing was that justice was being served.

When the news of Remember's capture reached him, Ethan outdid himself in dramatizing the affair for the readers of the *Courant.* Munro and his men were graphically depicted as sadistic, subhuman beasts, who brutalized Remember and his family, and, as a special touch, Ethan invented a dog for the occasion—"a large, spiteful, wilful, and very malicious dog, educated and brought up to their own Yorker forms and customs, who, being like those other servants of the devil, at that time all obedience, seized the said Baker." As Ethan told it, Remember's blood gushed forth by the gallon, staining the pure white snow of the New Hampshire Grants for miles around. A bit overdrawn perhaps, but it was undeniably very moving and left no doubt about the villainy of the Yorkers. Such stuff could hardly fail to win sympathy for the badly put-upon Wentworth settlers.

By early April, Ethan was once again back on the Grants, eager to resume his land transactions and, if necessary, deal the Yorkers another blow or two. For the time being, however, all was quiet. A standoff of sorts seemed to have been reached. The settlers had demonstrated their determination not to be pushed, and at the time it appeared that it would be no simple matter to change their minds. "They are set upon holding their land," Benjamin Spencer, Yorker justice of the peace for the Clarendon area, wrote to James Duane. "They say they will defend it with force."

Throughout the length and breadth of the west side, in Bennington, Shaftsbury, Arlington, Manchester, and "other gatherings about the woods," the situation was much the same. A determined front of re- sistance had been formed. Everywhere the great majority of the men of the Grants were armed and resolute, and woe be unto those Yorkers or Yankees who might be foolish enough to give precedence to a New York land title or otherwise fail to conform to Wentworth orthodoxy. "Some are beaten in a most shameful manner," Spencer reported. "There are four men in Socialborough that settled under New Hampshire title that would willingly purchase confirmation but dare not do it for fear of endangering their lives." Clearly the time had arrived for the Province of New York to use force to put down the rampant lawlessness that had seized the Grants, and to establish legitimate authority over the area.

In May of that year, 1772, it appeared for a while that New York intended to do just that. At that time the news reached Ethan, then in Bennington, that a large contingent of troops, including British regulars, had begun moving up the Hudson from New York City. It was reported that these troops were en route to the Grants, and that Governor Tryon himself was riding at their head. Ethan immediately sent out mounted messengers to alert the settlers, and not long thereafter members of the various Committees of Safety of the west-side towns began flocking into Stephen Fay's tavern to confer with the Colonel Commandant and his lieutenants. Scarcely had the delegates assembled, however, when it be- came apparent that opinion was dangerously divided. Many of the mem- bers of the committees, who had previously been willing enough to engage in strong talk and minor harassments, now paled at the prospect of having to stand up against an armed invasion—especially one in which British regulars were involved. This would be open rebellion, and the contemplation of the possible, if not probable, consequences of such an act was worrisome indeed. According to Ira, Ethan had a difficult time preventing the meeting from breaking up in confusion and indecision. In the end he managed to convince a majority of the committees that, in view of what the men of the Grants stood to lose, there was no reasonable course open to them save armed resistance. Force would be met with force, and plans were drawn up accordingly by Ethan and his staff for the approval of the committees.

First a spy must be sent to Albany to obtain information about the size and nature of the invading force, its route of march, etc. On the basis of this intelligence, strategic vantage points would be carefully chosen along the way where squads of sharpshooters would lie in wait and snipe. Special care was to be taken by the snipers to cut down the enemy leaders, particularly Governor Tryon, in the hope that loss of leadership would have a demoralizing effect upon the troops. Then, at the proper moment of fear and confusion, the Green Mountain Boys would emerge from out of nowhere and sweep down upon the invading army with as much force and fury as they could muster.

Chosen for the job of spying on Tryon's troops was Ira Allen, Ethan's youngest brother and the runt of Joseph and Mary Allen's large litter. Born a dozen or so years after Ethan, Ira had spent his childhood on the family farm in Cornwall. There this undersized, deceptively fragile-looking youth made his way as a precocious tag-along to his older brothers, who called him Stub and taught him the ways of the farm and forest and what the world expected of an Allen. He learned his lessons rapidly and well. He always would.

At sixteen Ira went to live with Heman in Salisbury, where he remained for nearly three years working in and about the general store. Sometimes he took to the woods for extended periods, searching for hides or hemlock bark for Heman's tannery, or driving his brother's hogs to fatten in the beech groves of southern Massachusetts. At other times he worked in the store, buying and selling and keeping accounts. From it all he managed to accumulate, in addition to a world of experience, modest sums of money which, on Ethan's advice, he invested at a penny or two an acre in wild lands on the New Hampshire Grants. By late 1770 he held Wentworth titles to sizable stretches of property north and east of Poultney, and in the autumn of that year he moved permanently onto the Grants in order to oversee and promote his expanding land operations.

By the time of the invasion crisis in early May of 1772, Ira had been on the Grants for a year and a half and, although barely twenty-one years old, was already recognized as a person of some standing in the area. A quiet, mature young man of considerable property, the brother of Ethan Allen, and himself a lieutenant in the Green Mountain Boys, he was well enough known and respected by his west-side neighbors to be singled out now for the difficult and hazardous job of spying on Governor Tryon's invasion force. It was Ira's first public assignment—but not his last.

For the journey to Albany, Ira was given a brace of pistols, the fastest horse in Bennington, and many a God-speed. As matters turned out, however, he needed none of these. Upon his return to Fay's tavern on the following day, he reported that although large contingents of troops were indeed moving up the Hudson, they were not bound for the Grants but for the relief of the British garrisons at Niagara and Detroit. The crisis that was not a crisis had passed. The two venerable cannons and a mortar recently acquired from the ruins of Fort Hoosick could now be put back under wraps, and the Green Mountain Boys could return home to start their spring planting. Had it all been for nothing? Not at all. The invasion scare had resulted in a useful drill for the men of the Grants and, more important, had provided them with an opportunity to prove to themselves and others that they would not be demoralized by a show of force. In defense of their property they would stand an engagement on the field of battle if need be, even against British regulars. "This alarm," Ira later noted, "answered every purpose that a victory possibly could have done, without shedding blood."

Actually, Governor Tryon, quite unaware of the flurry of excitement among Ethan and his friends, had already decided upon a more temperate approach to the problem of the Grants. Perhaps influenced by rumors that the Home Government was less than pleased with his lack of progress in resolving the Grants controversy, Tryon sent off a peace-feeler on May 19 to "the inhabitants of Bennington." In a letter drawn up with the approval of his Council, Tryon stoutly reaffirmed New York's political authority over the Grants and denounced the recalcitrance of the settlers. At the same time, however, he indicated a desire to avoid "compulsive measures" and to follow "lenient methods . . . to give such relief as the nature of your situation and circumstances will justify." Generally conciliatory in tone, the governor's message invited the settlers to send representatives to New York City to present their grievances before the provincial authorities. The governor was willing and anxious to receive anyone the settlers should choose to speak for them, excepting Ethan Allen and his fellow outlaws. On the whole it was a friendly letter and seemingly a generous one, but it was also clearly meant to be an ultimatum of sorts to which the men of the Grants would do well to accede. "I flatter myself you will cheerfully improve this final offer of reconciling yourselves to this government. I am your friend— Wm. Tryon."

The governor's message reached the Grants not long after the invasion scare and was received with great enthusiasm by the settlers, who only a short while before had been busy planning the best way to shoot down His Excellency from ambush. At a public meeting held in Bennington on June 5, it was decided to accept the invitation and send Stephen Fay and his son Jonas to represent the Wentworth proprietors before Tryon. A letter was then composed which contained strong professions of loyalty to New York authority, but at the same time firmly upheld the settlers' right of soil under the Wentworth titles. The controversy over land ownership, it was conceded, was indeed a thorny one, resulting, no doubt, from confusion and misunderstanding. One day soon the problem would be finally resolved by His Majesty's great wisdom. In the meantime, "we most earnestly pray and beseech your Excellency would assist to quiet us in our possessions."

A good enough letter perhaps, but a little too moderate to suit Ethan. Consequently, he wrote one of his own which, although somewhat pompous and long-winded, gave an excellent statement of the settlers' position. Filled with dramatic references to "our undoubted rights and privileges as Englishmen," "tyrannical exertions of power," etc., Ethan's reply to Tryon left no doubt that while the men of the Grants were steadfast in their loyalty to the King and the government of New York, there was a line beyond which they would not go. "Our properties are at stake—this we contend for." Sounding more like John Locke than a frontier land-merchant and outlaw, Ethan then presumed to lecture Tryon on the nature of law:

> Laws and society compacts were made to protect and secure the subjects in their peaceable possessions and properties, and not to subvert them. No person or community of persons can be sup-

posed to be under any peculiar compact or law, except it presupposeth that the Law will protect such person or community of persons in his or their properties; for otherways the subject would, by Law, be bound to be an accessary to his own ruin and destruction, which is inconsistent with the law of self-preservation; but this Law being natural as well as eternal, can never be abrogated by the Law of men.

Like his Bennington friends, Ethan professed to believe that the trouble on the Grants had arisen and was being kept alive by misinformation and a lack of a true understanding on the part of Governor Tryon and his Council. And small wonder, for "your Excellency's ear has been much abused by subtle and designing men . . . who manifest a surprising and enterprizing thirst of avarice after our country." It was against these "intreaguers," and certainly not against the authority of the Province of New York, that "our breasts glow with a martial fury."

After getting his fellow outlaws, Remember, Seth Warner, and Robert Cochran, to join him in signing the letter, Ethan gave it to the Fays who took it along with the other to present to the New York Governor and Council. Three weeks later the landlord and his son returned to Bennington with glad tidings. They had been received cordially by Tryon, who although refusing to accept the settlers' view of things, had agreed in the presence of his Council to show "great tenderness to a deluded people" by postponing all proceedings involving right of soil until His Majesty's pleasure became known. The governor also indicated his willingness to suspend action against all persons on the Grants, including Ethan and his friends, charged with crimes supposedly committed in defense of the Wentworth titles. In other words, a general moratorium. While London continued to ponder the problem, "the settlers on both sides shall continue undisturbed."

There was great rejoicing in Bennington over Governor Tryon's generous offer. After accepting the truce terms by "a full and unanimous vote" in public meeting, the settlers celebrated the occasion in proper fashion. "The whole artillery of Bennington [those two rusty cannons and the mortar from Fort Hoosick] together with small arms were several times discharged in honor to the Govr & Councill of N. York," and the flowing bowl passed freely among His Majesty's loyal subjects. Health was drunk to the King, to the good governor and his Council, and to "universal Peace and Pelenty, Liberty, and Property." It was a fitting way to herald the coming of a brighter day on the New Hampshire Grants—fitting but premature, for at that very moment, far to the north, things were happening that would shatter the truce before it really had a chance to go into effect.

While the Fays were in New York consulting with Governor Tryon, Ira had been off on one of his lonely expeditions into the wilderness, searching out choice land. Near Bolton, in the vicinity of present-day Burlington, he chanced to come across a Yorker survey team headed by William Cockburn—the same William Cockburn whom Ethan had driven from Pittsford just a year before, and now here he was back on the Grants again with his transit and chain and obviously up to no good. Ethan, then in Castelton, was immediately notified, and he dispatched a small contingent of Green Mountain Boys, headed by Seth Warner and Remember Baker, to seize Cockburn. This they did, and more. On their way northward the Boys passed by the lower falls of Otter Creek in what is now Panton. There they found several families of Jerseyites who had just recently been brought to the area as tenants of Colonel John Reid, holder of New York title to a large tract of land in the vicinity of the falls.* Since these newcomers obviously had no right to be there, they were unceremoniously set upon by the Boys and driven into the woods amidst warnings, loud and profane, never to return.

As for Cockburn, he was captured easily enough. He was found not far from where Ira had first spotted him, and was trussed up and carried down to Castleton to appear before Ethan. Fortunately for the New York surveyor, Ethan had just learned of Governor Tryon's truce offer, and he therefore released Cockburn without punishment and provided that he be escorted safely off the Grants. But the damage had already been done. When Tryon heard about the seizure of Cockburn, and particularly about the ouster of Colonel Reid's tenants, he was more than a little upset. The whole business was shocking, he wrote to the people of Bennington. He found it difficult to understand "this breach of faith and honor made by a body of your people." He had attempted to deal honestly and leniently with the men of the Grants, but "during the very moment" of negotiation, "a daring insult to government, a violation of public faith" had been committed by some of the very people he had been laboring so hard to accommodate. It was all very disappointing

* Not the same John Reid whom Ethan had driven from Rupert the previous autumn.

and disturbing to His Excellency, and he hoped that the decent, law-abiding settlers of the area would alleviate his distress by restoring the dispossessed tenants to their lands. This would be one way, in fact the only way, by which the men of the Grants could reassure the governor of their good faith and honest intentions.

Immediately upon the receipt of Governor Tryon's angry letter, the Committees of Safety of the various Grants towns convened at Manchester to ponder the new situation and decide upon a course of action. It was not the first such meeting, nor would it be the last, but it held a special significance for the future because of the presence of a few representatives from towns east of the mountains. For the first time settlers of the east side, although not as yet directly threatened to any significant degree by the land controversy, had begun to show interest and act in concert with their more exposed neighbors to the west. It was a small beginning, but a beginning nonetheless, to cooperative action between the two sections against the growing Yorker menace.

For a time it appeared that the more conservative (Ethan called them fearful) members of the convention would succeed in persuading the towns to accommodate Tryon by restoring Reid's tenants to their property, thereby disavowing the recent action of the Green Mountain Boys. Eventually, however, Ethan and his supporters were able to convince the meeting that to give in on this matter would be to weaken the position of the Wentworth proprietors and encourage the Yorkers to make future encroachments. Better than that, Ethan managed to get himself elected clerk of the meeting and as such was charged with the responsibility of writing a reply to the New York governor. And what a reply it was, bristling with denials, charges, and counter-charges! It was all the governor's fault that this recent trouble had occurred. It was he, Ethan insisted, and not the settlers, who had been guilty of bad faith, and it was he, not the settlers, who should now apologize. After all, while talking peace His Excellency had permitted a surveyor to be sent onto the Grants to parcel out land for the New York land-jobbers, and the Green Mountain Boys had acted only in retaliation.

All things considered, this was not the sort of letter calculated to soothe Tryon's ruffled feelings, especially in view of the fact that it was written by the chief of the Grants outlaws. His Excellency found it "highly insolent and deserving of sharp reprehension," and sent it along to London as a good example of a bad thing. But good or bad, Ethan's letter left no doubt about how matters stood on the Grants. It made it clear that the settlers were notably lacking in contrition and still as defiant as ever. On September 8, 1772, two weeks after Ethan had written his explosive reply, Tryon and his Council concluded that the Wentworth settlers were "highly unworthy of that Lenity discoverable in the Terms so lately offered them" and declared an end to all negotiations. The Tryon truce was a thing of the past, without really ever having had a chance to amount to much, and no one was more responsible for its untimely ruin than Ethan Allen.

It may be that Ethan deliberately subverted the Tryon truce. Perhaps he saw it as a possible threat to his holdings. It was well known that the government of New York had long looked with some sympathy upon those holders of Wentworth titles who had actually settled on their property. In fact, for many months there had been rumors abroad that a generous accommodation might be offered them—perhaps confirmation without fee. For those Wentworthites who had not settled their lands, however, there had been no such signs of solicitude. Quite the opposite. The New York authorities had on more than one occasion made it clear that they were not very kindly disposed toward them, especially those like Ethan who held large acreage for speculation. In other words, the settlers were in a distinctly more favored (or less unfavored) position than the non-resident proprietors, and were therefore more likely to be receptive to the blandishments of Tryon and his Yorker friends. In time, all of this could conceivably lead to some sort of amicable arrangement between the settlers and the government of New York Province, which would leave the non-resident proprietors in the hopeless position of having to stand alone in their defense of the Wentworth titles. If it had been given half a chance, the Tryon truce could have proved to be a long step in this direction, and for that very reason Ethan might have wrecked it purposely. Who can say?

Whatever Ethan's real feelings may have been about it, and whatever his reasons, if any, for demolishing it, the Tryon peace offer in no way interfered with his land dealings. He continued to traffic in speculation with unbated zeal, buying when he could, selling when he must, and plowing most of his profits back into the business. So far he had operated pretty much on his own, constantly straining his resources to add what he could to his rapidly expanding domain. But in the autumn of 1772, not long after the shattering of Tryon's truce, Ethan's land transactions began to take on a new dimension.

The idea came from Ira, as so many ideas did. Not long before leaving Connecticut in late 1770, Ira, then only nineteen, had set himself up in a new profession by purchasing a secondhand transit and a set of chains, and studying under a master surveyor for a period of seven days. Upon his arrival on the Grants he proclaimed himself an expert surveyor whose services were available to anyone—except Yorkers—for a reasonable fee. Jobs were not slow in coming. At that time there was plenty of surveying to be done on the New Hampshire Grants, especially in the north country where the boundaries of holdings were for the most part known only by approximation, if at all. Ira, it soon became known, was extraordinarily good at his work. Later he would become the first surveyor-general of the independent Republic of Vermont and prove himself, beyond any question, the best surveyor in the Republic and the worst keeper of records.

From dozens of Wentworth proprietors, including several non-residents he had known back in Salisbury, Ira received assignments that took him over much of the Grants area west of the mountains. A great part of his time was spent in the north country in the vicinity of Mount Mansfield, where he often ran lines across land that had never before been visited by a white man. His journals written during this period tell in a most matter-of-fact way a story of appalling hardship and loneliness, and of the incredible courage, stamina, and enterprise of a young man who had a job to do and meant to do it. In return for his services he collected a tidy sum in the aggregate, much of it paid in acreage rather than cash, and to a large extent it was this income earned from surveying other men's lands that enabled him to add substantially to his own holdings during his early years on the Grants. In addition to his fees, Ira's surveying brought him a knowledge of the north country that few men, if any, could match—an advantage that he would not fail to exploit to the fullest.

In the summer of 1772 Ira spent some time in the vicinity of the Onion (now Winooski) River, and his impressions of the place were so favorable that he became convinced that here was an area bound to become valuable, and at no distant time. Blessed with rich stands of timber, broad intervales, and a generous availability of water, plus easy access to Lake Champlain, this land would one day sell for a handsome figure. An ideal spot for speculative buying on the large scale. Why not form a partnership with Ethan, and perhaps others, and exploit the situation while the price and circumstances were right?

He put the idea to Ethan at Poultney and proposed that the two of them travel north together and inspect the area. Ethan was not particularly enthused over the prospects of becoming involved in a partnership with Ira or anyone else. He figured that he was doing pretty well on his own. Besides, he was already stretched rather thin and didn't want to run the risk of taking on more than he could handle. However, he did agree to go up north with Ira on a hunting trip and take a close look around. Late in the autumn the two brothers packed up their gear and headed for the Onion River to bag a few deer and sniff out the land. What they saw must have convinced Ethan that Ira had been right all along, for by the time they returned to Poultney, Ethan was ready to admit that Ira's plan had much to recommend it.

In the winter of that year, Ethan and Ira got together with Heman and Zimri at the general store in Salisbury. Also on hand was Remember Baker, who had come down from the Grants at Ira's urging. For the better part of two days Ira's project was carefully examined and discussed. Ethan was by now completely sold on the idea. So was Remember. But Heman was not, and neither was Zimri, who tended to follow Heman's lead in most matters. To do the thing right would require a great deal of money, Heman argued, perhaps more than all of them together could raise, and with the future of Wentworth land titles very much in doubt, they ran the risk of total loss. On the whole, he had serious doubts about Ira's plan and at first refused to go along with it. In the end, however, he relented. He was an Allen after all, and if the others were willing to take the gamble, damned if he and Zimri would be standoffish. Thus was formed among the four brothers and their cousin the new partnership of Allen and Baker, soon to become known as the Onion River Company. There were, Ira would later recall, no contracts and no stated capital—just a friendly, informal family agreement to pool their resources, such as they were, and buy land for speculation in the Onion River area. From these meager beginnings there would develop an uncommonly enterprising business venture that within two years would obtain title to more than one hundred square miles of the choicest land in the north country.

The plan of operation was simple enough. The partners would immediately buy up as much land as possible near the mouth of the Onion River and from that base would fan out as fast and as far as circumstances would permit. Ira and Remember would station themselves up north and handle the company's affairs at that end. Among other things, they were to build a store near the falls of the river and cut a road through the wilderness to the southern settlements. Heman and Zimri would act as agents for the company in the Salisbury–Sheffield area where interest in Grants land continued to run high. As for Ethan, it was agreed that he would operate out of Bennington, from where he could best serve the company's interests by "managing political affairs." In other words, he was to continue to do what he could in defense of the Wentworth titles against the Yorkers—a defense that must not fail if the Onion River Company were to avoid disaster.

Soon after the formation of their partnership in Salisbury, the Allens and Baker set about the business of acquiring acreage in the Onion River area. Much of the land near the mouth of the river was known to be in the hands of "Edward Burling and associates," a group of New York speculators who lived in the neighborhood of White Plains. A decade earlier, Governor Wentworth had granted the Burling associates some 20,000 acres in the immediate vicinity of what is now Burlington, plus extensive tracts in Essex, Jericho, and New Huntington (now Richmond). Here was an attractive and sizable block of choice land, a fitting nucleus about which the Onion River Company might build its empire, and in February of 1773 all of the partners save Zimri set out for White Plains to see what could be done about obtaining it.

Mindful of the fact that two of their number, Ethan and Remember, were outlaws with rewards posted for their capture, and that White Plains was in enemy territory a scant twenty miles from Tryon's capital in New York City, the three brothers and Cousin Remember approached the situation with caution. Fully armed and disguised as British officers they made their way on horseback to White Plains where they put up at the local tavern. There they remained for the better part of three days while dickering with Burling and his partners for as much land as they could get. They got plenty—upwards of 40,000 acres in all, and at an average price of less than ten cents an acre. Here was an excellent bargain indeed, made possible mainly by the fact that Ethan and his friends had faith in the Wentworth titles, whereas Edward Burling and his associates did not. The Onion River Company was off to a promising start, and the fact that this initial triumph had been scored under the very nose of the New York governor must have made it all the sweeter.

Not long after the trip to White Plains, Ira and Remember were back on the Grants making preparations to move north to Onion River and begin work on the store and the road. Ethan stayed on for a time in Salisbury, however, to help drum up business for the new company. The Burling purchase had put a severe strain upon the treasury, and it was imperative that money start coming in as soon as possible. To this end, Ethan wrote up an advertisement for the Onion River Company and rode down to Hartford to place it in the *Connecticut Courant*. The ad, which appeared in late May, told of a northern paradise that fairly reeked of fertility and natural beauty. The forests abounded in choice timber and game; the rich intervales beckoned enticingly to the plow; and the Onion River itself was crowded with "a diversity of sorts of excellent fish particularly the salmon. . . . There is no tract of land of so great quantity between New York and the government of Canada, that in a state of nature can justly be denominated equally good. . . . The land will be sold at a moderate price." And then, with less than complete candor, Ethan added: "Said purchase and settlement is insured on a title derived from under the Great Seal of the Province of New Hampshire."

Meanwhile, Ethan and Heman were making the rounds among their friends and neighbors in Litchfield County, and with some success. In mid-May they sold 1,200 acres to a group of Salisbury residents, who agreed under bond to repair to the Onion River area within a year and immediately begin clearing the land. It was the first sale made by the new company, and it would turn out to be an especially significant one for among the purchasers was Thomas Chittenden, who would play a most important role in the subsequent development of the Grants area. Before long he would occupy a commanding position among the founding fathers of the Republic of Vermont. He would, in fact, serve as the Republic's first and, save for one brief exception, its only president during the dozen or so years of its existence.

Although close to illiterate and somewhat rough around the edges, "One-eyed Tom" was a person of rare quality. Possessed of no special talents of his own, he had, nevertheless, the ability to marshal the talents of others and direct them toward a common purpose. By all accounts he was the great cohesive factor of Vermont's most critical years. Men trusted him. They rallied behind him. Without him it is unlikely that the Republic of Vermont would have survived its infancy. It was said of him that he rarely made a mistake in judging men, and if this is true, then it may be worth noting that he would remain from first to last, through good times and bad, a devoted friend and staunch ally of the Allen boys.

By the time Ethan had arrived back on the Grants in the late spring of 1773, Ira and Remember, working with a small crew of hired men, had already made a good beginning on their road. With remarkable energy and speed they continued to chop away at the dense wilderness throughout the summer months, cutting a narrow and tortuous swath almost due south along the line of least resistance. From time to time Ethan would appear upon the scene to look over the operation and nod approval, but the moving force behind this ambitious undertaking was Brother Ira, who determined the road's course with his transit and provided general supervision for the project. By early autumn the road had been completed. Running approximately along the route of the present-day highway from Burlington to Castleton by way of Middlebury, the road, nearly seventy miles long, was really little more than a pack trail, but it was good enough to serve the purpose for which it was intended. The Onion River country was now accessible to the outside world, and first to take advantage of the fact was Remember Baker who proceeded to move his family up to the vicinity of the falls, thereby becoming the first permanent settler in the Burlington area. Others would soon follow. "Thus in a short time," Ira later remarked with understandable pride, "I led a people through a wilderness of seventy miles; about the same distance that took Moses forty years to conduct the children of Israel."

During that same summer the store was constructed. Actually it was a blockhouse of sorts which was meant to serve mainly as a fort and only incidentally as a general store and office headquarters for the company. The building was designed for strength and durability rather than comfort, and with Indians and Yorkers on the prowl, the effort that went into its making represented a judicious investment. Constructed at the falls of the Onion River, the fort measured thirty-two feet by twenty and was made of hewn hemlock timbers, no one of which was less than eight inches thick. The second story, with an overhang of two feet, was pierced by thirty-two portholes for small arms, and the roof was so attached that it would be taken off in case of fire. Inside the fort was a natural spring which, along with the food-stuffs stashed on the shelves, would enable a small group to withstand a prolonged siege. As it turned out, the fort was never used for defense, but its rugged presence was a splendid morale factor and doubtless did much, along with the road, to increase the value of the Onion River property and hurry settlers into the area.

While pushing their road through the wilderness, Ira, Remember, and their crew passed close by New Haven township, located at the lower falls of Otter Creek directly across from  Panton. Here they discovered that Colonel John Reid, whose Jerseyites had been driven from Panton by Warner and Baker during the truce of the summer before, had again settled the falls area with tenants, this time on the New Haven side. These new tenants were Scots, recently arrived in the Colonies from the Old Country. They had been brought to the Grants in early June by Reid himself, who, after driving off two Wentworth settlers, had re-affirmed his ownership of the New Haven–Panton area and assured the Scots that they had nothing to fear because the authority of the mighty Province of New York stood behind them. Reid had then retired to New York and safety, leaving his unsuspecting tenants to their own devices. In all, there were not more than a dozen families of them—strangers far from home, alone now in a new and awesome land. It must have been a terrifying experience for them when the Green Mountain Boys fell upon them in August of that year.

Upon learning of this new encroachment by the Yorkers, Ira sent word to Ethan in Bennington, who immediately mustered a force of more than one hundred Green Mountain Boys, including most of Seth Warner's company. This was many times the number needed for the job at hand, but the greater the show of strength the more indelible would be the impression made upon the intruders and upon others, including Governor Tryon, who would be bound to hear of the affair sooner or later. After a four-day trip the main body of troops, moving up from the south, reached a point across the creek from Reid's settlement where they were joined by Remember and Ira and their road crew. Crossing over by canoe, the Boys fell with full fury upon the terrified settlement and began a systematic destruction of everything of value. Letting loose their horses to destroy the corn in the fields, Ethan's troops spent the better part of two days in spreading ruin and terror throughout the little community. The houses of the settlers were burned to the ground; their corn sheds and haystacks were destroyed; the gristmill was entirely demolished and its millstones smashed to bits and thrown into the creek. No injury was done to any person—Ethan saw to that—but men, women, and children, some of them infants, were left without shelter and only enough food to see them off the Grants. Even so, they must have considered themselves fortunate, for there had been some careless talk about tying them all to trees and skinning them alive.

On the evening of the second day, after the devastation and harassment had been completed, Ethan announced to the Scots that it would be unwise of them, or anyone else for that matter, to attempt to rebuild. If Reid were to send any more settlers into the area, they would get the same sort of treatment and would be whipped into the bargain. And if the Green Mountain Boys ever managed to get their hands on Reid himself, they would surely cut off his head. Count on it. Ethan expected to be around for a long time to see to it that the Yorkers kept their distance. "I have run these woods in the same manner these seven years past and never was catched yet." And then he surprised the burned-out settlers, and perhaps himself as well, by offering them some of his own land free if they cared to settle it. For all of his brusqueness and occasional bursts of violence, Ethan was not an insensitive person. He seems to have been a man of basically generous impulses who more often than not was apt to temper his ferocity with some unexpected and sometimes highly illogical act of compassion. It was probably this charitable strain in his behavior that caused some of Ethan's earlier biographers to see him as a sort of Yankee Robin Hood—possibly a not altogether unfitting comparison, although it is not recorded that Robin ever speculated in wild lands. As for the Scots, there was little enthusiasm shown for Ethan's generous offer. Only one of Reid's tenants decided to accept and start life anew as a free man on land of his own. The others had seen enough of the New Hampshire Grants to last them a lifetime.

With the ruins of the New Haven settlement still smoking, Ethan and his Boys recrossed the creek and began their long march southward. For most of them, this expedition against Reid's tenants had involved considerable sacrifice, for it had taken them from their farms for more than a week during the long days of midsummer. But it had all been worth the effort. Once again the Yorkers had been routed, and although the means employed had been somewhat brutal, they had also been effective. The area had been purged of a dangerous contaminant. The unfortunate Scots would make no attempt to reestablish themselves, nor would Colonel Reid ever again trouble the region around the lower falls, or anywhere else on the Grants. Within a few weeks Ira's road would be open all the way to Castleton, and the land that Reid had twice tried to settle with Yorker tenants would soon be taken over in fee simple by Yankee farmers moving up from the south with their Wentworth titles. Some of these titles would be purchased from Ethan Allen, who, it so happened, held ownership in his own name to a sizable acreage in the vicinity of the falls, including some of that which Colonel Reid had been brash enough to attempt to settle with his Scottish tenants.

The Onion River Company continued to grow and prosper until the spring of 1775 when the outbreak of the Revolution brought a sudden suspension of all activity. By that time the company had become solidly established as a going concern. A considerable amount of acreage had been sold, mainly to individuals and groups intent upon settling the land in the near future. In most cases a provision was included in the sales contract whereby the purchaser agreed to begin clearing his land within a year. In this way Ethan and his partners deliberately discouraged speculative buying. They were, after all, not primarily interested in reaping the short gains from quick resale, but rather in waiting for the infinitely more wholesome profits to be had from a long-range increment in land prices which they believed would certainly come. The day of handsome returns could be hastened, not by selling to speculators who would be apt to hold the land fallow for months or years, but by attracting settlers, whose improvements and very presence would enhance the value of the surrounding area. By the spring of 1775, perhaps as many as fifty families had made their pitches in the Onion River country, and more were on their way to help settle the nearly 17,000 acres of choice land that Ethan and his partners had already sold. Since an average acre of this land, which only two years before had been purchased by the partners for ten cents, was selling in early 1775 for somewhere around five dollars, the Onion River Company was obviously making a substantial profit. While selling, however, the partners continued to add to their holdings by buying up wild lands in adjacent areas, with the result that by the eve of the Revolution they were able to claim holdings in excess of 60,000 acres, valued at a total of $297,000.

In March of 1775 the members of the Onion River Company held their first and only business meeting. Assembling at Ethan's place in

Sheffield, the four brothers and Cousin Remember had good cause to congratulate themselves. In a little more than two years they had developed Ira's dream into an impressive reality with assets of more than a quarter of a million dollars. On paper they were all rich men, and they saw no reason why they should not become richer. It was agreed that they should "continue said business" and meet at Sheffield the following spring to take stock of things, and at that time either dissolve the partnership and divide the assets or plan for future expansion. This second meeting was never held, however. War would intervene and cast a long shadow over the lands and personnel of the company. For many years the Onion River country would be completely behind British lines, and not until after the signing of the peace treaty in 1783 would the company be able to fully resume its activities. By then, of the original partners only Ethan and Ira would still be alive to pick up operations where they had been left off in the spring of 1775.

# V. The Enforcer

IN HIS dual, yet single-purpose role of Colonel Commandant of the Green Mountain Boys and "manager of political affairs" for the Onion River Company, Ethan had his hands full during the years just prior to the outbreak of the Revolution. After the collapse of Tryon's truce hardly a week went by when his special talents were not called upon to put down some threat, real or imagined, to the Wentworth titles. It would have been worrisome enough if all of the trouble, or even most of it, had come from the direction of Albany or New York City, but by mid-1773 there were disturbing signs that all was not well on the home front. It was apparent that many of the men of the Grants, including several who had stood four-square with Ethan only a few months before, had begun to weary of the long contest and were inclining more and more toward seeking an accommodation with the New York authorities. For most of the more seasoned settlers, the hardships of the early years had passed. By now their fields had been largely cleared; permanent homes had taken the places of the earlier huts and hovels, and in general, the commitment of these men to their lands had increased manyfold. Furthermore, there was among them a burgeoning prosperity of sorts that made the price of confirmation seem less outrageous than it once had. Many of these better established settlers had even managed to accumulate a fair amount of cash by selling pearlash to the neighboring colonies, and with money on hand with which to pay to have their lands guaranteed them, the thought of jeopardizing everything by continuing to resist the power of New York no longer seemed very reasonable.

The tactics employed by Governor Tryon further weakened their spirit of resistance. Following the end of the truce, Tryon increased his pressure on the Wentworth holdings by issuing several new grants under New York titles. Most of these grants covered land already held by New Hampshire proprietors, including Ethan, and a few of them overlapped settled areas. The fact that he had been specifically forbidden by the Home Government to make further issues until the King's will were made known did not hinder the Governor at all. If anything, it probably had the opposite effect, for he seemed to be in a great hurry to grant as much acreage as possible—thereby strengthening New York's tenuous hold on the Grants—before His Majesty could find out what was going on. By the spring of 1775, Tryon and his acting-governor, Cadwallader Colden, had issued patents to approximately 2,000,000 acres of Grants land, or about one-third the total area of present-day Vermont.

At the same time that he was pressing in on them with new grants, Governor Tryon made it considerably easier for the Wentworth settlers to come to terms with New York by offering to confirm their lands at half-fee. This too, of course, was against the King's pleasure, for the Decree of 1767 had ordered the suspension of all grants, including those of a confirmatory nature. Still, King's pleasure or not, it was probably a wise move on Tryon's part. The Grants settler could now obtain confirmation for his 100-acre holding for seven or eight Spanish dollars, and such an attractive offer as this put Ethan at an added disadvantage. In spite of everything he and his Boys could do, with each passing month it became increasingly more difficult to prevent defections. Time and attrition, the improved fortunes of many of the settlers, and Tryon's half-fee policy were dangerously eroding the Wentworth position. The Yorkers were winning the war of the Grants, and they were winning it mainly from within. By the spring of 1775, ninety-two towns had applied for confirmation under the Seal of New York, and forty of these were on the west side in Ethan Allen country.

Ethan had no intention, however, of losing the struggle by default. Both as Colonel Commandant of the Green Mountain Boys and official enforcer for the Onion River Company, he had to do his level best to defend the Wentworth proprietors, large and small, resident and nonresident, whether they wanted him to or not. No one was more aware than he that the Grants situation was becoming increasingly grave, but there was some comfort in the realization that it had never been especially promising. From the very beginning Ethan had been engaged in a desperate holding action, playing for time until something—perhaps the long-awaited decision from London—would come along to save the day for the Wentworth titles. Actually, very little had changed. He must still fight for time, only now he must fight harder; and he must fight without being quite sure of who his friends were. Already a few of his closest comrades had openly declared their intention of seeking an accommodation with the Yorkers, and Ethan did not doubt for a moment that others would follow their example. But neither did he doubt that he could slow down the process of defection, and to do this he would not be reluctant to use a little muscle if the occasion seemed to warrant it, even against so-called friends.

Thus, during the two years prior to the Revolution, as the Wentworth prospects grew noticeably bleaker, Ethan stepped up his war against the Yorkers and all those others whose actions or attitudes tended to promote the Yorker cause. Those who were not his friends became his enemies, and his enemies did not fare well before Ethan's wrath. Consider the case of Benjamin Spencer and his Clarendon neighbors. For some time Clarendon, a small west-side town about a dozen miles east of Poultney, had been a bone in Ethan's throat because of the Yorker sympathy prevalent among its inhabitants, many of whom had come from New York and settled the area under New York titles. On several occasions the Green Mountain Boys had made known their displeasure toward the town by issuing warnings of one sort or another and subjecting the settlers to minor harassments. Haystacks had been burned and fences toppled, and, as a special touch, a dog belonging to a Clarendon resident had been seized by the Boys, killed, and cut up into pieces because his master had been thoughtless enough to name him "Tryon". "Thus will we do to Tryon," proclaimed Ethan as he and his men paraded the dismembered parts through the town.

If these forays were meant to frighten the townspeople into better behavior, they failed of their purpose. In spite of them, or perhaps partly because of them, the people of Clarendon continued their perverse ways. It was bad enough that they had recently taken to calling their town Durham, a name assigned to it by the government of New York, but it was far worse that many of the town's more prominent Wentworth settlers were reported to be seeking New York confirmation of their lands. This was too much to be endured. Something had to be done to teach the people of Clarendon better manners.

In November of 1773, Ethan and about one hundred and thirty of his men fell upon the town in the dead of night. Singled out for special attention by the raiders was Benjamin Spencer, Yorker justice of the peace, who was generally considered to be the ringleader of the Yorkish faction in town and who had performed his duties as a New York official much too zealously to be permitted to go unmolested. He was, in fact, with the exception of Squire Munro of Shaftsbury, the most outspoken and adamant Yorker partisan west of the mountains, and it was at his house that the Green Mountain Boys made their first visit. After smashing in the door with axes, Ethan and Remember Baker, along with several armed men, rushed into the house and seized Spencer in his bed. "You are a damned old offender," Ethan thundered, and the whole town was a "hornet's nest" that needed cleaning out. Spencer was ordered to get dressed, and when it appeared that he was taking too long about it, Ethan dealt him a smart blow on the head with his gun butt in order to hurry him up.

According to Spencer's later deposition, he was taken a couple of miles down the road to the home of a loyal New Hampshireman, and there he was held under armed guard for the better part of two days, being subjected to "frequent threats and many insults by the most opprobrious language." Meanwhile, Ethan and his friends were busy demonstrating to Spencer's neighbors the error of their ways. At least two houses were burned to the ground and their owners forced to "consult their safety by flight." A few other residents were physically abused, although none severely. But this was only a sample of things to come if the inhabitants of the town continued their Yorkish behavior. If the Green Mountain Boys should find it necessary to make another visit to the place, Ethan shouted out loudly enough for the entire town to hear, they would "reduce every House to ashes and leave every Inhabitant a Corpse." If, on the other hand, the deluded people of Clarendon would come to their senses and support the Wentworth cause, they could count on generous treatment from their Grants neighbors and, of course, the protection of the Green Mountain Boys.

As for Spencer, obviously an example must be made of him. On order of the Colonel Commandant he was escorted back to Clarendon and brought to trial in his own front yard, where the people of the town were forced to assemble in order to witness the proceedings. A "judgment seat" was erected for Ethan and fellow judges, Seth Warner, Remember Baker, and Robert Cochran, and the defendant was brought before it to hear the list of charges against him. It was a long list, but what it came down to was that Justice Spencer had been over-zealous in his "respect and obedience" towards the Province of New York. Did the defendant have anything to say? Only that the charges against him were all true, but he saw no reason to apologize for anything he had done. He had performed his duties of office in strict compliance with New York law and his own conscience. "Have I been unfair to any man?" he asked. "No, I give you that," Ethan replied. "You have been fair." But that, of course, was not the point.

Spencer was found guilty on all counts and his house was ordered burned as a public nuisance. Remember urged that the Justice also be whipped, but Ethan and the other judges ruled against this. It would be enough to burn out "the old rat," and so amidst "great shouting of Joy and much Noise and Tumult," torches were applied to the eaves of Spencer's house. As the fire devoured the roof, however, Ethan had a change of heart and ordered the roof knocked off in order to save the rest of the house. Spencer had seen enough to know that the Green Mountain Boys meant business. They expected him to behave himself from now on, and he could begin by resigning his Yorker commission. In the future, let him refrain from acting against the best interests of his neighbors, else Ethan and his men would return and inflict upon him "the severest punishment." That was the way things stood, and if Spencer didn't like it, he could complain to Tryon. Damn Tryon anyway, and damn the whole government of New York, Ethan declared. "Force is force in whatever hands, and we have the force and power to protect ourselves."

Squire Spencer gave no more trouble. He replaced his roof, resigned his commission, and curbed his enthusiasm for the Yorker cause, thereby sparing himself the unpleasantness of a return visit from the Green Mountain Boys. What had happened to him was no worse than the treatment given dozens of others on the Grants whom Ethan and his men saw fit to punish for their Yorkish ways. Indeed, some of Ethan's victims were handled much more roughly than Spencer. So it was with Spencer's Clarendon neighbor Benjamin Hough, Baptist minister of the town and avid Yorker. Soon after Ethan's raid on Clarendon, Hough journeyed to New York City where he met with the Governor and Council to give in detail his eyewitness account of the outrage committed against his town and the government of New York by "the Bennington mob." He urged that New York send troops onto the Grants to restore order and protect the "friends of Government," and he warned that special efforts should be made to capture Ethan Allen and his fellow terrorists who were turning the Grants into a land of violence and fear. Having presented his case and found his listeners sympathetic and apparently determined upon strong measures, Hough began his long trip back to the Grants, but not until after he had agreed to take over the job of justice of the peace left vacant by Spencer's sudden resignation.

The Reverend Benjamin Hough almost made it back home—almost, but not quite. He was within sight of his house in Clarendon when he was seized by two of Ethan's men, who hustled him onto a sleigh and drove him thirty miles south to Sunderland. There he was held in confinement for the next three days until Ethan and Seth Warner, along with a few men from Warner's company, were able to make it up from Bennington to sit as a court of judgment. Since the members of the court were both accusers and judges, it did not take them long to find Hough guilty of having been an obnoxious busybody and carrier of tales, and of having accepted a commission from the government of New York with the intention of acting against the interests of the Grants settlers. For his crimes, Hough was to receive two hundred lashes well laid onto his naked back.

The sentence was carried out to the last lash, and Hough, his back horribly mutilated, was cut free from the tree to which he had been bound and carried to the home of a nearby doctor, who attended to his wounds and provided him with a bed for the night. Early the next morning Hough was brought before Ethan and orderd to leave the Grants immediately and never return. Hough asked that he be allowed to go home first to see his family and collect a few belongings, but permission was denied him. He had been on the Grants too long already, and it was high time he departed from the sight of respectable people. Let him betake himself to his beloved New York and stay there. If he were ever to return to the Grants, the Green Mountain Boys would "ketch" him and give him twice two hundred lashes and then some. Ethan then handed Hough a note which read:

This may certify the inhabitants of the New-Hampshire Grants that Benjamin Hough hath this day received a full punishment for his crimes committed heretofore against his Country, and our inhabitants are ordered to give him, the said Hough a free and unmolested passport toward the City of New York, or to the Westward of our Grants, he behaving as becometh. Given under our hands, etc.

Ethan Allen
Seth Warner

And so, racked with pain and barely able to stand, the Reverend Benjamin Hough set out on foot that cold winter's morning to leave the Grants at the request of the Green Mountain Boys. As he stumbled away he heard Ethan say that he supposed the New York authorities would soon be hearing about what had happened to another of their magistrates. Well, let them hear. "They are all a bunch of damned cowards, or they would have come against us long before."

Ethan's treatment of Hough was an undeniably brutal bit of business, but it must be remembered that he was engaged in a desperate struggle against long odds, and upon the outcome of his running battle with the Yorkers depended in a very large way the fortunes of several thousands of people settled on the Grants under Wentworth titles. If some of these people now found themselves ready to come to terms with New York, there were many others who were in no position to do so, and thus were likely to suffer the sorrowful fate of Andrew Graham. In 1767 Graham had made a small pitch in Windham County on the east side of the mountains. With help from his family, he built a log house and proceeded to endure "all the hardships and Calamities of bringing in a new farm out of the howling wilderness." For several years he worked as hard as any man could, often having to carry in provisions for himself and his family on his back through sixteen miles of forest. And then one day in 1774, after he had proved up nearly forty acres, he was driven off his land without compensation by a group of Yorkers who confronted him with a New York title to his property and the local sheriff to back them up. Thus, without quite understanding how or why, Graham lost everything that he had labored for seven years to acquire. And for him there was no recourse. There was no Ethan Allen on the east side of the mountains.

On the west side there were many settlers whose circumstances were not far different from those that had cost Graham his farm. Some of them, especially the newcomers, could simply not afford to pay the confirmation fee, even at Tryon's bargain rate. To men grubbing away among the stumps and stones of a half-cleared acre or two, straining desperately to provide enough food for the table, cash was a rare commodity indeed. Seven Spanish dollars? Might as well be seven hundred. To many other settlers, like Graham, confirmation was out of the question anyway, cash or no cash, for their lands had already been granted to others under New York patents. These settlers, who for one reason or another were unable to obtain confirmation, made up what was probably a sizable majority of the westsiders. For them the validity of the Wentworth titles was a matter of survival, or something close to it. Like Graham, they stood to lose everything they had worked so hard to acquire. But unlike Graham, they could claim a champion working mightily in their behalf. From men of this sort, and there were many, Ethan received his principal encouragement and support. To them he was neither bully, brute, nor outlaw. He was a hero and a friend, whose name was spoken with considerable reverence.

By early 1774 Ethan's behavior had brought Governor Tryon's patience to the breaking point. The governor was especially upset over Ethan's rough handling of Spencer and Hough. Such outrageous abuse of New York officials must not go unpunished. All persons associated with these crimes should be called to account, and the number of these persons was obviously not a small one. It was now clear to Tryon that the acts of rowdyism committed by Ethan and the "Bennington mob" had received support, or at least friendly acquiescence, from a substantial segment of the Grants settlers. In the past the governor had chosen to deal gently with these people, showing them great charity and forbearance in the hope that they would accept the realities of the situation and reach a peaceful accommodation with the authority of New York Province. But they had chosen instead to allow and, it would seem, even encourage vicious elements among them to conduct a campaign of violence against the law and those appointed to enforce it. The time had now come to put the people of the Grants on notice that they, all of them, must expect to bear full responsibility for any and all crimes committed against the Colony of New York and the King's peace.

To show that he meant business, Tryon issued a proclamation on March 9, 1774, increasing the rewards offered for the Grants outlaws. The price on Ethan now stood at one hundred New York pounds, or about two hundred and fifty Spanish dollars—a considerable sum of money. At the same time, on orders from the governor, the New York Assembly passed "An Act for preventing tumultuous and riotous Assemblies . . . and for the more speedy and effectual punishing of the rioters." By any reasonable reckoning, this Act was more of an emotional outburst than a rational approach to the troubled situation on the Grants. Many of its provisions were extreme, to say the least. Henceforth, assemblies of three or more persons for "unlawful intent" were to be proscribed throughout the Grants, and any person involved in such an assembly would be liable to one year's imprisonment. Officials charged with the responsibility of enforcing this provision might use whatever means they considered necessary, and were explicitly absolved from any blame or penalty for injuring or even killing persons who might prove refractory. Anybody who interfered with a magistrate or his assistants in the execution of this proscription, or any other official duty, would be attainted of felony and would be liable to suffer death. The Act also included a long list of other capital offenses. Among them were such relatively minor infractions as the burning of haystacks and the destruction of fences and outhouses.

As for Ethan and his fellow outlaws, the "harbouring, abetting, or succouring" of these bandits was to be considered a crime against the Province of New York punishable by a year's imprisonment. If the governor so chose, he could now, under a special provision of this Act, issue a decree calling for the Grants outlaws to surrender themselves before the New York authorities within a period of seventy days. If they failed to comply, they could then be shot on sight like so many mad dogs. Actually no such decree was ever issued by Tryon or his acting-governor, Cadwallader Colden, but the provision that authorized it is illustrative of the convulsive nature of the New York Assembly's infamous "Outlawry Act." It was, according to an angry and somewhat exaggerated appraisal written twenty years after the fact by the venerable Samuel Williams, Vermont's first historian, "an act which for its savage barbarity is probably without a parallel in the legislation of any civilized country." Half a century later Jared Sparks, Ethan's first real biographer, matched Williams' indignation by referring to the Act as "the most extraordinary specimen of legislative despotism that has ever found a place in a statute-book."

Whatever else the Act may or may not have been, it was certainly grist for Ethan Allen's propaganda mill. He immediately dubbed it "the Bloody Act," and by that name it became known throughout the Grants. Here was an excellent blunder on the part of his Yorker adversaries that presented him with a rare opportunity. To the issue of property rights, which for many of the settlers had lost some of its intensity, was now added the awful element of political oppression. There was much to rail against in this latest Yorker atrocity, and Ethan proceeded to rail loudly and well. "Tyrannical," "written in blood by villains and sons of whores," "replete with malicious turpitude," etc., this evil Act was clearly the work of modern Dracos who were bent upon "verifying" their laws in blood while casting the pall of slavery over the Grants. Well, now, let them do their damnedest to enforce their awful contrivance. They would not find it an easy task. The men of the Grants were not going to be legislated out of their rights as free men. "We shall more than three, nay, more than three times three hundred, assemble together if need be to maintain our common cause," Ethan declared in a defiant letter to Tryon. And as for threats of capital punishment, "Printed sentences of death will not kill us. . . . We will kill and destroy any persons, whomsoever, that shall presume to be accessory, aiding or assisting, in taking any of us."

The Bloody Act caused Ethan's stock to rise precipitously. Prior to its passage he had been fighting a losing battle in his attempts to hold the Wentworth settlers in line, but suddenly the tide seemed to have turned dramatically in his favor. Actually, this change would prove to be only transitory. Within a few months, after Tryon had left on an extended visit to London and it became apparent that Acting-Governor Colden had no intention of enforcing the Act, the excitement would subside and many of the Grants settlers would once again think longingly of an accommodation with New York—and in some cases even plan for it. But for a while at least, during the spring and early summer of 1774, the men of the Grants with few exceptions appeared to stand almost solidly behind Ethan. Even those older and more conservative settlers who had earlier been inclined to temporize, and had considered Ethan something of a hoodlum, now tended to look upon him as a champion of their liberties. A champion and a prophet, for from the very first he had warned them that the Yorkers would stop at nothing, and it now appeared that he had been right all along.

In mid-April, a few weeks after the news of the Bloody Act had reached the Grants, the committees of the various west-side towns, together with a sprinkling of representatives from across the mountains, met in Manchester to decide what to do about the "hostile resolves of the New York Assembly." At this meeting Ethan was clearly in charge of things. Riding the crest of his new popularity, he had little difficulty in persuading the members of the convention to take a strong stand. In a spirited statement prepared by Ethan himself and adopted by the convention as its official report, the delegates declared their "fixed determination" to maintain their rights and their possessions, and to "stand by and defend our friends and neighbors at the expense of our lives and fortunes. . . ." Among such friends and neighbors, of course, were Ethan and his fellow outlaws, and just to be sure that this fact was generally understood, Ethan spelled it out in the convention's report: "For the future every necessary preparation will be made, and . . . our inhabitants will hold themselves in readiness at a minute's warning to aid and defend such friends of ours, who, for their merit to the great and general cause are falsely denominated rioters."

Of even greater significance was a resolution passed unanimously at the Manchester session which forbade all inhabitants of the Grants to "hold any office of honor or profit under the colony of N. York," and those who already held such office were ordered to suspend their functions "on pain of being viewed" by the Green Mountain Boys. This proscription against New York officials was tantamount to a total denial of New York's political jurisdiction over the Grants. The controversy had obviously entered a new phase. To question the validity of Yorker land titles was one thing, but to renounce New York's political right to rule the area, a right that had been clearly confirmed by the King in 1764, was a long step in the direction of open rebellion. It was also, as matters would turn out, the first major move toward independence for the land that would one day become Vermont.

No sooner was the Manchester convention adjourned than Ethan took up quarters in Stephen Fay's tavern in Bennington, where he would spend much of his time during the spring and summer of 1774 preparing a long pamphlet that was intended to be the final word on the controversy between the men of the Grants and the government of New York. It is likely, but not certain, that this tract was written at the request of the Manchester convention and probably at Ethan's suggestion, although (interestingly enough) the printing costs were paid by the Onion River Company. This was not the first of Ethan's political writings, nor would it be his last, but in many ways it was the best. Certainly it was by far the most substantive. Entitled *A Brief Narrative of the Proceedings of the Government of New York Relative to Their Obtaining the Jurisdiction of that Large District of Land to the Westward of the Connecticut River,* etc., etc., Ethan's pamphlet was neither brief nor a narrative. It was instead a two-hundred-page polemic that bristled with claims and counter-claims in support of the Wentworth position. Brother Ira pronounced it "invaluable in educating the people of other colonies and uniting our people at home," but Ira had a way of exaggerating the achievements of his big brother. Actually, probably very few people ever bothered to read the pamphlet. Certainly this was true of Ethan's neighbors on the Grants, many of whom could read only with great difficulty, if at all, and most of whom would have preferred to fell a hickory rather than fight their way through a page of print.

Still, Ethan's *Brief Narrative* should not be dismissed lightly. Whatever else it was, it represented the first definitive statement of the Wentworth proprietors' side of the argument. Prior to this time many refined and educated gentlemen such as James Duane, John Tabor Kempe, and Cadwallader Colden, had delineated the New York cause in long and fluently written accounts for the world and posterity to scrutinize. Now here was the other side of the case, presented for the written record by the king of the Grants himself, that arch-villain Ethan Allen, who was presumptuous enough to enter boldly into an arena in which words, rather than clubs and torches, were the weapons of combat. On the whole he did remarkably well, too. It is obvious that he spent a great deal of time and effort on his pamphlet, for it indicates a lot of homework, both in the gathering of materials and in their presentation. Essentially, he based his case on justice rather than formal legality. He appealed not to the laws of man but to that higher law of nature which allowed, indeed commanded, every person to protect himself in the possession of his life, liberty, and property. He replaced Blackstone with John Locke, and in so doing made the legalistic arguments of the Yorkers seem petty and irrelevant.

Ethan's pamphlet was undeniably a commendable piece of work. If he mixed a few metaphors along the way, at least he managed to develop his points in a clear and spirited manner. There was a great élan about Ethan which couldn't help but spill over into his writings and make them sparkle. His *Brief Narrative* stands in striking contrast to James Duane's works on the same subject. Whereas Duane in his many pamphlets and articles amply demonstrated his faculty for making even the most exciting matter seem dull, Ethan seemed to give a special luster to every line. But there was more than style and spirit in Ethan's development of his material; there was also a considerable amount of thought, the sort of patient, reflective thinking that one would not ordinarily expect of a frontier strong man. It was a work, remarked Ethan's first biographer, which contained "many evidences of a mind accustomed to observe and think and draw its own inferences." It was also a work of some courage, for in keeping with the recent resolve of the Manchester convention, Ethan's pamphlet went beyond the matter of property rights and denied New York's right to political jurisdiction over the Grants until such a time as "His Majesty's final pleasure be known." Here was rebellion in print.

Ethan finished his pamphlet in the early autumn and left the Grants soon after to take the manuscript down to Hartford. After depositing it with the printer, he retired to his farm in Sheffield to spend the final few weeks of the year with his family while waiting for the *Brief Narrative* to clear the press. By early January of 1775 the printer had finished his work, and Ethan headed northward for the Grants once again, distributing copies of his pamphlet along the way. Priced at four shillings, sixpence a copy, the pamphlets were not exactly snapped up by the farmers of western Massachusetts as Ethan passed their way, but he did manage to lighten his load a bit by leaving a couple dozen copies on consignment with landlords and storekeepers along his line of march. Once back on the Grants he distributed them as widely as he could, often as gifts, among his friends and neighbors; to his brother Levi, who happened to be passing through Bennington on his way to Portsmouth, he gave a few copies to scatter among the right people in New Hampshire. Never the most modest of men, Ethan was inordinately proud of what he had written. Understandably, he hoped for a wide readership, and in one way or another he intended to get it.

On February 1, only a few days after his return to the Grants, Ethan attended another meeting of the town committees, again held at Manchester. Here he discovered that the attitude of the delegates had changed considerably since the convention of the spring before. Now the fire of defiance burned with a lesser ardor. Governor Tryon's Bloody Act, which had not so long before loomed menacingly over the Grants, had faded into the background. No serious attempt had been made by the Yorkers to enforce it, and it was commonly believed that none ever would, now that Tryon had left for England. All in all, things had been going well on the New Hampshire Grants. Many months had passed during which the sun had shone more often than not; crops had been harvested, fair to middling-good; children had been born who would one day inherit the fruits of their fathers' labor; and throughout the Grants, outrage seemed to have given way to something approaching complacency.

As usual, Ethan was able to dominate the convention, mainly because there was nobody else who was able or willing to step forward and take charge. Not even he, however, could rekindle that spirit of bold defiance that had characterized the meeting of the past spring. Among the incomplete records of this convention there is some evidence to suggest that he actually attempted to persuade his colleagues to declare complete independence from New York. He got much less. In fact, it was only with great difficulty that he was able to prevail upon the members to reaffirm the resolution against New York magistrates which had been passed at the previous meeting. Once again the sentiment of his Grants neighbors was obviously moving in the direction of accommodation with the Yorkers. Once again Ethan must be on guard against the enemy within.

Soon after the adjournment of the Manchester convention, Ethan made one of his frequent journeys through the north country in search of game and likely land. It was midwinter and the earth lay still and white under a heavy blanket of snow—a time of exquisite beauty and solitude. On occasions such as this, as he wandered alone through the wilderness, he could not have been unaware of his great danger. The forest was a friend he had known intimately since his boyhood, but he knew that even friends could be cruel and capricious. A disabling fall or illness could leave him a helpless feast for wolves, while an unexpected meeting with a catamount could easily mean a more sudden end.

A far greater hazard, potentially at least, was the human element. The Indians were safe enough, except for an occasional renegade. Could as much be said, however, for the white settlers? Many of them were appallingly poor, living on the very margin of starvation, worn down to desperation by the attrition of the frontier. Often Ethan would come upon their cabins in the middle of nowhere and bed down before their fires for a night or two. They also, like the forest, were his friends, but unlike the forest they were not impervious to the glitter of gold. With a price of £100 on his head, Ethan's person represented many times the wealth most of these people would accumulate during a lifetime of hard work and privation. To some of the more desperate or daring among them there must have been a strong temptation to seize Ethan and turn him in for the Yorker reward. And yet, despite many romantic tales to the contrary, there were no known attempts by his Grants neighbors to capture him and spirit him away to Albany, and no wonderful, hair-raising escapes. The chief of the outlaws was apparently secure enough among his own people. At any rate, he saw no cause to worry about the situation. He came and went on the west side of the Grants as he saw fit, and he slept with both eyes closed.

In early March, Ethan left the north country and went directly to Sheffield to sit in on the previously mentioned meeting of the Onion River Company. He had been south only a few days, however, when a report reached him which sent him racing back to Bennington. Blood had finally been spilled on the Grants. One man was dead and another lay dying. Oddly enough, though, the trouble had occurred on the east side of the mountains where the settlers, nearly all of whom had hailed from the more conservative and affluent regions of eastern Connecticut and Massachusetts, had proved themselves for the most part to be sober, law-abiding, and generally well-behaved. Not only had they shown a marked willingness to accept New York's political jurisdiction over the area, but to a far greater extent than their west-side neighbors they had also agreed to seek Yorker confirmation of their Wentworth land titles. As a result of this accommodating attitude, and the fact that only a small number of overlapping land titles had been issued by New York for the region east of the mountains, the eastern settlers and their Yorker officials had, on the whole, gotten along reasonably well with one another. Ethan considered most easterners to be little more than Yorker stooges, while they, in turn, tended to look upon the west-siders as so many wild men ruled by a pack of outlaws.

What happened in Westminster on the evening of March 13, 1775, was quite unrelated to any of those issues over which Ethan and his friends had been carrying on their long running battle with the Province of New York. In essence "the Westminster Massacre," as it is generally known in Vermont history, was just another anti-court riot, the likes of which were common enough in frontier areas of eighteenth- and nineteenth-century America. Times had been bad in the east side's Cumberland County for the past few months, and in an attempt to forestall legal foreclosures on farms and other property, a sizable body of settlers had gathered in the shire town of Westminster to protest, and if possible prevent, the opening of the spring session of the Cumberland County Court scheduled for the following day. In the course of an angry demonstration at the courthouse, the crowd got out of hand, shots were fired by the Yorker sheriff and his deputies, and two men died—martyrs to something or other. No one knew exactly what.

In New York City, Acting-Governor Colden was visibly shaken by the news from Westminster. It was obviously a local disturbance that had nothing to do with political jurisdiction or land titles. "These Rioters have not pretended to raise up such a Pretence for their Conduct," he wrote to London. But the governor was not deluded. "I make no doubt they will be joined by the Bennington Rioters who will endeavour to make one common cause of it, tho they have no connection but in their violence to Government." The old governor was right, of course. Ethan immediately dispatched Robert Cochran with a company of Green Mountain Boys to the troubled area. These troops were neither needed nor expected, but they were gratefully received by the east-side settlers. So also was Ethan's offer to come in person to Westminster and do what he could to help out. Ethan was finally in a good position to gain valuable allies among the easterners, now that they too had suffered a taste of oppression. Perhaps he could even join the two sections of the Grants solidly together in a common front against the Yorkers. Naturally he intended to exploit this promising situation to the hilt.

On April 11, less than a month after the "massacre," committees from several of the east-side towns met in convention at Westminster to protest the recent atrocity committed by the Yorkers against His Majesty's loyal and peaceful subjects of Cumberland County. In attendance by special invitation (which he had taken pains to promote) was Ethan Allen from west of the mountains, who, although an outsider, would play an important role in the proceedings. With Ethan there to prod them on, the east-siders passed a number of strongly worded resolutions, including one calling upon settlers on both sides of the mountains to unite in renouncing and resisting the administration of the Government of New York." This was almost too good to be true—much more than Ethan had dared hope for. At last it seemed that the west side would no longer be alone in its struggle against the Yorkers. But the convention's work did not end there. Caught up in Ethan's oratory and their own momentum, the members voted to remonstrate directly to the King against the government of New York, and to beg "his most gracious

Majesty in his royal wisdom and clemency" to remove the people of the New Hampshire Grants "out of so oppressive a jurisdiction" and permit them to be "either annexed to some other government or erected and incorporated into a new one."

To prepare this bold remonstrance to the King, the convention chose a committee of three men, of whom Ethan was one. In view of the fact that he was not even a legal delegate, his selection was something of a tribute to the west-side outlaw. It was also a rare opportunity. For the first time an open declaration in favor of complete separation from the Province of New York was to be entered more or less officially into the records, and Ethan was more than pleased to have the chance to figure in so noble an undertaking. For some time he had been convinced that the Grants controversy could be satisfactorily resolved only by removing the area from under Yorker jurisdiction. At first he had favored annexation, or "re-annexation," to New Hampshire, and in 1772 he had joined several of his west-side neighbors in preparing a petition to that effect for the consideration of the King's Council. As time passed, however, he had inclined more towards the establishment of the Grants as a separate colony. Naturally it would have been unwise of him at that early date to have declared himself openly on such a delicate subject. He doubted that many of his neighbors were prepared to go so far so soon. But from time to time Ethan had talked the matter over among a few of his friends, including the influential Major Philip Skene.

Skene was a retired British officer who had received a military grant of 30,000 acres of prime New York land situated at the head of Lake Champlain in the vicinity of present-day Whitehall. He had subsequently developed his holdings into an impressive backwoods manor called Skenesboro, and had come to be recognized as one of the most powerful men north of Albany. Skene had first met Ethan in the early 1770's when Ethan was spending much of his time in Poultney, only a few miles east of Skenesboro. The two men had immediately taken a liking to one another, and even after Ethan had been declared an outlaw and Skene had become a Yorker justice of the peace, they had remained on friendly terms.

During the two years just prior to the Revolution, Skene and Ethan corresponded frequently, and on one point they obviously saw pretty much eye to eye: the establishment of a separate province was a thing greatly to be desired and sought after. Beyond this there was some disagreement, at least at first. Ethan favored a new colony to be made up of the Grants and a narrow fringe of land immediately to the west of Lake Champlain. Skene was far less modest. What he had in mind was a province that would stretch all the way from the Connecticut River to Lake Ontario, bounded on the south by the Mohawk River and on the north by the 45th parallel. The capital of this new colony would, of course, be Skenesboro, and what better man could be found to serve as governor than Major Skene himself? The more the Major thought about the idea the better he liked it, and in time he was able to bring Ethan around to his way of thinking. Thus, on a day late in 1774, Major Skene left with Ethan's blessing to see what could be done about promoting such a proposal among his influential friends in London.

And so it happened that at the very moment Ethan was nudging the Westminster convention toward separation from New York, Major Skene was laying his plan for a new colony before the British Board of Trade. As matters turned out, both men might just as well have spared themselves the bother. Less than a week after the adjournment of the Westminster convention, while Ethan and his committee colleagues still labored over the east-side remonstrance to King George, guns fired and men died not many miles away in Middlesex County, Massachusetts. The complexion of matters had suddenly changed. New forces had been unleashed which would call a halt, temporarily at least, to the long battle of the Grants. The miracle that Ethan had always counted on had finally arrived.

# VI. A Fortress Falls

WITH THE OUTBREAK of the Revolution, the men of the New Hampshire Grants suspended for a time their contest with New York and gave their not inconsiderable support to the common cause against the British. That they responded to the Revolutionary crisis with great alacrity and courage can hardly be denied. There remains, however, the question of why they responded in the direction they did. Actually, they had little to gain and much to lose by throwing in their lot with the Colonies, including, of course, the predatory Province of New York. By all that was right and reasonable they should have remained loyal to the King. They had no direct grievance against the Crown. They had suffered none of the adversities of Boston or Virginia. No port had been closed, no legislature dissolved. Quite the contrary. Since the opening of the Grants, the Home Government had been the Wentworth settlers' most consistent and valuable ally against the pretensions of New York. Had it not been for proscriptions from the Crown, the entire area would doubtless have been swallowed up by the Yorkers at an early stage. Furthermore, it was generally rumored and believed throughout the Grants that a decision favorable to the Wentworth settlers was about to be issued in London. All things considered, the men of the Grants had good reason to feel kindly and appreciative toward the Home Government, and to continue to look toward it as their main hope of protection against Yorker abuse. And yet, scarcely had the smoke cleared at Lexington and Concord when they committed themselves to the Colonial cause in no uncertain terms by conducting the first offensive action against the British in the War of the American Revolution.

While it is undoubtedly true that the Grants settlers were influenced to some extent by the pro-Patriot leanings of most of their Connecticut relatives and friends, it seems likely that the main reason they took up arms against the Mother Country is that Ethan Allen wanted it that way, and when Ethan wanted a thing badly enough he usually managed to get it. In this instance, although he certainly had no mandate from the people to do so, he simply decided, with a little prodding from outsiders, that he wanted to launch a frontal attack against the British Empire. He then proceeded to call upon his Boys for that purpose, and out of loyalty, camaraderie, and just plain boredom, about two hundred of them showed up, mainly from the Bennington area. This was not a very large or representative segment of the more than 25,000 settlers then living on the Grants, but it was enough to do a deed that would commit the New Hampshire Grants, probably against the wishes of a sizable majority of its people, to open rebellion against the Crown.

But all of this still fails to account for why Ethan himself decided to act as he did, and here indeed is a subject that, as is so often the case with questions of motivation, lends itself to far-flung conjecture. To those who have looked upon Ethan with favor, his actions stemmed from a deep-seated ideological commitment to the rights and dignity of man. Ethan himself, by tongue and pen, did much to encourage this view during his own lifetime. In writing a few years after the event about his decision to attack Fort Ticonderoga, Ethan explained:

> Ever since I arrived at the state of manhood and acquainted myself with the general history of mankind, I have felt a sincere passion for liberty. The history of nations, doomed to perpetual slavery, in consequence of yielding up to tyrants their natural-born liberties, I read with a sort of philosophical horror; so that the first systematical and bloody attempt, at Lexington, to enslave America, thoroughly electrified my mind, and fully determined me to take part with my country.

It could very well have happened that way. Here was a chance to strike a blow for John Locke against the timeless forces of grinding oppression —or so at least it might have seemed to Ethan who, after all, was something of a zealot on the subject of freedom, especially his own.

A less flattering assessment of Ethan's motives has him acting out of carefully reasoned self-interest. According to this view, Ethan was convinced in his own mind that sooner or later the Home Government would reaffirm New York's political jurisdiction over the Grants while at the same time validating the land titles of all settlers in actual possession of their lands. However, the claims of those Wentworth proprietors holding lands for speculation would almost certainly not be recognized, all of which meant that Ethan and his fellow speculators, including his Onion River partners, would be left in a desperate position. With their titles invalidated by direct order of the British Crown, and with the support of the settlers stripped from them, what chance would the speculators have to hold onto their lands? Very little, if any.

Obviously such a situation should not be allowed to develop, and one way, perhaps the only way, to prevent it was to drive the British presence from the scene while there was still time. If this could be done, the danger to Ethan and his fellow investors would be considerably lessened. They would still have to deal with New York, but at least they would not be called upon to do battle, alone and unaided, against the might of the British Empire. And Ethan had no doubt that the British would not hesitate to use regular troops if need be. On two occasions before, in 1772 and 1774, the Home Government had refused Yorker requests to send troops onto the Grants to put down disorders, on the grounds that these disorders were local matters of an internal nature and should therefore be handled by the New York constabulary. There was little question, however, that regular troops would be quick to appear in the area if a royal decree were defied, and all this could have but one ending—a very unhappy ending for the Wentworth speculators. It was perhaps with this in mind that Ethan decided in the spring of 1775 to take up arms against the British Empire.

Of course, it could easily be that there was no rationale for what he did. In view of the brash and expansive nature of the man, is it too much to suppose that he acted simply out of impulse? Is it inconceivable that he attacked the fort for no more complex and mystifying reason than that at that particular time he wanted to do so, perhaps just for the gratification of his tremendous vanity or lust for adventure? For several years he had passed by Ticonderoga in his wanderings. He had examined its formidable bastions looming like giant sentinels a mile or so across the narrow neck of the lake. What a majestic, awe-inspiring sight, and what a great triumph it would be to seize such a prize! In his mind he must have captured it more than once, and when the opportunity finally presented itself in reality, perhaps he simply could not refuse himself the chance to meet such an exciting challenge, and decided to make the effort just for the sheer swashbuckling hell of it.

Whatever his motives may have been, and they were probably mixed, confused, and not even clear to Ethan himself, there can be no denying that the attack upon Ticonderoga by a small contingent of poorly armed, undisciplined, rag-tail frontier farmers was a bold undertaking—both in its conception and in its execution. It was also an invaluable stroke for the American cause, for upon the possession of Fort Ticonderoga depended to a great extent the military fortunes of the United Colonies.

Tucked neatly in between New York and Vermont lies Lake Champlain, named after the famous French explorer who discovered it in the early 1600's. It is a long lake, more than one hundred miles from its southern tip at Whitehall, New York, to its northern extremity at the head of the Sorel (now Richelieu) River, through which it funnels its waters into the St. Lawrence. Historically, it has also been an exceedingly important lake, for this elongated waterway and its tributaries to the south formed the main avenue for traffic between Canada and the Hudson River Valley, and here men fought and died as rival armies and empires contended for more than a century in their attempts to penetrate farther to the north or to the south. Sooner or later, in virtually all of these contests, the action came to center upon the narrow eminence of land guarding the main approaches from Lake Champlain to Lake George, a couple of miles or so to the southwest, and it was at this place in 1755 that the French, working under the gifted military engineer, Sieur de Lotbinière, erected the fort that would come to be called Ticonderoga.

De Lotbinière named it Carillon because from it could be clearly heard the musical rapids of the nearby stream that tumbled down from Lake George. The French were mighty pleased with their stronghold, as well they might have been. Situated on Champlain's western shore, some twenty miles down-lake from the head of deep-draught navigation, and at a point where the lake is only a mile wide, Carillon occupied one of the most strategic positions in North America. Like some arrogant giant it stood astride the most important north–south highway on the continent, controlling all water traffic that moved beneath its imposing ramparts. Without its permission, nothing of consequence could pass in either direction.

Built from plans that had been drawn up three-quarters of a century earlier by the brilliant French military architect and engineer, Marshal Sebastien Vauban, Fort Carillon was a rugged, star-shaped structure of earth, timber, and stone, perched on high ground not far from the water's edge. Although designed to billet a garrison of four hundred men, the fort could hold many times that number during periods of emergency. That Fort Carillon was no mean obstacle to contend with may be indicated by the fact that the Marquis de Montcalm, with a force of fewer than 4,000 defenders, turned back an attacking army of more than 15,000 British and Colonial troops during the ill-fated northern offensive launched by the British in the summer of 1758. The fortunes of war were such, however, that in the following year the French were forced to surrender the fort to British General Jeffrey Amherst and were never able to regain possession. With the signing of the Peace of Paris in 1763 the fort officially became the property of the British Empire.

The British changed its name to Ticonderoga, which is said to be a corruption of an Indian word meaning "the place between two waters." They gave it little else besides its new name, however. With the French menace finally removed from North America, with the Indians of the area successfully cowed, and with the British Treasury badly straitened from the long strain of the Seven Years' War, the Home Government was not especially anxious to pay out the large sums of money needed for the proper maintenance of this "Gibraltar of the wilderness." As a result, for more than a decade Fort Ticonderoga was badly neglected and allowed to fall into a state of shameful disrepair. "I beg leave to inform you that the commissary's room is fallen in," the commandant of the fort wrote to his superior less than a year before the outbreak of the Revolution. "The Fort and Barracks are in a most ruinous situation."

As relations between the Colonies and the Mother Country became increasingly strained during the spring and summer of 1774, however, the British military command in North America started to press for a strengthening of Ticonderoga, with the result that wheels began to turn in London. But they turned slowly and it was not until late autumn of 1774 that Lord Dartmouth, the Colonial Secretary, finally ordered that the fort be put into "a proper state of Defence." Since Dartmouth's letter did not reach America until well after Christmas, an impossible time of year for undertaking military movements in the northern interior, no action was taken on the Secretary's order until the following spring. Finally in early April, after the ice had cleared from the lake, a small contingent of not more than a half-dozen men, together with a meager quantity of gunpowder and lumber, began to move up the lake from Montreal. This modest expedition was meant to be the vanguard of larger bodies of men and materials to follow during the next few months. In fact, elaborate plans had already been drawn up in British headquarters at Boston, to provide for a thorough refurbishment of the fort and to increase its garrison to between 1,500 and 2,000 men by midsummer of that year. As matters turned out, however, there would be no further reinforcements for Ticonderoga. Only those feeble offerings sent up the lake in April would have time to reach the fort before its capture by Ethan Allen in early May. Characteristically enough, the Home Government had waited too long to give adequate attention to what was probably its greatest single strategic asset in the American Colonies.

At the time of Ethan's attack, therefore, Ticonderoga was far less formidable than it should have been, or would have been a few months later. With its garrison badly understrength, its materials of war in short supply, and its fortifications in need of repair, the fort was far from fighting trim. Nevertheless, it was still a mighty presence. Nearly half a hundred British regulars guarded its ramparts, and at least two dozen working cannons poked their muzzles menacingly outward in all directions, ready to discharge withering blasts of grapeshot or ball if the occasion warranted. To take such a stronghold, weakened though it was by a decade of neglect, would be no easy matter—especially for a small and haphazard assortment of untrained farmers.

But the fort must be taken. That much was clear. Otherwise the entire northern flank of the American Colonies would be in a position of serious military disadvantage and jeopardy. "The Fort not only secures communication with Canada," British General Frederick Haldimand wrote to Lord Dartmouth from Quebec in the spring of 1774, "but also opens an easy access to the back settlements of the Northern Colonies and may keep them in awe, should any of them be rash enough to incline to acts of force and violence." For these reasons and for many others, some of them too unpleasant to dwell upon, possession of Ticonderoga by the Colonies was little short of imperative. The fort had to be seized, and it would not do to move too slowly, for if the British were allowed to provide Ticonderoga with substantial reinforcements there would be little chance for the Americans to capture it. The time was obviously now, and, just as obviously, the person in the best position to do the job was Colonel Commandant Ethan Allen, who, with his pack of Green Mountains Boys, had a military force of sorts already in being within easy striking distance.

Actually, however, Ethan needed to be prodded a bit before moving into action, and for understandable reasons. After all, bullying a Yorker justice of the peace was one thing, but making a direct and open assault upon Crown property was a far different thing indeed. To attack the King's fort was to attack the King himself, and Ethan may be excused for having hesitated for a moment or two. As he himself later explained his few days of indecision following receipt of the news from Lexington in late April, he wanted to ponder the situation awhile and "explore futurity" before assaulting the British Empire. Among other things, he wanted to be certain that the outbreak at Lexington was something more than just a local disturbance. If he were to attack this fort he wanted to do so as a leader of a revolutionary movement rather than as a Grants hoodlum, and he wanted to feel at least halfway certain that his wild work would be endorsed and supported by some authority higher than his own. Ethan Allen was impulsive, but he was no fool.

The prod that set Ethan moving and culminated in the seizure of Ticonderoga was not long in coming, and there is some irony in the fact that it originated with Benedict Arnold. Less than a week after the fracas at Lexington, Arnold, then a captain in the Connecticut militia, had donned his handsomely braided uniform and set out for Boston at the head of a company of Connecticut Footguards to help out against the British. On the way he happened to run into Samuel Parsons, a prominent member of the Hartford Committee of Correspondence and a Connecticut assemblyman, who was returning to Hartford from a business trip in Massachusetts. In the course of a brief roadside conversation, Parsons indicated his deep concern over the Patriots' critical need for artillery in their siege of Boston. The British would never be driven out, Parsons contended, unless heavy cannons could be brought to bear upon them. Arnold agreed. Small arms were next to worthless in such a situation. The Colonists must get cannons, and Arnold knew where there were cannons aplenty. He went on to tell Parsons of stories he had heard about a powerful array of iron and brass guns at Ticonderoga, guarded only by a skeleton garrison. Dozens of heavy cannons—all there for the taking. What a pity they could not be seized and put to use against the British at Boston!

By the time Parsons arrived home in Hartford, he had concluded that Captain Arnold's remarks merited serious attention, and he hastened to put the matter before a small group of his friends, all of them persons of political prominence in Connecticut and of unquestioned dedication to the Patriot cause. The little council decided at once and without dissent that Arnold's remarks should be acted upon and that no time should be lost in the process. Consequently, Parsons and the others proceeded to set the wheels in motion by drawing £ 300 out of the Colonial treasury, a highly irregular bit of behavior in view of the fact they had been given no authority to do so. Parsons later explained that although public funds were used this was strictly a private venture, entered into quickly and quietly by a half-dozen men from the Hartford area acting entirely on their own. True, all of them were assemblymen and all were members of the Hartford Committee of Correspondence, but what they did was done without the approval or even the official knowledge of either body. "We procured the money, and men, etc., and set out on this expedition without any consultation with Assembly or others."

It was a bold undertaking, and a precipitous one. Within twenty-four hours after the Hartford meeting, eight mounted men were on their way to the Grants to organize and finance the capture of the King's fortress at Ticonderoga. With them they carried the money that had been "borrowed" from the Connecticut treasury, and perhaps the fate of the Colonial cause. As they moved northward through western Connecticut and Massachusetts, they picked up fifty or more recruits along the way, all but a few of whom were members of Colonel James Easton's militia company from the area in and about Pittsfield, Massachusetts. They also sent word forward to Ethan Allen, informing him of their plan and asking him to ready his Green Mountain Boys. By the early evening of Tuesday, May 2, the Connecticut promoters and their contingent of Massachusetts militia had reached Bennington, and shortly thereafter a number of them met with Ethan and a few of his friends and officers at Stephen Fay's tavern. Here plans were drawn up for "laying in Bisket and Pork" and other necessary supplies, including powder and ball, and a general plan of operation was arrived at.

It was agreed that the Connecticut and Massachusetts people should remain in Bennington for a day or so to await the coming of the supplies, which were supposed to arrive soon from Albany and Williamstown. Meanwhile, Ethan, who had by now decided to call out his Green Mountain Boys, was to leave and take charge of mustering them and getting them to the rendezvous area at Castleton, fifty miles to the north, by the following Sunday. He was also to see to it that all roads leading to the fort were blocked off, in order to prevent intelligence from getting through to the British. Surprise would be the attackers' most potent weapon; it must not be lost through carelessness. And so at 11:00 on the following morning Ethan rode northward out of Bennington to collect his Boys and begin the greatest adventure of his uncommonly adventurous life.

By late afternoon of Sunday, May 7, the Connecticut-Massachusetts contingent of about sixty men had reached the rendezvous area at Castleton. It is recorded that the sun shone brightly down on Castleton that beautiful spring day, but military spirits were not correspondingly bright, for during the past couple of days rumors had been circulating that the British troops at Ticonderoga had been alerted to what was going on and were preparing a bloody reception. Shortly after 5:00 P.M., however, Ethan came riding into town, bringing with him one hundred and thirty of his Boys and a report, just received, that the British suspected nothing.

This much had been ascertained by Noah Phelps, a member of the Connecticut group, who had gone directly from Bennington to spy out the fort. He had done his job well. Disguised as a woodsman, Phelps had entered the fort on the pretext of getting a shave from the garrison's barber. While there he heard and saw a great deal, and he left convinced that the garrison not only was unaware of the planned attack but also, incredibly enough, was still uninformed of the fact that hostilities had broken out between the Crown and the Colonies. All this was most reassuring to the nearly two hundred men milling about in the field outside Zadok Remington's Castleton tavern on that Sunday in early May of 1775. "The men are resolute and want to proceed," one of them noted in his journal that evening.

Early the following morning the officers of the little army met to declare themselves a Committee of War and to organize the campaign against the fort. Edward Mott of the Connecticut group was elected chairman of the committee; a good choice since he seems to have been trusted and respected by all. Noah Phelps, just returned from his spying assignment, was chosen commissary, another good choice since he had the money, or what was left of it, in his saddlebags. As for field commander, there was no question about who should get the job. Ethan was chosen unanimously, again a logical selection and probably an unavoidable one in view of the fact that two-thirds of the troops were Ethan's own Green Mountain Boys.

Having chosen their leaders, the officers of the Committee of War then proceeded to draw up a specific plan of attack, and, just to be on the safe side, a plan of retreat as well. It was decided that daybreak of the following Wednesday, May 10, would be the time of attack. As for the place from which to launch it, the committee, acting on Ethan's advice, chose Hand's Cove in Shoreham, a sheltered little inlet some twenty miles to the northwest that seemed ideally suited to serve as the place of embarkation. Accordingly, at 10:00 that morning the committee ordered the troops to move out in the direction of Shoreham along the old Crown Point road, but not until after thirty of them had been detached and placed under the command of Ethan's friend Sam Herrick. It would be their job to hurry over to Major Skene's place at Skenesboro, about a dozen miles from Castleton, seize the manor and its tenants, and sequester any boats they could lay their hands on. At the same time Asa Douglas, another of Ethan's Boys, was sent to visit his brother-in-law who lived at Crown Point and was known to have a couple boats that he occasionally rented out to the King's troops at Ticonderoga. Douglas' job was to get these boats, by fair means or foul, and bring them up to Hand's Cove under cover of darkness in time to help make the crossing. The fate of the entire expedition depended upon the successful procurement of boats. Boats must be had, they must be had soon, and it was up to Herrick and Douglas to get them.

Late Monday morning, even before the Committee of War had completed its deliberations, Ethan set out for Shoreham in order to take charge of operations there. By the latter part of the afternoon the other members of the committee had finished their business and were ready to move out also. The first phase of the campaign had been completed, and there was good reason to be pleased with the way things had progressed. Thus far there had been nary a hitch, and there was no cause to suppose that there would be any, given a reasonable amount of good luck. But then, suddenly and without warning, a majestic new presence descended upon Castleton. With everything just about in readiness, with the mechanism of attack about to be triggered, who should appear upon the scene, handsomely mounted and uniformed, escorted by a body servant, and waving a commission of command, but Benedict Arnold!

After his conversation with Samuel Parsons, Arnold had continued his journey to Boston at the head of his Connecticut Footguards. Along the way he must have given considerable thought to the matter of Ticonderoga, for by the time he reached American headquarters at Cambridge he had come to an important decision: if Ticonderoga were to be seized, he should be the man to seize it. Accordingly, he proposed a plan of operation to the Massachusetts Committee of Safety in Cambridge, which was then acting as the provisional government of the Colony, and within a day or so he received authorization from the committee to go ahead and make the attempt.

Obviously Arnold's scheme was a chancy one at best, but in view of the high stakes involved it seemed deserving of such support as the committee could afford to give. Furthermore, Arnold was a difficult man to say no to. Brilliant, imperious, and courtly, he commanded attention, and more often than not deference, from those he had dealings with. At the time of the outbreak of the Revolution he was in his mid-thirties, about three years younger than Ethan, and was well established in his native Connecticut as an apothecary, bookseller, and ship-owner. He had long shown a preference for military life, however. In fact, he had an abiding compulsion for command, which he gratified up to a point by keeping his militia company in a state of readiness and discipline. When the Revolution came, he answered the Patriot call immediately and enthusiastically, and the fact should not be overlooked that until late in the war he served with unexcelled courage and brilliance. Few gave more to the American cause and few suffered so much. In the end he would sell his loyalty, but until then Benedict Arnold was a Patriot soldier, and a good one.

On May 2, the Massachusetts Committee of Safety appointed him colonel and presented him with an official commission to seize Fort Ticonderoga. To support him in this undertaking, the Committee provided him with ten horses, £100 in cash, as much ammunition as could be spared, and authority to raise four hundred men, to be placed under officers of his own choosing. Thus outfitted, Colonel Arnold left Cambridge on the morning of May 3 for western Massachusetts where he intended to do most of his recruiting.

As he approached Berkshire County in the western part of the Colony, reports began to reach him that another attempt was already under way to capture the fort. Leaving his officers behind to recruit, he hurried northward to Bennington. There he picked up the trail of Parson's Connecticut party and headed at once for Castleton, where he arrived shortly before 4:00 on the afternoon of Monday, May 8, just as the remaining members of the Committee of War were about to set out to join Ethan in Shoreham. Presenting his credentials to the committee, Arnold claimed to be in charge of the expedition. Somewhat bluntly he pointed out that he, and only he, had been duly commissioned to seize the fort, and, as Chairman Mott later angrily explained, "presumed to contend for the command of those forces that we had raised." Well, he wouldn't get it, commission or no commission. The Committee informed him in no uncertain terms that the command had already been assigned to Ethan Allen, and that it was unlikely the troops would be willing to serve under any other leader.

Arnold was not one to give in easily, however. Early the next morning he left with his valet for Shoreham and a confrontation with Ethan himself. Following not far behind were the members of the Committee of War, who were plainly worried that Ethan might weaken in the face of such imposing authority and give up his command. As it happened, they may have had some cause for worry, for when Arnold arrived in Shoreham shortly before noon and displayed his commission, Ethan did indeed appear to waver. He was impressed by Arnold's solid-looking credentials which clearly bespoke a higher authority than any Ethan could claim. In fact, now that the matter had been so bluntly brought to his attention, Ethan was forced to admit, at least to himself, that he really had no authority at all save for what had been granted him by that dubious little group that called themselves the Committee of War—and not even that was in writing. Furthermore, he could not help but be awed by Arnold's brilliant appearance. Dressed in the splendid blue uniform of the Connecticut Footguards, Colonel Arnold was a rare sight to behold, especially since his valet was on hand to insure his impeccability. By comparison, Ethan's uniform must have seemed shabby and dull. And Ethan had no valet de chambre. In fact, he had never even heard of one before.

Temporarily daunted, perhaps, Ethan called out the troops and announced that Colonel Benedict Arnold would lead them into battle. But this need not cause them any alarm, Ethan explained. The plan of attack would remain unchanged, and they would still receive the same amount of pay—about two dollars each. The men refused to hear of such a thing, however. Damn the pay. They weren't going to serve under a stranger. In fact, they weren't going to serve under anybody except

Ethan himself. Ethan would lead them or they would go home. It was as simple as that. And then to show that they meant what they said, they stacked their arms to await Ethan's assurance that he would remain in command.

Ethan could not have been very surprised. Indeed, this may have been what he had had in mind all along. He was aware of his popularity with the men, and it is not unlikely that he anticipated what their reaction to his announcement would be. At any rate, it proved to be an effective way of resolving the controversy over command. Colonel Arnold was outraged at this defiance of authority, but there was little that he could do about the situation. Ethan, reassured by the Committee of War and by the support of his troops, was firmly in control again. As a sop to Arnold, however, he agreed to allow him to come along on the expedition, although not in a position of command, and to enter the fort alongside Ethan himself. Arnold was not satisfied, but since it was the best he could expect, he accepted Ethan's offer. This was a charitable gesture on Ethan's part, and it was also a wise one. For the record, it would be nice to have Arnold along, standing beside him at the head of the troops. After all, Colonel Arnold was the only one in the entire lot who had any claim to legitimacy of command.

By the time this question had been settled it was nearly dark, and the troops began moving out toward the embarkation point at Hand's Cove about three miles west of Shoreham Center. During the afternoon and early evening they had been joined by more than fifty late-comers and now numbered two hundred and thirty officers and men. This was not a very awe-inspiring force with which to capture one of the most powerfully fortified positions in America, but it would have to do. Surprise was still the critical factor. If the British garrison remained unaware of what was going on, two hundred and thirty men would be more than enough to do the job. If word had leaked through to the fort, however, twice that number would probably be too few.

By 11:00 P.M. the entire force had assembled at the cove and was waiting in readiness. Across the narrow neck of Lake Champlain and a mile to the south loomed Ticonderoga. There still remained the problem of how to make the crossing, however. Obviously, nothing could be done without boats, and thus far no boats had arrived. Apparently the men sent to procure them had run into some kind of trouble, with the result that Ethan Allen's little army was now poised at the water's edge ready to attack the great bastion across the lake but unable to get there. This was all very embarrassing for Ethan, and the situation was getting worse by the minute. He had counted on at least four hours to get his men across, but as late as 1:30 the next morning he was still without a single boat. With sunrise only three hours away, he was about to postpone the attack until the following night, but at what must have been very close to the last minute he managed to obtain a large batteau and another boat of much smaller size. Neither of these was exactly what he had had in mind, but they were all he could find. Looking back on the Ticonderoga attack a few years later, Ethan singled out the procurement of boats as the most difficult problem of the entire expedition—a problem which, by the way, could almost certainly have been alleviated by more competent planning on the part of Ethan and the other members of the Committee of War. No matter. With a little luck and a lot of daring, things were eventually made to come out all right.

With only two boats on hand and the hours of darkness fast disappearing, a more reasonable man would have postponed the attack. Ethan was anxious to push ahead, however, and he therefore decided to take the great risk of going into battle with only a small part of his army. Even before the second boat had arrived at the cove he started the batteau across, loaded close to the waterline with forty men who were landed about a quarter-mile north of the fort. A second crossing was completed by the batteau an hour and a half later, this time accompanied by the smaller boat. Between them they were able to ferry across forty-three more men and a modest quantity of supplies. And this was all. Seth Warner would bring the main body across after the attack had begun. Until then, with daybreak only an hour or so away, there must be no further activity on the lake for the sake of surprise. The eighty-three men who had already made it across would have to do the job by themselves.

On the far side of the lake, just north of a little jut of land called Willow Point, Ethan drew up his troops in three ranks facing the shore. Then, as he later remembered it, he proceeded to regale them with remarks that went something like this:

> Friends and fellow soldiers, You have, for a number of years past been a scourge and terror to arbitrary power. Your valor has

been famed abroad. . . . I now propose to advance before you, and, in person, conduct you through the wicket-gate; for we must this morning either quit our pretensions to valor, or possess ourselves of this fortress in a few minutes; and, inasmuch as it is a desperate attempt, which none but the bravest of men dare undertake, I do not urge it on any contrary to his will. You that will undertake voluntarily, poise your firelocks.

Actually, it is unlikely that he said anything of the kind. None of the journals kept by men who were there with him makes any mention of pre-attack speechifying by Ethan or anyone else. In fact, with the fort within possible hearing distance, it would have been risky at best to speak above a whisper. Still, real or fanciful, it was a rousing speech, and by including it a few years later in his account of the capture of Fort Ticonderoga, Ethan added something to the dramatic quality of the occasion.

At Ethan's command, the men executed a right face and in columns of three began their brief march to the fort. Dressed haphazardly in buckskin and homespun, armed with rifles, muskets, knives, and pistols, and largely unfamiliar with the formalities of military formation, this little band of New England frontier farmers must indeed have been a sight to behold. At the head of this motley array marched Colonel Ethan Allen, clothed in his uniform of command and weighed down by a huge sword that hung from his left side. Beside him was the somewhat undersized Colonel Benedict Arnold of the Connecticut Footguards. In the east the first traces of light were beginning to appear. It was nearly four o'clock, May 10, 1775. Hundreds of miles away in Philadelphia a few Colonial notables were already starting to stir and ready themselves for an eventful day. In a matter of hours they would present themselves and their credentials at the handsome brick State House on Chestnut Street for the opening of the Second Continental Congress. Out of their labors a new nation would be born, and it is perhaps not too much to suppose that they were aided somewhat in their efforts by Ethan Allen and his small following of Yankee farmers, who in the early days of the American Revolution took it upon themselves to separate King George III from his property at Ticonderoga.

The men quietly made their way past the old grenadiers' battery which sat perched upon a slight bluff overlooking the lake. They then passed under the east ramparts, beyond which they turned to the right and proceeded until they arrived at the south side of the fort. Here a section of outer wall had been ruptured several years before and never adequately repaired. Incredibly enough, there was no sentry guarding the breach and the men were able to climb through undetected. From that point it was just a short stone's throw to the wicket gate that opened onto the inner quadrangle. One lone sentry stood guard before the gate.

Why the fort's commandant, Captain William Delaplace, had failed to provide for greater security is beyond all comprehension. In view of the strained relations that had existed for some time between England and the Colonies, trouble of some sort was much more than a remote possibility. The Home Government had certainly thought so. In December of the year before, it had ordered Commanding General Gage in Boston to place the entire American theatre in a condition of alert, and Gage had immediately relayed these orders to Delaplace. Two months later Gage had sent Delaplace a similar order, again admonishing him to exercise special caution in and about the fort. It appears, however, that Captain Delaplace had failed to take these orders very seriously. He had seen no sign of trouble, and if trouble should come he supposed he could handle it well enough. Thus he continued to carry on as he had before, giving more attention to his little vegetable garden outside the walls than to the security of his command. His lack of proper military precautions virtually invited disaster, and in the early morning hours of May 10 disaster came.

Once through the breach in the outer wall, the attackers made a rush toward the wicket gate. According to Ethan, the startled sentry had just time enough to snap his fusee before beating a retreat through the covered entranceway that opened onto the parade ground. The intended target had been Ethan himself, and since the sentry had fired at him point-blank, it was a happy thing for Ethan that the piece had fouled and failed to discharge. Followed by his men and with Arnold at his side, Ethan rushed onto the parade ground and had his troops level their guns at the barracks that housed the sleeping garrison. Then he had the Boys give three mighty huzzas in order to roust the rascals out. At this moment another British sentry suddenly appeared and bravely but foolishly lunged with his bayonet at one of the men standing beside Ethan and Arnold. Immediately Ethan wheeled about and dealt him a fierce blow on the head with the flat of his sword. The sentry crumpled to the ground, stunned but not seriously injured, and Ethan agreed to spare his life if he would lead the way to the commandant's quarters. The sentry took him to a stone stairway on the west side of the quadrangle, and Ethan, with Arnold still beside him, rushed up, followed by a half-dozen of his men.

As they neared the top of the stairs, Ethan shouted to the commandant to come out and surrender the fort or he would kill every man in it. In an instant Captain Delaplace appeared upon the landing, holding his breeches in his hand and demanding to know by what authority the King's property was being assaulted. "In the name of the Great Jehovah and the Continental Congress," Ethan replied. Thus was the famous surrender scene described some four years later in Ethan's written record of the event, and thus has it gone down in the history books ever since. Actually, however, it did not happen exactly that way.

In the first place, the trouserless officer who appeared in the doorway of the officers' quarters was not the commandant, as Ethan at first believed, but a lieutenant who, having been roused from his sleep by the ruckus below, had come to see what the trouble was. It was to this junior officer, Jocelyn Feltham, and not to Delaplace, that Ethan made his surrender demand, and it must have been rather embarrassing for Ethan when he later learned that he had demeaned his dignity by dealing with a mere lieutenant. Perhaps this is why Ethan's account states that it was Delaplace who first came to the door.

And then there is the question of what Ethan actually said on this occasion. There were later recollections among those who had been at the fort with him that he had shouted out: "Come out of there, you damned old Rat." Others claimed that it was: "Come out of there you sons of British whores, or I'll smoke you out." Nobody except Ethan seemed to recall anything about the Great Jehovah. Still, perhaps Ethan should be taken at his word, for although there is little to substantiate his "Great Jehovah" version of the surrender, it certainly has a better ring to it than the others. Furthermore, there is much about the logic of the situation to suggest that Ethan really did say what he later claimed. He may very well have shouted out something less eloquent as he raced up the stairs, but in the official confrontation he was probably more proper. After all, he could not have been unaware that, in the event of victory, his name would go down in history, and it would obviously be appropriate for him to have something resounding, something memorable, to say at the moment of triumph. Ethan was too much of a showman to miss such an opportunity for the dramatic, and it is unlikely that he did. So it would perhaps not be unreasonable to assume that he did evoke the Great Jehovah and the Continental Congress, even though, as one Vermont historian has pointed out, he had a commission from neither one.

Lieutenant Jocelyn Feltham probably had about as much respect for the Continental Congress, if indeed he had ever heard of it, as Ethan had for Jehovah, but what could he do? Still befogged by drowsiness, carrying his officer's breeches over his arm, and confronted by a mad giant waving a huge sword wildly about, Feltham could think of nothing better to do than stall for time. "I asked them a number of questions," he later explained in his official report, "expecting to amuse them until our people fired which I must certainly own I thought would have been the case." Among other things, he asked Ethan and Arnold by what authority they had presumed to attack the King's fort. This apparently was the occasion of Ethan's introduction of the Great Jehovah, although Feltham's report mentions only that Arnold presented his Massachusetts credentials while Ethan announced, quite inaccurately, that he was acting under orders from the Province of Connecticut.

Ethan was not to be put off by words for very long, however. He was interested in victory, not conversation, and once again he demanded the surrender of the fort. It was then that he learned that Feltham was not in command, and with an angry rush he pushed past the lieutenant and began beating on the door to the officers' quarters. According to Feltham, Ethan would probably have forced the door and dragged Delaplace out bodily if he had not been restrained by protests from Arnold, who behaved himself in a much more "genteel manner" than Ethan. No matter. A few seconds later the commandant, dressed in full uniform, appeared on the landing to suffer the humiliation that his disregard of security measures had so flagrantly invited.

By the time Captain Delaplace had come out of his quarters, the fort was lost. Ethan's men had already seized all but a few of the British troops and were in the process of rounding up the others. The surprise had been complete—so complete that not a shot had been got off, and, save for the reckless sentry whom Ethan had flattened with his sword, no one on either side had received so much as a scratch. Below him on the parade ground Delaplace could see the greater part of his garrison, unarmed, half-dressed, and groggy, guarded man-for-man at gunpoint by Ethan's troops. There was nothing for him to do but recognize the situation for what it was. Without further delay he presented his sword to Ethan and ordered the garrison to parade unarmed before the victors. It was all over.

"Thus," commented the American historian George Bancroft three-quarters of a century later, "Ticonderoga, which cost the British nation eight million sterling, a succession of campaigns, and many lives, was won in ten minutes by a few undisciplined volunteers, without the loss of life or limb." The almost-unbelievable had happened, and it had happened almost unbelievably. "Very unfortunate," remarked Lord Dartmouth when the news reached him at the Colonial Office in London. "Very unfortunate indeed."

# VII. On to Canada!

As Ethan later remembered it, "the sun seemed to rise that morning with a superior lustre." The great gamble had paid off handsomely, and no one was more exultant than the Colonel Commandant of the Green Mountain Boys. By ten o'clock the rest of the troops had arrived from across the lake and Ethan, in company with Seth Warner, had finished inspecting the spoils of war, including Captain Delaplace and Lieutenant Feltham. "This person Ethan Allen and Warner are as great villains as any on earth," Feltham later reported to his superiors.

There was still work to be done, however. A few miles to the north, at Crown Point, was a small British garrison that needed capturing, and to this job Ethan assigned Warner and a detachment of forty-five men. At one time the fort at Crown Point had been a truly imposing structure. Built originally by the French, many years before Ticonderoga, and later enlarged and strengthened by the British at a cost of millions of pounds, it had served as General Amherst's headquarters during the final stages of the French and Indian War. Now, however, it was in reality no longer a fort at all. Like Ticonderoga, it had been shamefully neglected during the dozen years following the Peace of Paris in 1763, and to make matters worse it had been ravaged by a fire in 1773 that all but destroyed it. At the time of the outbreak of the American Revolution it was little more than a pile of rubble, which served as a way-station for lake travelers and as a storage depot for ordnance and provisions. Still, it was an important military objective, not only because of its stores but also because of its strategic potential, which was almost as great as that of Ticonderoga itself. To allow it to remain in British hands would be to invite disaster. It had to be taken, and it would be best to take it before its garrison could learn of the outbreak of hostilities and destroy the precious stores of arms and other supplies.

On the day following the seizure of Ticonderoga, after much hard rowing against contrary winds, Warner and his men arrived at Crown

121

Point, just in time to meet Remember Baker at the head of a small party coming up-lake from the north. It had taken several days for Ethan's muster call to reach Baker at the Onion River Company's headquarters in Burlington, but, once alerted, Cousin Remember had lost little time in getting under way. It was a great disappointment to him that he arrived too late to be of any help in taking Ticonderoga. He at least had the satisfaction, however, of giving an assist in the reduction of Crown Point, although in view of the fact that the place was defended by only one sergeant and eight privates, his presence was scarcely needed. The garrison surrendered without a shot, and "great quantityes of stores" were captured, along with some fifty cannon, many of them in usable condition.

At about the same time that Warner and his men were taking possession of Crown Point, word reached Ethan that Herrick's expedition had successfully captured Skenesboro and had seized large amounts of supplies and several boats, including Major Skene's schooner. With Ticonderoga and its dependencies at Crown Point and Skenesboro now in the hands of Ethan's men, the upper lake was completely cleared of the enemy's presence. The battle of the narrows had been won, and victory had brought with it gratifying results. Boats, foodstuffs, building materials, gunpowder, and other military supplies had been seized in impressive quantities. More important, however, was the heavy ordnance that the French and British had transported at such great cost and effort from Europe to the interior wilderness of the American Colonies. According to an inventory prepared by Colonel Arnold a week after their capture, Ticonderoga and Crown Point yielded up approximately two hundred cannons, howitzers, and mortars, more than half of which were in usable or reparable condition. For the American Colonials, whose artillery during the early months of the war was virtually non-existent, these guns would prove to be of inestimable importance. In time, just as Benedict Arnold had envisioned it, many of them would be taken to Boston where they would be instrumental in enabling General Washington to drive the British out of the city.

Less impressive than the captured materials was the motley assortment of prisoners. Counting the two or three civilians seized by Herrick at Skenesboro, about sixty men were taken, all but a dozen of whom had belonged to the garrison at Ticonderoga. Numbers alone, however, tell only part of the story, for it appears that many of the British defenders were far from prime-quality fighting men. According to Lieutenant Feltham's report, only twenty-three of the British soldiers stationed at Ticonderoga were wholly "serviceable," and at Crown Point only two. The others either were "wore out and unserviceable and very few that can stand fatigue," or were "middling"—not a particularly powerful array of personnel with which to uphold King George's authority in the region of the upper lake. Besides the men, there were about forty women and children seized in the attacks, all of whom were treated with great solicitude by Ethan and his Boys, even after the rum had started to flow, as flow it did before the sun was very high on that triumphal morning of May 10, 1775.

But Ethan's seizure of Ticonderoga and its dependencies had a much greater importance than any that could be measured in cannonballs, barrels of flour, or prisoners of war. Despite its comic-opera aspects, the capture of the upper lake early in the war must be considered a major military victory, for it drastically altered the power potential in the northern Colonies and may very well have meant the difference between success and failure for the Revolutionary cause. Had Ticonderoga remained in British hands, there would almost certainly have been a hurried implementation of those orders, sent out earlier from London, to repair the fort and reinforce its garrison. As a result, the British would have had the advantage of a formidable base of operations, well within American territory, from which they most likely would have been able to make their thrust southward into the Hudson Valley in the summer of 1776, rather than having to wait until the following year when the likelihood of success was considerably less. In other words, it is because of the use that the British *might* have made of them, rather than the use, or lack of it, to which the Colonials actually put them, that the seizure of Fort Ticonderoga and its dependencies early in the war has often been considered one of the truly decisive strokes of the Revolution.

With the military situation under control, there was no reason in the world why Ethan and his Boys should not relax and savor the fruits of their victory. In this case the most immediately enticing fruits were ninety gallons of rum which Ethan found cached away in the cellar beneath the officers' quarters and which he proceeded to sequester "for the refreshment of the fatigued soldiery." When Captain Delaplace complained that the rum was his own personal property, Ethan presented him with a receipt for the total value which, Ethan supposed, the captain might be able to cash in against the Connecticut treasury at some future time.* At any rate, the rum was not to be denied the conquering heroes, and they wasted little time in putting it to use. "We tossed about the flowing bowl," Ethan later recorded, "and wished success to Congress, and the liberty and freedom of America." By mid-afternoon most of the men were more than a little drunk, and Ethan was probably no exception.

For the next twenty-four hours or so, until the rum supply had disappeared, Ticonderoga was a place of great merriment. In disposing of Captain Delaplace's liquor, the troops received help from crowds of thirsty visitors who, for reasons of curiosity and perhaps pillage, had begun streaming into the fort within a few hours after its capture. By early morning of May 11, the day following the surrender, there were nearly four hundred men milling about the fort in a totally disorderly manner, many if not most of them at least partially drunk. Under the circumstances it was only natural that the troops and their visiting friends and neighbors should help themselves to everything that caught their fancy—and there were few things that did not. "The plunder," reported Lieutenant Feltham, "was most rigidly perform'd as to liquors, provisions, etc., whether belonging to his majesty or private property."

Ethan took all of this in stride. He neither interfered nor objected. The men had done a hard job and had done it well, and now, in Ethan's judgment, they deserved a little indulgence. Colonel Arnold felt otherwise, however. To Arnold, who prided himself on his soldierly qualities, the complete breakdown of discipline among the men was appalling, and he was determined to restore order. At first he attempted to deal directly with the troops, but it soon became apparent that the men had no intention of obeying his orders. Worse than that, they made it clear that they would blow his head off if he didn't stop bothering them. All in all, Arnold noted in his Journal, they were insulting and threatening. Two of them even fired at him in attempts to frighten him, and another poked a musket into his ribs and demanded that he leave the fort. This Arnold resolutely and very courageously refused to do, since it would be "inconsistent with my duty, and directly contrary to the opinion of the colonies."

* In the library of the Connecticut Historical Society at Hartford can be found "A General Account of the Expenditures by the Province of Connecticut . . ." for the Ticonderoga expedition. Among the various items listed: "To Captain Delaplace for liquors supplied the garrison . . . 18–11–9."

Having failed to accomplish anything with the troops, except to stir up their rancor, Arnold went directly to Ethan and demanded once again that his credentials be respected and that he be given command of the fort. Ethan was totally unimpressed. Well, at least then, Arnold insisted, he should be recognized as holding joint command. After all, he argued, this had been the arrangement agreed upon at Hand's Cove just before the attack. Not so, replied Ethan, and he was probably right. Despite Arnold's insistence to the contrary, accounts found in the journals of men who participated in the attack suggest very strongly that at no time did Ethan concede more to Arnold than permission to enter Ticonderoga at his side. This arrangement was far from one of joint command, but after the capture of the fort, Colonel Arnold tried his best to parlay it into that. As for attempting to persuade Ethan, however, he might as well have spared himself the bother. The fact was that Arnold had no men, and how could he aspire to a position of command—or even joint command—when the men belonged to someone else? And as far as his credentials were concerned, they were not so all-fired important as he might think. Ethan could get credentials of his own—and he did. At Ethan's bidding and with the approval of the Committee of War, Chairman Mott sat down and wrote out the following commission:

To Col. Ethan Allen

Sir, Whereas, agreeable to the Power and Authority to us given by the Colony of Connecticut, we have appointed you to take the command of a party of men and reduce and take possession of the garrison of Ticonderoga and its dependencies, and as you are now in possession of the same,—You are hereby directed to keep the command of said garrison, for the use of the American Colonies, till you have further orders from the Colony of Connecticut or from the Continental Congress.

Signed per order of Committee
Edward Mott Chairman Committee

Ticonderoga, May 10, 1775

There! Now Ethan had a commission too. Of course, it had no real authority behind it, but it was nice to have. It gave him a feeling of legitimacy and it also provided him with something to wave back at Arnold. Finally, after realizing that Ethan would not be budged, Arnold retired to a quiet corner of the officers' quarters and sulked. To his

Journal he complained: "When Mr. Allen, finding he had a strong party, and being impatient to control, and taking umbrage at my forbidding the people to plunder, he assumed the entire command, and I was not consulted for four days." It was a humiliating and frustrating experience for the proud Benedict Arnold, but there was nothing that could be done about it. The men, for the most part, were Ethan's, and as Arnold himself would later concede, even though this obnoxious clodhopper knew nothing about military command, "he is perhaps a proper man to head his own wild people."

During that glorious day of May 10, as the fort reeled in a revelry of rum and plunder, Ethan somehow managed to arrange for the prisoners to be taken southward to Connecticut and to send out a half-dozen or more letters announcing to the world his great achievement.* One of these was dispatched by courier to the Continental Congress in Philadelphia. The others were sent out to neighboring Colonies. The fact that some of these letters were so effusively and erratically written would seem to indicate that Ethan was either very tired or not entirely sober at the time. In all of them, though, the message was clear enough: the fort had fallen as a result of the "great fortitude," "resisless fury," and "uncommon ranker" of the attackers, but if Ticonderoga and its dependencies were to be held, Ethan would need plenty of help and he would need it soon. "You know Governor Carlton of Canada will exert himself to retake them," he wrote to the Albany Committee of Correspondence. "I am apprehensive of a sudden and quick attack; pray be quick to our relief & send us five hundred men immediately, fail not." It would not take long for word of what had happened to reach the British in Canada, and before the enemy could launch a counterattack, measures would have to be taken by the northern Colonies, working together for the common defense, to strengthen the fort. Otherwise, in Ethan's judgment, it would surely fall before the first enemy wave. "We are in want of almost Every Necessity (Courage Excepted)," Ethan added. "We earnestly request your Immediate Relief, by Troops, Provisions, Arms, Ammunition, etc."

Actually there was little likelihood of any immediate attempt by the British to recapture the fort. Although Ethan had no way of knowing it, the military power of the enemy in Canada was next to nothing. In all of Canada there were fewer than eight hundred and fifty regular troops,

* Some of these letters were mis-dated May 11.

enough perhaps to conduct harassing operations, but certainly far too small a force to carry out a major campaign against an entrenched garrison over one hundred miles from the nearest British base. True, the British might conceivably have recruited additional manpower among the French settlers (the habitants), but this was not a very promising prospect in view of the cool relations that existed between the settlers and their British rulers. Even if enough troops had been available, however, they would have been of little offensive value to General Sir Guy Carleton, the Canadian governor, for he was sorely lacking in the ships and supplies necessary for a successful invasion. There was therefore small probability of a counter-operation from the north in the spring of 1775. In fact, there would be no significant threat to the upper Champlain region from that direction, or from any other, for the better part of a year thereafter.

But to Ethan, from his position near the head of the lake, the danger seemed very real and imminent, and it was in order to lessen this danger that he and the Committee of War determined upon a bold stroke. As soon as the sequestered boats could be brought down from Skenesboro, a raiding expedition would be sent far northward by water to destroy the small but ominous British military base at St. John's, situated at the foot of deep-draught navigation some twenty miles down the Sorel River. A more significant objective would be the capture or destruction of all British shipping in the lower-lake region. Of special concern to Ethan and his fellow officers was a British armed sloop which was known to be operating out of St. John's and which could cause a great deal of trouble if permitted to remain in enemy hands. The plan was both ambitious and dangerous. Much would depend upon whether or not the little expedition could do its work before the news of Ticonderoga's capture reached the lower lake and alerted the British. If the secret could be kept, the Colonials would have the great advantage of surprise and might well succeed in their mission. Otherwise they would probably be blown into oblivion by His Majesty's sloop.

Once again Ethan and his friends were plagued with boat trouble. Because of contrary winds and a series of time-consuming blunders, more than four days were required to move the captured craft from Skenesboro down to Ticonderoga, a distance of only twenty miles. Consequently, some of Ethan's staff favored abandoning the St. John's operation because of the likelihood that the advantage of surprise had been lost. Finally, however, on Sunday evening, May 14, the Committee of War decided that the attack should be made anyway. Major Skene's schooner would be used to carry a contingent of handpicked men to their down-lake destination, and to command the expedition the Committee of War chose none other than Colonel Benedict Arnold, who had only a few hours before emerged from his seclusion and begun to figure prominently in the decisions of the committee.

The sudden rise in Arnold's status had resulted not from any charitable impulse on the part of Ethan or the others, but rather from considerations of military reality. Earlier that same day more than one hundred of his recruits had arrived upon the scene from Massachusetts, and now at last he had what he had so conspicuously and embarrassingly lacked before—his own troops. Indeed, with many of Ethan's Green Mountain Boys already returned to their farms and with more of them chafing to leave, Arnold probably had a more numerous and reliable soldiery than any of the other officers at the fort. Add to this the fact that he alone could claim experience in handling large ships, and it is understandable why the committee should accede to his demand that he be given command of the St. John's expedition. Thus, on Monday, Arnold's contingent of about fifty men left Ticonderoga to see what could be done about sweeping the British from the lower lake. By 6:00 on Thursday morning they had won an easy victory. They had surprised and razed the military base at St. John's, seizing large quantities of provisions together with the entire British garrison of thirteen men. More important, they had made a clean capture of the British sloop, an impressively armed vessel of seventy-odd tons which the raiders swooped down upon and boarded as it lay at anchor a mile or so up-river from St. John's. In addition, nine large batteaux were captured, "four of which being out of repair we destroyed."

Arnold's victory was complete and unqualified. He had accomplished his mission, and in the process he had neither lost a man nor sustained a scratch. It was one of the first naval victories of the Revolution for the Colonials, and although diminutive, it was not without significance. For a time at least the Americans would be able to exercise total control over the lake, north and south. It must have been especially gratifying to Arnold to have handled the expedition so successfully. He had come a long way in search of victory, and now here it was, and there was no need to share it with anyone. Or was there? Shortly after nine o'clock, "at the completion of our business," Colonel Arnold, now riding the sloop and hauling his other prizes in tow, began his return south. By noon he had reached a point several miles above St. John's when he spied in the distance a strange procession approaching from up-river. Ethan Allen had decided that he too would like a share of the St. John's excitement and had accordingly set out from Ticonderoga for the British base not long after Arnold's departure.

With nearly one hundred of his Green Mountain Boys crowded into four batteaus, Ethan had proceeded to the foot of the lake by oar and makeshift sail. The trip had taken two days and nights of exhausting effort, and by the time he met Arnold returning from his successful raid, Ethan had some cause to wonder about the wisdom of what he was doing. His men were worn out—worse, they were hungry because in his haste Ethan had failed to provide enough food for the expedition. Now here they were nearly a hundred miles away from their base, confronted by the fact that victory had already been won by others. A lesser man, or a more rational one, would have accepted the realities of the situation and turned back, but Ethan had come this far and was determined that he and his Boys would have something to show for their ordeal.

Arnold was in an expansive mood. He invited Ethan to come aboard and inspect the captured sloop, and Ethan, probably half-choked with envy, did so. The two men drank "several loyal Congress healths" and then took dinner together in Arnold's cabin. Over dinner Ethan told his host that he planned to go on and occupy St. John's. Arnold was much opposed to the idea and attempted to dissuade Ethan by pointing out that it would be impossible for such a small contingent to hold St. John's because of its proximity to Montreal. It was probable that word of Arnold's raid had already reached Montreal, only fifteen miles cross-country from St. John's, and that regulars were even then being readied to re-garrison the base. Furthermore, why bother? Now that British shipping had been eliminated, the enemy's presence at St. John's could pose no threat for some time to come. At the moment the place had no military significance. Let it go. Arnold even volunteered to tow Ethan and his men back up the lake, an offer that must have cut painfully across the grain of Ethan's immense pride.

Perhaps it was the awful prospect of being towed back by Arnold that hardened Ethan's determination to continue northward and occupy St. John's; perhaps it was simply his characteristic stubbornness asserting itself. Or it may have been that Ethan sincerely believed that he could hold the town until the Americans could muster enough strength to invade Canada. Even at this early date he was mulling over the possibility of a full-scale Colonial attack against Canada, and the more he thought about it, the more feasible and desirable it seemed. For such an enterprise, St. John's would be an excellent base of operation. At any rate, despite Arnold's warnings, Ethan returned to his batteau, determined to lead his men northward. Arnold wished him well and gave him as much food as he could spare. Then he went below to the captain's cabin and informed his Journal that "100 mad fellows are going to take possession of St. John's. . . . A wild, impractical expensive Scheme. Of no Consequence."

As matters turned out, Ethan would have done well to have followed Arnold's advice and gone back in tow, for his attempted seizure of St. John's proved to be something less than a success. In fact, it ended so badly that Ethan conveniently forgot to mention it in his later written narrative of the lake campaign. After leaving Arnold, Ethan and his men made their way down the Sorel River and by nightfall had reached a promontory about a mile south of St. John's on the west bank. Here they disembarked and immediately began making preparations to advance upon the town. As they were about to move out, however, a scout brought back word that a relief column of upwards of two hundred British regulars was already on its way from Montreal. Arnold had gauged the situation correctly. Ethan and his Boys obviously had their work cut out for them.

For a time Ethan gave some thought to laying an ambush, but it was all too apparent that his men were in no condition to do battle against twice their own number of British regulars. In fact, after their long and arduous trip down the lake they were so tired that they weren't much good for anything at all. Ethan therefore decided to evacuate his force to the east side of the river in order to rest the men in preparation for something or other on the following day. This was probably the only wise decision he made throughout the entire course of his campaign against St. John's. As soon as they reached the opposite shore, the men crumpled into an exhausted sleep, Ethan included. No attempt was made by any of them to take cover, and no sentries were posted. To a man, Ethan's troops simply collapsed where their feet first hit dry land, and lay stretched out in long, exposed rows along the riverbank.

At daybreak Ethan and his men were given the rudest sort of awakening. During the night the British reinforcements had arrived at the opposite shore and had drawn up their cannons along the bank. At dawn they opened fire with savage blasts of grapeshot against the sleeping Americans. "The Musick was both terrible and delightful," Ethan later reported. Still groggy with sleep, confused, and terrified, the Boys piled into the boats, every man for himself, and rowed up-river at top speed. Because of the extended range of fire, none of the troops were seriously wounded, but in the haste to get away, three of Ethan's men were left behind. One of them was soon captured by the British. The other two eventually managed to make their way back to Crown Point, feeling none too kindly toward their comrades in arms and especially their Colonel Commandant.

It was a sorely chastened, hungry, and generally disgusted lot of Green Mountain Boys that pulled into Crown Point two days after their rout from St. John's. The expedition had been gone for five days and during that time had harvested nothing besides hard work and humiliation. Ethan had bungled, and he had bungled so obviously and so completely that no one could doubt the fact. He had exposed himself and his men to great risk and distress in order to engage in a stupid, useless bit of theatrics, and as a consequence his reputation for military command that he had won so impressively at Ticonderoga only a week and a half before was now seriously tarnished. Here was a blunder that would not go unnoticed by Ethan's friends and neighbors, and in due time would cost him dearly.

At Ticonderoga, Benedict Arnold was just sitting down to supper on Sunday evening, May 21, when the news reached him that Ethan had returned in defeat to Crown Point. It is not unlikely that Arnold was secretly pleased. Certainly he was not surprised. "It happened as I expected," he noted in his Journal.

Not long after Ethan's inglorious return to the upper lake, what remained of his soldiery began to melt rapidly away. For the time being the Green Mountain Boys had seen enough of war and now were returning to their farms to concern themselves with the more immediate neces-

sity of spring planting. By the final week of May, Colonel Commandant
Allen could claim only a handful of men still on the scene, most of them
officers, and his authority had decreased accordingly. Arnold, not
Ethan, was now clearly in command.

With their positions reversed, Ethan insisted that since he had captured Ticonerdoga he should remain in command, but Arnold reminded
him of the Committee of War's earlier decision: "no troops, no command," and the best Ethan could do was to grumble and give way. On
May 27 he made the best of a bad situation by announcing publicly that
out of deep concern for the common cause he was stepping down in
order to permit Colonel Arnold to exercise full command in the Champlain area. But this was to be merely a temporary arrangement, Ethan
declared, which would remain in effect only until the command situation
could be clarified by "some suitable higher authority." In the meantime
he would remain upon the scene in some capacity or other in order to
keep an eye on things. He was hopeful, he remarked to one of his fellow
officers, that the Continental Congress would soon name "a commander
for this department. . . . Undoubtedly we shall be rewarded according
to our Merit—in this or the Coming World."

To lose command was galling enough, but an even worse blow was to
come. Initially, the news of Ethan's seizure of Ticonderoga had been
received with great rejoicing. "The event," British historian George
Trevelyan would later comment, "caused an extraordinary outburst of
pride and gratification throughout the entire Confederacy." After the
first enthusiasm had waned, however, the fact became apparent that
Ethan's triumph had also brought about a situation  fraught with much
uncertainty and embarrassment for the Colonies. The capture of the fort
had been an exceedingly brash move. Unlike the more-or-less spontaneous defensive action at Lexington and Concord, it could hardly be
viewed as anything other than a deliberate act of premeditated aggression against the King. In other words, this was a clear case of rebellion,
and with the Colonies still loudly professing loyalty to the Crown, there
was an understandable hesitancy among them to act as the receiver of
what could aptly be construed as the fruits of treason. New York, within
whose jurisdiction the fort was situated, at first flatly refused to have
anything to do with the captured property, and for a time appeared to
pretend that it did not even exist. As for Massachusetts and Connecticut, they were willing to admit to their joint involvement in the seizure

of the fort, but they refused to accept the responsibility for maintaining possession of it. Here was a matter, they argued, for the Continental Congress to handle.

Congress, however, was also less than happy with the prospect of falling heir to Ethan's prize, and proceeded to act accordingly. Not long after receiving word of Ticonderoga's surrender, Congress agreed, by implication at least, to exercise authority over the fort and its dependencies, but at the same time it declared that the action against the British in the Champlain area had been purely defensive and that the property of King George III would be scrupulously protected. By resolution, Congress then called upon the northern Colonies to cooperate in removing the cannons, munitions, and other supplies to the south end of Lake George where they would be inventoried and held for safekeeping "in order that they may be safely returned, when the restoration of the former harmony between Great Britain and these colonies, so ardently wished for by the latter, shall render it prudent and consistent with the over-ruling law of self-preservation."

All this, of course, was tantamount to abandoning the fort, and when the news reached Ethan he was outraged. Immediately, on May 29, he fired off a strong letter to Congress, protesting a move which would leave the upper lake unprotected and the people of the Grants and the adjacent areas of New York Province entirely defenseless. One thousand or more families, according to Ethan's estimate, would be exposed to the ravages of the enemy. The fort must not, under any circumstances short of the restoration of peace, be abandoned, Ethan argued. In fact, instead of forfeiting this great advantage which he and the Green Mountain Boys had provided the Colonies, Congress should exploit it by strengthening Ticonderoga with additional men and arms. Such a move would not only secure the upper lake and block the invasion route from Canada to the Hudson Valley, but would also establish a strategic base of operations from which the Colonials could launch a campaign against Canada sometime in the future. And if the British should be upset by any of this, then let them be. In such matters, Ethan cautioned Congress, "it is bad policy to fear the resentment of an enemy."

Ethan's letter, which was read before Congress on June 10, was a forceful and courageous one. It was also sound and had particular appeal to the northern Colonies, who, although they had been reluctant to accept responsibility for the fort, were generally opposed to Congress' timid decision to strip it of its defenses. Even Arnold supported Ethan's stand by recommending to Congress that the defenses of the fort be kept up to fighting strength. Only those pieces of ordnance that could be spared should be removed, and they should be sent to assist the Colonials in Boston, as Arnold and the Massachusetts Committee of Safety had originally intended, rather than be placed in storage to await the King's pleasure. Both Arnold and Ethan wrote to the neighboring Colonies in order to marshal support against Congress' foolish scheme, and before long, because of mounting persuasion from the north, the delegates at Philadelphia reversed themselves and declared the ordnance and supplies seized by Ethan to be spoils of war, liable for use in defense of the common cause.

It was not enough for Ethan, however, that Congress should decide to keep up the defenses of Ticonderoga. By this time he had become dead set in favor of an invasion northward. During early June, as he scurried back and forth between Ticonderoga and Crown Point, scarcely a day passed when he did not write to someone or other in an attempt to promote a major expedition against Canada. He was now convinced, as a result of reports brought in by travelers from the north, that his earlier fears of enemy strength in Canada had been unjustified and that the entire Province of Quebec was in an almost totally defenseless state. A military thrust northward at this time would almost certainly succeed. To New York, Massachusetts, Connecticut, New Hampshire, and the Continental Congress he sent repeated pleas for men and supplies with which he might mount an immediate offensive. Canada must be taken. And Canada could be taken without any great difficulty. Now was no time to hold back. "A vast continent must now sink to slavery and poverty, bondage and horror, or rise to inconquerable freedom, immense wealth, inexpressible felicity, and immortal fame. . . . I will lay my life on it, that with fifteen hundred men, and a proper artillery, I will take Montreal."

Benedict Arnold considered Ethan a bit too sanguine, and chose to believe that he was motivated more by solicitude for his exposed land in the Onion River area than by considerations of patriotism. Still, he had to go along with Ethan's eagerness for a Canadian operation. The military logic of the situation demanded it.

While Ethan was busy attempting to stir up enthusiasm among the Colonials for a Canadian invasion, he was also doing what he could, by means of propaganda, to soften the enemy's position. It was apparent that the fortunes of any military attempt against Canada would depend to a great extent upon the attitude of the French settlers and of the Indians who inhabited the area of the upper St. Lawrence and lower lake regions. The settlers, or Canadians, constituted virtually all of the white population to the north. Although Canada had been under British control since the Peace of Paris in 1763, England's authority there was a very tenuous one indeed. A small scattering of British officials, supported by a few undermanned units of British regulars, exercised control over an extensive area settled by nearly a hundred thousand French habitants, most of whom had experienced some difficulty in adjusting to British rule.

Even though England had dealt leniently with the Canadians and had for the most part respected their traditions and ancient privileges, there was still unrest among these people who looked with suspicion, if not hatred, upon anything and anyone British. The implementation of the Quebec Act on May 1, 1775, only a week or so before the seizure of Ticonderoga, had tended to increase the uneasiness of the habitants who feared (quite unjustifiably) that the new measure would uproot their old ways. On May Day eve, as an expression of their disapproval of the Act, several Canadians paraded through the Place d'Armes in Montreal and urinated on the statue of King George III—"a most disgraceful behavior" in the opinion of the British authorities. Here was a spirit of defiance, "a sullen discontent," that Ethan considered worthy of exploitation.

In late May and early June, Ethan sent a number of letters northward by travelers and scouts to Canadians in the Montreal and St. John's area. In essence these letters, at least two of which were intercepted by the British, all contained the same message: We Americans "subscribe ourselves your unfeigned friends"; we have a common enemy; therefore, we should fight together, or, failing that, we should at least refrain from fighting against one another. What Ethan had to say made a good deal of sense, and all this may have had some temporary influence upon the Canadians.

Actually, however, for a multitude of reasons Ethan's letters proved to be of decidedly limited consequence. Under the circumstances they could hardly have been otherwise. For one thing, most of the Canadian priests inclined towards the British, and as agents of the Almighty the priests spoke with an awesome voice among the habitants. Furthermore, in addition to their spiritual role the clergy constituted what little community leadership there was among the French settlers. Even if the habitants had been willing to defy the word of God, without their priests they would have been hard put to organize anything approaching an effective effort against the British, or even to assume a concerted position of benevolent neutrality towards the Americans.

But worse than that, as far as Ethan's hopes were concerned, was the plain fact that although the Canadians did not think much of the British, they cared even less for the Americans—especially the New Englanders —who had traditionally made no secret of their anti-French, anti-Catholic feelings. For most of the Canadians there was really not much choice between the British and the Yankees, and as a result they lacked a feeling of involvement in the struggle between the Colonies and the Crown. They therefore did not feel inclined to take great risks one way or the other. In the end, a goodly number of Canadians would take up arms in support of the British or the Americans (or sometimes both), but few would fight very long or very hard, and their choice of sides would be determined without much reference to Ethan's fine words about freedom and brotherhood. To them, the important factor was the prospect of personal gain, and they would understandably tend to support that side which, at a given moment, appeared to offer them the better chance of obtaining it. Nevertheless, the more Ethan thought about it, the more convinced he became that the Canadians were so unhappy under British rule that they would rise up to a man and fight tenaciously alongside the Americans as soon as an invading force appeared upon the scene. This was a sad miscalculation on Ethan's part which would in time cost him dearly.

While Ethan was attempting to win over the Canadians, he was also making bids for the support of the northern Indians. These "French" Indians inhabited the region south and west of Montreal, and although they numbered fewer than 3,500 in all, they were nevertheless a power to be reckoned with. The most important of the French Indians were the Caughnawagas, whose "castle" was located about nine miles upriver from Montreal and whose hunting grounds extended over onto the eastern shores of Lake Champlain. Although a small tribe with probably no more than two hundred warriors, the Caughnawagas were highly respected for their fighting ability. Descended mainly from Iroquois stock, they were clever and bold and could boast effective organization and leadership. More often than not they set the course for neighboring tribes to follow, and for this reason their help against the British could prove to be an invaluable asset for the Colonials. It was to secure their support—or, failing this, their neutrality—that Ethan sent scouts to their castle carrying messages such as the following, which was intercepted by Governor Carleton:

> I always love Indians and have hunted a great deal with them I know how to shute and ambush just like Indian and want your Warriors to come and see me and help me fight Regulars—You know they stand all along close together Rank and file and my men fight so as Indians do and I want your Warriors to join with me and my Warriors like brothers and ambush the Regulars, if you will I will give you money, blankits Tomehawks Knives and Paint and the like as much as you say because they first killed our men when it was Peace time. . . . we are obliged to fight but if you our Brother Indians do not fight on either side still we will be Friends and Brothers and you may come and hunt in our woods and pass through our country in the Lake and come to our post and have Rum and be good friends. . . . I hope your Warriors will come and see me it may be at Crown Point or Saint John's and possibly at Montreal if I have good heart and fight well. So I bid all our Brother Indians farewell.

Ethan knew the Caughnawagas well enough not to be deluded, however. Among other things, it was clear to him that they enjoyed reasonably good relations with the British, while at the same time they held a rather low opinion of the Colonials, who had frequently treated them badly and had attempted to push them off their hunting grounds. But with the Caughnawagas, as with most other Indians, the principal consideration in matters of this sort was military realism. In the final reckoning they would be impressed more by power than by professions of friendship, and could be counted upon to do their best to end up on the side of the winner. "They act upon political principles," Ethan wrote in early June to the Massachusetts Legislature, "and are inclined to fall in with the strongest side." It was, in fact, at least partially to impress these Indians with American strength that Ethan urged a major campaign northward as soon as possible.

On a day in early June, Colonel Arnold, piqued by a minor incident that he considered an affront to his authority, kicked one of Ethan's officers in the rump and ordered him to leave the area. This was too much. Calling together what remained of the Committee of War, Ethan complained bitterly about the command situation and about the inexcusable failure of the Colonies to make preparations for an invasion of Canada. The time had come to straighten matters out, and in Ethan's judgment the best way to do this was to present the facts of the case before the Continental Congress. The committee agreed and chose Ethan, Warner, and Remember Baker (who later begged off) to go immediately to Philadelphia and attempt to get Congress moving. Among other things, Ethan was explicitly instructed by the Committee of War to seek authorization from Congress for the formation of a regiment of Green Mountain Boys, which would be incorporated as a regular unit into the Continental Army. To help Ethan along, his fellow officers affixed their signatures to a letter heartily endorsing his fine qualities of leadership. Ethan probably composed the letter himself, but, be that as it may, it was a good thing to have on hand. It spoke in glowing terms of his singular behavior and remarkable courage, and commended him "to the whole Continent."

On the morning of June 11, Ethan and Seth Warner set out from Crown Point on horseback for Philadelphia where they arrived late on June 22. The next day they appeared at the State House on Chestnut Street and were immediately granted permission to lay their business before Congress. With Ethan doing most of the talking, they proceeded to present their case to the government of what had by that time become known officially as "The United Colonies of America." There is no record of their remarks, but they must have argued very effectively, for later that same day Congress resolved:

> That it be recommended to the convention of New York, that they, consulting with General Schuyler,* employ in the army to be raised for the defence of America, those called Green Mountain Boys, under such officers as the said Green Mountain Boys shall chuse.

At the same time Congress resolved that the Province of New York be urged to pay Ethan and his Boys at Continental Army rates for their

---

* General Philip Schuyler was one of four major generals appointed by Congress soon after the outbreak of the Revolution. At this time he was in command of the Northern Department, which included the New Hampshire Grants.

expedition against Ticonderoga and its dependencies. As for Canada, the members of Congress at first refused to commit themselves to an invasion, out of fear that such a move might "appear aggressive." Four days later, however, after much squabbling, the delegates timidly gave their approval to launching such an operation "if General Schuyler finds it practicable and if it will not be disagreeable to the Canadians." In view of the timing of this decision, it is not unlikely that Ethan's appearance and arguments before Congress had a major effect in persuading that body to put aside some of its former doubts and adopt a more realistic policy towards the British presence in Canada.

Soon after Congress had haltingly declared itself on Canada, Ethan and Seth Warner left for New York City, carrying with them copies of the congressional resolutions and a letter of endorsement from President of Congress John Hancock to the New York Provincial Assembly. Since both Ethan and Warner had been for some years past on less than friendly terms with their Yorker neighbors and were, in fact, still officially listed as notorious felons with prices on their heads, they probably approached the New York Assembly with some feelings of trepidation. They had no guarantee that they would not be pounced upon immediately and thrown into a Yorker prison, or worse. Still, the odds were on their side. The old regime of Tryon, Colden, etc., had ceased to be, temporarily at least, and in view of this and the other great developments of the past couple of months, including belligerency against a common enemy, it seemed likely that the Yorkers would be willing to forgive and forget. Furthermore, there was some comfort for Ethan and Warner in the knowledge that they came well recommended by the Continental Congress. All things considered, the risk seemed worth taking, and they took it. In fact, it was a thing that had to be done if life were to be breathed into the resolutions so recently passed in Philadelphia. The Continental Congress may have given its blessings to Ethan's plan for a regiment and for back pay for the Ticonderoga campaign, but the implementation of both those resolutions depended upon New York's willingness to foot the bill.

On July fourth the chief of the Grants outlaws and his lieutenant knocked at the door of the Provincial Assembly in New York City and asked for permission to enter and be heard. At first their reception was far from cordial. In fact, they were made to wait outside the chamber for over an hour while the Assembly debated the propriety of admitting them. It was finally decided, however, that they should be allowed to come in and state their case. Once again they must have argued well, for in short order the Assembly responded by passing enabling acts to implement the resolutions of Congress. The Green Mountain Boys were to go ahead and activate, at New York's expense, a regular regiment of not more than seven companies, totaling five hundred men, and Ethan and his comrades in arms were to receive back pay in full for their part in capturing and holding Fort Ticonderoga. Here in New York, as in Philadelphia, things had turned out very well for Ethan. He could hardly have expected more.

On their way back to the Grants the two men stopped off to visit with Ethan's shamefully neglected family in Sheffield—but not for long. There was a war to be fought, and Ethan, who was never very happy at home anyway, was anxious to get moving. By July 12, a week after their departure from New York City, he and Seth were back in Bennington, spreading the good news among their neighbors. For Ethan the next two weeks were filled with great excitement and anticipation. For a day or so following his return, he put up at Fay's tavern and spent many exacting hours drawing up plans for the composition of the regiment and for the military campaign that he supposed would follow within a short time.

Having completed his plans, he rode northward to present them for approval and action to General Schuyler, who had by this time taken up headquarters at Ticonderoga. Then, after billeting himself at the fort on Schuyler's invitation, Ethan sat back to await new glory. He could doubtless picture quite clearly his triumphal entrance into the Place d'Armes in Montreal, handsomely mounted at the head of his own regiment. There was real challenge ahead; there were battles to be fought and won; but Ethan did not for a moment doubt that the Green Mountain Regiment under his leadership would prove more than equal to the task.

It would not do to wait too long in launching the invasion, however. Reports were coming in from the north that the British regulars were frightened and demoralized and that the Canadians and Indians were eagerly awaiting the arrival of American troops, whom they would surely join against a common enemy. Ethan, because he wanted to, chose to accept these reports at face value and to reject any information to the contrary. The time for invasion was now. Clearly, conditions would never be better. Delay would serve only to permit the British to strengthen their garrisons and thereby perhaps cow the Canadians and Indians into irrevocable submission.

Ethan was an impatient man, especially when he saw (or thought he saw) golden opportunity staring him in the face, and as the days passed and July neared its end, it became increasingly difficult for him to sit stupidly inactive while New York and Schuyler appeared to be doing little or nothing by way of activating the regiment or making any other sort of preparation. Still, Ethan had little choice but to wait. Occasionally he would confide to a friend, as he did to Governor Trumbull of Connecticut, that he was tempted not to wait upon the formation of the regiment, that he was thinking seriously of calling up his Green Mountain Boys and leading them northward to invest Montreal. Surely those brave troops who had captured Ticonderoga could take Montreal easily enough. In fact, Ethan assured Trumbull, were it not for the recent favors bestowed upon him by Congress and the New York Assembly, and the obligations he accordingly felt toward them and General Schuyler, he would gather up his Boys and set out "forthwith."

All of this was pure bluster on Ethan's part, and he knew it. It was one thing to have captured by a sudden surprise attack the semi-dilapidated fortress at Ticonderoga, so conveniently located within easy striking distance of the settled areas of the Grants. It would be a far different matter, however, to mount an offensive northward through a hundred miles of wilderness and wage war against an alerted and entrenched enemy. For such an operation a sustained military effort of considerable size would be needed, and it was eminently clear that nothing of consequence could be done without the supplies and money promised by the Province of New York. Ethan would simply have to curb his impatience and hold himself in check until New York and General Schuyler had completed their preparations. When that would be, who could say? General Schuyler had never been widely known in the past as a man given to precipitous action, and there was nothing in his behavior at Ticonderoga that summer to suggest that he had changed his ways. As far as Ethan could determine, precious days were being squandered. He was becoming increasingly concerned over the delay. And with good reason. Subsequent events would prove that his impatience was justified.

And so Ethan chafed. But despite his mounting anxiety, he remained in a generally sunny mood. Looming always before him during these midsummer days was the happy prospect of leading his own regiment of regulars, and he was filled with feelings of warmth and gratitude to all those who had helped make such a good thing possible. He was especially appreciative of the generosity shown him by his old adversary, the government of New York, and he could not resist the temptation to tell his Yorker benefactors how much he treasured their new friendship.

In a letter written at Ticonderoga on July 20, he thanked the members of the New York Assembly and praised "the union that hath lately taken place between the New York government and those its former discontented subjects in making a united resistance against ministerial vengeance and slavery." And as far as ancient antagonisms were concerned, Ethan hoped that bygones would be bygones, and that "no gentlemen in the [New York] Congress will retain any preconceived prejudice against me." This was obviously a broad hint that Ethan would welcome an official pardon from the New York Assembly, but there was no pardon forthcoming. Despite the fact that he had been given permission to raise troops under the authority and with the support of the Yorker government, Ethan's name would remain on the New York records as an outlaw with a price on his head. No matter, however. Ethan, for his part, was willing to forgive New York, and he said so.

Finally, on July 26, the first real step was taken in the actual raising of the Green Mountain Regiment. On that day, pursuant to the congressional resolution of more than a month before, and at the request of General Schuyler, a convention of the committees of the west-side towns met at Dorset to elect officers for the regiment soon-to-be. What took place at the meeting was not recorded—save for the results of the voting. In all, twenty-three officers were elected by the convention. Among those chosen, the Allen presence was apparent enough. Heman, who had come up from Salisbury that spring to help his older brother take Ticonderoga, was to be a captain, and young Ira a first lieutenant. Conspicuously absent from the list of officers, however, was the name of the greatest Allen of them all. By a landslide vote of 41–5, Ethan's neighbors had seen fit to entrust the command of the new Green Mountain Regiment to Seth Warner.

For Ethan, there was nothing at all, not even a lieutenancy.

# VIII. "A Day of Trouble, if Not Rebuke"

ETHAN'S REJECTION by the town committees must have come as a terrible blow. He had long been the acknowledged military leader of the Grants, or so at least he had fancied himself, and until now nobody had questioned his preeminence. It had been he who had kept the Yorkers at bay for five years, and who had led his friends and neighbors in the dramatic capture of Fort Ticonderoga. Afterwards it was he, admittedly with some help from Warner, who had successfully sold the idea of the Green Mountain Regiment to the Continental Congress and the Government of New York. Naturally he had assumed that he would be the commander of the new unit. By all that was right, the regiment belonged to him and it had never crossed his mind that anyone might think otherwise. To be rejected for command by the people he had served so well was disappointing, to say the least. But to be rejected by such an overwhelming vote, and, worse still, to be omitted entirely from the list of officers, was little short of shattering. More stunned than angry, Ethan wrote to Connecticut's Governor Trumbull soon after the blow had fallen in a painful attempt to explain what had happened:

> Not withstanding my Zeal and success in my Countrys Cause the old Farmers on the New Hampshire Grants who do not incline to go to war have met in a Committee Meeting and in their Nomination of Officers for the regiment . . . have wholly omitted me. . . . I find myself in favor with the Officers of the army and the young Green Mountain Boys. How the old men came to reject me I cannot conceive inasmuch as I saved them from the incroachments of New York.

Actually, the decision of the Dorset convention was understandable enough. A fair number of Grants settlers, including many of the more

143

affluent and well-established, had never been very favorably disposed towards Ethan. As Ethan was well aware, they had long regarded him not as their savior but as an irresponsible troublemaker who stood in the way of a reasonable settlement with the Yorkers. But this group, important as it was, represented only a nucleus of discontent about which there clustered during the weeks following the seizure of Ticonderoga a number of new recruits, who for one reason or another had become disenchanted with Ethan and his brand of leadership. In fact, by mid-summer of 1775, probably a sizable majority of the Grants settlers had lost much of whatever enthusiasm they had once had for Ethan, and, tacitly or otherwise, had either arrayed themselves against him or adopted an attitude of indifference. Clearly, Ethan had, at least temporarily, lost his hold over his neighbors, and the reasons for his eclipse are not hard to find.

By all accounts, Ethan's behavior since his capture of Ticonderoga had been less than edifying. Victory and the sudden fame that had come with it had seemed to accentuate his natural inclination toward boastfulness and arrogance, with the result that he had, in the opinion of many of his Grants neighbors, become intolerably overbearing. His loud and tiresome bragging and his imperious posing, plus his peevish bickering with Arnold had, in fact, caused many of his former supporters to wonder about the true measure of this man whose lead they had so often followed. Wide attention was now given those critics of Ethan who had long denounced him as a selfish, vain, arrogant, unprincipled adventurer who could be relied upon to act for the common good only if his own ambitions were served by so doing. Perhaps they had been right all along. Certainly, Ethan's recent conduct had tended to indicate that, whatever else he may or may not have been, he was an incurable egotist who was more than a little interested in personal aggrandizement.

Above and beyond all this, however, was the fact that Ethan's reckless and entirely ill-advised attempt to occupy St. John's had given rise to serious doubts as to his military abilities and judgment. It was true that as a frontier vigilante chieftain he had done well enough at spreading terror among the Yorkers, and as the leader of a pre-dawn sneak attack against an undersized garrison of sleeping Britishers, he had triumphed dramatically. But to command a regiment of five hundred men in a planned military operation of some complexity required something more than the skills of a skirmisher. A very special capacity for military leadership was needed, and in the St. John's expedition—his only genuine campaign—Ethan had proved himself woefully ill-equipped with that commodity. Here was a fact that understandably loomed large in the reckoning of the men of the west-side towns, many of whom would be serving in the new regiment.

And so the decision of the Dorset convention was at least partly a vote of no-confidence in Ethan, but it was also a vote of approval for Seth Warner—and a wiser and more logical choice of commander for the new regiment could hardly have been made. Warner, with his quiet ways and steady habits, was looked upon with great favor by the men of the Grants, particularly the older settlers who saw in him many things that Ethan lacked—including a settled residence on the Grants and membership in the Congregational Church. Although not the sort of person to excite great affection, he commanded respect and confidence from all who knew him. Notably lacking in dash and bluster, he moved in an unspectacular manner and with a somewhat plodding step. But he moved wisely and well, and, what was perhaps most important, he could be absolutely counted upon to give his best to any cause assigned to his care. Credit mattered little to him. Getting the job done was the thing, and with Seth Warner there would be no quitting until the final reckoning. Few men would perform so devotedly and well in behalf of the American cause.

The record of his military service is filled with accounts of the remarkable heroism of a man who never questioned a command, argued with a superior, or claimed an ounce of glory for himself. On more than one occasion Warner saved the northern department from probable disaster by fighting hopeless rear guard delaying actions against far superior British forces. And when in the late summer of 1777 America's destiny hung in the balance in the fields outside of Bennington, Warner was there in the thick of it, fighting gallantly at the head of his pitifully decimated regiment. That he more than justified the faith placed in him by the delegates at the Dorset convention is clearly written in the annals of the Revolution. It is doubtful that Ethan would have done nearly as well.

It is greatly to Ethan's credit that whatever his other faults, he was certainly not a poor loser. Although his towering egotism and bluster often made it difficult for him to cope with success, they enabled him to take defeat pretty much in stride. Never was he known to sulk or bear a grudge for any length of time, and the idea of feeling sorry for himself simply didn't occur to him. He was not a brooding, introspective man who allowed set-backs to gnaw at his viscera, and least of all was he inclined to blame or question himself when things went wrong. Let other men concern themselves with self-doubt and self-appraisal. Ethan knew what he was, and he approved mightily. If things happened to turn out badly now and then, he was sure that they had gone wrong through no fault of his own.

In this instance, the town committees at Dorset had obviously made a great mistake, but Ethan was ready to forgive them. He also forgave Warner, and never did he utter a word of recrimination against his friend and former lieutenant. All of this was very generous of Ethan— and very natural. He had never learned the conventional responses to defeat, and, approaching forty, he was certainly too old to learn them now. It is not surprising, therefore, that he appeared before Schuyler a few days after the Dorset vote and offered to serve under the general in any capacity, commissioned or otherwise, that would best contribute to the success of the forthcoming invasion of Canada.

Aside from Ethan, nobody was more surprised by the decision of the town committees than General Schuyler. Like Ethan, he had supposed that the selection of commanding officer for the new regiment was a foregone conclusion. He had even directed his paymaster to advance Ethan £200 against his colonel's pay. Actually, however, the patrician Schuyler was anything but chagrined over Ethan's rejection. He had never liked Ethan, and although he had refused to interfere in the election, he was clearly relieved by the outcome. To his way of thinking, Ethan was too brash and impulsive to assume a major command, and was as likely as not to prove insubordinate and disruptive of military discipline. It is understandable, therefore, why Schuyler at first refused Ethan's offer to accompany the army northward. "I always dreaded his impatience of subordination," Schuyler wrote somewhat later to John Hancock, President of the Continental Congress.

But Ethan was not without friends, including Warner and the other officers of the new regiment, and they finally prevailed upon Schuyler to allow Ethan to join the expedition in the capacity of civilian scout. Schuyler agreed to this, he later explained, "only after a solemn promise, made me in the presence of several officers, that he would demean himself properly." And so, although holding no military rank of any kind, and claiming less than the complete confidence of the Commanding General of the Northern Department, Ethan was permitted to participate in the invasion of Canada that he had done so much to promote. For several weeks he would conduct himself in a most seemly manner, but eventually he would forget his promise to Schuyler and do a very foolish thing.

While it is true that Ethan was less than a model of patience and moderation, it also is true that the man to whom the Canadian campaign had been entrusted was painfully deliberate and methodical. A well-intentioned man was Philip Schuyler, but obviously lacking in the power of decision, perhaps because he sensed what many others knew—that he was at best a second-rate leader of men. Even in his prime he had manifested few outstanding qualities of leadership, and although only in his early forties at the time of the Canadian campaign of 1775, he was already well beyond his peak. Long a victim of what was then called retrogressive gout, an exceedingly painful affliction, he was clearly an ailing man whose drawn features reflected the attritional effects of great suffering. In body and spirit, pain had ground him down and made him much older than his years, and among those persons who knew him best there was the whispered suspicion that his mental faculties had been somewhat dulled by his long and cruel ordeal.

Still, during those early days of the Revolution, when command potential was in such short supply in the Colonies, his appointment to one of the Continental Army's highest offices was reasonable enough. He had, after all, gained some experience fighting the French twenty years before, and for a while he had stood high in the New York militia. More important, however, was the prestigious position he occupied as a powerful landholder and political influence in pivotal New York Province. Descended from an early Dutch patroon, he ruled over an extensive empire, and when he spoke the Province of New York did well to listen. This had been true under royal government, and it was even more true now that the Colonies had taken up arms against the Mother Country, for at a time when many of the wealthier families in New York and elsewhere were declaring for the King, Philip Schuyler was conspicuous for his loyalty to the Colonial cause. He was a good man and true, and despite the fact that his florid, puckered face suggested a tyrannical spirit, he was in reality a gentle and courteous person. He was, in effect, as one of his biographers has remarked of him, "just the man to lead a quadrille at a county ball." He was less well equipped to lead a full-scale invasion of Canada, and he could certainly have profited from some of Ethan's impetuosity.

During most of the month of August, Schuyler remained in a state of immobility. True, almost from the very beginning his efforts at preparation had been plagued by a multitude of maddening delays, some of which he could not have foreseen or avoided, and as a result the strength of his command had increased less rapidly than he had anticipated. Shipments of flour and other food supplies from the south had reached the staging area at Ticonderoga decidedly behind schedule; powder and shot had proved surprisingly hard to come by; the construction of boats had lagged, as had the repair and readying of ordnance. Many of the troops that had been promised Schuyler had also been slow in assembling, including the Green Mountain Regiment, which Warner and his officers had a difficult time raising because of lack of volunteers.

Delays of this sort were, of course, not actually Schuyler's fault, although it seems likely that a more forceful leadership might have managed to obtain faster and better results. What was Schuyler's fault, however, was his refusal to budge until conditions were perfect, or nearly so, in his very conservative military judgment. By insisting upon optimum conditions within his command before setting out to meet an outnumbered, confused, and nearly defenseless enemy, Schuyler allowed precious days and weeks to slip by, and thereby squandered the most irredeemable of military assets—time, and in so doing he contributed as much as any other person to the disastrous American defeat in Canada. Ethan had been right all along, and events were soon to bear him out. Time was of the essence.

As matters turned out, Ethan's ardent wish for a Canadian campaign would eventually come true, but it would come true too late. By the end of August when the American invasion expedition left the upper lake, too much time had passed since Ethan's seizure of the initiative in early May. During this period of almost four months the enemy forces in Canada, although still badly neglected by Britain in matters of supply and troop reinforcement, had regained much of their composure and had dug in to make a fight of it. Far worse, though, was the fact that by adhering to his policy of delay, Schuyler had put off launching the campaign until too late in the season. The enemy would soon be gaining a formidable ally.

In a land where frost usually comes on the first full moon in September, if not earlier, and snow can come at any time thereafter, there is an ominous quality about the days of late August. The nights are colder than they have any right to be, and in the low places the foliage takes on the first touches of autumn color. There will be more warm days ahead, but those who know the region well are not deluded. Winter is on its way and may be expected to arrive before very long. It is not a propitious time of year to begin long-term outdoor projects, for by late August time is clearly running out. In the officers' quarters at Ticonderoga, General Richard Montgomery, second in command to Schuyler, was not unmindful of this fact. "Good God," he wrote in exasperation to a friend." A winter campaign in Canada! Posterity won't believe it."

Had it not been for a flare-up of Schuyler's gout, the expedition might never have got under way. By late August Schuyler's condition had become so painful that he was forced to repair to his home in Saratoga. From time to time during the next few weeks he would return to rejoin his troops, but on each occasion he would remain for only a brief period before being driven back home by the grinding pain of his affliction. From late August on, the actual direction of the invasion force would fortunately be in the hands of the very capable Montgomery, who, then in his late thirties and an almost exact contemporary of Ethan Allen, was a seasoned soldier and an excellent leader of men.

Soon after Schuyler's departure, it fell to Montgomery to make the decision that his superior had been unwilling, perhaps unable, to make. On August 28 word reached the upper lake that the British at St. John's were feverishly engaged in constructing a fleet. Here was an ominous development, which if allowed to go unchecked could dangerously alter the military situation in the Lake region. Thus, at six o'clock that same evening General Montgomery, acting entirely on his own initiative, set out from Ticonderoga at the head of a flotilla carrying twelve hundred American troops on the first leg of that ill-starred Canadian invasion from which he and so many others would never return. "Moving without your orders I do not like," he wrote to Schuyler as he began his thrust northward, "but the prevention of the enemy is of the utmost consequence; for, if he gets his vessels into the lake, it is over with us for the present summer." Schuyler immediately wrote back endorsing Montgomery's action. In fact, the tone of Schuyler's letter suggests that he was much relieved that somebody else had made the decision for him.

For the next six days nearly fifty boats, most of them batteaux loaded to the water's edge with rawboned Yankees and up-river Yorkers fresh from the plow, made their way northward by sail and oar. Halting each night to regroup and rest and care for the sick, which at one time numbered nearly three hundred, the expedition made painfully slow progress. But that this highly chaotic array managed to move at all was something of a tribute to General Montgomery, whose patience was inexhaustible and whose qualities of leadership won him the admiration of all, including Ethan—who appears to have had a high regard for Montgomery and to have got along with him very well. As the troops neared the lower narrows, word reached them that the war in the Champlain region, begun by Ethan at Ticonderoga nearly four months before, had finally claimed its first victim. Ethan's cousin and good friend, Remember Baker, was dead. On a scouting expedition not far from St. John's, he had been set upon by a band of Caughnawagas and beheaded.

Understandably proud of their trophy, the Indians carried Remember's head to St. John's and paraded it through the town on the end of a pole. In time the British officers of the garrison were able to persuade the Indians to part with it, for a price, and subsequently returned the head to the place of Baker's death and buried it beside his body. Thus, a few months past his thirty-eighth birthday and many miles removed from his native Woodbury, Connecticut, died the interpid frontiersman Remember Baker who did more than his share in taming the wilderness and shaping the early development of what would one day become Vermont. Back at the Onion River Company headquarters in Burlington his wife, Desire, and his young son, Ozzie, would find it hard to believe that he was dead. To them and all others who knew him he had always been the indestructible man.

On the evening of September 4, an even week after their departure from Ticonderoga, the Colonial troops took possession of undefended Ile aux Noix, preparatory to their attack on St. John's fifteen miles to the north. On the following day Ethan with a half-dozen men was sent out into enemy territory to spread the word among the Indians and the Canadian settlers that a great American army was coming, and to invite all freedom-loving men among them to rise up and join their American friends in toppling British tyranny. This was the sort of thing that Ethan was particularly good at. With his boundless enthusiasm and confidence and his powerful gift of persuading others to follow his lead, he could hardly have been otherwise, and it is not surprising that his proselyting attempts brought results which, at least at first, were very gratifying. "Colonel Allen has been very serviceable in bringing in the Canadians and Indians," one of Montgomery's officers wrote to a friend. "The Indians of all the tribes and the Canadians who join us, have all learned English enough to say Liberty and Bostonian, and call themselves Yankees. The Indians boast much of it and will smite on their breasts, saying 'me Yankee.' " In his headquarters at Montreal, Governor Sir Guy Carleton was well aware of what Ethan and his small party were up to. Reports of their successful recruiting reached him almost hourly, and the governor was clearly disturbed. "They have injured us very much," he wrote to Lord Dartmouth in London.

Returning from his mission after eight days in enemy territory, Ethan joined the Americans outside of St. John's where they had already begun to invest the town. To General Montgomery, Ethan freely proffered advice on how best to "lay a line of circumvallation around the fortress of St. John's." In fact, let the General but say the word and Ethan would gladly lead a charge against the town. Montgomery was grateful for this generous offer but pointed out very tactfully that Ethan's services among the Indians and Canadians had been so helpful that he could best serve the cause by returning into enemy territory to continue his good work. It was a dangerous assignment, Montgomery well understood, and one which few men were brave enough and enterprising enough to carry out. Ethan did not argue the point. He would have preferred to remain at St. John's and help with the siege, but "my esteem for the general's person, and my opinion of him as a politician and brave officer, induced me to proceed." And so on the morning of September 18, Ethan set out again. This time he would be gone for nearly three years.

For the first few days after leaving St. John's Ethan's successes were brilliant, if his own accounts of the mission can be believed. Accompanied by eight or ten Americans and a couple of Canadian interpreters, he progressed northward under specific orders "to raise a regiment of Canadians" in the triangle formed by the confluence of the Sorel and St. Lawrence Rivers. Moving down the Sorel, he paused from time to time to "preach politics" among the Indians and scold them for certain scattered acts of hostility they had recently committed against the Americans, including the murder of Remember Baker. The Indians were inordinately friendly and filled with remorse over their transgressions. They really hadn't wanted to do anything bad to their good friends the

Yankees, but the British officers at St. John's had got them drunk on rum. They would certainly behave better in the future.

Upon reaching the mouth of the Sorel, Ethan and his party doubled back southward and began moving up the near bank of the St. Lawrence in the direction of Montreal. Everywhere they went they met with great success in raising troops among the French settlers. On September 20 Ethan reported to Montgomery by runner:

> I am now in the parish of St. Tuors, four leagues from Sorel [Parish], to the south; have two hundred and fifty Canadians under arms; as I march, they gather fast. . . . You may rely on it that I shall join you in about three days, with five Hundred or more Canadian volunteers. I could raise one or two thousand in a weeks time, but will first visit the army with a less number, and if necessary will go again recruiting. Those that used to be enemies of our cause come cap in hand to me; and I swear by the lord I can raise three times the number of our army in Canada, provided you continue the siege. . . .

In addition, Ethan reported, he had been able to purchase from the Canadians substantial amounts of foodstuffs and rum which he had already ordered sent back to the siege forces at St. John's. Things were going very well indeed—too well for a person of Ethan's boundless self-confidence.

Whatever prompted him to exceed his orders and attack Montreal can only be guessed at. As he and his small party roamed openly and with impunity to within a few miles of the city, recruiting Canadians at will, the possibility of a successful assault on the thinly defended City must have crossed his mind more than once. For the man who had captured Ticonderoga would this be such a difficult feat? Certainly it would be a tremendous coup if he could bring it off—a real feather in his cap. It would prove once and for all, beyond any question, that he was a man of exceptional military gifts. At one stroke it would erase the stain of his earlier St. John's fiasco and would demonstrate to his Grants neighbors that they had committed a great blunder in rejecting him for command.

According to Ethan, however, the thought of attacking Montreal had never even occurred to him until the matter was brought up by his supposed friend John Brown, a major in Montgomery's army who had served under Ethan with the Massachusetts contingent at Ticonderoga. It was just after Ethan had left the St. Lawrence, three or four miles north of Montreal, and had begun to cut cross-country on his way back to St. John's that he came unexpectedly upon Brown and a few of his scouts and interpreters. Like Ethan, Brown had been sent out by General Montgomery to recruit among the settlers, and like Ethan he had met with great success. In fact, less than ten miles south of that very spot, Brown had (or claimed to have) a force of almost two hundred men assembled, for the most part Canadians. Ethan, who had already sent many of his recruits to St. John's still had nearly half that number. Taken altogether, here was a fair-sized body of troops, already within easy striking distance of Montreal. In the front room of a nearby farmhouse, just outside the little French parish of La Prairie, Ethan, Brown, and a few of their men pondered the potential of the situation, but not for long. The opportunity was obviously too rare to miss. It was agreed that the two forces would cooperate in a double-pronged attack against the city, and that the operation would be begun that very night. Under cover of darkness Ethan was to cross the river from a point a couple of miles north of Montreal, while Brown would cross at about the same distance to the south. At daybreak, after exchanging "three huzzas," the two contingents would converge upon the city and seize it before the inhabitants could brush the sleep from their eyes.

It was a bold plan attended by great risk. After all, Montreal was no mere hamlet. It was, in fact, with a population of nearly nine thousand, one of the largest cities on the continent. Still, the idea of seizing it was not so entirely mad as some of Ethan's critics have made it appear. Through information received from friendly Canadians, Ethan and Brown were both well aware of the extreme weakness of the city's defense capabilities. The British had chosen to make their stand at St. John's and had committed most of their strength, such as it was, to a defense of that point. As a result, there were at the time fewer than sixty regulars in Montreal and little else in the way of military manpower that could be safely relied upon. The loyalty of the French inhabitants of the city was shaky at best, and the English civilians able to bear arms numbered only in the dozens. Furthermore, the news recently received of the American investment of St. John's had deeply disturbed the city —so much so that a sudden show of force at the gates might throw the place into a panic. The odds were therefore not really so long as they might have been, and, of course, the prize was tremendously enticing.

Nevertheless, Ethan's decision to advance upon Montreal was, besides being contrary to his orders, a foolish one at best, for the plain fact of the matter was that there was no military necessity for such a move. Once St. John's fell, as fall it almost certainly would, then Montreal was automatically lost to the enemy. It was as simple as that, and in view of the very obvious military realities of the situation, a reasonable man would have avoided needless risk and been content to await the inevitable. But Ethan was not always a reasonable man, especially when glory appeared to be within his reach.

Immediately after his meeting with Brown, Ethan returned to the St. Lawrence a few miles below Montreal to prepare for the attack. Along the way he encountered a scouting party of twenty or more Americans whom he persuaded to join him, thereby bringing his total strength to about one hundred and ten men. More than eighty of this number were Canadians, whose enthusiasm for the attack appeared to stand very high, perhaps mainly because of Ethan's promise that each of them would receive "thirty coppers a day and an equal share in the plunder." Unfortunately, however, aside from their apparent eagerness, they had little to recommend them as troops. For the most part they were poorly armed, ragamuffin farmers who knew little about military matters and probably cared even less. All things considered, they did not constitute a prime-quality fighting force, and Ethan knew it. Still, with nearly thirty Americans spaced in among them, likely as not they would work out well enough. At any rate, they would have to do.

Shortly before midnight on that same day, September 24, Ethan began ferrying his troops across the river, about a mile south of Longueil Parish. As at Hand's Cove a few months before, so here again there was an awkward shortage of boats. The best that could be found in the brief time available was an odd collection of canoes and square-end dugouts, and precious few of those. Three crossings were necessary to get all of the men across, and none of them was easy. The wind had come up not long after dark, and the river had responded with an angry choppiness that spanked heavily against the small craft. As a result, the crossings were considerably slower and more treacherous than they ordinarily would have been, but they were conducted without loss or mishap, and well before dawn the entire force was safely across the river and moving quietly towards the city.

At a point about a mile north of the city, Ethan halted and rested his troops while he awaited daybreak and Brown's signal. Daybreak came soon enough, but the signal did not. Thinking that perhaps Brown's contingent had been delayed by the turbulent waters, Ethan continued to wait until the sun was two hours high in the sky. By that time, however, it was sadly clear to him from reports brought in by his scouts that Brown, who commanded by far the larger force, had unaccountably failed to make the crossing. Here was a very unpromising situation. "I began to conclude," Ethan later commented, "that I was in a premunire," which was another way of saying that he was in something of a fix:

> I had no chance to flee, as Montreal was situated on an island. . . . I would have crossed the river back again, but I knew the enemy would have discovered such an attempt; and as there could not more than one third part of my troops cross at a time, the other two-thirds would of course fall into their hands. This I could not reconcile to my own feelings as a man, much less as an officer; I therefore concluded to maintain the ground, if possible, and all to fare alike.

This was a noble decision and one which, if carried a step further, might have brought Ethan a spectacular victory. For a brief time during the mid-morning hours, after the presence of his troops had become known within the city, Montreal reeled in a state of panic. Rumor had it that the Americans had arrived in force and were about to begin a cannonade, and in response to the awful prospect of hot shot descending upon them from the skies, the inhabitants scurried about helplessly in a frenzy of fear and confusion. At one time Governor Carleton was, by his own later admission, on the verge of ordering all official records and personnel evacuated to the British armed schooner *Gaspée,* anchored in the river. If at this moment of great turmoil, Ethan had shown his customary brashness and launched an all-out attack, Montreal would probably have fallen to him by default. Understandably, however, given the circumstances as he saw them, Ethan chose to stay put and hope for a miracle. Not even Ethan Allen could have been expected to storm Montreal with only a hundred men. This would have been madness, and although in this instance madness would probably have won the day, Ethan had no way of knowing or even suspecting it.

And so he sat still and waited, and as time passed without any sign of activity on the part of his miniature siege force, the city regained something of its composure and began to take a closer look at the situation.

What it discovered was most reassuring. From Canadians who had slipped by Ethan's roadblocks, information on the true size and nature of the American force reached the town shortly after eleven o'clock, and from that moment Ethan was doomed. Within the next two hours Governor Carleton was able to rally a substantial number of the inhabitants to support the regulars, and by two o'clock that afternoon an impressive force of over three hundred British, Canadians, and Indians had poured out of Montreal to do battle with Ethan and his hapless little army one-third that size. "When I saw the number of the enemy as they sallied out of the town," Ethan later reported, "I perceived it would be a day of trouble, if not rebuke. . . . I thought to have enrolled my name in the list of illustrious American heroes, but was nipped in the bud."

# IX. Captivity!

WHY Major Brown failed to join Ethan before Montreal has never been satisfactorily explained. According to one account, he did make an attempt to cross the River as planned, but was turned back by the roughness of the water. This seems somewhat implausible, however, in view of the fact that only a few miles down-river Ethan, despite admitted difficulties, was able to make the crossing without mishap. It is also rather unreasonable to suggest, as some have, that at the final moment Brown's nerve failed him and he purposely left Ethan in the lurch in order to save his own skin. Throughout the Revolution, from the earliest days with Ethan at Ticonderoga until he was killed in battle in 1780, Brown consistently proved himself a person of great bravery, and there is no cause to suspect him of having been cowardly in this instance. Ethan himself in his later account of the Montreal fiasco had no recriminations to make against Brown, nor did he offer any explanation. He simply told of Brown's failure to appear, and let the matter go at that. One thing seems clear, though: had Brown's force appeared at the proper time, Montreal would probably have fallen, and Ethan would have wallowed in that military glory he so consummately craved. As it was, without the aid of Brown's substantially larger contingent of troops, Ethan was quite right in anticipating "a day of rebuke."

For almost two hours Ethan managed to hold off Carleton and his men. By all accounts, including those of British regulars, he put up a stiff fight. But as the enemy pressed in, nearly all of his Canadians, plus a few of the Americans, threw down their arms and fled, and in the end there was nothing for Ethan to do but surrender. Of his original force of one hundred and ten men, only thirty-eight were still with him at the finish. All the others had disappeared. Aside from the long list of Ethan's "missing-in-action," however, the casualties on both sides were light. In fact, once the smoke of the battle had cleared, it became apparent that the contest, although fiercely waged, had taken a surprisingly small toll. Only two men, both on the British side, are known to have been killed, and scarcely more than a dozen wounded. "I never saw so much shooting result in so little damage," Ethan remarked afterwards.

Following their surrender, Ethan and the pitiful remnants of his little army were herded together and, guarded by an escort of British regulars, were marched into the City. It was not the sort of entrance into Montreal that Ethan had envisioned, but at least he was alive, and that was something to be grateful for. Furthermore, for a brief time at least he was on center stage, the focus of all attention, a fact which probably did something to take his mind off the unpleasantness of his predicament. Whatever else he may have been, Ethan was a showman, and before an attentive audience he seldom failed to rise to the occasion. And certainly now he had an appreciative multitude of onlookers— Canadians, British, and Indians—all of whom viewed the arrival of this notorious giant with much wonderment and comment. It was not such a sight as one would behold every day. Even Montreal's officialdom was impressed. According to the records of the Canadian Military Command, "that uncouth illiterate backwoodsman . . . presented a strange appearance wearing as he did a deerskin fur cap adorned with an eagle's feather, coarse homespun clothing and heavy cowhide hobnailed boots of the rudest make."

Immediately upon his arrival at the Place d'Armes he was brought before General Richard Prescott, commander of the British garrison. As Ethan recalled the occasion when writing about it some three years later:

> No abuse was offered me 'till I came to the barrack yard . . . where I met General Prescott, who asked me my name, which I told him: He then asked me, whether I was that Col. Allen, who took Ticonderoga. I told him I was the very man. Then he shook his cane over my head, calling many hard names, among which he frequently used the word rebel, and put himself in a great rage. I told him he would do well not to cane me, for I was not accustomed to it, and shook my fist at him, telling him that was the beetle of mortality for him if he offered to strike; upon which Capt. M'Cloud of the British, pulled him by the skirt, and whispered to him, as he afterwards told me, to this import; that it was inconsistent with his honor to strike a prisoner. He then ordered a serjeant's command with fixed bayonets, to come forward, and kill

the thirteen Canadians who were included in the treaty [of surrender].

It cut me to the heart to see the Canadians in so hard a case, in consequence of their having been true to me; they were wringing their hands, saying their prayers, as I concluded, and expected immediate death. I therefore stepped between the executioners and the Canadians, opened my clothes, and told General Prescott to thrust his bayonet into my breast, for I was the sole cause of the Canadians taking up arms.

The guard, in the meantime, rolling their eyeballs from the General to me, as though impatiently waiting his dread command to sheath their bayonets in my heart; I could, however, plainly discern, that he was in a suspense and quandary about the matter: This gave me additional hopes of succeeding; for my design was not to die, but to save the Canadians by a finesse. The general stood for a minute, when he made me the following reply; "I will not execute you now; but you shall grace a halter at Tyburn, God damn you."

General Prescott's promise of a halter at Tyburn was another way of telling Ethan that he would be sent to England to be hanged for treason. This was not the best news in the world, but "I was, notwithstanding, a little pleased with the expression, as it significantly conveyed to me the idea of postponing the present appearance of death." At Prescott's order, Ethan was then taken aboard the schooner-of-war *Gaspée,* where he was locked in irons and cast into a makeshift cell in the lowest part of the hold. There, under heavy guard, deprived of all but the barest necessities of life, he remained in solitary confinement for nearly five weeks. Sharing with him the semidarkness of his dank, little prison were a crude wooden chest which served as his chair and bed, and an excrement tub. These were his only companions, except for various types of vermin and, of course, his relentless shackles, which weighed close to thirty pounds and caused him great discomfort.

Here was an ordeal that might well have broken the spirit of a lesser man, but Ethan did not break, nor did he bend. From time to time he roared for better treatment. He never begged, however; he demanded. Above all, he insisted that his irons, which cut deeply into his wrists and ankles, be removed or at least loosened. But on all accounts he might better have saved his breath. From his guards he learned that General Prescott had specifically ordered that the prisoner be treated "with much severity," and under no conditions were his shackles to be loosened. "They were," Ethan later reported, "mean-spirited in their treatment of me."

The news of Ethan's capture and subsequent imprisonment spread rapidly. The British, of course, were delighted to have taken such a rare prize. Aside from the natural gratification derived from seizing the notorious rebel chief who had so recently affronted the King's property at Ticonderoga, there was the happy realization that Ethan's capture could scarcely help but have a sobering effect upon the Canadians. "This little action has changed the face of things," gloated a Britisher who had taken part in the skirmish against Ethan. "The Canadians before were nine-tenths for the Bostonians. They are now returned to their duty, many in arms for the King."

As for the American reaction, there was notably more anger and worry than sorrow expressed over Ethan's misadventure. It was generally agreed that Ethan had done a very stupid and irresponsible thing that would be bound to have evil repercussions because of its unfortunate effect upon the Canadians. How serious or permanent the injury would be, no one could say, but certainly damage had been done. "His defeat hath put the French people into great consternation," Colonel Seth Warner remarked in reporting on Ethan's capture to Montgomery from an advanced position just outside of Montreal. And when the bad news became known among the American forces besieging St. John's, who were already experiencing more than their share of trouble, there were few kind words spoken in Ethan's behalf. Not even the pious chaplain, Benjamin Trumbull, could muster up any Christian compassion for Ethan—only blame. "This rash and ill concerted measure of Colonel Allen," Trumbull complained to his journal, had done great harm to "the affairs of the united Colonies in Canada," and had succeeded in "disheartening the army and weakening it, and in prejudicing the people against us . . . , making us enemies and losing us friends."

The usually charitable and unruffled Montgomery made no attempt to conceal his feelings of disappointment and outrage. To Schuyler he fired off an angry note in which he denounced Ethan bitterly as an egotistical glory-seeker who, for the sake of achieving personal recognition, had done considerable injury to the American cause. Schuyler was visibly upset by the news, but not especially surprised. He had feared that something like this would happen, and he cursed the day he had ignored his better judgment and permitted Ethan to join the expedition. "I am very apprehensive of disagreeable consequences arising from Mr. Allen's imprudence," he wrote to President of Congress John Hancock, as soon as the word of Ethan's capture reached him.

But amidst the loud professions of anger and dismay, there may also have been an occasional sigh of relief, for there were those in high positions who were probably happy to be rid of Ethan. He had, after all, been something of a nuisance—and a very durable and persistent nuisance at that. True, he had been handy enough to have around during those first few days of the Revolution when there was a need for an Old Testament stalwart who could wield the jawbone of an ass, but as one historian has so aptly put it, "now that the war had gone to a stage altogether beyond the tactics of the Book of Judges . . . it would have been far from easy to find Ethan Allen employment which would both suit and satisfy him." The hero of Ticonderoga had become something of an embarrassment to the Colonial Command, and his seizure by the British, whatever else it may have accomplished, neatly solved the problem of what to do with an unwanted Samson. Furthermore, his capture may have had some value for the Americans as a good example of a bad thing. Commented General Washington: "His misfortune will I hope teach a lesson of prudence and subordination to others who may be ambitious to outshine their general officers, and regardless of order and duty rush into enterprises which have unfavorable effects on the public and are destructive to themselves."

Late in October, as the Americans began to press in upon Montreal, Ethan was shipped down-river to Quebec where he was transferred to the dispatch-carrier *Adamant,* and soon after sent on his way to England. From this point until his parole on Long Island a year later, what is known of Ethan's adventures is derived almost entirely from the narrative of his captivity, written by Ethan himself more than three years after his capture. Clearly this account is not entirely above suspicion. On some occasions truth and objectivity have obviously been sacrificed for braggadocio, even to the extent of inserting a whopping big lie now and then. On the whole, however, it is probably an essentially accurate record of what actually happened. At least, on nearly all of those points (admittedly few) for which collateral evidence has been found, Ethan's account bears up very well. As a historical document it is perhaps as reliable as most—and it is infinitely more interesting.

The crossing to England took forty days—forty days of indescribable torment for Ethan. The best that could be said of it was that he was no longer in shackles. He was also no longer alone, although it would perhaps have been better if he had been. Along with him now, deep in the hold of the *Adamant,* standing practically elbow to elbow in the poorly ventilated and almost totally dark pen no larger than twenty feet square, were crowded thirty-three other prisoners, all of whom had been captured with Ethan at Montreal. The congestion was almost unbearable, and amenities were nonexistent. There were no bunks. Sleeping was done on the deck, when space could be found for it. The food was coarse, although apparently plentiful enough. Drinking water was in short supply, but each prisoner was given a gill of rum daily, a rare kindness which according to Ethan was "of utmost service to us and probably was the means of saving several of our lives." Worst of all was the incredible squalor of the place. With no water for washing, and only two excrement tubs to serve nearly three dozen men, many of them afflicted with diarrhea, the little prison soon became surfeited with filth and vermin and the stinking vomit of men made wretchedly sick by the tossing of the vessel. "What is the most surprising thing," Ethan later remarked, "is that not one of us died in the passage." Added to all this, of course, was the sobering realization that, almost certainly for Ethan and perhaps for the others as well, the end of the voyage would mean a short rope on a British gallows.

Towards the end of December, probably the twenty-second, the *Adamant* put in at Falmouth, England, where Ethan and his companions were unloaded and marched through the streets to the prison quarters at Pendennis Castle, about a mile or so outside of the city. According to Ethan, "multitudes" of the inhabitants of Falmouth turned out to witness the procession—and a pitiful procession it was, composed of men who had known little but horror for nearly three months, whose clothes were tattered and encrusted with filth, whose bodies and brains reeled from prolonged mistreatment, and whose eyes could barely stand the light of day. If the people of Falmouth were shocked by what they saw and smelled that day (and many were), they clearly had every right to be. It was not a thing of which they could be proud.

The prisoners were herded into Pendennis Castle where they at once began to receive considerably better treatment. Their stay at the castle was to be a brief one, however, for within three weeks Ethan and the others would be moved again, and happily not to the gallows as they had feared, but onto a British man-of-war which would carry them back to America. This surprising turn of events was the work of the Duke of Richmond and other highly placed persons, both in and out of government, who, immediately after the arrival of the prisoners at Falmouth, had set important wheels in motion which would soon bring about a decided improvement in the prospects of Ethan and his friends.

Among these powerful benefactors (and they included members of both parties) there was no great feeling of solicitude for the American prisoners, who in their assault upon Montreal had clearly committed wanton aggression against the Crown and in the process had killed two of the King's loyal subjects. The leader of this rabble had infinitely more to answer for, including the unprovoked seizure of Fort Ticonderoga. Surely His Majesty's Government would be justified in hanging the lot of them. And yet, as odious as they were, they were still British subjects, and as such they were entitled to the rights of all free-born Englishmen, including the right of trial by jury. If it were the intent of the Crown to treat these men as criminals, then they must either be charged with their crimes and brought to trial before their peers, or be released on habeas corpus. If, on the other hand, they were to be considered prisoners of war, and thereby rendered eligible to be held in confinement for an indefinite period without trial, then they should be treated as such. Let all talk of hanging cease, and send them back to America where they belonged.

The question of what to do with Ethan and the others caused much soul-searching among the more thoughtful and sensitive members of British officialdom. There was no right answer to the problem. To grant them prisoner-of-war status would be to permit these outrageous scoundrels to escape the halter they so richly deserved. Worse still, it would be tantamount to recognizing the Colonials as bona fide belligerents rather than a band of irresponsible outlaws. It would obviously lend a dignity to the American rebels which the British were most reluctant to see them gain. Against all this, however, was the palpable fact that whether or not His Majesty's Government cared to admit it, Ethan and his men had been acting as soldiers, and to treat them as common felons would be bound to cause considerable awkwardness for the British Government both at home and abroad.

The British Army in North America would be particularly embarrassed by such a move, for the Americans naturally looked upon the captured men as prisoners of war and could be expected to retaliate if Ethan and his companions were badly done by. Reports had already reached England, in fact, that General Prescott, who had been seized by the Americans during their recent capture of Montreal, had been cast into irons "in company with common Malefactors and the most Notorious Villains" because of his brutal treatment of Ethan. There would certainly be more mischief of this sort, and worse, if the British should insist upon following a hard course on the matter of Ethan Allen and his fellow captives. Let punishment be inflicted upon these men, the Duke of York warned in the House of Lords, and "the consequences might be dreadful."

Here was a thorny problem indeed, but it was solved, as so many problems were in the England of those days, by the personal intercession of George III. Shortly after Christmas the King informed the Colonial Secretary, Lord George Germain, of his wish that the captives be sent back to America as prisoners of war. Germain passed the royal word on to the Admiralty, and less than two weeks later Ethan and his party were again at sea, this time headed in the opposite direction across the Atlantic. There is some evidence, but not much, to suggest that just prior to Ethan's departure from England, attempts were made to persuade him to let bygones be bygones and agree to perform, for a fair price of course, certain unspecified services for the British Crown upon his arrival back in the Colonies.

Certainly there were people in high position in London who were thinking along these lines. "Something more might be done than merely return him as a prisoner to America," the King's Solicitor-General wrote to the chief of the Royal Secret Service at this time. Why not dangle a few enticements before Allen and see what would happen? It was no secret that he was not very happy with the situation on the New Hampshire Grants. His holdings there were still under a cloud. He had recently been deeply disappointed by his own people. Offer him a full pardon and a chance to fight on the winning side. Put him in a fancy uniform at the head of a company of Rangers. Free his friends. Promise him clear title to his lands, and if necessary give him gold as well. In other words, apply precisely the same sort of tactics that His Majesty's Government had worked with such unblushing frequency and transcendent skill during much of the eighteenth century: buy out the opposition.

Why Ethan was not approached on this matter before he left England (and he almost certainly was not) is something of a mystery. Perhaps the British simply did not get around to it. In time they would, however, and their efforts in this direction would eventually find Ethan not altogether unreceptive.

On January 8, 1776, the frigate *Solebay,* carrying Ethan and his men, sailed out of Falmouth harbor on the first leg of a crossing to America that would take nearly four months. Although the British government was not yet ready to announce the fact officially, from that moment forward Ethan and his friends and all other captives taken or to be taken in the American Rebellion were to be dealt with as prisoners of war rather than as criminals. This was a decision of great advantage to the Colonials and their cause, and since he had been so largely responsible for bringing it about, it was only fitting that Ethan should be among the first to benefit from it. And benefit he did. Not only had the halter been snatched from his neck, but also the treatment accorded him from now on would be somewhat more humane. This is not to say that the remainder of his imprisonment would be a time of gracious living. Far from it. But despite the fact that hardships aplenty lay ahead, he would at least, save for rare occasions, no longer be subjected to the extreme sort of abuse that had characterized the first few months of his captivity.

In early February the *Solebay* put in at Cork, Ireland, where it rendezvoused with five other men-of-war and some forty transports—a truly imposing lot of sails which, Ethan later discovered, were to carry Lord Cornwallis and his invasion force to the Carolinas. At Cork, Ethan learned to his great satisfaction that his fame had preceded him, and that not all of his friends (or, better, not all of England's enemies) lived on the other side of the Atlantic. As soon as it became known that Colonel Ethan Allen, the hero of Ticonderoga, was aboard the *Solebay,* a collection was taken up among a number of "benevolently disposed gentlemen" of the town to provide Ethan and his men with clothes and "other necessaries" which might ease their distress. Through the generosity of the good people of Cork, each of Ethan's fellow prisoners was outfitted with a new suit and overcoat and was given ample quantities of tea and sugar. Ethan fared much more handsomely. In addition to a ready-made suit and enough broadcloth to make two more, he received such "grandeurs and superfluities" as:

> . . . eight fine Holland shirts and socks ready made, with a number of silk and worsted hose, two pairs of shoes, and two beaver hats, one of which was sent me richly laced with gold. . . . The Irish gentlemen furthermore made a large gratuity of wines of the best sort, spirits, gin, loaf and brown sugar, tea and chocolate, with a large round of pickled beef, and a number of fat turkeys. . . . And to crown all, they did send me fifty guineas, but I could not reconcile receiving the whole to my feelings, as it might have the appearance of avarice; and therefore received but seven only.

As a parting gesture, Ethan's Irish benefactors even offered to provide him with a few head of livestock and the wherewithal to support them during the crossing to America, but, sensing that such an arrangement might be displeasing to the ship's captain, Ethan graciously declined to accept.

As it was, the captain was none too happy when he returned from two days ashore and discovered what his junior officers had permitted to go on during his absence. As Ethan later remembered it, the captain went into something of a rage. "He swore by all that is good, that the damned American rebels should not be feasted at this rate, by the damned rebels of Ireland." Consequently, although the prisoners were allowed to keep their new clothing, most of their other recently acquired treasures were taken from them and distributed among the crew. Included in the items confiscated was Ethan's priceless supply of liquor, save for a couple of gallons he managed to conceal below-deck. Here was a display of British barbarism which Ethan could describe only as "abominable." But not even this staggering disappointment could dull the luster of the splendid generosity shown him by the men of Cork. Ethan sent them a thank-you note expressing his "highest sense of gratitude" for their great humanity, and ever thereafter he would hold a special warmth in his heart for the Irish and permit no man to speak against them.

For nearly a year after leaving England, Ethan remained aboard one or another of His Majesty's prison ships. In early May the fleet carrying Lord Cornwallis' invasion force arrived off Cape Fear, North Carolina, where Ethan and most of his party were moved to the frigate *Mercury*.

In command of the *Mercury* was Captain James Montague, a lout of a man whom Ethan soon concluded was "underwitted" and weighed down by a grudge against the world "which was in no instance liable to be diverted by good sense, humour, or bravery." Because of his shameful neglect of the prisoners entrusted to his care, Captain Montague would prove to be an evil spoke in what Ethan liked to refer to as "the transitory wheel of my fate."

Bound for Halifax, the *Mercury* lay over at anchor for three days at the Hook off New York City, where it took on supplies and, shortly before its departure, played host to a group of visiting dignitaries from shore. At the head of these distinguished visitors were Ethan's old adversaries, Governor Tryon and Attorney-General Kempe. Ethan had met Kempe once before, during the Albany ejectment trials nearly six years earlier. Tryon he had never laid eyes on, but he needed no introduction to the man who had put such a handsome price on his head, and he was pretty certain that Tryon, doubtless having been alerted by Kempe and the ship's captain, knew well enough who he was. As Tryon and his entourage strolled the deck with the captain, the governor caught a glimpse of Ethan on the other side of the ship. For Governor Tryon, who had suffered so much abuse and embarrassment from this arrogant backwoodsman, the temptation to gloat must have been strong indeed. But His Excellency chose not to demean himself. He looked at Ethan for an instant "with a stern countenance," but gave no sign of recognition. "What passed between the officers of the ship and these visitors I know not," Ethan later reported, "but this I know that my treatment from the officers was more severe afterwards."

In late June of 1776, the *Mercury* put in at Halifax, where the prisoners were transferred to a small sloop that had been brought alongside and placed under Captain Montague's command. At this point Ethan's fortunes reached a lower ebb than at any other time since his crossing to England several months earlier. Food aboard the sloop was desperately scarce for prisoners and crew alike, so scarce that Ethan and his companions were put on one-third rations—hardly enough to keep a man alive. Worse yet, scurvy soon broke out, and although its effects on the crew were bad enough, it proved to be infinitely more ravaging among the prisoners, who, after the rigors of nearly nine months of confinement, had become so debilitated that they were easy prey for almost any affliction.

During their six weeks at anchor in Halifax harbor, many if not most of Ethan's men came down with scurvy, a few of them with such severe cases that their lives were all but despaired of. From this awful scourge, and from the epidemic of dysentery that tormented most of his men, Ethan himself was spared. Here in Halifax, as on so many occasions before, he was well served by that amazing physical toughness that helped set him apart from ordinary men. Endowed with uncommon strength and remarkable reserves of energy, his body was indeed a superb bit of machinery. Had it been otherwise, more than likely Ethan would not have lived to record the story of what befell him during his nearly three years as an involuntary guest of His Britannic Majesty.

But he was mortal nonetheless, and there was no mistaking the fact that by the summer of 1776 the effects of his long ordeal had begun to show on him. Ever since leaving England he had sensed that his strength was being gradually but inexorably sapped away. Prolonged imprisonment had worn him down and made him a lesser man than he had once been—so much so that when confronted by the grim conditions at Halifax, he wondered if he could withstand the test. For the first time the thought occurred to him that he might starve or rot to death in the hold of some stinking prison ship, if not this one then perhaps the next, and the idea of such an unspeakable end filled him with revulsion. But it was the revulsion of disgust rather than fear. The vision of dying by inches in such an inglorious and unmanly fashion affronted his great vanity. It was a far from fitting end for one such as he.

And yet, what could he do? To Captain Montague, who had left the *Mercury* for pleasanter accommodations ashore, Ethan wrote several letters demanding more humane treatment for himself and his men. But there was never any reply. The captain was obviously too busy being entertained by his friends to bother himself with the welfare of a few misbegotten rebels. Having failed with the captain, Ethan then tried to strike a spark of humanity among the junior officers aboard ship, but he might as well have spared himself the trouble. The junior officers lacked the means, the authority, and apparently the disposition to do anything about alleviating the prisoners' suffering. They even refused Ethan's request that those of his men who had come down with scurvy be taken ashore periodically, and, as was the custom then, be buried up to the neck in dirt for a few hours to relieve their pain. "I assure you," an angry Ethan wrote at this time to friends in Connecticut, "that this rascally English treatment . . . has wholly erased my former feelings of parent state, mother country, and, in fine, all kindred and friendly connexion with them." It would doubtless have done him some good had he known that only a few weeks before, his countrymen had officially proclaimed the same sentiments and had punctuated them by severing once and for all their former ties with Great Britain.

In mid-August, as a result of the personal intervention of the Governor of Halifax, who was forced to go over the head of the ship's captain, Ethan and the others were moved from the sloop and taken ashore to the city jail. By this time only thirteen of the men who had been seized with Ethan at Montreal were still with him. A few had died. Some, at the insistence of the governor, had been taken belatedly to the Halifax hospital. Others had escaped. As for Ethan, he was still alive and thankful to be in the Halifax jail where conditions, although bad enough, were much less desperate than they had been aboard ship. The food was now better and more plentiful, and occasional baskets of vegetables and fruit brought to the prisoners by sympathetic townspeople were the means of putting a thankful end to the scurvy.

Ethan's health continued to decline, however. Shortly after his transfer to the jail he was seized with a severe attack of nausea which seriously dehydrated him and prevented him from getting any nourishment from the small amounts of food he was able to force down. He became progressively weaker and more listless and seemed no longer able to rise up in protest. "The malignant hand of Britain had greatly reduced my constitution with stroke upon stroke." And now as he lay in torment on the prison floor at Halifax, the question that loomed more and more ominously before him was: How much longer could he go on in this manner, with the endless rigors of imprisonment picking away mercilessly at his emaciated frame and draining off what little remained of his vitality? It would have been a proper time for despair and self-pity, but from Ethan came neither. His spirit was at least a match for his body, and his spirit refused to yield.

Actually, the worst was about over for Ethan. In time his sickness passed, and not long thereafter he and his remaining men were taken from the jail and once again put aboard a British man-of-war, this time the *Lark,* which happily turned out to be a far cry from the *Mercury.* Aboard the *Lark,* Captain Smith commanding, the prisoners received attentive care and uncommon courtesy. Their treatment was, in fact, nearly too good to be true, and almost sufficed to erase the awful memories of Captain Montague and the *Mercury*—almost, but not quite. Ethan was especially well used. He was provided with a comfortable berth and almost complete freedom to stroll the deck. Even more surprising, he was frequently invited to join the captain in his cabin for food and drink. He could scarcely have asked for greater consideration, and he was duly grateful. "This was so unexpected and sudden a transition," Ethan later remarked, "that it drew tears from my eyes, which all the ill usage I had before met with, was not able to produce." After a week or so at sea and several pleasant sessions at Captain Smith's table, Ethan could sense that his body had begun to rally. He could feel his old vitality returning, and the world seemed brighter than it had for some time past.

In late October the *Lark* put in at New York harbor, at a time when the British Army under General William Howe was engaged in mopping-up operations against the remnants of Washington's troops still hanging on in the outlying regions. By the end of the following month, the New York area was again securely in the hands of the British, and Ethan and his fellow prisoners were moved ashore, where the enlisted men were assigned to the Provost Jail and Ethan himself was at long last placed on parole. This meant that as an officer, and supposedly a gentleman, he was put on his honor and permitted to roam at large during daylight hours, provided he remained within a given area and observed certain other restrictions. It was not exactly freedom, but it was a marked improvement over what he had become accustomed to during the fourteen months that had passed since his capture at Montreal. Despite the run-down condition of his health and the fact that he was being turned out without a copper in his pockets to make his own way in a strange city occupied by the enemy, Ethan could not help but feel that a better day had dawned. And he was right.

During the first month of his parole, December, 1776, Ethan was confined to lower Manhattan where he soon fell in with several other paroled officers, most of whom had been captured recently in the Battle of Long Island. Since his new friends were for the most part younger men and more or less unaccustomed to captivity, Ethan naturally assumed a position of seniority among them and proceeded to give them the benefit of his wisdom by regaling them with tales of his amazing experiences. All of this helped to pass the idle hours, of course, and at first Ethan's stories were probably as fascinating for his listeners as they were for Ethan himself, but in time they tended to wear a trifle thin. "Dec Tues the 10th Col Allyn came in," one of the parolees noted in his diary with a discernible yawn, "and repeated to us again the Story of his taking Ticonarogue & also many other of his Adventures."

Still, it was generally conceded that Ethan was a good man to have around. He was usually hearty and good-natured, and there was a noisy self-assurance about him that seemed to rub off onto the others and help buoy up their sometimes sagging spirits. In a word, he was, as always, a towering presence. Several years later Captain Alexander Graydon, one of the paroled officers in New York, would remember Ethan distinctly as having been a colossus in their midst:

> His figure was that of a robust, large-framed man, worn down by confinement and hard fare; but he was now recovering his flesh and spirits; and a suit of blue clothes, with a gold laced hat that had been presented to him by the gentlemen of Cork, enabled him to make a very passable appearance for a rebel colonel. . . . I have seldom met with a man, possessing, in my opinion, a stronger mind, or whose mode of expression was more vehement and oratorical. Notwithstanding that Allen might have had something of the insubordinate, lawless frontier spirit in his composition . . . he appeared to me to be a man of generosity and honor.

While in Manhattan, Ethan meandered from here to there, living off the bounty of townspeople sympathetic to the Revolution. As a hero and something of a martyr, he himself fared well enough, but the scenes of human suffering he encountered as he wandered about the city were "incredible for their horror." Thousands of American prisoners, captured in the New York campaign, had been herded into lower Manhattan and crowded into churches and other makeshift prisons. There amidst filth, disease, and lack of food, death became commonplace and often merciful. The stench of rotting men hovered over the town, and the groans of torment never ceased. Occasionally Ethan, often at some risk to himself, managed to visit one or another of the prisons where invariably he found conditions that staggered belief:

> I have seen several of the prisoners in the agonies of death, in consequence of very hunger, and others speechless and very near death, biting pieces of chips; others pleading for God's sake for

something to eat, and at the same time shivering with the cold. Hollow groans saluted my ears, and despair seemed to be imprinted on every of their countenances. The filth . . . was almost beyond description. The floors were covered with excrements. I have carefully sought to direct my steps so as to avoid it, but could not. They would beg for God's sake for one copper, or morsel of bread. I have seen . . . seven dead at the same time, lying among the excrements of their bodies.

In time, Ethan discontinued his visits. With no money or influence he could do nothing to help, and although he had known hard times himself, the sight of others undergoing such great suffering "was too much for me to bear as a spectator."

It was at this unlikely moment, with Ethan sickened and outraged by what appeared to him to be a calculated policy of British brutality, that His Majesty's Government chose to initiate its campaign to purchase his services for the Crown. What happened next is best told by Ethan himself:

A British officer of rank and importance . . . sent for me to his lodgings and told me "That faithfulness, though in a wrong cause, had nevertheless recommended me to general Sir William Howe, who was minded to make me a colonel of a regiment of new levies, alias tories, in the British service; and proposed that I should go with him and some other officers, to England, who would embark for that purpose in a few days, and there be introduced to Lord G. Germaine, and probably to the King; and that previously I should be clothed equal to such an introduction, and, instead of paper rags, be paid in hard guineas; after this, should embark with general Burgoyne, and assist in the reduction of the country, which infallibly would be conquered, and, when that should be done, I should have a large tract of land, either in the New Hampshire grants, or in Connecticut, it would make no odds, as the country would be forfeited to the crown." I then replied, "That, if by faithfulness I had recommended myself to general Howe, I should be loth, by unfaithfulness, to lose the general's good opinion; besides, that I viewed the offer of land to be similar to that which the devil offered Jesus Christ, 'To give him all the kingdoms of the world if he would fall down and worship him; when at the same time, the damned soul had not one foot of land upon earth.' " This closed the conversation, and the gentleman turned from me with an air of dislike, saying that I was a bigot; upon which I retired to my lodgings.

This was a clear enough rebuff to such a dishonorable overture. Ethan had made it eminently plain that he was not for sale. But the bait had been dangled before him. A beginning had been made, and perhaps at a later time under different circumstances the matter could be pursued more fruitfully.

In January, the paroled American officers were moved from Manhattan to King's County on Long Island. With money sent to him by his brothers and friends, Ethan was able to obtain decent board and lodging at the home of a Dutch farmer in New Lots where he would remain for the next seven months. This was a long step up for Ethan. For the first time since his capture he was able to live in comfort, and for a while he reveled in it. He stuffed himself with clams, porridge, and buttermilk. He surfeited himself with sleep, and when he felt like it, he wandered freely about the little town, breathing the fresh, clean air.

Not infrequently his wanderings would take him to the local tavern where he was almost certain to find a group of fellow officers with whom he could visit for a time. Visit and talk. From a diary kept by one of the New Lots parolees, it is clear that Ethan had lost none of his zeal for sharing what he knew (or thought he knew) with others. Reads one entry: "Among us was Col Allen, who entertained us with a very learned lecture on the Art of Generalship, etc." And another: "Col Allen came to see us, with whom we had some peculiar conversation, & observations on Divine Providence, on Inevitable Fate, etc., which was somewhat entertaining." And then, of course, there were endless stories about his captivity and his seizure of Ticonderoga and his close friendship with the fallen Montgomery. It was all rather pleasant.

But as the weeks passed, Ethan grew restless. There was more to life than talk and clams, and with his vitality now somewhat restored, Ethan longed for some kind of action. By mid-spring New Lots had become an awful bore for him. His life there had grown "irksome" and "painful," Ethan wrote to the Connecticut Committee of War in late April. He had been reduced to a "mere cipher, exempted from danger and honor," and he longed for the day that he would be exchanged and allowed to function as a full-fledged human being once again. When that day would come (if ever) was a matter apparently in the lap of the gods and the

British, but if it didn't come soon he would surely go mad. Danger and hardship he could stand up to, but boredom was another thing. It eroded his spirit and soured his disposition. It made him less than a man.

In June, Ethan's distress was compounded by the sorrowful report that his eleven-year-old son Joseph had died of smallpox. For Ethan the news came as a painful blow to "the tender passions of my soul, and by turns gives me the most sensible grief." True, he had never been much of a father to the boy. In fact, for the past decade he had been little more than a stranger to his family. Still, his grief on this occasion was real enough. He had always put much stock in his son and had great plans for his future. And now suddenly the boy was gone, taken from him forever. "I had promised myself great delight in clasping the charming boy in my arms," Ethan wrote his brother Heman, "and in recounting to him my adventures. But mortality has frustrated my fond hopes, and with him my name expires—My only son, the darling of my soul—who should have inherited my fortune, and maintained the honour of the family."

During the summer months of 1777, grief and boredom gnawed away intolerably at Ethan, and he responded with a mounting uneasiness that sooner or later was bound to get him into trouble. He became increasingly impatient with New Lots and everything in it, including the other parolees, who now found Ethan more often than not peevish and short-tempered. "Col Allen was here," Ethan's diarist friend noted on a day in early summer, "and he was not in the most moderate mood neither." In time the situation became so unbearable for Ethan that he took to wandering a little farther afield—too much farther to satisfy the conditions of his parole. On several occasions he was so bold as to cross over to New York and walk the streets in broad daylight before the very eyes of the British. It was almost as if he were courting a comeuppance, and a comeuppance is what he got. On August 25 a contingent of British troops descended upon him in the tavern at New Lots and carried him away to the Provost Jail in lower Manhattan. For the record, Ethan cried out loudly that he had been framed. "I was apprehended under the pretext of artful, mean and pitiful pretenses." To friends, however, he admitted confidentially that although he had certainly honored the spirit of his parole, he may have been guilty of a minor infraction or two, and if the British wanted to be narrow-minded about it, technically they had the right to reconfine him.

Ethan remained in the Provost Jail from August, 1777, to early May of the following year. During that time he was reasonably well treated, and although he complained bitterly that his life was being wasted away, "my very prime," it appears that he was actually less miserable there than he had been in New Lots. Perhaps this was because he felt that by being something of a burden and a nuisance to his British warders he was now, at least in a small way, actively involved with the fortunes of American arms, rather than being a mere onlooker. And these fortunes were obviously taking a decided turn for the better. Within a couple of months after Ethan's return to prison, word arrived in New York of General Burgoyne's total defeat at Saratoga, a stunning American victory that had been contributed to in no mean measure by Ethan's neighbors on the Grants. And then in the spring of the following year came the grand news of the French Alliance. The Americans had found a powerful friend who would certainly help put a new face on things. Ethan was exultant:

> My affections are Frenchified. I glory in Louis the sixteen, the generous and powerful ally of these states; am fond of a connection with so enterprising, learned, polite, courteous and commercial a nation, and am sure that I express the sentiments and feelings of all the friends of the present revolution.

Who could doubt now that the British would soon be routed from American soil and pushed back to their contemptible little island?

In early May of 1778, Ethan was exchanged for a British officer of equal rank, after a long series of negotiations between General Washington and the British North American Command. Actually, attempts to obtain Ethan's release had been begun not long after his capture at Montreal and had been persistently pushed by Washington on orders from the Continental Congress. But the wheels had turned slowly. On several occasions when success had seemed virtually assured, negotiations would break down, often over trivial differences, and would have to be begun again. There was, for example, the question of Ethan's rank, if indeed he held any rank at all. Should he be exchanged for a full colonel, a lieutenant colonel, or a civilian? Since the Americans themselves seemed somewhat uncertain on this matter, the British claimed a right to classify him as they saw fit and thereby drive as hard a bargain as possible.

A more serious obstacle was British resentment of what they considered to be exceedingly brash and boorish behavior by the American negotiators. In the British view of things, the Americans were attempting to rush pell-mell into what was really a very complex and delicate matter. After all, officers were not to be exchanged on mere whim or impulse, like so many sacks of grain. There was proper procedure to be followed. There were long-established rules that had to be adhered to. Certainly the Americans were aware of all this, and yet they gave no indication of it. In their attempts to obtain the release of their backwoods hero, they had from the beginning behaved with an arrogant impatience that was remarkable for its lack of sensitivity. General Washington, in fact, had been an absolute churl. His letters had been little short of abusive. They had accused the British of calculated brutality in their treatment of Colonial Allen and had charged the British Command with bad faith in negotiating for his exchange. At one point General Howe became so incensed over Washington's "insolence" that he called a temporary halt to all communications having to do with the exchange.

Finally, however, the conditions of the exchange were agreed upon, and on May 3, 1778, Ethan received word that he was to be swapped for a lieutenant-colonel in the British regulars. On the evening of that same day he was taken from the Provost Jail and transported to British headquarters on Staten Island. Here for two days, while waiting for the final few touches to be added to the exchange arrangements, he was treated very generously and was even permitted to join the British officers at their table. "As I was drinking wine with them one evening," Ethan reported afterwards, "I made an observation on my transition from the provost criminals to the company of gentlemen, adding that I was the same man still." Bathed, shaved, and clad in clean clothes, he was not ungrateful for the kindnesses shown him by his British hosts during these final few hours of his captivity. He later conceded that he had to give the British credit for "two days good useage." But, he added, "it was a poor amends."

On May 6, 1778, Ethan was ferried across the Hudson to Elizabethtown and there bidden goodbye and God-speed by his British escort. The long ordeal was finally over. After an imprisonment of nearly thirty-two months, Ethan was once again a free man. "In a transport of joy, I landed on liberty ground, and as I advanced into the country, received the acclamation of a grateful people."

# X. Return of the Hero

ANY OTHER MAN would probably have headed straight for home after an enforced absence of nearly three years, but Ethan had different plans. General Washington had labored long and hard to obtain his release from prison, and Ethan was not ungrateful. It seemed only fitting, therefore, that he should pay his great benefactor a visit and personally offer to serve under the General's command. For Ethan, who had always had a lofty opinion of his own military prowess, there could be no better manner of expressing his feeling of gratitude, which in the flush of his new freedom was well-nigh overwhelming. This would also be an excellent way of getting back at the British for their rascally treatment of him.

By May 8, Ethan had crossed through New Jersey and arrived at Valley Forge where Washington and the pitiful remnants of his army had just spent a disastrous winter. Ethan was deeply moved by what he saw there. He was assured by everyone he talked with in the camp that conditions had improved immensely since the coming of spring. Warm weather, the arrival of desperately needed supplies, and just lately the news of the French alliance, had combined to put a much brighter face on things, particularly as far as morale was concerned. Still, the scene that confronted him at Valley Forge was a distressing one. Everywhere he turned he saw the effects of the awful winter that had just passed. Washington's army had been reduced to a small collection of ragged scarecrows, terribly debilitated by long months of hunger, exposure, and disease. It was not a very pretty sight to behold. And yet, had not Ethan himself experienced much worse during his long captivity? At least these poor creatures at Valley Forge had undergone their agonies as free men and soldiers—an infinitely better thing than rotting away stupidly in a British prison. In a way he envied them.

Washington received him graciously and treated him as handsomely as he could under the circumstances. From the first Ethan was much taken with the General, and in his stolid, undemonstrative way, Washington appears to have been favorably impressed by Ethan. "His fortitude and firmness seem to have placed him out of reach of misfortune," Washington wrote a friend soon after Ethan's visit. "There is an original something in him that commands admiration; and his long captivity and sufferings have only served to increase if possible, his enthusiastic zeal." But as for Ethan's offer of military service, Washington obviously had some reservations. He recalled only too well Ethan's foolish behavior at Montreal and the difficulties it had caused. Of course, a man could change. Perhaps Montreal had taught Ethan a lesson. Perhaps his long imprisonment had led him to reflect ruefully upon his folly and to resolve upon a saner course for the future. Perhaps, but only perhaps. Could he really be relied upon now to behave responsibly in a position of command, or would he be apt to revert to his old, impetuous ways and try to win the war all by himself? There was a palpable risk here, and General Washington, who was a fair judge of men, was certainly not unmindful of it.

Then too, there was the awkward fact that Ethan was still a civilian. He had never been anything else as far as the Continental Command was concerned. For the purposes of exchange he had been assigned the simulated rank of lieutenant colonel, but actually he held no position, commissioned or otherwise, in any military organization. To accept his services now as a regular lieutenant colonel in the Continental Army could pose certain problems of delicacy and precedence and probably create some hard feelings. To accept him at a lower rank would be tantamount to demotion—a poor return for what he had been through. All things considered, there were reasons enough for Washington to wish that Ethan had gone straight home.

Still, there was much to be said for Ethan's great enthusiasm and courage and for the exemplary way he had conducted himself while in captivity. Certainly his offer was at least deserving of attention, and it was probably for this reason that Washington advised him to write to Congress for a commission. Ethan did so just before leaving Valley Forge for home, and the General enclosed a few words of his own in support of the application:

> He appears very desirous of rendering his services to the States, and of being employed; and at the same time he does not discover any ambition for high rank. Congress will herewith receive a letter

from him; and I doubt not that they will make such provision for him, as they think profitable and suitable.

It was not the strongest endorsement in the world, but it was enough to bring Ethan's case immediately before the Continental Congress, and within a few days he was awarded a brevet commission as full colonel and voted military pay of seventy-five dollars a month.

Actually, the brevet commission was less than Ethan had hoped for. It meant in effect that he had been assigned to reserve status and would play no active role in the war until Congress should see fit to call upon him. In other words Ethan, who hankered for an immediate command, had been filed for future reference, and when the news of this fact reached him shortly after his return home, he was at first not altogether pleased. But after some reflection he concluded that perhaps a brevet was just the thing. After all, he was really in no great hurry to return to battle. He was not in the best of health and could use a month or so "to recruit my Constitution." In the meantime, he had the satisfaction of knowing that he held a position of high rank and honor in the American Army, fair evidence of the fact that his uncommon military talents were widely recognized and appreciated. And there was also the seventy-five dollars a month, a pleasant sum that would prove helpful to him in improving "my greatly reduced circumstances."

Eventually, Ethan had no doubt, his call would come and he would take to the field in the service of what he now referred to as "my country." As matters turned out, however, this was not to be. The ensuing months and years of conflict would come and go, carrying with them great and frequent shifts of military fortune, but throughout the remainder of the Revolution, Ethan would remain on the shelf. He would never be called to active service, probably because nobody really wanted him or dared use him. In time, the monthly payments would fall in arrears and then would cease altogether. In other words, Ethan's role as an officer in the Continental Army would be a totally inactive and meaningless one. Still, it is important to bear in mind that he held onto his commission until the last shot was fired. He neither gave it up nor had it taken from him. From the date of its issue in mid-May of 1778 until the end of hostilities, he was a bona fide American officer, a fact that adds a special dimension to his strange flirtations with the British during the late years of the war.

On May 10, after a three-day visit at Valley Forge, Ethan left for home in company with General Horatio Gates, who had been conferring with Washington on matters concerning the Northern Department. Gates had commanded the American forces in the smashing victory at Saratoga the autumn before, and at this time was at the peak of his military reputation. Ethan was much impressed by Gates, and flattered by the attention the general paid him. This was characteristic of Ethan. From beginning to end, he was strongly attracted to the great and the near-great. He was invariably pleased to find himself in their company, and went to some pains to seek them out and impress them. Despite his loud professions of faith in the worth and dignity of the common man, Ethan preferred the company of the not-so-common, perhaps because he sensed that only they could fully appreciate his higher qualities. As for his roughhewn neighbors on the Grants, there is no question that Ethan felt a great affection for them and a genuine solicitude for their interests. Still, his feelings towards them were marked by a discernible trace of paternalism. They were his people, to be sure, but they were not really his *kind* of people. In Ethan's letters there is evidence aplenty that he placed himself above the commonalty—approachable, but obviously superior. He was a gentleman and they were not. He was literate and they were not, or barely so. He was a philosopher-prince and they were honest but humble peasants who looked to him for wisdom and virtue. He had no doubt that they loved him and honored him, but they could never understand him because they occupied a lower plane. In other words, Ethan, for all of his backwoods earthiness, was something of a snob.

The journey northward with Gates was a leisurely and pleasant one. The general treated Ethan "with the familiarity of a companion and generosity of a lord," and listened attentively as Ethan regaled him en route with tales of "striking circumstances which occurred in the course of my captivity." At Newburgh on the Hudson, Ethan parted company with Gates and struck out northeastward to visit Heman in Salisbury, where he arrived on May 25, only to learn that less than a week earlier his favorite brother had died after a hard and lingering illness brought on by wounds suffered at the Battle of Bennington the summer before. Ethan was deeply affected. Since the beginning of the war, he had lost heavily from among those closest to him. First to go had been Cousin Remember, cut down by Indians only a few weeks before Ethan's capture. Then in the following spring Brother Zimri had died while still in his twenties. Next after Zimri had been Ethan's son Joseph, only a boy. And now Heman, with whom Ethan had travelled shoulder to shoulder for many a mile since their growing-up days in the Cornwall hills. In many ways his death was the hardest of all to bear.

A day or so later a despondent Ethan set out northward on a horse borrowed from Heman's widow. Ordinarily he would have stopped along the way in neighboring Sheffield to visit for a time with his family, but soon after the death of Zimri, who had kept the farm going, Mary and the children had moved to Arlington on the Grants where they were taken in and cared for by Ira. Ethan therefore headed directly for Bennington on what would be the final leg of his long journey home from captivity. In the three weeks since his release by the British, he had traveled a distance of two hundred and fifty miles, much of it on foot. This would have been simple enough if he had been his old self, but after three years of captivity he was not in the best of health. Those final few months, when he was caged in the Provost Jail in New York, had nullified much of the recovery he had made during his days on parole at New Lots and had greatly impaired his physical powers and stamina. "He was terrible thin and worn," Heman's widow would later recall. She had hardly recognized the emaciated giant when he appeared at her place in Salisbury a few days after her husband's death.

Upon his arrival in Bennington on the last day of May, 1778, Ethan found that many changes had taken place during his absence. The area that had formerly been known as the Grants had in early 1777 declared its independence of all outside political authority and, now calling itself the Republic of Vermont, was asking for admission as a co-equal state into the American Confederation. A constitution had been drawn up for the infant Republic, and a very liberal constitution it was—the first in America to provide for unrestricted manhood suffrage and the immediate abolition of slavery. By the time of Ethan's return, elections had been held; the Assembly had met in its first session; and the Republic of Vermont, shaky though it may have been, was a going concern. Naturally, Ethan was pleased. Since before the onset of the Revolution he had dreamed hopefully of complete independence for the land between the Connecticut River and Lake Champlain. Now the deed was done, and although Ethan's absence from the scene had disqualified him from any rightful claim to founding-fatherhood, he certainly felt that by having prevented the Yorkers—and later the British—from swallowing up the area, he had at least contributed something to the establishment of this new order of things.

Understandably, the State of New York was less than happy over what was going on in its eastern counties. At first New York's Governor George Clinton seemed determined to send troops into the area and quash this great impertinence at its source. Upon reflection, however, it became clear to him that this would not be a very wise thing to do. To have put an end to the trouble on the Grants would have necessitated, among other things, the withdrawal of a sizable number of New York troops from the Northern Department of the Continental Command, a move that would have left the frontier defenses in the Champlain area seriously weakened. This the governor was not willing to do. Whatever else George Clinton may or may not have been, he was certainly a dedicated patriot. Since the outbreak of the Revolution, he had given vigorous support to the American position, and he didn't intend to jeopardize it now by mounting a military attack against his own countrymen, no matter how badly they were behaving.

Instead of force, therefore, the governor decided to use words to combat the secession on his eastern flank, and during those early months when Vermont was slowly getting set under its new constitution, a torrent of protest poured forth from the governor's mansion at Poughkeepsie. Of course, words alone would accomplish little against the ambitious designs of the Vermont rebels, and it is doubtful that Governor Clinton ever really believed that they would. At a later time, once the smoke of the Revolution had cleared, he could register his disapproval in a stronger manner. In the  meantime he was making it clear to the Vermonters themselves and the world at large that the State of New York did not intend to acquiesce in what was going on, and that sister states would do well to refrain from extending aid, comfort, or encouragement of any kind to the self-styled Republic of Vermont.

It was especially important to Clinton and New York that this new regime not be extended recognition by the Continental Congress. Indeed, if recognition were given, then all would be lost, for Vermont's admission into the Union as a sovereign state would be bound to follow in short order. But none of this was very likely to happen. True, the Vermonters could count upon some support in Congress, mainly from among the New England delegations, but among a substantial majority of the congressional delegates there was an understandable reluctance to offend the sensitivities of a member state as powerful and as important to the Revolutionary cause as New York. Thus, when in the summer of 1777, only a few months after declaring its independence, Vermont petitioned Congress for recognition, its request was peremptorily dismissed. "Congress," explained the official Journal, "will not by any of its proceedings do or recommend or countenance any thing injurious to the rights and jurisdiction of the several communities which it represents." And so it would go, with slight variations, for the next fourteen years, with Vermont persistently knocking at the door of the Union, asking for admission, and New York just as persistently blocking the entranceway.

Actually, Vermont could scarcely have chosen a less promising time for going it alone. By the spring of 1778, when the machinery of government began moving under the new constitution, the military situation in the area had been eased somewhat by the withdrawal of the British garrisons from Ticonderoga and Crown Point. But they had not gone far. Poised in readiness at their bases in Canada, not so many miles to the north, the enemy forces hovered menacingly, casting a shadow over the new state. At any moment they might return up-lake and conceivably ravage the west-side towns. In the meantime they could and would keep themselves amused by conducting raids, usually in company with their Indian allies, against the far-flung outlying settlements of the infant Republic. If for no other reason than that of survival, this would have been an excellent time for Vermonters to have kept their ties with the Yorkers close and cordial. As it was, the new state was in the precarious position of not really daring to call upon its irate parent for protection against the British, for in view of Governor Clinton's strong feelings against Vermont and Vermonters, the presence of New York troops in the area was obviously a thing to be avoided at almost any cost. If the Republic were to be defended against the British, it would presumably have to do the job without the help of its powerful neighbor to the west. This, in the judgment of those Vermonters who were willing and able to take a hard look at reality, would admittedly be no easy task, especially now that Seth Warner's regiment had been withdrawn from the region and attached to General Gates' headquarters on the Hudson many miles to the south.

But if the military situation were perilous, and indeed it was, the economic conditions facing the young Republic were even more so.

From the beginnings of settlement, poverty had been the standard lot of most of the settlers. Many of those who had migrated to the area, especially those who had pitched west of the mountains, had been failures or near-failures in one or another of the older, established colonies and had struck out for the Grants, sometimes in desperation, to start a new life. Often carrying their entire wealth, on ox-cart or sled, they staked down on the Grants with few material possessions to sustain them in their battle for survival. In time, as ax and plow and human toil worked their change, the fortunes of most of the settlers brightened somewhat, but by the outbreak of the Revolution only a few of them had progressed very far beyond the outer limits of subsistence. And then came the war, with its cruel demands and dislocations—husbands and fathers taken from the farm for months at a time, and not a few forever; deprivations and atrocities committed against the countryside by angry armies on the move; the family's precious savings spent for ball and powder instead of seed.

By the spring of 1778 the economy of the region was probably at its lowest ebb since the earliest days of settlement. Money had virtually disappeared from circulation. What little there was had long since gone into hiding, cached for the most part in the coffers of a fortunate few on the east side. Barter exchange had become the way of things, and fortunate indeed was he who had anything left over to barter after providing for the barest necessities of his family and farm. In a word, the economic conditions confronting Vermonters at this time were desperate. For even the most securely established government, these conditions would have been difficult to contend with. For the shaky, embattled, upstart Republic of Vermont, they were well-nigh impossible.

Adding to the Republic's woes was a sizable element of internal dissatisfaction with the new government. This dissatisfaction, which expressed itself in many ways and varying degrees, was found mainly but not entirely among the more affluent settlers, and was centered in the area adjacent to the Connecticut River on the east side of the mountains where relations with the Yorkers had traditionally been less embittered. From the very beginning a large number of easterners, together with a substantial scattering of settlers on the west side, had made no secret of their opposition to the independence movement. To most of them, many of whom held their land under New York title either through original purchase or confirmation, separation from New York even under the most ideal conditions would probably have seemed very ill-advised, for it would have meant a step away from order and security. But to launch a new state now in the face of such palpable military and economic peril was nothing short of madness.

And where was the provocation for such a rash move? There was none; at least none worthy of the attention of honest and reasonable men. True, some years earlier there had been occasional friction between the Yorkers and some of the Grants settlers, but since the beginning of the Revolution former antagonisms had all but disappeared. Relations between the Grants and the government of New York had, in fact, reached a new high of cordiality. Yorkers and Yankees had fought side by side against a common foe; together they had succeeded in driving the enemy forces back into Canada. And now that the Grants had been reclaimed from British occupation, Governor Clinton was reportedly ready to recommend to his Legislature that all New Hampshire land titles held by actual settlers be confirmed without fee under the Great Seal of New York. What more could be asked for? Surely there was no rational explanation for this reckless experiment in state-building now under way, no explanation at all except, of course, the most obvious one: all of this was the work of a small group of grasping, ambitious men who were out to promote their own fortunes by seizing political control over the area—a clear-cut power-grab impelled by the mean and selfish motives of a small clique of unprincipled adventures, many of whom held wild lands for speculation.

And perhaps those who looked upon the new regime with some suspicion were right. Certainly there was much about the birth process of the Republic to suggest that independent Vermont was something other than the product of a widespread popular enthusiasm. Of the more than fifty towns on the Grants, only seventeen had been represented at the convention that had declared for independence in January of 1777, and scarcely more than that had been directly involved in framing and adopting the constitution six months later. More notable still was the failure of Vermont's founding fathers to submit their constitution to the people for ratification, a highly irregular bit of political remissness which caused many of the Grants settlers to wonder if this were not perhaps a calculated omission designed to prevent a popular vote on the document. Apparently it was precisely that. Many years later Ira Allen, one of the prime movers in the founding of Vermont and a shrewd politican whose ear was never far from the ground, stated flatly that the constitution had been deliberately kept from the people. Why? For the simple reason that it would have been rejected by them. Whether or not this was an accurate appraisal of the situation is anybody's guess. It appears, however, that the founders of the new government were convinced that the opposition, although largely unorganized, constituted an element powerful enough to pose a serious threat to the fortunes of the young Republic.

So it was that when Ethan returned from captivity in May of 1778, only a month or so after the Republic had begun operating under its constitution, there was strong reason to doubt that the new government could last more than a few months at best. Plagued with military and economic problems of frightening proportions, and a large and surly dissension within, the Republic of Vermont was already in a precarious position, and its prospects for the future were all bad. If it were to survive, it would surely need a stout heart and the blessings of a benign Providence. It would also need an uncommon amount of enterprising leadership.

As befits a returning hero, Ethan was received with great rejoicing upon his arrival in Bennington on the evening of the last day of May, 1778. Somehow word had preceded him from Salisbury that it was he rather than Heman who had died. Thus the cause for celebration was twofold: Ethan had been delivered up not only from British captivity but, in a sense, from the grave as well, and on the very night of his return the Bennington militia toted its three ancient cannons out of storage and discharged them to announce the happy tidings. On the following day Ethan's old comrade in arms Sam Herrick, now a colonel in the Vermont militia, ordered a fourteen-gun salute to be fired—thirteen for the states of the Union and one for the new Republic—in celebration of Ethan's safe deliverance. It was an extravagant thing to do in view of the acute shortage of powder in the Republic, but Ethan was clearly worth every bit of the fuss being made over him. He was indeed the man of the hour.

The warmth and enthusiasm of his reception must have been very gratifying. It was apparent that his time away in prison had done much to obscure his earlier blunders at St. John's and Montreal and those former displays of egotism and bombast that had alienated so many of his neighbors. More than that, it had added a new luster to his image. The British had provided him with an Elba of sorts, and now, his long exile at an end, he was home again—acclaimed and honored by his own adoring people. Ethan was visibly moved by it all, and so were the good citizens of Bennington, many of whom accompanied him up the hill to Stephen Fay's Catamount Tavern where, Ethan later reported with obvious satisfaction, "we passed the flowing bowl, and rural felicity, sweetened with friendship, glowed in every countenance."

After a day of revelry in Bennington, Ethan set out for Arlington, a dozen miles to the north, to visit his family at Ira's place. Along the way he could not help but be struck by the great changes that had taken place during his absence. Although in the early years of the war immigration onto the Grants had slowed almost to a stop, Bennington County had nevertheless experienced a substantial population growth. This had been brought about mainly by the flight of hundreds of frontier families who, for safety's sake, had been forced to abandon their farms in the northland. Some of these refugees, stripped of their land and virtually all of their other possessions, had returned in defeat and despair to live off the bounty of relatives in Connecticut and Massachusetts. But most of them, perhaps because they had no place else to go, had resettled in Bennington County, where they had somehow managed to acquire small parcels of wild land. Here, removed from the immediate threat of British and Indian depredations, they had begun again the relentless battle against the forest.

As a result, much of the countryside, especially in the more southerly parts of the county, had taken on a new appearance. The land was more open now. Handsome stands of giant hardwood had fallen before the persistent attack of the settler's ax, and in their place were ugly acres of stark, jagged stumps, interspersed now, in early June, with the tender green shoots of young corn. Near the center of each new clearing was a shelter of sorts, usually a small cabin that had been hurriedly pieced together out of logs or roughhewn timbers. And above the cabins and the half-cleared fields, thin ribbons of smoke diffused and drifted eastward toward the mountains, while, below, the sound of children's voices proclaimed that man had come and laid his claim upon the land. Bennington County had indeed filled in during the early years of the war, and to a man like Ethan who reveled in the unencumbered freedom of the forest, this was not an altogether good thing.

At Arlington he found his family much as he had left them, save for the absence of his son, a painful matter that Ethan did not care to dwell upon. His three daughters, who ranged in age from fifteen down to three, seemed well enough, although not so robust as they might be. His wife had changed little, except to grow noticeably older. Ethan's years away had done nothing to sweeten her disposition or soften her complaints about her health, her husband, and her world in general. It was not the happiest of domestic scenes, but Ethan, who had not expected anything better, was able to put up with it for nearly two days before leaving with brother Ira for more pleasant surroundings.

Ira was still Ira, only more so. He was still a young man, and he continued to live the spartan, uncluttered life of a backwoods bachelor, although as one of the handsomest men around he must have been much sought after. To Ethan he remained, as he always would, the baby of the family, and he conducted himself accordingly by showing his older brother a proper and probably genuine deference. But there was no mistaking the fact that Ira's station in life had risen dramatically during the nearly three years since Ethan had last seen him.

Early in the war he had moved down from the Onion River country to take over the operation of a gristmill in Arlington. Soon after, he built a sawmill in the same town, and, between these two enterprises, managed to do rather well. He had also turned a few profitable land deals by buying low at the time of the British invasion in the summer of 1777 and selling high after their defeat at Saratoga and subsequent withdrawal northward. At the moment of Ethan's return, Ira, anticipating a brisker traffic in land, was announcing in the *Connecticut Courant* the imminent opening of the Ira Allen Land Office in Arlington. All in all, he had prospered during the hard times of the early war years by working on the sound assumption that men would always need, in good days or bad, flour, lumber, and land—and by taking a few well-calculated risks that his neighbors could not or dared not venture. He was still far from wealthy. That would come later. Nevertheless, at the age of twenty-seven, he was already a man of substantial property, nearly all of which he had gained through his own considerable energy and enterprise.

It was as a public figure, however, that Ira had gained his greatest prominence during Ethan's absence, and it was to matters of state that he now gave most of his time and attention. As one of the five or six men most responsible for launching the new government, Ira occupied a place of importance and power in the Republic. In fact, at the time of Ethan's return he held several positions, official and otherwise, which combined to make him certainly the most active and probably the most influential member of the small clique that directed the destinies of young Vermont. Councilor, Treasurer, unofficial Secretary of State, and soon-to-be Surveyor-General, Ira was indeed a power to be reckoned with. Unfortunately, however, he was notably lacking in that magical quality called leadership. For all his brilliance, his good looks, and the power of his many offices, he had no hold upon the people. More often than not they admired him for his obvious abilities, but they could never quite bring themselves to trust him. Perhaps this is why old Tom Chittenden, rather than Ira, was chosen to occupy the presidency of the new Republic.

Although not the brightest or most assertive of men, Chittenden had an almost mystical rapport with the people. He liked them and, what was more important, he understood them, and they in turn gave him their respect and trust, confident that One-eyed Tom would always do his best by them. Clearly he had the stuff of leadership, but in the truest sense of the word he was not a leader, for he failed to lead his people; he merely rallied them, and this was not enough. If the Republic were to survive, it would have to move ahead. Cohesion was only something to build upon. Dynamism was needed now, and who indeed was more richly equipped with that commodity or more willing to lavish it upon the infant Republic than Ethan Allen, man of the people and hero extraordinary?

From soon after his return to the Grants in the late spring of 1778 until the defeat of Cornwallis at Yorktown in the autumn of 1781, Ethan was unquestionably the most powerful figure in Vermont. With the instinct of a natural leader he immediately sensed the void at the top and proceeded to fill it with remarkable effect. Never before in his tempestuous career had he shown such enterprise and dash, and never again would he be so able to carry everything before him as during the three years following his return from prison. Here, clearly, was Ethan at his best, and Ethan's best was nothing to be scoffed at. Even his most hostile critics, then and now, have had to concede that in the early days of the Republic of Vermont, Ethan Allen was a host in himself. Without him it is unlikely that the young Republic would have lived through its first few rickety years.

The extent of Ethan's power and influence at this time is a difficult thing to assess, for he customarily operated outside the regular avenues of authority. During these years he held no civilian office, elective or otherwise, save for an occasional ad hoc appointment of usually brief duration. In fact, it was only through his command of the Vermont militia, to which he was elected in the spring of 1779, that he could claim anything resembling official prominence in the young Republic. But official or otherwise, his power was considerable, to say the least. No other man in the Republic wielded so much influence, for no other man could come close to matching his hold on the imagination and affections of the people. It was this fact and the general recognition of it that for three years or more enabled Ethan, with or without the vestments of office, to rule over Vermont pretty much as he saw fit.

It has often been said that Ethan was inhibited from holding office by his outspoken religious heterodoxy. Perhaps so. Certainly he would have found it awkward to meet either the letter or the spirit of the religious qualifications for office-holding, for his God was a far cry from the Old Testament Avenger to whom all Vermont officials were required by the constitution to take a solemn oath of reverence. Still, if all this were indeed a factor in keeping him away from public office, it was probably not a very important one. If Ethan had actually wanted this position or that, he would doubtless have found a way to get it, oath or no oath. He was not a man to allow technicalities to stand in his way. With his uncommon enterprise and resolve he could surely have made his way through, over, or around such a petty obstacle if he had so chosen. In some instances he obviously did so choose; otherwise he would have been unable to take over command of the militia, or to accept a varied assortment of special assignments he saw fit to undertake for the Republic from time to time.

It seems more likely that Ethan purposely tended to shy away from public position because he preferred to stay on the outside and operate as a free agent, unencumbered by the fixed dimensions of office. He may have felt that office-holding would only cramp his style, as indeed it probably would have. Better to remain off-stage and direct things from the wings. And this is precisely what he did. Working in a manner that was too loud and too conspicuous to obscure the fact, he ran the Republic of Vermont for more than three years by pulling the strings that made things happen. That his job was made easier by the fact that most of the Republic's important offices were held by trusted friends who generally shared his view of things can hardly be denied, but even without them he would doubtless have found a way to translate his great popularity into effective political power.

To most of today's Americans the folk hero is a total stranger. The great mass and speed of modern life have made him, like the ox-cart and the double-bitted ax, an incomprehensible relic of the past. If he is seen at all now, it is only for an instant, and the stage on which he struts is usually a minute one, far removed from the main currents of a society in which individual relationships have, for better or worse, lost much of their intensity and meaning. But it was not always so. There was a time, not so very long ago, when men depended upon other men, rather than institutions, for much that was important in life and much that was not. In the absence of anything better, men customarily turned to their neighbors for help and sympathy, news and entertainment, and sometimes a word or two of hope for the future. And how one man responded to the call of another, be it the call of desperation or only whimsy, was apt to be his measure for as far as his name was known.

Most men met the test well enough, perhaps because, in the world that they knew, it never occurred to them not to. But every so often there arose among these people accustomed to helping one another a man so extraordinary in the generosity and efficacy of his response that in time he became set aside as a special member of the community. If to such a quality as this, the proper temperament and enterprise were added, a man could go far. He could loom larger than life among his contemporaries, who would delight in swapping tales about his prowess and nobility. He could even become a legend in his own time.

And so it was with Ethan who, in a paternalistic way, cared deeply for his people and delighted in playing the role of benefactor to them in large matters and small. He was seldom too busy to lend his mighty shoulder to a cabin-raising, or to amuse the boys with a story or two he had picked up in his many travels, or join them in a friendly toast to the future, the present, or old times. But most important of all, Ethan was never known to disregard the cry of the anguished. When trouble came or threatened, he could be counted upon to come forward and do his level best by his friends and neighbors. He was known far and wide as a man who would pitch in when the going became perilous or rough, and he was richly deserving of his reputation. Consider the following incident, too well documented to be doubted.

On an afternoon in late May, 1780, Eldad Taylor of Sunderland reported that his two small daughters, ages seven and four, had wandered off into the woods a few hours earlier and had failed to return. By nightfall a large search party of more than a hundred men, Ethan among them, had assembled at Taylor's place and begun fanning out through the surrounding woods. The hunt continued throughout the night, the next day, and the next, but by mid-afternoon of the third day, the last of the searchers had returned without having discovered any trace of the children. Exhausted by their long ordeal and convinced that the little girls were by now dead, the men had all but decided to give up and return to their homes when Ethan Allen mounted a stump and, "in a manner peculiar to himself," demanded to be heard.

The girls were not dead, he insisted. The weather had been unseasonably warm since their disappearance; and with the wolves and catamounts long since driven from the nearby area, there was nothing in the forest that would be apt to harm the children. They were still alive. They were somewhere out there waiting to be found, "perishing with hunger and spending their last strength in crying for their father and mother." What parent, yea, what man, could fail to go out again into the woods and do what had to be done? For his part, Ethan did not intend to leave until the children were found. He would continue to hunt if he had to do so alone, but he supposed that others would join him rather than return home and live forever with the knowledge that they had done less than their best by these little girls and their grief-stricken parents. And, of course, Ethan was right. To a man the searchers returned to the woods, and before the sun set that evening the children had been found alive and returned to their home. Needless to say, from that day on, nobody spoke ill of Ethan Allen in the presence of Eldad Taylor, nor were the scores of men who had been involved in the search likely to forget that it was, after all, Ethan, who by giving something extra, had saved the children of a neighbor from starving to death less than two miles from their home. Small wonder that there developed about Ethan the luster of legend, the stuff of the folk hero. And if he chose to be boastful about it or exploit it for political advantage—well, what was wrong with that?

After the brief but adequate visit with his family in Arlington, Ethan set out for Bennington in company with Ira who, as a member of the Council, was expected to be on hand for the meeting of the Vermont Assembly, then about to be opened in the Bennington Meeting House. On the outskirts of town they were joined by their friend Tom Chittenden, who early in the war had been driven from his Onion River farm by the British advance and, like Ira, had come to settle in Arlington. At this time a capital had not yet been chosen for the new state, nor would one be for several years, and consequently the Assembly "met around," usually alternating its sessions between Windsor and Bennington on opposite sides of the mountains.

For all intents and purposes, however, the Republic had its capital at Arlington during these early years, for here, besides President Chittenden and Ira, lived the fiery Matthew Lyon and at least one other member of the Council of State, and here the affairs of early Vermont were pretty much decided upon by a small group of neighbors meeting informally from time to time over a round of rum in Chittenden's or Ira Allen's kitchen. Of course, their decisions were eventually submitted to the Assembly for approval, but the Assembly seldom saw any reason to balk. For the most part its members, elected by the towns, were content to concern themselves with such lesser matters as fixing bounties on wolves or regulating fishing on the White River. On weightier issues they seemed only too willing to defer to the greater wisdom of the President and his Council, probably because they preferred to make things as easy for themselves as possible and thereby save their time and energy for the more important business of wringing a living out of the Vermont soil. This tendency on the part of the Assembly to duck its obligations meant in effect that the political destiny of the Republic was in the hands of a very few men, all of whom were well disposed toward Ethan. And at the head of this tidy structure sat old Tom Chittenden, whose friendship with the Allen boys dated back to the old days in Salisbury. All very handy for one about to take over the reins of leadership.

Ethan and the others reached Bennington midway through the first week of June, just as the Assembly was beginning its proceedings. It was the second session of the Assembly—its first on the west side of the mountains—and the meeting was well attended, despite the fact that it was being held at a time of year when most of the legislators might better have been back in their fields nursing their shoots and seedlings. Naturally, Ethan dropped by the hall to pay his respects to the delegates, who greeted his appearance with tumultuous applause. Before his departure, a Resolution was passed unanimously by the Assembly, congratulating him on his return—all of which must have pleased Ethan immensely. The last time his friends and neighbors had voted on him, they had done him out of his regiment. But that was long ago and now all but forgotten.

From the Meeting House, Ethan made his way up the hill to the Catamount Tavern for a visit with his friend Jonas Fay. Jonas had been trained, more or less, as a physician, and as the only doctor in town he had for several years been kept busy physicking and bleeding his neighbors. Of late, however, he had all but abandoned his practice, for with his father Stephen getting along in years, Jonas had taken over the running of the Tavern. This was a happy development for Ethan, for his thirst was often more robust than his purse, and Jonas, much more so than his father, was willing to carry Ethan on the books. But Ethan's affection for Jonas went back to an earlier time, long before Jonas had risen to the position of tavern-keeper. From their first meeting many years before, the two men, almost exact contemporaries, had struck it off well with one another, and until the end their ties would remain close and strong. Together they drank and confided, and together they performed many estimable services for the Republic. At the risk of belaboring a point already made, it should be mentioned that Jonas and his younger brother Joseph, both of whom liked Ethan and saw things his way, were also members of the all-important Governor's Council. Good men for the job, as far as Ethan and his enterprises were concerned.

After a day or so as Jonas' guest at the Catamount, Ethan managed to find a house not far down the hill, and here he lived for the better part of the next two years, apparently renting the premises and an adjacent pasture from one of his Bennington friends. Occasionally he would venture up to Arlington to visit his family or sit in on a meeting of the Council, but Bennington was his headquarters, and for understandable reasons: Bennington was the gateway from the south. It was also the largest and most prosperous (or least unprosperous) town on the west side of the mountains—a veritable metropolis compared with Arlington and the other towns to the north. Granted, Arlington was the political nerve-center of the Republic, but Bennington was the hub of excitement and action, and it was here, close to the joys of the Catamount Tavern and safely removed from the strident whines of his wife, that Ethan apparently preferred to be.

At the time of his arrival in Bennington, Ethan found the town in a flurry of excitement. Of course the Assembly was in session, and that in itself would have been cause enough for a livelier tempo of things, but in addition, there was the happy prospect of a very special sort of entertainment: a man was soon to be hanged on the Bennington green. The intended victim was David Redding, a recent arrival in Vermont, who had been found guilty of collaborating with the British by selling them powder and ball that he had stolen from one of the public arsenals. For such "enemical conduct" he had been sentenced by a jury of his peers to be executed on June 4. It was to be Vermont's first public hanging, and it was Bennington's good fortune to have been selected as the site of execution. Naturally the promise of an event such as this had occasioned something of a holiday air in the town. From all over the county a large number of the citizenry had flocked into Bennington to attend the spectacle. And then suddenly, at the last moment, the execution was postponed for a week in order that Redding might be given a new trial because of an irregularity in the original proceedings.

Understandably, the people were much upset by all of this. They had been looking forward to the event with great anticipation. Many of them had come a long way in order to witness it, and now it looked as though they were going to be cheated out of a good show by legal shenanigans. For a time they seemed determined to have their hanging anyway, even if they had to do it themselves, but it appears that they were dissuaded from doing anything rash by the timely intervention of Ethan Allen. According to accounts given by several persons present at the time, Ethan shouldered his way into the midst of the angry crowd, shouting "Attention to the whole!" and proceeded to bring the people under control by promising them that Redding would get what he deserved and at no distant time. In fact, they could absolutely count on having a hanging if only they would be patient. Go home, he urged, and come back in a week. "If Redding is not then hung, I promise you that I will hang myself," Ethan is reported to have said. And he probably did. It would have been unlike him to miss such an obvious opportunity to step forward and exert a touch of authority over his people. And it certainly would have been consistent with his style for him to josh them out of their meanness and send them away laughing.

Thus, Redding was saved for the time being, but not for long. Just to make sure that there would be no slip-up in the retrial, Ethan had the Council appoint him prosecuting attorney. It would, after all, be embarrassing, to say the least, if Redding were allowed to escape the noose. There really wasn't much danger of this, however. Retrial or not, Redding was doomed, and Ethan was able to secure a conviction without seriously taxing his legal talents. At one o'clock on June 11, the Vermont Assembly recessed for the afternoon to witness the execution. Great numbers of people from far and near filled the Bennington green to overflowing. And, of course, very much in evidence among them was Ethan himself, who, as a result of his dramatic role in the production had, as one Vermont historian would later put it, "considerably enhanced his popularity as a leader and public benefactor."

This was good fun, the hanging and all, but it did not really do much to improve the rickety condition of the Republic. The difficulties facing the new government were many and immense, and not the least of these was a critical shortage of money. How to raise the funds necessary for carrying on state business was a perplexing problem that demanded a fairly immediate solution. Taxation might have been tried, but what good would a tax program be when most of the people lacked the wherewithal to pay? Of course, there was the possibility of operating under some sort of barter system, and for a time this was seriously contemplated by the Council before being ruled out as too cumbersome to be practical. Several months before Ethan's return, the Republic had set up a public loan office in Bennington and had advertised for money in several of the New England newspapers, with repayment guaranteed at 6 per cent within a year's time. The response had been weak, however, and what little money had come into Vermont through this channel had only postponed the eventual day of reckoning. A more substantial source of revenue would obviously have to be found.

The confiscation of Tory property had been begun in the summer of 1777, even before the new government had been set in operation under its constitution. At the suggestion of Ira, the provisional Committee of Safety, which then governed the state, had initiated the practice of confiscating and auctioning off the estates of Loyalists who, in fleeing to the safety of British lines, had left their property unattended. The sales had from the first been successful, offering as they did very generous bargains in choice land, a great deal of it improved. Much of what little capital there was left in the state, together with sizable sums of outside currency, poured into the Vermont treasury, and within fifteen days after the sales had begun, enough money had been raised to provide equipment and bounties for Vermont's brand new militia regiment. "Hence," Ira would later comment, "it was found that those who joined the British were benefactors of the State, as they left their property to support a government they were striving to destroy." By the time of Ethan's return, however, all of the abandoned property had been sold— one hundred and fifty-eight estates in all—and, alas, the proceeds had long since been spent, leaving the public treasury as bare as before.

It was Ethan, with the aid of Ira, who convinced the Council in June of 1778 that the business of confiscation had not been pushed far enough, that there was still much that could be squeezed out of the operation by adopting a more realistic view of what constituted Toryism. Obviously, Ethan insisted, not all Tories had fled. There were many others still living in the Republic, especially on the east side, who were clearly pro-British in their sentiments if not their actions, and the fact that they had chosen to remain rather than flee made them even more dangerous and reprehensible than those who had left. Surely such vipers should not be permitted to escape the righteous resentment of their patriotic neighbors. Let the confiscation be broadened to include them as well. In this way the Republic could all but eliminate its financial problems. At the same time it could make it emphatically clear that Vermont did not intend to tolerate disloyalty to the American cause.

Thus, only a few days after Ethan's return from captivity, President Chittenden and his Council persuaded the Assembly to pass the so-called Banishment Act, a sweeping and rather ill-defined measure which, among other things, authorized the establishment of confiscation boards for the various counties of the Republic. These boards, empowered to hear and decide upon charges of disloyalty brought against residents of the Republic, would remain in operation throughout the remainder of the war and would yield in excess of £190,000—more than all other sources of public revenue combined. Largely as a result of the work performed by the confiscation boards, the Republic of Vermont was able to get along without having to resort to taxation until 1781, a fact that did much to endear the new government to its people and to attract many immigrants into the state.

In response to Ethan's request, the Assembly named him as one of the five judges authorized to try "any person or persons charged with being guilty of any inimical treacherous or treasonable conduct or conspiracies against this and the Independent States, within and for the County of Bennington." He was also given permission to select his four colleagues—a generous concession which perhaps indicated something of the influence he already wielded within the councils of state. Naturally he packed the board with his friends, including Jonas Fay's young brother Joseph, and just as naturally he threw himself into his new assignment with great enthusiasm and bluster, moving from town to town to decide upon the loyalty of his neighbors, and, if circumstances warranted, to strip them of their property and order them from the state. And why not? "It is," Ethan commented, "a game of hazard between whig and tory. The whigs must inevitably have lost all, in consequence of the abilities of the tories, and their good friends the British; and it is no more than right the tories should run the same risk, in consequence of the abilities of the whigs." In short, do unto others what they would do unto you if they had the chance.

During his stint on the Bennington Board of Confiscation, Ethan convicted eight "enemical persons;" not a bad score in view of the fact that he served for less than two weeks before being called from the bench by other duties. For his services the Assembly paid him about £20, "as money went in 1774." He also received the satisfaction of knowing that, in addition to aiding the American cause, he had given a good start to a program that held great promise for the Republic of Vermont. Lesser men could carry on now that he had shown the way.

In accordance with the provisions of the Banishment Act, the Tories convicted by Ethan's court were expected to leave the state immediately with no property save what they could carry on their backs. To make sure that a proper precedent would be established, Ethan took personal charge of ushering them out. Arriving in Albany in early July, he turned his prisoners over to General John Stark with the request that they be sent through to enemy lines. This was all right with Stark, but before he could take action, the news of Ethan's Tories had reached the ear of Governor Clinton who immediately demanded that the captives be turned over to him. The prisoners, it seems, had protested to Clinton that they were not Tories at all but merely good Yorkers who, because of their lack of sympathy with the self-styled Republic of Vermont, had been criminally despoiled of their property.

Clinton chose to take the prisoners at their word, and he may have been right in doing so. Ethan himself was making no secret about the fact that he had not been very fussy about separating one sort of "Attrotious Villain" from another. "These enemical persons are Yorkers as well as Tories," he wrote to a friend. Besides, what difference did it make what they called themselves? They were all enemies of Vermont; Vermont was doing its best to hold back the British; and so it followed logically (although Ethan did not say this in so many words) that anybody who was hostile to the Republic of Vermont was an ally of the British and therefore deserving of the worst.

There was more involved here, however, than the question of the prisoners' loyalty to the American cause. What disturbed Governor Clinton most was the fact that the entire matter was a blatant affront to the authority of his state. The governor was quick to point out that although the pretended Republic of Vermont might presume to set up courts of law, these courts obviously had no meaning. How could they, when there was no Vermont and never had been? The Grants were still very much a part of New York and subject therefore to New York law. To hold that the proceedings against Ethan's Tories had been in any way legal would be taking a long step toward recognizing the independence and sovereignty of an area that New York still claimed for its own. This, of course, Clinton had no intention of doing, nor did he mean to have others do so. Tories or otherwise, the prisoners must be turned over to him to be tried, if at all, under Yorker jurisdiction.

Unfortunately for Governor Clinton, John Stark was a Yankee, and like most of his breed he had little affection for Yorkers. He was furthermore a very stubborn man, perhaps the stubbornest of his generation. Not only did he refuse to turn over Ethan's Tories to the governor but he made it clear that he intended to carry out "the commands of the Courts of the State of Vermont." To a delegation of Yorkers sent by the governor to reason with Stark, the general was less than cordial. "He informed us," the delegation reported back to Clinton, "that it was none of our busines to interfere with Tories from another State." In an angry mood, Clinton wrote to General Washington demanding that Stark be ordered to surrender the prisoners and that he be disciplined for his "unwarrantable conduct." But Washington chose not to get involved. He had too many problems of his own. He also had too few good generals on the line, and Stark, although independent as a hog on ice, was a good officer; not even Clinton would deny that. Consequently, General Washington turned the entire matter over to the Continental Congress where, he assured Clinton, careful consideration would in due time be given the governor's complaint. In other words, in his hassle with Stark, Clinton was to be left to his own devices, and there was obviously nothing much he could do about the situation but grumble.

Eventually the prisoners, under the command of one of Stark's officers, were driven southward from Albany to General Gates' headquarters at White Plains, from where the intention was to send them to the British lines. At the last moment, however, General Washington intervened. As a gesture of generosity towards the prisoners, and probably as a sop to Clinton, Washington ordered the captives taken to Fort Arnold at West Point and held there under easy arrest. "I do not mean that their confinement should be close or rigorous," he wrote to the fort's commanding officer. "Yet they must not be suffered to escape." Thus the prisoners were to remain within American lines and were to be comfortably treated, but they would be prisoners all the same, and that was the important point. Despite the protests of New York, the findings of a Vermont court had been substantially upheld by the Commanding General of the Continental Army, who also happened to be the most powerful and respected man in the country. All this was a bitter blow for Clinton and a source of great satisfaction for Ethan, who recognized the political importance of what had happened  and rejoiced in the embarrassment it had brought the Yorkers.

Throughout the remainder of the war, Ethan would continue to be involved in the Republic's confiscation program, although he would never again serve officially as a judge. As the mainstay of the Republic's economy, and as a powerful weapon for use against the enemies of the state, confiscation had a vital significance for Vermont, and it was important that Ethan keep a close eye on its implementation. That he was instrumental in pushing the program can hardly be denied. Often he acted as spotter for one or more of the county Commissions of Confiscations, sniffing out some hapless miscreant and then turning him over to the board of judges. In fact, so diligently did he apply himself to the job of ferreting out Tories, real or supposed, that on one occasion he found himself initiating confiscation proceedings against his own brother, Levi.

This was indeed an odd sort of operation for Ethan to be involved in. The bonds among the Allen brothers had always been strong, and it was almost unthinkable that one should turn against another, especially in public. To make the matter even more surprising there was the sizable debt of gratitude that Ethan owed his brother, for during those long and cruel years of captivity it had been Levi more than any other person who had exerted himself in behalf of Ethan's welfare. It was Levi who had written time and again to General Washington and Congress, prodding them to work for Ethan's exchange; it was Levi who had made a long and futile journey to Halifax in a quixotic attempt to buy his brother's release; and it was Levi who, at some inconvenience and peril to himself, had visited Ethan on several occasions and provided him with money during his parole in New York. All things considered, Levi had good reason to expect something better from his brother than he received during the early winter of 1779.

But there was much that was questionable about Levi. In the first place, he was a clown, and a cynical clown at that. Unlike his brothers he was a confirmed pessimist and misanthrope who insisted upon looking on life as a bad joke to be laughed at out of the corner of his mouth. Perhaps it was for this reason that his character was not what it might have been. Honor and integrity were not his strongest suits. In the abstract he had nothing against them, but he was seldom known to permit them to stand in the way of a likely opportunity for pleasure or gain. He was often apt to forget such matters as debts and promises, and it appears that at the time of the confiscation proceedings against him he was in the process of attempting to swindle Ethan and Ira out of a sizable portion of land in northern Vermont—a characteristic bit of Levi-ism that doubtless contributed to Ethan's determination to chasten this "accursed rogue." All in all, Levi Allen was not an entirely lovely figure, a fact which helps explain why at the time of his death in a debtors' prison many years later, nobody, not even his children, would come forward to claim the body.

In addition to all this was the fact that Levi was obviously no friend of the Revolution. Ethan called his brother a "Goddam devilish Tory," but Levi was actually no more Tory than he was Patriot. He simply lacked strong convictions on American independence and related matters. As far as Levi was concerned, the war presented a splendid opportunity for making money, and he had no intention of permitting ideology or sentiment to interfere with business. In other words, he was apolitical at a time when most men had committed themselves to one side or the other. "I boast not of loyalty," he once remarked. "Nor have I in the least concerned myself with Revolutionary principles. There are in all governments the ins and the outs at Court; the latter are ever grumbling." True, for one brief moment at the outset of the conflict he had served with Ethan at Ticonderoga, but since then he had concentrated on shouldering a profit rather than a musket. Leaving behind substantial landholdings on the Grants, some of which he had purchased jointly with Ethan and Ira, he had moved early in the war to Dutchess County, New York, from where he periodically sallied forth to trade with anyone who could afford to buy his wares. Frequently his business ventures took him inside enemy lines, where he was well received and handsomely paid.

Levi was halfway to Virginia when the bad news reached him. He had just been released from a Connecticut prison where he had spent six months for trading with the British on Long Island, and he was not in the best of humor. Upon learning that his Vermont lands had been snatched from him and that his own brother had been behind it all, he turned angrily about and headed north to see what could be done about recouping his losses. Arriving back in Dutchess County, he proclaimed himself the innocent victim of an ungrateful brother's spleen and avarice, and vowed that he would eventually get his lands back, by one means or another. In the meantime he intended to let the world know something of the malignity of Ethan Allen and the so-called Republic of Vermont. In a long letter to the *Connecticut Courant,* Levi described in detail the great injustice that had been done him by the Vermonters. He was ready to concede that "the convenient remedy of confiscation is an excellent institution for a *blooming State,*" but he found it difficult to understand why this weapon should be turned against one who had in no way done injury to the pretended state or its people. Of course, hardest of all to bear was the fact that his own brother, whom he had always revered and deferred to, had initiated the proceedings against him. "How can this be possible?" Levi asked:

> Can this be the man for whom so many were ready to drop a tear while he endured chains and captivity for his oppressed country? Or is he no sooner at liberty, than unmindful of his benefactor, like the serpent in the fable, he would sting him to the heart? Let him confess, let his letters show who it was that laboured by continual application for his relief and enlargement. Can he forget my voyage to Halifax, afterwards to New York, and the insults,

imprisonments, and sufferings sustained, and the cash advanced, merely to restore him to his country and friends?

When Ethan read Levi's account in the *Courant* he must have blanched a bit. The fact was that Levi had indeed done all of these things, and Ethan could not forget how much they had meant to him in those times of great want and desperation. "But God damn it all," Ethan explained, "under cover of doing favours to me, when a prisoner at New York and Long Island, he was holding treasonable corispondence with the Enemy."

Not so, Levi fired back. An out-and-out lie! And he challenged Ethan to a duel.

Fight a Tory, a traitor, on the field of honor? Never, thundered Ethan.

"I have no doubt he would have fought me," Levi later commented after his temper had cooled a bit, "but all his friends jointly put in their argument that Levi was only mad."

And so it went for two months or more, with brother shouting at brother over a distance of a hundred miles, until business called Levi to South Carolina where he passed through British lines and remained to trade with the enemy until the war ended. When he returned northward in 1783, he discovered that the passage of time and dramatic political shifts within the Republic of Vermont had softened Ethan's feelings toward him; so much so that within a year after his return he was once again in the full good graces of his big brother. Best of all, he was able with Ethan's help to retrieve his land, which for some strange reason the Confiscation Commission had not got around to putting up for auction. Thus all ended happily for the wayward Levi, who by the late 1780's was operating as a full-fledged partner of Ethan and Ira in many of their business dealings.

After depositing his Tories at General Stark's headquarters in early July of 1778, Ethan traveled down to Salisbury where he remained for a few days to help Ira close out Heman's books. As joint executors of their late brother's estate, Ethan and Ira discovered that the amiable storekeeper's accounts had been left in a sad state of disarray. It seemed as if virtually everyone in Litchfield County owed Heman money, and some of his debtors were into him for sizable amounts, including one account outstanding for 5,000 Connecticut pounds—no trifling sum even in those days of highly inflated currency. To set matters right would take a great deal of doing, and so the entire business was turned over to Salisbury lawyer John Knickerbocker, with instructions to bear down hard on the debtors and if necessary have them cast into prison. Attorney Knickbocker obviously took his job very seriously, with the result that during the next few months Ethan and Ira were frequently called upon to make the long ride down from Vermont to Salisbury to appear as complainants before one or another of the Litchfield County courts. All of this was bothersome, to say the least, but it was something that had to be done. After all, a debt was a thing to be paid, especially if it were owed to an Allen.

In Salisbury Ethan and Ira learned that Heman had willed them jointly one-half of his holdings in the Onion River Company, the other half going to his widow. A year earlier the unmarried Zimri had bequeathed his company holdings equally to each of his brothers and sisters, and before that, Remember Baker's share had passed on to his widow and son. Thus, ownership in the company had diffused considerably since its inception five years earlier, but at the same time the interest held by the two surviving original members, Ethan and Ira, had increased from 40 per cent to nearly 60 per cent. Exactly how much land the Onion River Company held title to at this time is unknown, but it was almost certainly in excess of 70,000 acres. Unfortunately, however, all of the company's holdings were in the north country, well behind enemy lines, and therefore of little value to the Brothers Allen and associates, for the time being at least.

But for Ethan the British presence in the north was not an unmixed evil, for it had the effect of raising land values in the southern part of the state where he held considerable acreage, purchased during the days of easy prices before the war. In midsummer of 1778, for example, he was able to sell a 300-acre spread in Tinmouth, a few miles south of the Castleton defense line, for a pre-war pound an acre—nearly one hundred times the amount he had paid for it five years before. With the proceeds from the sale of this and other property in the settled southern area, he purchased additional land in the north country, much of which he later turned over to the company at a respectable profit to himself. Apparently he was not especially troubled by the fact that he was investing heavily in the doubly risky business of buying New Hampshire titles to land still claimed by New York and actually occupied by the British. With his characteristic optimism (or foolhardiness) he pushed resolutely ahead as if there were not the slightest doubt in his mind that someday, somehow, things would work out to his advantage.

Back in Vermont by the latter part of July, 1779, Ethan closeted himself in his quarters at Bennington, where for the next two or three weeks he devoted most of his time to preparing one of his many political pamphlets. A few months earlier, Governor Clinton had issued his long-expected proclamation forgiving the people of the Grants for their past transgressions and confirming the titles of all persons in actual possession of their land. In return the governor asked only that the settlers recognize and respect New York's political jursidiction over the area. This was not an ungenerous gesture on Clinton's part, and if it had been made two years earlier it might conceivably have healed the breach between the Grants and the government of New York. Coming now, however, after Vermont had set itself up as a sovereign state, the offer was downright insulting, and Ethan intended to say so.

He completed his pamphlet on August 9, and on the following day sent it down to Hartford to be printed. He called it: *An Animadversory Address to the Inhabitants of the State of Vermont; with Remarks on a Proclamation, under the Hand of his Excellency George Clinton Esq; Governor of the State of New York,* a title ponderous enough to satisfy the fashion of the day and probably frighten away all but the most fearless readers. But, happily, the pamphlet was better than its title. In fact, it turned out to be a spritely and highly engaging piece of work—vintage Allen from beginning to end. Taking aim first at Clinton's proclamation, Ethan announced in no uncertain terms that the Republic of Vermont was a fact, whether the governor of New York liked it or not, and it was quite ridiculous of him to issue "romantic proclamations . . . calculated to deceive woods people" on this point. Governor Clinton and his land-grabbing friends might just as well recognize the cold realities of the situation: the area that had formerly comprised the eastern counties of New York but was now, and had been for nearly two years, the sovereign state of Vermont, was forever lost to the Yorkers, and for the governor or anyone else to pretend otherwise could lead to all sorts of unpleasantness.

So much for Clinton and his "folly and stupidity." Ethan next addressed himself to his fellow Vermonters with grandiloquent passages obviously intended to arouse passions of pride and patriotism and incite the great bird of freedom to soar:

> You have experienced every species of oppression which the old Government of New-York, with a Tryon at its head, could invent and inflict; and it is manifest that the new government are minded

to follow in their steps. Happy is it for you that you are fitted for the severest trials! You have been wonderfully supported and carried through thus far in your opposition to that government. Formerly you had everything to fear from it, but now little; for your public character is established, and your cause known to be just. In your early struggles with that government, you acquired a reputation for bravery. This gave you a relish for martial glory, and the British invasion opened an ample field for its display, and you have gone on conquering and to conquer until TALL GRENADIERS are dismayed and tremble at your approach. Your frontier situation often obliged you to be in arms and battles; and by repeated marchings, scoutings, and manly exercises, your nerves have become strong to strike the mortal blow. What enemy to the State of Vermont, or New-York land monopolizer, shall be able to stand before you in the day of your fierce anger.

A little overdone, perhaps, but basically sound to those who chose to read it with a sympathetic eye.

All things considered, the *Animadversory Address* was one of Ethan's most successful writings and a product of which he was unblushingly proud. Done in a breezy, humorous, and yet forceful manner, it was a timely and competent bit of political propaganda for the fragile new state. Intended primarily to put Governor Clinton in his place, it also managed to present a sympathetic picture of the Republic and its uncommon people to the outside world, while at the same time giving Vermonters themselves a boisterous and reassuring pat on the back at a moment when their morale was much in need of repair. Copies of it were distributed widely. Ethan saw to that. Several of them were sent to Congress, where this spirited statement of Vermont's position might conceivably make important friends for the Republic. In time, of course, the pamphlet came to the attention of Governor Clinton, and the governor was understandably upset by it. Ethan Allen had called him a fool and a liar and many things in between, and for a time Clinton was sorely tempted to lash out with military force and put an end to this insolence once and for all. In the end, however, he merely issued another proclamation, which in essence was not much different from the first and just about as insulting to the independent Republic of Vermont. "Rather childish than manlike," Ethan called it in the pages of the *Courant*. "Impudence and treason," Clinton countered. And so it went, with much huffing and puffing but little else.

Now, ordinarily all of this would hardly be worth the telling. After all, Yankees and Yorkers had been growling at one another off and on for many years, and the whole thing had become rather commonplace, if not tiresome. On this occasion, however, the angry exchange between Ethan and Governor Clinton took on a special significance, for it was being carefully noted and weighed by the crafty apparatus of His Britannic Majesty's Secret Service in North America. From New York, agent Andrew Elliott dispatched a detailed account of the controversy between "Governor" Allen and Clinton to his home office in London. "Allen will be superior to Clinton and of course extend his views," Elliott concluded, unless the Continental Congress should decide to send troops into Vermont in support of New York. If this were done, then who could say what the consequences would be? The British might even find themselves in a favorable position to develop important friendships among the people of northern New England. At any rate, here in this angry squabble between Vermont and New York was a situation that would bear close watching, and, conceivably, lend itself to fruitful exploitation by His Majesty's Government.

# XI. Courtship with Congress

DURING THE YEARS immediately following its declaration of independence, until its ardor was finally dampened by repeated rebuffs, the Republic of Vermont was unrelenting, if not always wise, in its attempts to win recognition from Congress and admission as a sovereign state into the American Union. For years the Confederation was kept under a constant barrage of petitions and promises from the Vermont authorities; congressional ears were bent and arms twisted, and on occasion men in high Continental office, both civilian and military, were offered thinly veiled bribes of Vermont land to help set their thinking straight. In Philadelphia, where the final decision on Vermont's application would have to be made, agents from the Republic were a common and often bothersome presence. Ethan himself made three separate trips to the capital during the year following his return from captivity, and would have made more if he had met with any real encouragement.

All attempts at obtaining recognition and admission were totally unsuccessful, however, mainly because Governor Clinton continued to stand foursquare in the way. Always sensitive to criticism and intolerant of insubordination, Clinton had developed a strong personal hostility toward the Vermont regime. After all, on more than one occasion he had been publicly affronted and ridiculed by its leaders. Furthermore, the governor held in his own name New York titles to sizable areas of wild lands on the Grants, all of which would become worthless if Vermont were to make good its secession and independence. But aside from his personal feelings, and probably more important, was the fact that George Clinton was the governor of New York, and as one who took his office and its obligations very seriously, he was determined to do all he could to preserve the territorial integrity of his state, which for more than a century had held legal jurisdiction over the entire Grants area. Above all else, he meant to frustrate any and all attempts by the pretended Republic of Vermont to obtain congressional sanction, and in

208

this, as has been mentioned, he was not without powerful backing in Philadelphia.

An important factor in marshaling congressional support for New York's position was the obvious vehemence of Clinton's feelings, and a resultant fear on the part of Congress that recognition of Vermont would so offend the governor that he might take some sort of extreme counter-action. He could conceivably lead his state out of the Union, or, worse yet, he might resort to an armed invasion of Vermont in order to regain the area for his state. This was a thing to be dreaded at any time, but during the pressing days of the Revolution it was unthinkable that such a calamity should be permitted to occur.

In addition to all this was a consideration that loomed particularly large among the southern states: namely, that secession in one area might give encouragement to the same sort of behavior elsewhere. In certain districts of Virginia, the Carolinas, and Pennsylvania there were already disturbing signs of separatist sentiment, and it would not do to permit Vermont to provide a successful example for potential insurrectionists in these sensitive areas. When a South Carolina congressman assured the New York delegation of his state's support in opposing Vermont's application, he explained that he and many of his southern colleagues believed that "the consequences of their [Vermont's] holding their independence would be a means of producing fifty new States, and therefore must not be allowed."

Naturally, Clinton would have preferred that Congress come forward with some sort of strong positive action against Vermont, rather than merely refuse to recognize its existence. Ideally, he would have liked the Confederation to dispatch Continental troops into the defected area—or at least authorize New York to send in troops of its own. But this was out of the question. One war at a time was enough. There were, however, measures short of armed intervention that might have been taken by Congress to bring Confederation pressure to bear against the Republic. An economic boycott, for instance, could have seriously weakened the Vermont regime, and on several occasions the New York delegation, prodded by Clinton, called upon Congress to undertake such a move.

But unfortunately for New York and Governor Clinton, the political situation in Philadelphia made it highly unlikely that any effective kind of repressive action against the Republic of Vermont would or could be authorized by the Confederation. Vermont had many friends in Congress, especially among the New England delegations, and while they were not numerous enough to do much about obtaining recognition for the young Republic, they were nevertheless in a strong enough position to shield it from congressional coercion, and they were obviously determined to do so. Thus, at the time of Ethan's return from prison in the late spring of 1778 and for some years thereafter, the Vermont situation in Congress was at a standoff. For all of its attempts at recognition and admission, Vermont could not break through the wall of opposition erected by New York and kept in constant repair by the inflexible Clinton. At the same time the governor, despite much smoldering and many strong words, was unable to employ the putative powers of the Confederation to any great effect in his unflagging efforts to regain control over the Grants.

Theoretically, the deadlock in Congress should have worked to Vermont's advantage, for time was the Republic's natural ally. Other things being equal, the longer the Republic was able to maintain its independence, the stronger became its arguments for recognition of that independence. In fact, it is conceivable that if Vermont had managed to keep up a reasonably respectable and friendly appearance, it would have won congressional approval long before the end of the war, New York and Governor Clinton notwithstanding. Unfortunately for Vermont, however, while its application lay before Congress in the late 1770's, certain unsalutary events at home succeeded in casting a long shadow over the Republic's image. Many of these were the result of just plain bad luck; others stemmed directly or indirectly from the impetuosity and arrogance of Ethan Allen and his friends of the Arlington junto. But deservedly or otherwise, Vermont during the late 1770's and the early 1780's was plagued by a long parade of misadventures, which, bad enough in themselves, often evoked decidedly unattractive responses from the overly sensitive and jittery government of the Republic. All of this tended to dim the luster of the Arlington regime, especially in the eyes of outsiders, and thereby did much to strengthen the hand of Vermont's enemies and seriously undermine its case before Congress.

Among the most troublesome and persistent sources of mischief for the young Republic was the problem of the sixteen towns. Although eventually this explosive situation would be deliberately exploited for purposes of political manipulation, it originally derived more from the nature of things than from devious intent on the part of the Vermont government or any of its leaders. But regardless of the cause, the Repub-lic's unfortunate involvement in this affair surely succeeded in tarnishing its reputation and alienating important friends. The trouble had begun in the winter prior to Ethan's release from prison, when several towns on the east side of the Connecticut River decided to secede from New Hampshire and cast their lot with the new state of Vermont. This was a natural enough decision. After all, rivers make notoriously poor boundaries, and the New Hampshire towns along the Connecticut felt much closer to their neighbors across the river than to the distant gov-ernment in Exeter, which neither shared nor understood their particular problems. Therefore, in early 1778, sixteen of these towns petitioned the Vermont government for admission into the Republic.

This was not the best of news for Governor Chittenden and his Coun-cil. Actually they would have preferred to leave the New Hampshire towns alone. Here was a risky bit of business that could obviously lead to great trouble. But there was so much sentiment for annexation among Vermonters east of the mountains, that to refuse the towns admission might have had evil repercussions in that area. With hostility toward the Arlington regime already rampant on the east side, Chittenden and his friends saw no reason to add to it. Therefore, when the rumor reached them that if the New Hampshire towns were not admitted, several of the river towns of Vermont might very well secede and join their neighbors across the Connecticut in forming a new state, the Arlington junto hastened to choose what appeared to be the lesser of two evils. In June of 1778, not long after Ethan's return from captivity, the Vermont Assembly, acting upon the recommendation of the Governor and Coun-cil, voted in favor of union with the New Hampshire towns. Thus was begun, as something unwanted, an adventure in expansionism which in varying degrees and ways would affect the fortunes of the Republic of Vermont for a half-dozen years to come.

Nearly two months later, at about the time Ethan was putting the finishing touches to his *Animadversory Address,* Chittenden received a letter from New Hampshire's President Meshech Weare, which, al-though couched in courteous language, left no doubt that his state was more than a little upset over Vermont's annexation of the sixteen towns. For many weeks, Weare explained, he had deliberately postponed writ-ing because he could not bring himself to believe that Vermont had actually committed an act of such great folly:

> When I consider the circumstances of the people west of the Connecticut River, the difficulties they encountered in their first settlement, their late endeavors to organize government among themselves, and the uncertainty of their being admitted as a separate state, I am astonished that they should supply their enemies with arguments against them.

The letter made it clear in a nice way that Vermont could expect plenty of trouble unless it released the towns—and soon. In fact, the possibility was strongly implied that New Hampshire would join forces with New York, since these two States now had similar grievances against the Republic of Vermont.

Weare's message was plain enough to Chittenden and his friends. It was also probably welcome, for by reacting as he was bound to do, President Weare was in effect allying himself with the Arlington junto. With good reason, Chittenden and his Council had from the very beginning been opposed to union with the New Hampshire towns. It had been obvious to them that this act of expansionism against a friendly neighbor would seriously injure the Republic's position and weaken its chances for favorable consideration by Congress. Besides this, however, was a more personal objection by the Vermont leaders: annexation of the sixteen towns would bring about such a dramatic increase in the wealth and population of that part of Vermont lying east of the Green Mountains, that almost certainly political control would soon come to reside there. If the Arlington faction intended to retain its hold on the Republic, it would do well to discourage any aggrandizement of the east side.

In early September, acting on the request of the Governor and Council, Ethan left Bennington for Philadelphia. More than three years before, in company with Seth Warner, he had taken the same route in order to sell the Continental Congress on his idea for a Green Mountain Regiment, which, as matters turned out, he had never been permitted to become a part of. But all that was an eon ago. Now in the late summer of 1778 he went again to the capital. Ostensibly his purpose was to explain and justify to Congress Vermont's recent act of union with the New Hampshire towns. Actually, however, it appears that his principal aim was to disavow the union and do what he could to prepare the way for its destruction by his friends at home.

He reached Philadelphia not a moment too soon. By pure chance, on

the very day of his arrival Congress was scheduled to consider a remonstrance submitted by New Hampshire against Vermont's high-handed
aggression. Wasting no time, Ethan sought out Josiah Bartlett, head of
the New Hampshire delegation, and persuaded him to withdraw the
resolution. The annexation of New Hampshire's river towns, Ethan acknowledged, had been a terrible mistake. He could scarcely understand
how such a thing could have happened, but he promised Bartlett that
Vermont would undo the mischief at once by dissolving the union. In
fact, if this were not done, Ethan Allen himself would petition Congress
against the union and use his influence in any other way that might help
set things right again with Vermont's good friend, New Hampshire. Of
course, he and the Republic of Vermont had no right to ask for any
favor in return. After all, they were only righting a palpable wrong and
they expected no reward for that. It would be gratifying, however, to
know that New Hampshire once again felt kindly toward them and that
the New Hampshire delegation would continue to do what it could for
Vermont in Congress.

Having made his point with Bartlett, Ethan then visited privately with
several other members of Congress, including its President, Henry
Laurens of South Carolina. He found them deeply disturbed almost to a
man by Vermont's recent behavior. Even so staunch a friend as Connecticut's Roger Sherman, who had consistently championed Vermont's
cause in Congress, was shocked by what had happened. Clearly the
union with the New Hampshire towns had done much to injure Vermont's position before Congress, and just as clearly something would
have to be done, and done soon, to repair the damage.

Ethan now had what he wanted—convincing proof that the union was
a blight upon the Republic of Vermont. Back in Bennington by early
October, he headed almost at once for Windsor on the east side where
the autumn meeting of the Assembly was just beginning. On the third
day of the session, he appeared before the Assembly and presented a
grim and considerably over-stated account of his findings in Philadelphia. In it he did his best to impress upon the delegates that disaster
would befall Vermont if the union with the New Hampshire towns were
adhered to:

From what I have heard and seen of the disapprobation, at congress, of the union with sundry towns, east of Connecticut river, I

am sufficiently authorised to offer it as my opinion, that, except this state recede from such union, immediately, the whole power of the Confederacy of the United States of America will join to annihilate the state of Vermont, and to vindicate the right of New-Hampshire, and to maintain inviolate, the articles of confederation, which guarantee to each state their privileges and immunities.

If, on the other hand, the union were dissolved and Vermont were returned to its earlier boundaries, the Republic could doubtless count upon a favorable disposition among most members of Congress. In fact, Ethan continued, the President of Congress himself, the Honorable Henry Laurens, had assured him that with the union out of the way, he as head of Congress would have no objection to Vermont's being recognized and admitted into the Confederation. Later, Laurens would brand this statement by Ethan an out-and-out lie, and he was probably right. But no matter; it helped strengthen Ethan's argument against the union, and in view of the strong support given the New Hampshire towns by the Assembly's east-side members, he needed all the ammunition he could muster.

A few days later, in spite of bitter opposition from the east-siders, the union was dissolved. Ethan and his Arlington friends had triumphed, thanks mainly to Ethan's skillful and rather sneaky maneuvering, and a good thing it probably was for the welfare of the Republic. In an especially ebullient mood, Ethan dashed off a letter to President Weare of New Hampshire, announcing the good news. This great folly that had been brought about by the machinations of "designing men" had been done away with. "The union which Impolitically was for a Time adhered to by a majority of this State is now in the fullest and most explicit manner dissolved." As matters turned out, however, Ethan was wrong in assuming that the last had been heard of the union. The New Hampshire towns had no intention of giving up their courtship of Vermont. Like spurned lovers, they would show a perverse talent for making a nuisance of themselves for many years to come.

Three weeks after the adjournment of the Windsor Assembly in late October, Ethan set out again for Philadelphia in order to report the good news of the dissolution of the union, and then do what he could about getting Vermont admitted into the Confederation of American States. Before leaving Windsor he had arranged for the Assembly to bestow upon him the title of "Agent to the Honble Congress when the Governor and Council Shall Judge Necessary," thereby adorning himself with an official dignity that he had lacked on his previous trip. But, given the way things were, more than a high-sounding title would be needed for him to do much good for Vermont before Congress.

Arriving in Philadelphia in late November, he soon discovered that he might as well have spared himself the journey. He did manage to have a reasonably friendly visit with William Whipple, Bartlett's successor in the New Hampshire delegation, who informed him (quite falsely) that New Hampshire was now entirely reassured and would not give another thought to the unfortunate business about the sixteen towns. Aside from this, however, Ethan was able to accomplish little, for it was clear that even though the union with the New Hampshire towns had been terminated, Congress still remained disinclined to give much favorable attention to Vermont's application for recognition and admission. New York, which certainly had not lost ground as a result of Vermont's recent misadventure, still stood massively between the Republic and congressional approval, and there was no sign that Congress had been sufficiently impressed by Vermont's renunciation of the union to deliberately antagonize Governor Clinton's powerful state. In fact, it appeared that the Confederation, now busy with more important matters, had all but forgotten about Vermont.

On December 4, Ethan left Philadelphia for home. He had failed to achieve anything of much importance on this second trip. Perhaps he had not really expected to, and had merely gone through the motions in order to impress the folks back home. It seems more likely, though, that Ethan who had the habit of believing only what he wanted to believe, had concluded somewhere along the line that once the union with the New Hampshire towns was dissolved, Congress would respond favorably to Vermont's application. If he actually had convinced himself of this, then he must have been sadly disappointed and felt not a little betrayed by the cold reality that confronted him at Philadelphia. Congress had greeted the news of the dissolution with an approving yawn— nothing more. Still, things were not so bad as they might have been. At least the union had been shattered, and regardless of congressional response, or lack of it, there was some satisfaction to Ethan in knowing that political control of the Republic of Vermont had been kept on the west side. The Arlington junto still reigned.

By mid-December Ethan was back home again, where he immediately dashed off a brief newsletter to the people of Vermont, assuring them that things had gone about as expected in Philadelphia and that their "superior lustre both in arms, freedom of constitution and government, and above all righteousness of cause" could not help but win out in the end. He then retired to his inner chamber where he would spend the winter writing up the story of his wartime adventures, from his capture of Ticonderoga in May of 1775 to his release from British prison three years later. It was a winter well spent, for before the frost had left the ground the next spring, he had managed to produce a masterpiece of exciting narrative that would take the country by storm and give a much-needed boost to the morale of the American Patriots, who by mid-1779 were growing mighty tired of their long, uphill struggle for independence.

Ethan called it: *A Narrative of Colonel Ethan Allen's Captivity . . . Containing His Voyages and Travels, With the most remarkable Occurrences respecting him and many other Continental Prisoners of different Ranks and Characters. . . . Interspersed with some Political Observations. Written by Himself and now published for the Information of the Curious in all Nations.* Its title notwithstanding, the book was a brief affair of about twenty-five thousand words which could hardly fail to capture the public imagination. Written in a highly romantic, colorful, and racy manner, it dealt in a grandly patriotic way with the experiences of a real-life, two-fisted American hero who had refused to bend before British brutality. A good, red-blooded tale it was, one that stirred its readers so profoundly that many of them saw fit to liken Ethan to Tom Paine. Of course, given the rousing nature of the story he had to tell, Ethan could scarcely have gone wrong. Still, there is no denying that his talents as a writer were equal to his material. With the skill of a polished professional he carried his readers along, exciting them, amusing them, shocking them, and above all completely absorbing them in his adventures. His style, described by one of his contemporaries as "a singular compound of local barbarisms, scriptural phrases, and oriental wildness," may have become a trifle pompous on occasion, but it never bogged down. Liberal dashes of Allen humor saw to that.

As a record of what actually happened, Ethan's *Narrative* leaves something to be desired. As mentioned earlier, it is far from a model of objectivity. Written throughout from an Ethan Allen point of view, the

book is richly laced with the author's towering prejudices and predilec-
tions, not a few of which are outrageously specious. Furthermore, although probably in the main a true account, the *Narrative* abounds in
errors and distortions of fact—some small and some not so small. Many
of these are doubtless honest mistakes resulting principally from the fact
that the story was written some time after the events described, and was
done almost entirely without benefit of notes or other written references.
In some cases, however, it is apparent that Ethan intentionally lied a
little (or a lot), or left important truths untold. Since he was the only
witness to much of what befell him, there is no way of knowing to what
extent he tampered with the truth, but tamper he surely did. And why
not? After all, it was his own story that he was telling, and as befits an
egotist of Ethan's stature, he wanted to appear in the best possible light.
Still, it was not very conscionable of him to make no mention of
Bendict Arnold's presence at the capture of Fort Ticonderoga, or to fail
to report that it was Seth Warner, rather than Ethan Allen, upon whom
the freemen of the Grants saw fit to confer command of the Green
Mountain Regiment in the summer of 1775.

Reliable or otherwise, Ethan's *Narrative* gave the American people
what they wanted to read at precisely the time they wanted to read it.
And why they were so mightily impressed by it is easy to understand.
Even today it is difficult to read Ethan's story without becoming deeply
moved by the heroism and more than a little amused by the wild his-
trionics of this swashbuckling American frontiersman who refused to
cower before the might of the British Empire. Consider, for instance, the
following passages, written about his confinement at Pendennis Castle,
where for more than two weeks he fully expected to be led out and
hanged at any time:

> I now clearly recollect that my mind was so resolved, that I
> would not have trembled or shewn the least fear, as I was sensible
> that it could not alter my fate, nor do more than reproach my
> memory, make my last act despicable to my enemies, and eclipse
> the other actions of my life. For I reasoned thus, that nothing was
> more common than for men to die . . . and that as death was the
> natural consequence of animal life to which the laws of nature sub-
> ject mankind, to be timorous and uneasy as to the event and man-
> ner of it, was inconsistent with the character of a philosopher and
> soldier.

But even while faced by the specter of the gallows, Ethan remained the inveterate showman, taking obvious delight in being the object of much public curiosity and attention:

It was a common thing for me to be taken out of close confinement, into a spacious green in the castle, where numbers of gentlemen and ladies were ready to see and hear me. I often entertained such audiences with harangues on the impracticability of Great Britain's conquering the then colonies of America. . . .

Among the great numbers of people who came to the castle . . . some gentlemen told me that they had come fifty miles on purpose to see me, and desired to ask me a number of questions, and to make free with me in conversation. I gave for answer that I chose freedom in every sense of the word. Then one of them asked me what my occupation in life had been. I answered him that I was a conjurer by profession. He replied that I conjured wrong at the time I was taken; and I was obliged to own, that I mistook a figure at that time, but that I had conjured them out of Ticonderoga. . . .

At one of these times I asked a gentleman for a bowl of punch, and he ordered his servant to bring it, which he did, and offered it to me, but I refused to take it from the hand of his servant; he then gave it to me with his own hand, refusing to drink with me in consequence of my being a state criminal: However, I took the punch and drank it all down at one draught, and handed the gentleman the bowl; this made the spectators as well as myself merry.

Later in Ethan's *Narrative* there appears an account of the great joy he experienced when, in early 1778 while imprisoned in the Provost Jail at New York, he learned that France had entered the war against England. As soon as the glorious news reached him, Ethan knew for certain that independence for young America had become a reality. Surely even the British, slow-witted though they were, could understand the immensity of what had happened. They had lost the war, and they had best recognize the fact:

Vaunt no more, old England! consider you are but an island! and that your power has been continued longer than the exercise of your humanity. Order your broken vanquished batallions to retire from America, the scene of your cruelties. Go home and repent in dust and sackcloth for your aggravated crimes. The cries of bereaved parents, widows, and orphans, reach the heavens and you are abominated by every friend to America. Take your friends the tories with you, and be gone, and drink deep of the cup of humiliation. . . . Your veteran soldiers are fallen in America, and your glory is departed. Be quiet and pay your debts, especially for the hire of the Hessians. There is no other way for you to get into credit again, but by reformation and plain honesty, which you have despised; for your power is by no means sufficient to support your vanity. . . . I have something of a smattering of philosophy, and understand human nature in all its stages tolerably well; am thoroughly acquainted with your national crimes, and assure you that they not only cry aloud for Heaven's vengeance, but excite mankind to rise up against you. Virtue, wisdom and policy are in a national sense, always connected with power, or in other words power is their offspring, and such power as is not directed by virtue, wisdom and policy never fails finally to destroy itself as yours has done. It is so in the nature of things, and unfit that it would be otherwise; for if it was not so, vanity, injustice, and oppression might reign triumphant forever. I know you have individuals who still retain their virtue, and consequently their honor and humanity. Those I really pity, as they must more or less suffer in the calamity, in which the nation is plunged headlong; but as a nation I hate and despise you.

The *Narrative* was published first in the tri-weekly *Pennsylvania Packet* of Philadelphia, where it ran in serial form during the late spring of 1779. It was then brought out as a book by a Philadelphia printer and immediately became a best-seller. Priced at ten Continental dollars, a modest amount at a time when Continental dollars were worth very little, the *Narrative* went through eight editions within the first two years. By 1854, seventy-five years after publication, it had appeared in nineteen different editions in eleven cities. If he had lived and written at a later time, Ethan might have collected a substantial sum in royalties, but in those pre-copyright days it is unlikely that the book brought him much in the way of money. It certainly paid off handsomely in acclaim and admiration for its author, however, and to Ethan this meant a great deal. Americans of high station and low read of his amazing adventures and marveled at them—and at him. In neighboring New Hampshire, the learned Jeremy Belknap, Congregational minister of Dover who would one day be ranked among America's foremost historians, wrote to a friend after reading Ethan's story in the *Packet:* "I think him an original in his way, . . . as rough and boisterous as the scenes he has passed through."

His friend agreed:

> Allen is really an original; at least I never met a genius like him. Had his natural talents been cultivated by a liberal education, he would have made no bad figure among the men of science; but perhaps his want of such an education is not to be lamented, as, unless he had more grace it would make him a dangerous member of society.

With the matter of the sixteen towns temporarily settled, Vermont's foreign relations entered a period of unusual tranquility. During the winter and early spring of 1779 the Republic was all but ignored by its neighbors and by the Confederation Congress. It was almost as if the outside world had conspired to forget that there was or ever had been such a thing as an independent Vermont. Even the British joined in the spirit of things by refusing to budge from their bases at Montreal and St. John's.

Within the Republic itself, the business of living went on for its now nearly forty thousand people. While children with bundles of hay bound about their feet traipsed through the snow to tend the stock and carry in cordwood, hard-bitten men dressed in homespun and deerskin used these cold, brief days to wrest another acre or two from the wilderness. Inside the roughhewn homes the womenfolk, confined to their little world of smoky semidarkness, made meals and clothes and candles and soap, and bore multitudes of children without much fuss or bother before the open hearth of a hardwood fire. And lest people such as these be tempted to stray from the path of righteousness, the Vermont Assembly that winter, in a move that could hardly fail to improve the Republic's image in the eyes of the Almighty (and perhaps the Continental Congress as well), passed a series of blue laws that provided stiff punishment for blasphemy, Sabbath-breaking, and a number of lesser outrages. Fortunately, the moral fervor of the Assembly was not fully shared in by the governor and his Council. As a result, although the laws would remain on the books for many years to come, mainly because it would have been politically unwise to repeal them, they were never seriously enforced by Governor Chittenden or his successors. The Code of Leviticus obviously had no place in the rough-and-tumble life of eighteenth-century Vermont, and a good thing for Ethan that it didn't. Otherwise, as one of the greatest blasphemers in the Republic, he could conceivably have spent the rest of his natural life in jail—or worse.

In early April, soon after completing his *Narrative,* Ethan rode up to Arlington to spend some time with his family and sit in on a number of meetings with the Governor and Council. Mary was pregnant again and due to deliver within a matter of a few weeks, but of greater interest to Ethan was the concern on the part of Chittenden, Ira, and the others over reports of growing unrest across the mountains. It was no secret that anti-government feeling had been building up for some time in the east side's Cumberland County. Yorker sentiment in this area had always been strong, especially among the more prominent settlers, and this in itself had been worrisome enough for the Arlington junto. Now it appeared that the Yorkers had been joined in their hostility towards the government by many of their neighbors who, having favored the union with the New Hampshire towns, had been left bitterly disappointed by its dissolution, and consequently disenchanted with the Republic—or at least with its leaders.

Evidence of this feeling had been manifested a couple of months before when, after delivering an angry remonstrance against the dissolution of the union, ten east-side members strode indignantly out of the Assembly. Since that time the situation across the mountains had worsened considerably. Ominous talk of secession and worse could be heard throughout Cumberland County, and it even appeared that several of the east-side militia companies had come under the control of the grumblers. Sooner or later serious mischief was bound to erupt in that quarter, and Ethan and his Arlington friends meant to meet it head-on.

Back in Bennington after his Arlington visit, Ethan had just put the finishing touches to a day or two of high revelry when news of the expected trouble reached him. Since May 3 had been the first anniversary of his release from prison, he had thought it appropriate to celebrate the occasion in a fitting manner. Dedicating the festivities to the good men of Cork who had so handsomely come to his relief during a dark hour, Ethan invited friends (and even enemies) from far and wide to join him for a little "rural felicity" at Fay's tavern. The response was heartening; so much so that Bennington took on something of a holiday air, and the long room of the Catamount rocked with the sounds of good fellowship, including, of course, the booming voice of Ethan Allen recounting one more time the story of his amazing adventures in captivity. It was a great party, and Ethan decided then and there that he would observe all future anniversaries of this important date in the same way.

Scarcely had the merriment died down when the governor's message arrived by dispatch rider from Arlington. It told of evil doings on the east side. Uprisings had broken out that previous week in Putney, and had spread rapidly to the surrounding towns of Hinsdale, Guilford, Brattleboro, and Westminster. Indeed, it appeared that most of Cumberland County was now in a state of insurrection that seriously threatened the "peace and dignity of the Republic." Actually, the agitation, which had been triggered by recent attempts on the part of the Arlington government to draft men for the Continental Army, was much less serious than reported. It was true that angry crowds had assembled in different parts of Cumberland County and had caused something of a ruckus. In a few instances they had even gone so far as to prevent proper enforcement of the law. But the disturbances had been largely unorganized and sporadic, and more in the nature of protest than rebellion. Thus far neither person nor property had been injured, but it was clear that the authority of the government had been openly challenged. Something would surely have to be done about that, and Ethan was obviously the man to do it:

> You are hereby commanded [read the Governor's letter to Ethan], in the name of the freemen of Vermont, to engage one hundred able bodied effective men as voluntiers in the County of Bennington, and to march them into the County of Cumberland to assist the Sheriff of said County to execute such orders as he has or may receive from the civil authorities of this State. . . .
> Hereof you may not fail. . . .
>
> Thomas Chittenden, Captain General

Ethan rose to the occasion in splendid fashion. Naturally. It was precisely the sort of thing that he was best at and probably enjoyed most. Despite the fact that his call for volunteers went out at the beginning of the planting season, he was able to recruit his little army with surprising speed. Within a few days he was proceeding eastward toward Cumberland County, impressively mounted at the head of a column of well over one hundred ununiformed troops carrying everything from fowling pieces to cutlasses. Along the route of march others joined him, until his force numbered nearly two hundred and fifty men, many if not most of them former Green Mountain Boys who had served with Ethan in the old days and now welcomed the opportunity to take the field under him once again. It appears, in fact, that the expedition against the east side in the spring of 1779 was something of a class reunion for those old irregulars who, with sprigs of evergreen jutting from their caps, had taunted the Yorkers so successfully before the Revolution and marched and plundered with Ethan at Ticonderoga.

About the middle of May, Ethan crossed the mountains and proceeded to descend with great swagger upon the wayward towns of Cumberland County. It was really a very simple operation, done in the style that had served Ethan so well in the past. Not a hand was raised against him as he roared through town after town, promising unspeakable retribution and frightening the inhabitants half out of their wits. At times, just to prove that he meant business, he would deliver a smart blow with the flat of his sword across the head or buttocks of someone unfortunate enough to rub him the wrong way, but this was the extent of the violence. Throughout the entire Cumberland campaign, nobody was killed and nobody was seriously injured. As so often before, Ethan brought men into line by bluster rather than bloodshed. He was obviously still an expert at cowing others into submission. People believed this noisy giant when he raised himself up high in the stirrups, brandished his huge sword about his head, and swore he would skin them alive if they did not behave. They believed him, and they behaved. "This Ethan Allen," remarked a frightened Brattleboro Yorker, "is more to be dreaded than Death with all its Terrors."

Under Ethan's supervision about three dozen of the more prominent Yorkers were arrested and confined in the county jail at Westminster. It was well known that most of them had been involved in encouraging acts of defiance against the Vermont government and in attempting to bring about a return of New York jurisdiction. Only two weeks before their arrest, many of them had been active in setting up committees throughout the various towns of the county for the express purpose of "opposing the pretended state of Vermont." Some had even gone so far as to appeal to Governor Clinton to send troops into the Republic in order to put an end to "the lawless rule of riatous men." Clearly these prisoners, or at least most of them, had in one way or another amply demonstrated their hostility toward the Republic. They, and such as they, had been the cause of most of the mischief on the east side, including the recent uprisings, and for all of this they should be made to pay. As matters turned out, however, they were made to pay surprisingly little, and might even have got away scot-free had it not been for a timely bit of browbeating by Ethan.

When a few days after their arrest the prisoners were brought to trial before the Vermont Superior Court at Westminster, it at once became apparent that the court was not disposed to deal very harshly with them. For all of their wicked behavior they were charged only with breaking the peace of the Republic, mainly because, according to Blackstone's *Commentaries,* the evidence against them would support nothing stronger. Furthermore, when held up to the legal light of Blackstone, the charges against three of the prisoners appeared so unsupportable that they were dropped at the outset of the trial on motion from the Prosecuting Attorney, Noah Smith. But these legal shenanigans were to be permitted to go only so far. When early in the trial the Judge ruled favorably on a motion by Defense Counsel Stephen Bradley, that charges against three of the other prisoners also be dropped, the decorum of the court was suddenly shattered by loud protests from Ethan Allen, who with mounting disgust had been witnessing the proceedings from the rear of the courtroom. Rising from his seat, the angry giant strode up the aisle to the front of the room, where he took a position before the bench and proceeded to lecture judge, jury, and lawyers alike.

Assuring his astonished listeners that he didn't care a good Billy-go-to-hell about Blackstone ("With my logic and reasoning from the eternal fitness of things I can upset your Blackstones, your whitestones, your gravestones, and your brimstones"), he warned all concerned that they would be making a grave mistake if they permitted the defendants to squirm free:

> Fifty miles I have come through the woods with my brave men, to support the civil with the military arm; to quell any disturbances that should arise; and to aid the sheriff and the court in prosecuting these Yorkers—the enemies of our noble State. I see however that some of them by the quirks of this artful lawyer, Bradley, are escaping from the punishment they so richly deserve, and I find

also that this little Noah Smith is far from understanding his business, since he at one time moves for a prosecution and in the next wishes to withdraw it. Let me warn your Honour to be on your guard lest these delinquents should slip through your fingers.

And so saying, he stomped out of the room, leaving the stunned court to ponder his remarks.

Shortly thereafter the rest of the prisoners were found guilty as charged and fined a total of £1,500, or about 5,000 Continental dollars. In addition to these prisoners, most of the militia officers of the Cumberland towns had been rounded up and incarcerated for a time, but then released without punishment after "a friendly admonition." All of this represented lenient treatment for insurrectionists, Ira later commented. Under the laws of the Republic, each of the guilty could have been inflicted with "not exceeding forty stripes save one," but in this case the offenders were totally spared the lash by a forgiving and warmhearted government. In the future, such leniency could not be expected. Not long after the Cumberland uprisings the Vermont Assembly decreed that thenceforth severe corporal punishment would mandatorily be meted out to all "opposers of the Republic." A special sort of treatment would be given those persons within the Republic who claimed to act as public officers under any other authority than that of the government of Vermont or the Continental Congress. Anyone so doing would be flogged, have his right ear cut off, and be branded on the forehead.

From Westminster, Ethan rode directly up-river to Windsor where the Vermont Assembly was just opening its spring session. There, after reporting on the Cumberland County trouble, he received the grateful thanks of the delegates and, because he now wished it so, was elected Commanding General of the Vermont Militia. Now he held a regular position within the officialdom of the Republic. It was his first, and also his last. Why he decided at this time to accept the responsibilities and restraints of office is not clear. Certainly he had not lacked for power in his role of friend and unofficial advisor to the Arlington regime. Indeed, since soon after his return from prison a year before, he had been first citizen of the Republic, and most everyone had recognized the fact— including Ethan himself. His influence on affairs of state had been, if not absolute, then surely unequaled. However, he was too much of a show-off to be content to work off-stage. This was Ira's way, but not Ethan's. Perhaps it was the excitement of riding at the head of his Boys once again that made him decide to take his rightful place in the limelight where he could be seen and applauded by all. At any rate, he was now an official figure, having been placed by his friends and neighbors in command of the Republic's military establishment, and he would play his new role for all it was worth.

The Cumberland County campaign cost the Republic about $4,000, including $80 in military pay to Ethan and nearly a quarter of that amount to each of his men.* Since the prisoners had been made to pay $5,000 in fines, the Republic, in addition to delivering a lesson in manners to the east side, had managed to make a slight profit on the operation. Unfortunately, however, the cost of the Cumberland campaign would not be reckoned solely in terms of inflated Continental currency. At precisely the time the leaders of the vulnerable young state should have been on their best behavior, they had committed an act of such undisguised aggressiveness as to stir up an almost unanimous indignation among the members of Congress. This time Ethan and his Arlington friends had gone too far to be ignored by the Confederation, and Governor Clinton meant to see to it that they were not.

On the same day that the news of Ethan's doings reached him, a very much aroused George Clinton sent off an angry letter to the President of the Continental Congress. The hour had come for Congress to quit stalling, Clinton warned. The situation in New York's eastern counties was obviously out of control; prominent persons had been abused and humiliated for their loyalty to the government of New York, and armed outlaws had terrorized the citizenry. Governor Clinton expected the Confederation to undertake measures against the pretended Republic of Vermont—NOW! Later that same day the Governor fired off a blistering note to the members of the New York delegation at Philadelphia, ordering them in no uncertain terms to get things moving against Vermont. They could begin by making it clear to their congressional colleagues that the governor of New York stood ready to detach one thousand troops from the Continental Army and send them to Cumberland County unless Congress took some positive action within the next few days. As he had on more than one occasion before, Clinton was calling upon the Confederation to do its duty by the state of New York, but this

---

* Apparently this was the first time that Ethan was paid for military services against domestic enemies. There is no evidence that he ever received any kind of payment for his pre-war activities against the Yorkers.

time he was not asking, he was demanding, and this time he would get results of a sort.

In early June, only a couple of weeks after the Cumberland County affair, the delegates at Philadelphia passed a resolution of apology to New York for their delay in attending to the Vermont matter, and ordered that a copy of the resolution be sent forthwith to Governor Clinton. At the same time Congress, by a virtually unanimous vote, appointed a five-man committee to "repair to the inhabitants of a certain district known as the New Hampshire Grants," and report back on the true nature of the situation there. All this was certainly a move in the right direction—much more than Congress had ever done before. President John Jay, himself a Yorker, thought it a very good thing indeed. At least the members of Congress had finally bestirred themselves and agreed to become directly involved in the Vermont controversy, and now that they had taken this first step, Jay wrote to Clinton, "they might with more ease be led to a farther and more effectual interposition."

But the still-smoldering Clinton was far from pleased. Neither in its resolution of apology nor in setting up its committee had Congress uttered a single word of reproach against the perpetrators of the recent atrocities in Cumberland County, "and what makes this silence the more extraordinary is that Ethan Allen, having the rank of Colonel in the Service of the United States, was a principal actor in this outrage." The governor would hold his troops in check for the time being, but he expected Congress to come up with something more than an investigating committee before it had finished with the matter. Just to be on the safe side, Clinton wrote to General Washington asking him to return the six brass cannons the state of New York had lent to the Continental Army, and alerting the General to the fact that New York flour and recruits intended for the war effort might have to be diverted for use against Vermont. Washington was gravely disturbed. He would return the cannons, of course, but he viewed the situation as "pregnant with very unhappy consequences. . . . Much is to be apprehended, if this State on whose wisdom and energy I have always had the strongest reliance, should turn its resources into a different channel."

Later that same month, just before the congressional committee arrived in Bennington to begin its investigation, Ethan and his good friend Jonas Fay set out for Philadelphia on orders from the Governor and Council. Their mission: repair if possible the damage done Vermont's position before Congress by the recent foray onto the east side, and, as always, attempt to give a push to the Republic's application for admission into the Confederation of American States. Having been notified by informers that Ethan Allen would soon be passing through New York, Governor Clinton gave long thought to having him seized. Feeling as he did about Ethan, Clinton would probably have liked nothing better than to have him thrown into the deepest dungeon in the state and kept there forever. But in the end the governor concluded that such a move, although entirely justified and certainly pleasant to contemplate, might have an unfortunate effect upon congressional opinion. Ethan and his friend were allowed to pass in peace.

Arriving in Philadelphia in early July, the two emissaries at once sought and obtained permission to lay papers before Congress, although not in person as Ethan had hoped. These papers, which, as it turned out, would be given only perfunctory notice by the delegates, represented the Republic's official version of "the late unhappiness" in Cumberland County. Prominent among them was a letter written by Ethan, with assists from Jonas in spelling and grammar, which rather arrogantly proclaimed that Vermont was not ashamed of what it had done and would welcome an investigation by Congress at any time. To those who were unacquainted with the realities of Vermont politics, and there were very few in Congress who still were, it must have seemed odd indeed that this Ethan Allen, a person who held no regular civilian office within the pretended Republic of Vermont, should presume to pronounce so authoritatively upon important affairs of state. To Ethan, however, it did not seem odd at all. It was a natural thing for the leader of his people to do.

That much taken care of, Ethan then hustled about among the congressional delegations, as he had on previous visits to Philadelphia, in an attempt to promote enthusiasm for Vermont's application. He must have known that he was operating at a decided disadvantage, for this was clearly not the most propitious time for selling Vermont to Congress. Still, he had always been a strong believer in pressing the offensive, even when the opposition appeared to have things pretty much under control, and he saw no reason now to do differently. Furthermore, on this occasion he had been authorized by the government of the Republic to promise Congress that if Vermont were admitted, it would assume its share of the Continental war debt from the beginning of the hostilities with Great Britain.

This apparently struck Ethan as being a particularly valuable bargaining point, but he soon discovered that no one else in Philadelphia, except Jonas, seemed to think so. In fact, although nobody would say as much in so many words, Congress at this time was obviously in no mood to have dealings with the Republic of Vermont on any terms or under any circumstances. Thus on this, his third trip to Philadelphia within a year, Ethan accomplished even less than he had before. Indeed, the situation, next to hopeless at the time of his arrival in the City, was probably even worse when he left. It doubtless would have been better for the Republic if he had stayed home, for his appearance in Philadelphia so soon after his blustering behavior in Cumberland County must have done more to antagonize than appease.

But the trip was not a total loss—at least not for Ethan. It was an experience which, taken together with his earlier visits to Congress, caused him to take a harder look at the way things were, or seemed to be, in Philadelphia. Three times he had gone to Congress on friendly and generous business for the Republic of Vermont, and three times he had received little or no satisfaction. Worse yet, three times he had been given rather short shrift. He had not even been permitted to appear on the floor of Congress to argue Vermont's case. Up until now he had allowed himself to be deluded by his own colossal optimism. He had told himself and the folks back home that sooner or later the Confederation was bound to recognize and admit Vermont. Now he was not so sure. In fact, all indications were that Congress was inclining more and more toward the side of the Yorkers. Barring a dramatic change of some sort, Vermont could probably expect little good and much bad from the American Confederation, and it behooved Ethan Allen and his Arlington friends to make their future plans accordingly.

# XII. Flirting with Treason

THE Cumberland County affair marked a turning point of sorts in Vermont's relations with the American States. Unlike the earlier dalliance with the New Hampshire towns, it would bring forth immediate and serious repercussions. Up to this time there had been good reason to suppose that, Yorker opposition notwithstanding, the Republic of Vermont would eventually receive recognition from Congress and take its place as a sovereign state alongside the other members of the American Confederation. Now, however, all this would change. From the moment the news of Ethan's east-side expedition became known, Vermont's prospects for recognition, or survival for that matter, grew steadily and dramatically worse. The arrival of the congressional committee in Bennington during the early summer of 1779 signaled this change, for although the committee would accomplish virtually nothing, its very presence carried an ominous significance. At last Congress had taken action on the matter of Vermont, and this fact alone would be enough to set in motion a number of forces and counter-forces that would cause considerable trouble and apprehension for the young Republic.

Not long after the committee's visit, New Hampshire, in a move that would have amused and delighted Benning Wentworth, reasserted its ancient claims to the Grants area. Shortly thereafter, Massachusetts followed suit by resurrecting its own claims, dating back to the early seventeenth century, to large sections of southern Vermont. The reason for all this is not hard to find. It was beginning to appear that the days of independent Vermont were numbered, and New Hampshire and Massachusetts, although having no strong feelings against Vermont and in fact holding certain sympathies for it, intended to get as large a share of the feast as possible. Their motives were partly those of land hunger —but only partly. Perhaps even more compelling was the fear of an aggrandized New York. As befitted all good Yankees, the freemen of Massachusetts and New Hampshire had little love for the Yorkers or their institutions, and they meant to see to it that the New York presence was kept as far away from home as possible. New Hampshire, which stood to share its entire western boundary with New York along the Connecticut River unless something could be done to prevent it, was especially upset by the prospect. Writing from Philadelphia, the New Hampshire delegation in Congress predicted an early judgment on the Vermont matter in New York's favor, and urged President Weare to present New Hampshire's claims before Congress as rapidly and forcefully as possible:

> We must exert every Nerve to Prevent a State by her vast extent of Territory, and still greater Claims, already Troublesome to her Neighbors and Tyrannical to the last degree over all such as are the unhappy victims of their resentment, from Extending jurisdiction so as to circumvolve the State of New Hampshire.

By mid-August both New Hampshire and Massachusetts were vigorously pressing their respective claims before the Continental Congress, much to the disgust of the New York delegation and the consternation of the Republic of Vermont.

With the problem of what to do about the New Hampshire Grants obviously becoming more critical, Congress resolved in late September that it would give its final decision on the matter on February 1 of the following year. In the meantime, by order of Congress, those three states directly involved in the dispute, together with the so-called Republic of Vermont, were to take no action to disturb the status quo. A special warning was given President Chittenden to refrain from attempting to exercise authority over persons unwilling to recognize the Arlington government, and to suspend all confiscation of property and granting of public lands. In effect, Congress was ordering Vermont to stop functioning as an independent State, at least until the Confederation Government could pronounce upon its fate, and the tone of this injunction certainly made it appear that Congress meant business.

When the news of all this reached Ethan, he had just returned to Bennington after a two-hundred-mile round trip to the little town of Dresden in Grafton County, New Hampshire. Here he had taken his most recent pamphlet to be printed by Alden Spooner, who a few months earlier had set himself up in business after having moved the venerable Stephen Day Press up from Cambridge, Massachusetts. Although living and working across the river in New Hampshire, Spooner served as the official printer for the Arlington government until Vermont got a press of its own in the early 1780's. Consequently, many of the early documents of the Republic, together with two of Ethan's pamphlets, were turned out on the Day Press, the oldest in America, and as a result are today much sought after by collectors of native incunabula.

Ethan's newest pamphlet, entitled *A Vindication of the Opposition of the Inhabitants of Vermont to the Government of New York and of their Right to form into an Independent State,* was largely a rehash of old arguments, but it was done in such a highly spirited style that it could not help but have an appeal of sorts, even to Vermont's enemies. Remarked that estimable Yorker, John Jay, after having studied a copy of it that had managed to reach his desk in Congress: "There is a quaintness, impudence, and Art in it." Written not long after Ethan had returned from his disappointing trip to Philadelphia in July of that year, the pamphlet was actually an attempt to take Vermont's case directly to the people. Obviously congressmen cared more for politics than for rectitude and justice, and Ethan had all but despaired of reaching them. Thus he addressed his *Vindication* to "the consideration of the impartial World," proclaiming for all to hear that Vermont was right and New York was wrong, but right or wrong the people of Vermont would continue to cherish their liberty and would never, nay, could never, live under New York jurisdiction. Published at public expense by order of the Governor and Council, the pamphlet was distributed widely among the various states and units of the Continental Army.

Brother Ira later remarked that Ethan's *Vindication* did much to strengthen Vermont's position in the eyes of the outside world, but in reality it probably changed little or nothing, for this was not a time when words—especially Vermont words—could be expected to have much effect. Still, in view of the repercussions following the recent Cumberland County affair, a statement of some sort from the Vermont authorities was certainly in order. It was a thing that really needed doing, and once again it was Ethan who did it.

Formal notification of Congress' restraining order was received by the Vermont government just as the Assembly was about to open its autumn session in the west-side town of Manchester. Sitting in on the session at the request of President Chittenden, Ethan soon discovered that the members of the Assembly had been noticeably shaken by the recent action of Congress, and with good reason, for the directive from Philadelphia was clearly intended to be an ultimatum. Congress expected Vermont to adhere strictly to the provisions of the September resolution. If Vermont failed to do so, Congress would "on pledge of faith" unleash punitive measures. In his *History of Vermont* written several years after Ethan's death, Ira described the atmosphere at Manchester as a decidedly apprehensive one. Obviously worried by the gravity of the situation, perhaps as many as nine-tenths of the delegates, according to Ira's reckoning, appeared ready to vote in favor of compliance with the congressional injunction.

Ethan saw to it that they did not, however. It took him the better part of two weeks to do so, but he finally managed to persuade the Assembly to resolve by unanimous vote that neither Congress nor anyone else had the authority to interfere in the affairs of the sovereign Republic of Vermont, and that "this State ought to support their right to Independence." If Ira can be believed, and there is no reason to doubt him in this instance, it was Ethan acting practically alone who succeeded in steering the Assembly away from a course of timid acquiescence. And a good thing that he was able to do so, for to have given in to Congress on this occasion would in all likelihood have resulted in further encroachments against Vermont's sovereignty, and eventually its total extinction. So at least believed Ethan Allen, and he was probably right. At any rate, he was able to make the members of the Vermont Assembly think so.

To make sure that Congress would have a proper understanding of Vermont's intentions, Ethan persuaded the Assembly to commit an act of unmistakable defiance. At his request, a three-man committee was set up for the purpose of preparing the way for the issuance of land grants. Although not even a member of the Assembly, Ethan was chosen to head this committee, which was instructed to "see what petitions there are on file in the Secretary's office that can be granted this session." Plenty of petitions were found, and before the Assembly adjourned on October 27, several thousand of acres of wild land had been granted, all in direct and open defiance of Congress. At the same time the Assembly also ordered that confiscation of property belonging to supposed Tories be continued, despite congressional proscription of the practice. The Republic of Vermont was giving clear notice that it meant to keep on its independent course, whether Congress approved or not.

Among those land petitions passed upon by the Manchester Assembly was the famous Two Heroes Grant, so called in honor of Ethan and his old friend of Ticonderoga days, Sam Herrick. Composed of two large islands in the northern part of Lake Champlain, the grant included a total area of 40,000 acres, or nearly sixty-three square miles. However, although his name stood conspicuously at the head of the list of grantees, Ethan was actually only one among three hundred and sixty-five co-equal proprietors. Consequently, his share of the grant came to little more than 100 acres—hardly an immense spread. And this is a point worth noting in view of the claims and innuendos that continue to circulate concerning the supposedly vast amounts of land granted to Ethan by the Republic of Vermont. The truth of the matter is that, for all of his extensive holdings, Ethan received very little land, directly or otherwise, from the Republic. He acquired most of his property through purchase of Wentworth titles, sometimes as a member of the Onion River Company and sometimes as an independent speculator.

It is true that over a period of years he submitted frequent petitions to the Assembly for grants which represented a very sizable acreage in the aggregate, but though he himself often headed (quite illegally of course) the land committee of the Assembly, few of his petitions came to fruition, perhaps because he neglected to take the trouble to follow through on them. In his position of first citizen during the years immediately following his return from prison, he could have got just about anything he wanted from the Republic, within reason. And obviously there were many things that he did get. There is no indication, however, that favored treatment in the granting of public lands was one of them. In fact, according to the Vermont Land Records, from 1779 until his death ten years later, Ethan received from the Republic a total of no more than 1,500 acres of land—on all of which he paid the customary fee. This was a considerably smaller amount than that received by at least a dozen other petitioners, and less than one-fourth of the acreage granted to his brother Ira during the same period.

Land, of course, was the Republic's greatest asset. It was, in a sense, like money in the bank, and the government of the Republic used it as such. Public debts were sometimes paid with it when the treasury was empty or low, and from time to time political wheels were greased by a judicious grant to the proper person. It was in the conduct of its "foreign policy," however, that the Republic showed its greatest adroitness in parceling out its wild lands. Fully aware of the fact that land spoke a persuasive language, the government of Vermont from an early date distributed grants liberally among important outsiders whose friendship might in some way and at some time prove helpful. Because the Republic very cleverly assigned minimal fees to these grants, they could not exactly be considered bribes, and were therefore accepted in good conscience (or otherwise) by men of recognized probity who would certainly have responded indignantly to the slightest suggestion of bribery. Still, the result was the same: for a price, the sympathy of great men was enlisted on the side of the Republic of Vermont.

Naturally, the beneficiaries of such a generous policy had to be chosen with great care, and Ethan, as chairman of the land committee during much of the time from 1779 to 1781, saw to it that they were. Ordered by the Assembly to "determine what persons will most conduce to the welfare of this State," Ethan's committee arranged for Vermont land to reach a number of the right people. Among them were members of Congress and many of the state governments, together with high-ranking officers in the Continental Army. Understandably disturbed by the news that two of his generals, Gates and Glover, had accepted Vermont land on bargain terms, Washington wondered to what extent Vermont's "very politic measures to enlarge and increase its influence" had already corrupted his army. How many other officers of the Northern Department held Vermont land titles? It was to be hoped not many. After all, the time might come when, at the order of Congress, Washington would have to call upon these very officers to lead Continental troops against the pretended government of Vermont. And then what? With how much enthusiasm would a man be apt to fight who stood to lose his land by winning?

All things considered, it was not, of course, very nice of Vermont to resort to such low tactics, but it is possible that the Republic's considerable success in distributing its lands in the right way among the right people meant the margin of survival for independent Vermont. Writing from Philadelphia in the autumn of 1780, Ethan's old land-jobbing enemy, James Duane, informed Governor Clinton that "the use made by Vermont of public land grants . . . have in my judgment had no inconsiderable weight" in preventing Congress from arriving at a "rapid and just settlement" of the Grants controversy. In fact, Duane had recently been told by a member of Rhode Island's congressional delegation that, as a matter of fixed policy, that state intended to continue its determined support of Vermont's claims to independence. Why? Because "many of the principal people in Rhode Island have accepted grants under the assumed State." The Rhode Island governor himself was deeply involved, and "he has desired the delegates to take care of his Interests." Naturally, rather than run the risk of "vacating our grants," the leaders of Rhode Island would do all they reasonably could to sustain the Republic of Vermont. And this, of course, was precisely what Ethan and his friends had counted on all along.

After having succeeded in persuading its members to defy the recent resolution by Congress, Ethan got the Manchester Assembly to send him to Massachusetts "and other places contiguous to negociate the public business." The intention was that he should act as a sort of minister plenipotentiary in an attempt to improve things between Vermont and its neighbors, especially Massachusetts and New Hampshire. As matters turned out, however, his experience in Massachusetts ended so badly that Ethan never did get to the "other places contiguous." Appearing before the General Court in Boston one cheerless afternoon in November, Ethan offered to buy out Massachusetts' claims to Vermont, in the hope that if Massachusetts agreed to bow out, New Hampshire would do likewise. Actually his mission was doomed from the outset, for Massachusetts had no intention of abandoning its claims, especially since it was now being rumored that a secret agreement had been reached between New Hampshire and New York to partition Vermont between them at the crest of the Green Mountains.

Exactly what happened to Ethan in Boston is not certain, but it is clear that his visit there turned out very unhappily. According to one report, when Massachusetts refused Vermont's offer Ethan lost his temper, berated the members of the General Court for their avarice and stupidity and "exposed himself to so much resentment that he thought it prudent to withdraw precipitously. Upon the whole his pompous person in Boston has ended in his own disgrace."

Whatever it was that happened in Boston, Ethan returned to Bennington in very ill humor. With an assist from his friend Jonas Fay he dashed off a brief pamphlet entitled: *A Concise Refutation of the Claims of New Hampshire and Massachusetts Bay to the Territory of Vermont.* Published as a State Paper by order of the Governor and Council, the pamphlet was not the best of Ethan's works, but it was certainly the angriest. Writing in a tone of great bitterness, Ethan accused New Hampshire and Massachusetts of having conspired with New York to swallow up Vermont. As a result the Republic found itself "under the disagreeable necessity of publicly exposing the imbecility and depravity of those governments." This was strong language, but no stronger than the situation demanded. Vermonters had no intention of giving up their independence which was "not of man or the will of man . . . but HEAVEN BORN." And then, in a direct slap at Congress, Ethan declared that the people of Vermont would not submit their freedom "to the arbitrament of any tribunal below the stars . . . but are determined to hold it fast, except it be torn from them by the hand of power." It was a smoldering statement from beginning to end. What it really amounted to was an emphatic notification to all concerned that the Republic of Vermont would fight its neighbors, Congress, and the world at large rather than surrender its sovereignty to outsiders.

One thing of value came out of the visit to Boston: Ethan was able to get himself fitted out in a new military tunic, complete with epaulettes and gold-plated buttons, all carefully designed to match the intricate pattern that adorned the dog-head pommel of his mighty sword. Such an elaborate outfit must have cost a great deal, but for the time being, at least, money seems not to have been one of Ethan's most pressing worries. Indeed, it appears that during the three or four years following his return from captivity he did very well financially as a servant of the state, despite the fact that he drew no regular salary. The early records of the Republic contain reference to a surprising number of payments made to Ethan by the Vermont treasury. Many of these were for his services as head of the militia; some had to do with his various trips to Philadelphia and elsewhere on business for the Arlington government; a considerable number were for nothing more specific than "general services rendered the Republic." In one way or another they all indicate that Ethan was well recompensed. To cover his trip to Boston, for instance, he asked for and received nearly $1,300, a liberal amount even when measured in depreciated Continental currency. This does not necessarily mean, of course, that Ethan exploited his powerful position in order to drain the public till. There is too little evidence at hand to suggest anything more than that he was generously provided for by a grateful Republic.

Certainly it can be argued, though, that Ethan earned every cent of his money, especially during those months immediately following his return from Massachusetts when he busied himself with the imposing task of putting Vermont's defenses in order. Perhaps because he thought it likely that a crisis was near at hand, he devoted most of his time during the winter and spring of 1780 to improving Vermont's military posture. It was a big job, and a discouraging one, even for Ethan who did not discourage easily. Many of the younger men had left the state to serve with Seth Warner in the Continental Army. Most of those who remained, it seems, had little natural liking for military life, and the conditions of service offered them by the Republic were not very enticing. A few months earlier, the Assembly had passed "An Act for Regulating the Militia, and for Encouragement of Military Skill, for the better Defence of the State," but had then failed to come up with enough money to buy adequate supplies of powder and ball and other essentials. Shortly thereafter the Board of War (as the Governor and Council had taken to calling themselves) solemnly ordered that militiamen be paid a daily rate of five pre-war shillings. Actual payment was left up to the individual towns, however, with the result that the average Vermont militiaman seldom received more than a single shilling a day.

Thus it happened that the frontier, which ran pretty much due east along a line from Castleton to the crest of the mountains and thence northeast to Newbury on the Connecticut River, a total distance of some seventy miles, was guarded by a pitifully small number of underpaid, often underequipped, and sometimes underfed militiamen, few of whom knew or cared much about military matters. At one time during the early spring of 1780, the garrison at Castleton on the western flank of the defense line contained only nineteen men. Ethan liked to boast of the seven thousand militiamen under his command, but all but a few of them were paper soldiers. It is unlikely that at any one time he had more than five hundred men under arms. This was not a very impressive response to crisis by the forty thousand inhabitants of independent Vermont. What made matters doubly bad, of course, was the possibility if not the probability that, given the predatory designs of Vermont's next-door neighbors and the angry feelings of Congress, an attack could come from any direction. Great Britain was certainly not the Republic's only enemy.

A year before, when relations between Vermont and Congress had been somewhat less strained, Ethan had written to General Washington (in vain, as it turned out), asking that the commander in chief send Continental troops to the Grants to assist in defending the northern frontier. Now, however, for reasons not difficult to understand, the Republic shied away from calling upon the American Confederation for help. It would not do to invite the wolf to guard the fold, and in Ethan's opinion, Congress of late had become decidedly wolf-like in its attitude toward the Republic of Vermont. Obviously General Allen would have to make do with the resources he had at hand, and the greatest of these resources seems to have been Ethan himself.

During that critical winter of 1779–80 he was everywhere. Operating out of his military headquarters at Rutland, Ethan was a familiar presence along the frontier line. Resplendent in his grand new tunic, he inspected and supplied garrisons on both sides of the mountains, shuffled his troops about in order to give the illusion of greater numbers, and generally did whatever else needed doing. Sometimes he was accompanied in his travels by Ira who, in addition to his other offices, was also the Republic's Surveyor-General and consequently spent much of his time moving about the wilder areas of the state. Together the two brothers roamed through the Vermont woods in the dead of winter, spending their nights stretched out beneath a makeshift lean-to or crouched in the shelter of an uprooted tree, and living for days at a time on hard biscuits and the bounty of the forest. Occasionally they would take advantage of new snow to track down a deer or two, which they would usually drag to the nearest garrison. Technically this was quite illegal, for in early 1779 the Vermont Assembly, in order to protect the dwindling herd, had outlawed the killing of deer during the first six months of every year—a sure and sad sign that civilization had come to the Grants. But the Allen boys had never worried much about laws they did not approve of, and they certainly did not approve of a law that said a man could not shoot a deer when he happened onto one.

Ethan's job of defending the Republic was made even more difficult in the midwinter of 1780 when Congress, in response to Vermont's insolent defiance of its restraining resolution, ordered the Continental Commissary at Bennington to issue no more supplies to the pretended Republic of Vermont. A few weeks later the Vermont Assembly, meeting across the mountains in Westminister, answered by prohibiting the export of wheat, flour, pork, and certain other commodities from the State. As it turned out, this measure, although passed mainly as a retaliatory gesture against the American Confederation, would also prove helpful in staving off a threatened food shortage in the Republic. However, Vermont still came out the heavier loser from this little exchange of incivilities. Suddenly the Republic found itself in the position of having to purchase war materials out of its own thin treasury, often at inflated prices and great inconvenience. This was not the happiest of arrangements, as Ethan himself would surely have been the first to admit. During the six months following the closing of the Bennington commissariat, he was forced to make three separate trips to Hartford and one to Boston to buy powder, flint, and ball, all at considerable expense to the Republic.

Aside from closing the Bennington commissariat, Congress did little to curb or punish Vermont's recalcitrance. Despite its strong words of the past autumn, it permitted the Republic to continue on its defiant course virtually undisturbed, and when finally confronted with the February 1 deadline that had been set the previous September as the time for Congressional solution of the Vermont problem, the gentlemen in Philadelphia conveniently found themselves bogged down in more important matters. This did not mean that Vermont's position before the American Confederation had improved, and Ethan and his friends were not bemused into thinking it had. Congress had simply found it "inexpedient" to act on the matter of Vermont at this time, all of which meant that the Republic had won only a reprieve rather than a victory. Even this was something to be grateful for, of course, but with New Hampshire and Massachusetts continuing to press their claims and New York now threatening to withhold taxes from the Confederation unless Congress did something about Vermont, how long could the reprieve be expected to last? Probably not very long. Trouble could come on short notice, and the Republic had better keep its guard up.

Meanwhile, within the Republic itself, the situation had grown increasingly ominous for the Arlington regime. The mounting pressures from without had done much to embolden the political enemies of the government and to confuse and frighten its friends. To the east of the mountains the Yorkers were again stirring up trouble, and their chorus, as before, was joined by many of those disgruntled east-siders who still longed for a union with the New Hampshire towns. On the west side too, where the Arlington junto had always claimed its strongest support, dissatisfaction was on the rise. There was grumbling aplenty, even in Bennington, to the effect that the government seemed bent upon a policy of destruction, and that something should be done to stop the Allens, Chittenden, and the others before it was too late. Out of all this there had begun to emerge in many of the west-side towns by the beginning of 1780 the discernible outlines of an opposition party that favored a more conciliatory policy toward Congress and the neighboring states, and would very soon make its presence felt in the Vermont Assembly.

For the time being, however, Ethan and his friends managed to stand firm against all enemies, foreign and domestic, and to maintain their hold upon the Republic. Still, by the spring of 1780 it must have been clear to anyone who cared or dared to think about it that the Arlington government represented a very poor risk. Beset by angry pressures from without and increasingly harassed by centrifugal forces tearing at it from within, it was obviously headed for troubled times. And its prospects were not brightened by reports reaching Bennington in early April that at long last, the British at St. John's were unmistakably up to something.

For the next year or so, little changed between Vermont and Congress. Although at times it appeared that Congress, its patience stretched thin by the surly insolence of the Arlington regime, was about to bear down with force upon the Republic, nothing of the kind actually happened. Months of continuing tension passed without retribution, and with them a half-dozen or more deadline dates, each of which had been solemnly set by Congress as the time for final resolution of the Vermont problem. Naturally New York continued to demand action. "The Yorkers push the matter almost beyond the bounds of modesty," remarked a Yankee delegate. But for a number of reasons, including a frequent lack of quorum, Congress repeatedly failed to muster the votes necessary for any positive move against Vermont. The most it could or would do was to let loose an occasional tirade of angry words against the "highly unwarranted and subversive" behavior of the Republic—to which Governor Chittenden and his friends invariably replied that the Confederation would do well to mind its own business and refrain from interfering with "the rights and prerogatives of an independent State." And so it went with Congress and Vermont during 1780 and the better part of 1781, while in the background New York, New Hampshire, and Massachusetts kept a watchful eye on their intended prey and on each other.

But all of this had lost much of its interest for Ethan. By the spring of

1780, if not earlier, he had concluded that the Republic was playing a losing hand. For months he had strongly suspected that Vermont would never be taken into the Confederation, and now he was all but convinced that, given the way things were going, it was just a matter of time, and probably not much time at that, until the Republic would be snuffed out by Congress or chewed to bits by its greedy neighbors—presupposing of course that it were not overrun first by the British and their Indian allies. With enemies threatening from all sides, independent Vermont stood naked and alone. If it were to survive it would have to have outside help, and it seemed likely that this help would have to come from some untried source. As to exactly what that source would be, Vermont was obviously in no position to be choosy or squeamish. It would have to find salvation where salvation was most apt to be, and Ethan had already decided that he knew where to look. "There is a North pole as well as a South pole," he had once been heard to remark, "and if thunder should threaten from the South, we will shut the door opposite that point and open the door facing North."

Exactly when and how Ethan's courtship with the British began is not clear. Shadowy transactions of this kind are not apt to be very lavishly or honestly recorded by their participants, with the result that available evidence is often so skimpy and suspect as to be of limited use to others in determining what actually happened. And so it was with Ethan's dickerings with the British during the latter part of the Revolutionary War, for although the so-called Haldimand negotiations are more amply documented than most, as affairs of this sort go, there is still much that can only be guessed at.

It appears that, at least as far as the British were concerned, the plan that would eventually come within an ace of enticing Vermont back into the Empire, had been germinating for a long time. It may be recalled that as early as December of 1775, during Ethan's brief stay in England, a plan to purchase him had been proposed by the King's Solicitor-General, and that a year or so later, while on parole in New York, Ethan was actually approached on the subject by one of General Howe's officers. It was not, however, until after the French had entered the war and hopes of an easy British victory had noticeably dimmed that a comprehensive plan to buy out the rebels came to be seriously considered by His Majesty's Government. Especially instrumental in promoting the idea was the King himself, who had long been a strong believer in purchasing the opposition and could not quite understand why such a policy should not work out as well in North America as elsewhere. At least it seemed worth a try. And so, largely in response to the royal wish, a master operation was conceived sometime during the late summer months of 1778, the object of which was to accomplish by more subtle and devious means what the British armies were so obviously failing to achieve on the field of battle. Of particular interest to King George was the area that had recently taken to calling itself Vermont, where, according to all reports, much good might result from a proper use of the right inducements.

The person whose responsibility it became to implement this program was the Colonial Secretary, Lord George Germain, and he was without any question an ideal man for the job—ideal, that is, for the Americans. There were in those days men of staggering inadequacy occupying key positions within the British government and military establishments. To these men Americans must forever be indebted, for had it not been for their remarkable deficiencies, the Revolution would doubtless have been crushed within a matter of a few months. High among these unsung heroes of American independence was Lord Germain, whose incompetency was so great that it exceeded even his arrogance and conceit. In the hands of a person of less extraordinary ineptitude the King's plan might have worked. With Lord Germain in charge, however, it never had a chance.

In December of 1778, after at least two false starts, Germain finally got a letter off to Sir Henry Clinton, Commander of British forces in North America, telling him officially and rather vaguely what the general had already learned months before from the Secret Service: that, in accordance with the King's pleasure, he was to do what he could to help the Colonial Office exploit the widespread spirit of disaffection known to exist among the Americans. Three months later the Secretary sent Clinton another letter. This one left no doubt that Vermont had been singled out for special attention by His Majesty's Government:

> The separation of the inhabitants of the country they call Vermont from the province in which it was formerly included, is a circumstance of which I should hope much advantage might be made by discreet management. I see no objection to your giving them reason to expect his Majesty will erect their country into a separate province and confirm every occupant that shall give proof of his

return to his duty, in possession of the ungranted lands he occupies. . . . I shall therefore only add upon this subject that the
restoring that country to the King's obedience would be considered
as a very important service, and that I am commanded by his Majesty to recommend it to your attention.

It would have been superfluous of His Lordship to add that the most
likely person to deal with in Vermont was Ethan Allen. Clinton had
already heard a great deal about Allen from the Secret Service and from
his own Intelligence apparatus. According to all reports the man was a
complete scoundrel, "a person of infamous character and wicked practices. . . . But under the present circumstances it may be that he can
be attracted."

Within days after receiving Germain's second letter, General Clinton
began preparations for opening negotiations with Ethan. It was a delicate business all around, and, of course, a dangerous one, and it is not
surprising that many months passed before an avenue could be opened
to Ethan from Sir Henry's headquarters in New York City. On at least
three occasions messages sent to Ethan failed to get through, and as late
as mid-spring of 1780 Clinton was forced to report to Lord Germain
that he had been unable to establish contact with "the Chief of Vermont." Still, Sir Henry felt confident that by this time Ethan had at least
grown "sensitive" to the fact that efforts were being made to reach him,
and this in itself represented progress of a sort.

If Ethan actually had become "sensitive" to what Clinton had in
mind, and he doubtless had, then he was certainly not alone. Indeed, by
the spring of 1780 the fact that Sir Henry Clinton had been making
attempts to woo Ethan was more or less common knowledge, and,
naturally, the basis for a multitude of rumors, some outrageously farfetched, some considerably less so, but all in essential agreement on one
important point: in one way or another the hero of Ticonderoga was
involved or about to become involved in shady dealings with the British.
In early July, for instance, the American spy Abraham Bancker reported
to General Washington from New York City that a person positively
identified as Ethan Allen of Vermont had been seen there on the second
of that month, moving about in the company of several high-ranking
British officers.

Upon receipt of this news from one of his most reliable agents, Washington immediately ordered General Schuyler of the Northern Depart-

ment to inquire into the matter and, if Bancker's reports were found to be true, arrest Ethan on the spot and seize his papers. Since Schuyler had never had much liking for Ethan anyway, he undertook the chore with an unaccustomed vigor. Two of his most trusted aides were sent at once to Bennington to gather information as secretly as possible on Ethan's recent doings. This they did for more than a week, and what they found left little room for doubt: Ethan Allen had positively not been in New York City on July 2, or at any other time during the period from mid-June to mid-July. In fact, he had not set foot off the Grants. There was no question about his whereabouts; his movements could be well accounted for—too well, as far as General Schuyler was concerned. In his official report to Washington he cleared Ethan, because the evidence left him no other choice, but personally he remained unconvinced. Although he really had nothing more than a hunch to go on, to his dying day Schuyler believed that Ethan had somehow arranged to be in two places at the same time.

The first direct contact known for certain to have been made with Ethan occurred, ironically enough, at about the same time he was being given a clean bill by Schuyler's agents. On an unseasonably chilly day in late July of 1780 as Ethan was walking down the highroad in Arlington, he was approached by a British courier, dressed in the clothing of a frontier farmer and bearing a letter from Beverly Robinson, a prominent Virginia Loyalist who commanded a Tory regiment known as the Royal Americans. The letter, which had taken nearly four months to reach Ethan from New York, had obviously been authorized and probably prompted by Sir Henry Clinton himself. It could scarcely have been more to the point:

> Sir—I am now undertaking a task which I hope you will receive with the same good intentions that incline me to make it. I have often been informed that you and most of the inhabitants of Vermont are opposed to the wild and chimerical scheme of the Americans in attempting to separate the continent from Great Britain, and to establish an independent state of their own; and that you would willingly assist in uniting America again to Great Britain and restoring that happy constitution we have so wantonly and unadvisedly destroyed. If I have been rightly informed and these should be your sentiments and inclinations, I beg you will communicate to me without reserve whatever proposals you would wish to

make to the commander-in-chief [Sir Henry Clinton] and I here promise that I will faithfully lay them before him according to your directions, and flatter myself I can do it to as good effect as any person whatever. I can make no proposals to you until I know your sentiments, but I think upon your taking an active part and embodying the inhabitants of Vermont in favor of the crown of England, to act as the commander-in-chief shall direct, that you may obtain a separate government under the king and constitution of England, and the men formed into regiments under such officers as you shall recommend, and be on the same footing as all the provincial camps are here. I am an American myself, feel much for the distressed situation my poor country is in at present, and am anxious to be serviceable toward restoring it to peace, and that mild and good government we have lost. I have, therefore, ventured to address myself to you on this subject and hope you will see it in a proper light, and be as candid with me. I am inclinable to think that one reason why this unnatural war has continued so long, is that all the Americans who wish and think it would be for the interest of the country to have a constitutional and equitable connection with Great Britain, do not communicate their sentiments to each other so often and freely as they ought to do. In case you should disapprove of my hinting these things to you and do not choose to make any proposals to Government, I hope you will not suffer any insult be offered to the bearer of this letter, but allow him to return in safety, as I can assure you he is entirely ignorant of its contents.

But if you should think it proper to send proposals to me to be laid before the commander-in-chief, I do now give my word that if they are not accepted of or complied with by him, (of which I will inform you,) the matter shall be buried in oblivion between us. I will only add that if you should think proper to send a friend of your own here with proposals to the general, he shall be protected and well treated here, and allowed to return whenever he pleases.

I can say nothing further at present but my best wishes for the restoration of peace and happiness in America.

And am your humble servant,
BEV ROBINSON, Col. Royal Americans

Ethan kept the letter and, after sending the courier on his way without an answer, proceeded to hunt up Ira and Governor Chittenden. Together the three men, and possibly one or two other members of the Arlington junto, studied Robinson's offer, and, as Ethan later put it, "agreed after mature deliberation, and considering the extreme circumstances of this State, to take no further notice of the matter." For the time being at least, it would be best to do nothing and say nothing about what had happened. Thus Ethan and his accomplices, by deliberately keeping the Robinson matter under wraps, placed themselves in a rather compromising position, and, consciously or otherwise, took a long step down that dangerous and devious road that would eventually lead them perilously close to treason.

Or was it treason? Many historians, including some who have dealt intricately with the Haldimand Affair (as Ethan's negotiations with the British came to be known), insist that it was nothing of the sort. To these scholars, most of them native or adopted Vermonters, Ethan was certainly at no time engaged in any sincere attempt to turn Vermont over to the British. To support their faith in Ethan's innocence and probity, however, has not always been easy for them. In fact, in view of the compelling evidence to the contrary, it has frequently involved them in a clumsy jockeying of reason and even of facts.

Of the many explanations offered for the Haldimand Affair by these writers who reject the notion of a traitorous Ethan, the favorite by far is the one which has it that Ethan and the others were never actually serious about delivering Vermont to the British. They were just pretending all along, leading the enemy on in order to worry Vermont's neighbors into a more cordial behavior and perhaps even frighten Congress into admitting Vermont into the American Confederation. It was a dangerous sort of operation all right, but in the end it redounded greatly to Vermont's advantage, thanks to the daring resourcefulness of Ethan, Ira, and Governor Chittenden, who most assuredly made fools out of the gullible British.

Where this imaginative version of the Haldimand negotiations came from is not hard to determine. It was offered up originally by Ethan himself when the negotiations suddenly broke down and left him dangerously exposed and very much in need of a handy explanation to present to the people of the Republic. Ethan's story was later elaborated upon by Ira in his *History* and subsequently parroted by successive generations of reverential historians determined to protect the image of Vermont's greatest hero. Concluded one of these in a typical remark: "The escutcheons of Ethan and Ira Allen are as free from the tarnish of wavering patriotism or inconsistency as those of any of the men of the Revolution whom we delight to honor." And another: "There never was any thought of disloyalty on the part of the Vermont leaders. . . . This was a strategic move, delicate, difficult, and dangerous, made only to protect Vermont in a desperate situation. It served the purpose intended and Vermont was saved." Thus, as a noted Yorker scholar once put it, when dealing with the Haldimand Affair these so-called historians of the filiopietistic school have managed, by spreading their wings before their eyes, to shield their sensitivities from unpleasant reality.

Reality in this case was obviously treason—or at least intended treason. The evidence surely supports this conclusion. It always has, and during the past generation or so, new discoveries have been made in the British archives which leave absolutely no room for doubt: Ethan and his Arlington friends were bent on delivering Vermont to the enemy. Not at first perhaps, but certainly their efforts eventually became aimed toward that end. In the early stages of the intrigue, Ethan, Ira, and the others were probably playing pretty much by ear, hoping that by becoming involved in negotiations with the British and allowing the outside world to sniff something of what was going on, Vermont would somehow manage to improve its position. It is actually not unreasonable to assume that during the early months of the Haldimand conspiracy, the Vermont leaders were indeed, as they themselves would later claim, deliberately playing off hostile forces against one another with the specific view in mind of bringing about a speedy recognition of Vermont by the American Congress.

But it is clear beyond any question that as the negotiations progressed and the pieces of this dangerous transaction began to fall into place, Ethan and his accomplices became firmly committed to the idea of taking Vermont back into the British Empire. By the late spring of 1781, the Arlington conspirators, with Ethan obviously in charge, were headed hell-bent for treason, and that they finally stopped just short of the mark was no fault of their own. "In the time of General Haldimand's command," Ethan remarked in a personal letter written several years later, "if Great Britain could have offered Vermont protection, they would readily have yielded up their independency and become a province of Great Britain."

In the story of the Haldimand Affair there occasionally appears the argument that whatever it was that Ethan and his friends were hatching with the British, it could not, by definition, have been treason, for since Vermont was not a part of the United States, it owed the United States no allegiance, and, owing none, it could betray none. Of course the only thing wrong with this argument is that Vermont's independence had never been recognized by anybody but the Vermonters themselves, and certainly not even all of them. As far as the rest of the world, including the American Confederaiton, was concerned, Vermont was still officially part of New York State, which meant that it was also part of the United States of America. The continued presence in the field of Seth Warner's regiment of Vermonters as a regular unit in the Continental Army served as a conspicuous reminder that whatever it chose to call itself, Vermont was actually part and parcel of the new America. And attesting to Ethan's own personal involvement in the American cause was the somewhat embarrassing fact that throughout his dealings with the British he continued to hold his brevet commission in the Continental Service.

But even if one were to accept the not entirely unreasonable view that despite a few inconsistencies, such as Warner's regiment and Ethan's commission, Vermont was a completely independent state with no attachments or commitments to its American neighbors, the doings of Ethan and his fellow conspirators still amounted to intended treason—in this case, against the Republic of Vermont. After all, Vermont was at war with Great Britain, and had been for many years. During that time it had suffered death and devastation from the English and their Indian allies, and consequently the majority of the settlers on both sides of the mountains, regardless of how they may have felt at the beginning of the conflict, now had little inclination to return to the bosom of the Empire. Personally they were not especially anxious to shoulder arms, as Ethan could well attest, but in the abstract at least they supported the war and the idea of independence from Great Britain for themselves and for the American Union, which most of them hoped they would one day join. Early in 1779, in order to leave no doubt of where the Republic of Vermont stood, the Assembly meeting at Bennington had passed an act which declared guilty of high treason all persons giving assistance to "any enemies, at open war against this state, or the United States of America, by joining their armies, or by inlisting or procuring . . . or carrying on a treacherous correspondence with them." A year or so later Ethan, who had been loud in his support of the Treason Act at the time of its passage, was working in direct violation of it—for whatever else he and his friends may or may not have been guilty of during their dalliance with the British, they were indisputably involved in "treacherous correspondence."

Call it treason against the United States, treason against the Republic of Vermont, or no treason at all, the fact is that beginning sometime in the summer of 1780 and continuing for some undetermined period, a small group of highly placed Vermont leaders worked toward the betrayal of their friends and neighbors on the Grants. For several critical months, while the Assembly debated ways to strengthen the Republic's defenses against the British and to improve relations with Congress, Ethan and his Arlington friends were moving covertly in the opposite direction. Unknownst to the people of Vermont (although strongly suspected by some of them), and in direct defiance of the popular temper, General Ethan Allen, his brother Ira, Governor Chittenden, and a half-dozen other prominent west-siders (two of them members of the Governor's Council), were unquestionably deeply involved in preparing the way for Vermont's return to the British Empire. From beginning to end it was an ugly, conspiratorial bit of business that would leave an indelible mark of shame upon its perpetrators, especially on Ethan Allen who, as usual, was in charge of things.

And yet it would be unfair to judge Ethan too harshly without first attempting to appraise his motives, and here the going becomes difficult and uncertain, for there is obviously no way of knowing for sure why men act as they do, particularly a man as notional and tempestuous as Ethan. It may very well be, as has frequently been charged, that his behavior at this time was determined mainly by the sizable financial stake he had riding on the future of the Grants. The way things were going he stood a good chance of losing a fortune in wild lands. If the Americans should win the war, New York, with the almost certain support of Congress, would be in a strong position to retrieve its lost territory and thereby invalidate Ethan's titles. If, on the other hand, the British were to win, he probably would not fare much better. And then, of course, even if the British were to recognize the independence of the American States, they might retain all or some of that territory occupied by His Majesty's troops, including northern Vermont where virtually all of the Onion River Company's holdings were located. In other words, if Vermont were to continue its present alignment with the American States, Ethan was liable to lose his northern lands no matter how the war turned out. Naturally he was aware of all this, and it is reasonable to suppose that he was influenced by it to some degree.

However, the contention that his property in the north was the principal, or even a major, determinant in deciding Ethan to throw in his lot with the British seems inconsistent with much that is known about him. Despite a well-deserved reputation for canny trading in land, there was nothing in his behavior, before or after, to suggest that he was a venal man. Quite the opposite, in fact. On earlier occasions in his dealings with the Yorkers and the British, opportunities had persented themselves for him to line his pockets by selling out his neighbors, but he had never succumbed to them or, as far as is known, even come close. Certainly personal gain in the material sense was as important to him as to the next man, perhaps even more so. After all, he was an Allen. But all indications are that there were some things he would not do to acquire it, and one of these was to sacrifice or compromise his honor—which in a pompous but nonetheless lofty way he appears to have treasured above all else. If it had been otherwise, he could surely have got a better price from the British than merely the security of lands he already owned. Given what he had to offer, he could have collected handsome amounts of gold guineas from Sir Henry Clinton and Lord Germain. Benedict Arnold did.

It seems much more likely that Ethan was moved to act as he did mainly by a genuine concern for the future of Vermont. Certainly the evidence, what little there is of it, points that way. Undoubtedly he had other reasons as well, not all of them very exalted, but the welfare of the Republic appears to have been uppermost in his mind. Pressured from all sides and harassed by enemies within, Vermont seemed headed for disaster, and a détente with the British appeared to offer a chance to ward off the worst of it—possibly the only chance. This, rather than narrow self-interest, was most likely what moved Ethan to put aside his hatred of the British and engage in a shamefully underhanded bit of skulduggery that was completely alien to his open nature, and this is why he was able to convince Governor Chittenden and the others to go along with him. Vermont needed saving, and Ethan thought he saw the way to do it. It was as simple as that. As for betraying the people, Ethan probably gave this aspect of the affair very little thought. He had never supposed that the people were really capable of looking after their own best interests. They needed to be taken care of by their betters, and this was precisely what he intended to do.

# XIII. The Haldimand Affair

SWEARING that he would "run on the mountains and live on mouse-meat" rather than submit to Yorker rule or the arbitrary dictates of an unfriendly Congress, Ethan became actively engaged in direct negotiations with the British sometime in the late summer of 1780. Although more or less controlled by the Colonial Office and channeled through Sir Henry Clinton's headquarters in New York City, these negotiations were actually conducted from the British end by Lieutenant General Frederick Haldimand, Carleton's successor as governor of Canada. This seemed like the safest and most convenient arrangement because of Haldimand's adjacency to the Grants and the consequent ease of setting up and maintaining a direct line of communications with the Vermont leaders.

The choice of General Haldimand was a good one, for he was a person of considerable intelligence, experience, and levelheadedness— all of which marked him as something of a phenomenon among the British officers of that day. He was also an honorable man with a reputation for fair dealing, and given the job he now had to do, this was an exceedingly valuable asset. In addition to all else, he was a conscientious keeper of records and writer of reports, and he insisted that his subordinates follow his example, with the result that very little of importance happened in General Haldimand's command without receiving detailed attention in his official papers. Some of these papers have been preserved, and fortunately so, for they offer about the only reliable evidence available on those highly controversial dealings that took place between the British and the Republic of Vermont during the late years of the Revolution. As for the Vermont records, official and otherwise, the less said the better. They are for the most part so beclouded with confusion and subterfuge as to be decidedly undependable. Consider, for example, the case of the two round robins.

In the original and presumably official collection of Vermont records pertaining to the Haldimand negotiations, early historians discovered a detailed statement signed by the Arlington conspirators which declares in a very positive manner that the negotiations were just a ruse. The entire transaction, according to this statement, was nothing more nor less than a clever scheme calculated to keep the British wolf away from the door while at the same time worrying Congress into recognizing Vermont and admitting it into the American Union. This document, of course, has been and continues to be seized upon by Vermontophiles as proof positive that Ethan and his friends were out to use, rather than join, the British.

A century later, however, a second statement was found, this one in the British Archives. In form it is almost identical with the first, and it bears precisely the same list of signatures. But the story that it tells is entirely different. According to this second document, it was the honest intent of the conspirators to take Vermont back into the British Empire, and their simultaneous overtures to Congress, such as they were, were simply a cover designed to lessen suspicion. This statement, which was apparently delivered to General Haldimand personally by Ira Allen, was meant to serve as the other half of a two-way insurance policy. Whatever their real intentions may have been, Ethan and his friends were obviously intent upon covering all bets, and it is mainly because of this understandable desire on the part of the Vermont leaders to protect themselves (and if possible their reputations as well) that the entire body of Vermont documents relating to the Haldimand Affair must be looked upon with considerable suspicion.

This much is unquestionably a fact, however: as far as the Vermont end of the negotiations was concerned, Ethan was the boss. True, it often appeared otherwise. With Ira and others rushing about conspicuously to parley with the British in Canada and elsewhere, Ethan sometimes seemed cast in a minor role, and for this reason a few historians have seen fit to discount his part in the Haldimand intrigue and mark him down as little more than a front for Ira and Governor Chittenden. Actually, however, among the Vermont leaders it was Ethan, and Ethan alone, who determined the direction of the negotiations, while the others served merely as his spokesmen and errand-boys. There was a tremendous amount at stake in what the conspirators were attempting to do, and the obstacles standing in their way were many and dangerous. To bring off this transaction successfully, whatever its true intent, would require the boldness and enterprise that only Ethan could provide.

Everybody recognized this, including Ethan himself, and he proceeded to act accordingly. It was he who made the big decisions. On this point there need be no mistake. General Haldimand said as much. And so did Ethan, who, incidentally, although repeatedly warned against doing so, sometimes dated and signed incriminating correspondence in his own hand.

In August of 1780, about a month after Ethan had received his interesting offer from the Tory Colonel Robinson, the Haldimand intrigue began in earnest with a letter from Governor Chittenden (actually written by Ethan) to General Haldimand proposing a truce for the purpose of exchanging prisoners. From what little evidence is available it appears almost certain that from the very beginning the swapping of prisoners was merely a pretext under which Ethan and his friends could go hunting for bigger game. A few weeks earlier, presumably to provide himself with a cover, Ethan had written to General Washington complaining of the treatment given Vermont prisoners of war and asking that Washington arrange for their exchange. When Washington, probably as anticipated, refused on the grounds that the Vermont prisoners must wait their turn, Ethan and his Arlington friends began to move ahead on their own.

Things went slowly at first, but when the British moved up the Lake in early October and deposited more than a thousand men at Ticonderoga and Skenesboro, the tempo of the conspiracy began to pick up. And properly so, for if the Vermont leaders were to reach an accommodation with the British, they would have to do so soon. Otherwise it would probably be too late. The newly arrived troops were thought to be only the vanguard of a much larger enemy force to come. Some estimates ranged as high as seven thousand. How could Vermont possibly defend itself against such an army as this? At that time Ethan had only two hundred and thirty men under arms, stretched out in little scatterings from Castleton to Newbury. Powder and ball were in short supply, and so was virtually everything else. To make matters worse, if that were possible, the New York militia had recently been withdrawn from the vicinity of the Vermont border, thereby removing any semblance of threat to the British western flank. It was, as Ira saw it, "a most forlorn situation."

Actually the military situation was not nearly so menacing as was generally supposed. There was no greater force under way, nor would there be one. In fact, according to Haldimand's own estimate, his total strength in men and materials at this time was not enough to allow for anything more than sporadic raiding activity. A full-fledged campaign was out of the question. Still, the important thing is that most Vermonters believed that the British were about to descend upon them in great numbers, and their leaders shared this belief. Besides, even if no more troops should come up the lake, those already in the area could foray at will, laying waste the countryside and setting a bad example for their Indian allies. News of recent Indian raids on a number of east-side towns, including the brutal destruction of Royalton, had left an indelible impression on most Vermonters, and it was not a pleasant one. All things considered, the prospects for the people of Vermont in the face of the British presence up-lake were unsettling, to say the least.

On a chilly, faded day in late October, a British agent bearing Governor Chittenden's letter and a flag of truce approached Ethan's headquarters at Castleton. The agent was Captain Justus Sherwood of the Queen's Loyal Rangers, a young man of uncommon talents and integrity, who was well known to Ethan. In fact, in the old days before the war he had for a time been a member of the Green Mountain Boys, and had helped rescue Remember Baker from Squire Munro and his Yorker band of kidnappers. When the war came, however, Sherwood refused to take up arms against the Mother Country and did what he could to influence others to follow his example. Consequently he was stripped of his property and banished from the Grants. He found refuge in Canada, and eventually became attached to Haldimand's command. Now, in the autumn of 1780, he was once again back on the Grants, attempting to persuade Ethan and his friends to bring Vermont back into the Empire.

At Castleton, Sherwood was taken before Ethan and a council of ten other officers. There he presented Ethan with Haldimand's reply to Chittenden's request for a cartel, which Ethan read to his fellow officers. On the whole it was favorable, but there were a few "discretionary" matters that obviously had to be worked out, and so with the approval of the others, Ethan and Sherwood retired for a private discussion. During the remainder of that day, the two men spent a good deal of time together, strolling through the autumn woods outside of Castleton. What they said to one another was carefully remembered by Sherwood and reported a few days later to General Haldimand.

Sherwood began by announcing to Ethan that he had some matters of special importance and delicacy to bring up, but first he wanted Ethan's promise of protection and immunity. Ethan, who must have had a pretty good idea of what was coming, agreed—provided it was "no damned Arnold plan to sell his country and his honor by betraying the trust reposed in him." Sherwood then got to the point by introducing what in essence was indeed an Arnold plan, or something mighty like it. He informed Ethan that General Haldimand was well aware of Vermont's unsuccessful attempts to gain recognition from Congress, and the general supposed that Ethan was too perceptive not to realize that Congress was only waiting for the opportunity to crush Vermont and turn it over to New York. Now was the time for Vermont to save itself by cutting free of the American States and resuming its former allegiance to the King. If this were done, the Crown would guarantee the people of Vermont "those privileges they have so long contested for with New York," including, of course, recognition of Wentworth land titles. Vermont would be established as a separate Province, and Ethan would be given command of a regiment of loyal Vermonters.

Ethan interrupted at this point, saying that as far as his own preferment was concerned, he didn't give a damn. He was not up for purchase at any price, and he thought that he had made that much very clear when he had refused a similar offer during his days in captivity. However, he could see that General Haldimand's terms might be of real benefit to the people of Vermont and should therefore be given serious attention. He would sleep on the matter.

When the two men met again in private on the following morning, Ethan admitted to Sherwood that he was "heartily weary of war," but assured him that he would go on fighting as long as necessary for the freedom of his people. It would take a great deal, he declared, to cause him to throw in his lot and Vermont's with that of Great Britain, but at the same time he realized that this might be the only way of guaranteeing Vermont's survival. Right now, though, he did not dare even think of such a thing. The people would have to be educated first, he stated, apparently warming to the idea. And this would take a lot of doing. Still, it could be done, he supposed. He himself could be their teacher. He could begin by issuing statements to them, explaining the unreasonable and threatening attitude of Congress, and in these statements he could intimate that if Congress were to continue to act toward them as it had in the past, then the people of Vermont would do well to look elsewhere for support and understanding. In Ethan's opinion, this would start the people thinking along new lines and would be a reasonable first step toward possible reconciliation with the British Empire. Of course, all of this would require time, and Ethan supposed that General Haldimand would find a way to give it to him.

Mid-afternoon of the second day, Ethan and Sherwood appeared before Ethan's staff to announce that arrangements for an exchange of prisoners had been agreed upon and that until the exchange had been completed a truce would be in effect all along the line. British troops were to be withdrawn from the upper lake and the Vermont militia was to be disbanded. The suggestion was made by one of the officers (probably prompted by Ethan) that those areas of New York adjacent to Vermont also be included in the truce, lest they be rendered more exposed to British arms because of Vermont's action. This was agreed to by Sherwood, who then set out for British headquarters—but not until after Ethan had met with him again privately to warn him of the need for utmost caution and secrecy. Here was a risky business for both of them. Only a month before, Benedict Arnold, Lord Germain's most eminent recruit, had been exposed as a traitor to the American cause, and a few days later his British contact, the hapless Major André, had been hanged for his part in the affair. Suspicion was running high in America. How many other Arnolds were there? People wondered and watched, and it would obviously be a good idea for Ethan and his British go-between to move carefully.

It was a somewhat discouraged Justus Sherwood who returned to Ticonderoga and thence to British headquarters at St. John's. What he had seen and heard had left him unconvinced of Ethan's sincerity, and he told General Haldimand as much. Haldimand was not surprised. He had not expected anything to come of the affair, for he had little faith in Ethan. "I am assured by all," he had written to Germain a month or so earlier, "that no dependence can be had in him—his character is well known, and his Followers, or dependents, are a collection of the most abandoned wretches that ever lived. . . ." In Haldimand's opinion Ethan was attempting to use the British in order to get recognition from Congress, and at this stage the general may very well have been right. Still, with winter coming on and military operations pretty much out of the question, the British might as well agree to a truce and continue to dicker with the Vermonters. The General had planned to withdraw his troops to winter quarters anyway, so no real harm would be done. And it was barely possible that something of value might develop out of all this. At least Lord Germain and Henry Clinton seemed to think so. Thus, in spite of his own misgivings, General Haldimand ordered a cease-fire and instructed Sherwood to keep on with the negotiations.

Word of the cartel was rushed southward to Bennington by Ethan himself. There the happy news was announced to the Assembly, then in session, by Governor Chittenden who, along with Ira and possibly a few others, was already aware of what was really going on. Having been warned by Ethan, however, that the people should be told as little as possible "and must be content with such conjectures as best suits," the Governor was uncommonly vague in his remarks to the Assembly—so much so that some of the members immediately took him to task. Unable to understand why the British should enter into such an obviously one-sided arrangement, these members, many of them east-siders, insisted on asking embarrassing questions of Chittenden and of General Ethan Allen himself, who was present at the session on invitation of the Governor and Council. Still, a substantial majority of the assemblymen clearly favored the arrangement without reservation. It would be good to get the prisoners back home again, and it would be especially nice to be protected by a truce while the exchange was being carried out.

The Assembly therefore voted by a respectable margin to ratify the cartel, and to furlough Ethan's far-flung militia until further notice—all of which was mighty convenient for Ethan since he had already sent his men home to put in their winter wheat. At the same time he had also sent out a message to Colonel Alexander Webster of the New York militia, informing him of the truce and of its application to the eastern strip of New York State. This was the first word of explanation the Yorkers had received of what was going on. They had, as Ira later commented, been understandably "much surprised to find that the militia of Vermont were returning home, and that the British troops were returning to Canada to winter quarters."

In November, Ira and Joseph Fay left under a flag of truce for British headquarters at St. John's on a well-advertised journey to make arrangements for the exchange of prisoners. They soon returned home, however, with the report that the ice was already two inches thick on the lake. They had found it next to impossible to make much progress by boat, and with the heavy snows apt to come at any time, travel by land would probably be every bit as difficult, if not more so. They would simply have to wait until spring. In the meantime, of course, the truce would remain in effect. Here was explanation enough for anyone who might wonder during the coming months about the surprising longevity of the cease-fire: the Vermont winter decreed it so—and, apparently, Ethan and his friends had planned all along that it should. After giving the matter further thought, however, Ethan sent word to Sherwood suggesting that, rather than maintain the truce over so long a period, it might be better for the sake of appearances to call it off for the time being and then reinstitute it in the spring. Since military operations during the winter months were not very appropriate anyway, there was really no need to keep the truce in effect, and suspicions might be somewhat lessened if it were lifted. Sherwood agreed, and so once again the Republic of Vermont and the British Empire were at war with one another, theoretically at least.

The winter that year was one of the worst in Vermont's history. The cold arrived early and stayed long, and in December a great snow fell that kept life slowed nearly to a standstill over much of the Grants until early May. Indeed, so severe was the winter of 1780–81 that spring planting had to be put off until June, and with the growing time of crops so shortened, a critical food shortage resulted that forced many of the west-side settlers to turn to the resources of the forest in order to keep alive until the harvest of the following year.

But through even the worst of the winter, communications were kept open between British headquarters at St. John's and the small town of Sunderland, five miles northeast of Arlington, where Ethan and his family, together with Ira, had moved a few months earlier. British agents were frequent visitors to the woods just outside the town. Here, after the 150-mile trek on snowshoes from St. John's, they met secretly with Ethan to deliver messages from Sherwood and Haldimand, the contents of which can only be guessed at. Indeed, so frequent and bold did their visits become that Ethan felt compelled to write to Haldimand in early 1781, urging greater caution. After all, Ethan pointed out to the general, if the people of Vermont were to find out what he was up to, they might very well chop off his head.

Despite all dangers and difficulties, then, the negotiations continued to move ahead during the long winter months, and it appears that by spring Ethan had come considerably closer to accepting what the British had to offer. Certainly General Haldimand, who was not usually given to self-deception, seemed to think so. Furthermore, the general had now come to believe that Ethan was dealing in absolute good faith with His Majesty's Government—or so at least he reported to Lord Germain. In fact, for some reason Haldimand's opinion of Ethan appears to have undergone a dramatic change during the winter of 1780–81. He still distrusted the other Vermont leaders, especially Ira, but he was now convinced that Ethan was an honorable, forthright (albeit somewhat posturing) man, who in both integrity and ability towered above his associates. Like many another, General Haldimand had obviously fallen under Ethan's spell—so much so that from now on, whenever major decisions were involved, he would, if at all practical, insist on dealing directly with Ethan himself and would accept the word of no one else.

Meanwhile, during the winter months the Vermont leaders took time out from dickering with the British to explore other avenues of opportunity, or at least give the impression of doing so. Governor Chittenden wrote conciliatory letters to Massachusetts and New Hampshire, asking that for the sake of harmony and friendship they drop their claims to Grants territory and support Vermont's application for admission into the American Union. Entreaties were sent out to other states as well, and in January a special delegation was dispatched to Philadelphia, ostensibly to attempt once more to soften the hard heart of Congress. Overtures were even made to New York by Chittenden and his Council, urging Governor Clinton and the Yorker Legislature to let bygones be bygones, concede Vermont its independence, and then cooperate in a joint military offensive against the British along the northern frontier. Surprisingly enough, it appeared for a time that this newest attempt to win Yorker acceptance might actually pay off. For one auspicious moment there was good reason to believe that the government of New York was at last ready to abandon its long obstinacy and recognize Vermont's claim.

Frightened by the mounting crescendo of rumor regarding Vermont's strange dealings with the British, and, according to Governor Clinton, outrageously corrupted by a generous distribution of Vermont land titles among them, the members of the New York Senate in late February voted to recognize Vermont's independence. A few days later the Lower House appeared to be ready to follow the Senate's example, but at this point an aroused Governor Clinton stepped in and threatened to prorogue the Legislature unless the Vermont matter were dropped at once. He would never, announced the governor, under any circumstances "permit acquiescence in another separate and independent Jurisdiction within what this State claims as its rightful territory." Thus, with a determined show of executive authority by George Clinton, this rather promising diplomatic thrust at the government of New York ended in sudden and total failure for Vermont. So, in fact, did all those other wintertime attempts by the Republic to gain advantage from the American States and the Confederation Congress—another round of rejections, which doubtless did something to move Ethan and his friends closer to the British.

It is difficult to understand how the Arlington junto expected much good to come of these efforts. Perhaps they didn't. Perhaps, as they assured Haldimand was the case, they were simply laying down a smoke screen to obscure their dealings with the British. Or, it may even be that they thought they saw in these overtures to their American neighbors a chance to actually hasten Vermont's return to the British Empire. This would help explain, among other things, some very odd behavior on the part of the Vermont leaders during those winter months of 1780–81, behavior which at best seemed insensitive and improper. In fact, so provoking were certain of their actions, that it would not be unreasonable to conclude that at the same time Ethan and his friends appeared to be making conciliatory gestures, they were in reality doing their level best to outrage the American States, especially those nearest home. In this way Vermont would become so odious to its American neighbors that its people would find themselves with little choice but to follow their traitorous leaders into the waiting arms of General Haldimand. A clever scheme indeed.

It is unlikely that Vermont's blustering behavior stemmed from any such subtle, calculated plan on the part of the Arlington government, however. Instead it appears that things happened as they did because Ethan and his confederates felt compelled to take steps, sometimes very reluctantly, which in their judgment were absolutely necessary for the continued well-being of the Republic—or their own positions of power, which was another way of saying the same thing. But whether or not consciously meant to be provocative, the conduct of the Vermont authorities during that cold and critical winter was certainly inconsistent, to say the least, with their simultaneous and purportedly sincere attempts to woo their American neighbors and Congress. It was not, after all, very friendly or ingratiating of them to come boldly forward at this time and annex sizable portions of New Hampshire and New York. This was a heavy-handed bit of imperialism that could scarcely be expected to add much luster to Vermont's image. Probably Ethan and the others would have preferred that none of this should happen, but once the process of empire-building had begun, they saw little choice but to continue it and attempt to steer it to their eventual advantage.

It all started with those pesky New Hampshire towns. By the autumn of 1780 they were once again demanding admission into the Republic of Vermont. And this time they were in a stronger position to be heard, for the Connecticut Valley was now speaking with one voice, and its message was plain enough: the towns on both sides of the river intended to join in political union, either under Vermont, New Hampshire, or a new state of their own making. As before, the Arlington junto looked with considerable disfavor upon the idea of annexing the New Hampshire towns. Still, it was obvious that the only alternative to accepting them into the Republic was the loss of much of the east side, an event which, of course, could not be permitted to happen. Thus, with Ira taking care of the details, Ethan, Governor Chittenden, and the other members of the Arlington faction arranged for the New Hampshire towns to be annexed to Vermont. On February 14, 1781, upon the recommendation of the Governor and Council, the Assembly sitting at Windsor made the so-called Eastern Union official by a one-sided vote of approval.

While all this was going on, attempts were begun by Ethan, with the somewhat halfhearted support of Chittenden, to set up a similar union west of the mountains by annexing the narrow oblong of territory lying between the Vermont border and the Hudson River. According to Ethan, this area, about eighty miles by twenty, should by rights belong to Vermont. It was inhabited to a considerable extent by Yankees who had drifted over from the Grants and from Berkshire County, Massachusetts, and everybody knew that it did not make sense for a Yankee to live under Yorker rule. Furthermore, the geography of the region made it clear beyond any question that this Hudson strip was meant by nature to be one with Vermont. In affairs of commerce and defense, for instance, the strip would obviously continue to be at a great disadvantage unless it were joined with the area to the eastward, and so, for that matter, would the Republic of Vermont. So went the arguments for the annexation of a sizable parcel of land which had never before this time been seriously considered as being anything other than an integral part of New York.

The real reasons for annexation were, of course, left unspoken. The most compelling of these appears to have been the determination on the part of Ethan and his friends that the political weight about to be gained by the east side through the addition of the New Hampshire towns must be offset by a corresponding gain for the west. Also probably of some importance in prompting the Vermont leaders to embark upon this bare-faced bit of land-grabbing was the belief that control over the strategically situated Hudson strip would put Vermont in a better bargaining position in its dealings with the British. An unchallenged approach to Albany could prove exceedingly useful to the British, and it doubtless occurred to Ethan that they might be willing to make attractive concessions to obtain it.

Whatever the motives behind it, there can be little doubt that the idea of a Western Union was mainly Ethan's, and that it was largely through his doing that within a surprisingly brief time the Union became a reality. In February of 1781, the Vermont Assembly voted, at Ethan's bidding, to "lay a jurisdictional claim" to the Hudson strip, and then went on to urge the inhabitants of that area to assemble in convention and petition for annexation to the Republic of Vermont. As Ethan was well aware, conditions at this time were certainly such as to incline the people of the strip toward political union with Vermont. In addition to the smoldering anti-Yorker bias that had long been prevalent among the large number of Yankees who had pitched in that area, there had lately arisen among Yankee and Yorker settlers alike a feeling of angry resentment over the fact that the government of New York had apparently abandoned them to fend for themselves against the British. "Nothing scarcely is talked of here but the bad conduct of the Legislature and the administration of government in this State," remarked a New York militia officer in reporting to Governor Clinton on conditions in the Hudson strip. "No troops on the frontier, nor no money, nor have the men got any ammunition, although an alarm is every day expected."

Contrasted to this obvious neglect by the government of New York was the solicitude that the Republic of Vermont had shown for its neighbors across the line. Poor and beset as it was, Vermont had on more than one occasion offered military aid to these people, and just recently it had demonstrated its concern for them by including them in its truce with the British. Here and there a Yorker voice could be heard protesting that the Vermont leaders had deliberately brought the strip under the truce for the specific purpose of preparing the way for its annexation, and perhaps this was so. Few of the settlers of the area seemed to care, however. To a very substantial majority of them the really important thing was that union with Vermont appeared to offer the best all-round hope for the future.

Lest the full meaning of all this be missed by some of them, Ethan Allen himself went among them frequently during the spring of 1781, showering them, according to on-the-spot reports received by Governor Clinton, with all sorts of wonderful promises, including "explicit assurances" that the people of the Hudson strip would not be molested by the British. A few of Ethan's listeners wondered how he could be so sure about what the British Army would or would not do, but most of the settlers were willing to take him at his word. In May the articles of union with Vermont were overwhelmingly agreed upon by the settlers of the Hudson strip, and midway through the following month, with the ratification of these articles by the Vermont Assembly, the Western Union became a reality.

To say that New Hampshire and New York were outraged by Vermont's grasping ways would be a classic understatement. They were wildly hysterical. To Congress, to each other, to the "pretended" government of Vermont, and to anyone else who would or should pay attention, they shrieked out their demands and threats. New Hampshire would leave the war and turn its forces loose against Vermont. New York would march immediately into the Hudson strip with five thousand men, and go on from there to crush the Vermont bandits, etc., etc. Ethan Allen and his cutthroat crew would be hanged, or worse, etc. etc. And so the agonized screams of the wounded states rent the northern air and reverberated with considerable volume for many months. But to little effect. Vermont's new acquisitions remained solidly in place, and Ethan and his friends showed not the slightest sign of being cowed by the furor they had provoked. In fact, it was "laughable and romantic," Ethan remarked contemptuously, for New Hampshire and New York to make "such a tedious outcry." For some time these two states had been attempting to devour the Republic of Vermont, and now Vermont was simply responding in kind, and it did not intend to have its work undone by noise. If the governments of New Hampshire and New York objected to what had been done, then let them seek redress by arms. Vermont was ready for the test.

But there was no test of arms, of course, nor did Ethan really believe there would be—at least not at this time. Through great daring and resourcefulness the Vermont leaders, not entirely of their own choosing, had created an empire of sorts, and this remarkable feat of expansionism had been accomplished entirely without violence of any kind. True, "Greater Vermont," as the imperium came to be called, would prove to be a rather brief affair, but the fact that it came into being at all, especially during a time of such great duress when the Republic was experiencing its most perilous hour, is something to be marveled at. "Even in the gulph of difficulties, and on the verge of ruin, she waxed strong and extended her wings," Ira would remark many years later when writing of Vermont's impudent expansion during that desperate winter of 1780–81. "The genius of Vermont was fruitfull in resources." And he might have added that not the least of these resources was his big brother Ethan, who on this occasion, as so often before and after, took it upon himself to decide what course the Republic of Vermont should follow, and then proceeded to persuade those lesser men about him to nod their approval.

On January 1, 1781, Colonel Warner's regiment was disbanded by an Act of Congress. Some of the officers and men were transferred to other commands within the Northern Department, but not Seth Warner. For over five years he had been more or less constantly in the field at the head of the regiment that Ethan Allen had always thought should have by rights been his. With Montgomery's motley array of Continentals, Warner had moved northward into Canada during the tragic winter of 1775–76, and, after Montgomery's death before the walls of Quebec, had held up the rear during the devastating American retreat. In the summer of the following year, while Ethan languished impatiently on parole in New Lots, Warner fought a stubborn rearguard action against the invading army of General Burgoyne at Hubbardton, buying desperately needed time for the Continental forces then massing for a defensive stand farther to the south. Falling back, he arrived in Bennington just in time to take his place beside General Stark, and perhaps accounted for the difference between victory and defeat in a battle that had to be won, and was. Stark later paid him great credit. So, in fact, did Ethan in his *Narrative*.

Only a week or so after the Battle of Bennington, Warner came down sick. He never recovered. The arduous campaigning of the previous two years had worn down his constitution, and during the remainder of his life he died by slow degrees. He continued in command, however, even though his condition grew increasingly agonizing. For more then three years after Bennington he remained with his regiment as it was shuffled from here to there throughout the Northern Department, often assigned to frontier duty, and sometimes forced to operate under conditions of great hardship. In the autumn of 1780, while Ethan was preparing to talk treason with General Haldimand, and Benedict Arnold was selling out his country for fifteen hundred guineas, Warner was painfully wounded in an Indian ambush near Lake George. Soon after this, he retired from the service, and at least partly because there was no one to take his place, the regiment he had commanded so long and well was mustered out.

By early 1781 Warner was back with his family in Bennington. His stay on the Grants would be brief, however. His lungs ravaged by tuberculosis, his joints grotesquely swollen with arthritis, and his mind inclined to wander now and then, Seth Warner, aged thirty-eight, was a used-up man. In a few months' time he would leave Bennington to return to his old home in Woodbury, Connecticut, where for the next two and a half years his life would drain out of him with terrible deliberation. Some time before the end his mind failed him, and he spent the final months strapped to his bed, fighting over and over again the battles of years gone by. When he finally died on the day after Christmas, 1784, the Reverend Thomas Canfield, a neighbor who had known Warner during better times, conducted the services. His remarks were taken from 2 Samuel I:27. "How are the Mighty fallen, and the weapons of War perished."

But before leaving the Grants for Woodbury, there was one more public service that Seth Warner felt compelled to perform. He had heard disturbing reports that his old comrade in arms, Ethan Allen, was engaged in some sort of shady dealing with the British, and he was determined to find out what was going on. Thus, on a day in early March of 1781, he rode up to Sunderland to see and talk with Ethan in person.

His timing was just about perfect, for only a few days before, Ethan had received a second letter from Tory Colonel Beverly Robinson. Although virtually the same in content as the first, this new message had a decidedly more positive tone to it and seemed more hopeful of success: "The frequent accounts we have had for three months from your part of the country confirms me in the opinion I had of your inclination to join the King's cause, and to assist in restoring America to her former peaceable and happy constitution."

Apparently Seth Warner had somehow or other found out about the letter. He must have, for he asked Ethan point-blank if he had recently received a secret communication from the enemy. At first Ethan flatly denied that he had received anything of the sort, recently or otherwise, and insisted that despite rumors to the contrary his involvement with the British had never gone beyond making arrangements for a prisoner exchange, and there was certainly nothing wrong with that. Finally, however, under Warner's persistent questioning, he admitted that he had received two letters from the British during the past year. One of them, he lied, he had burned. The other, just recently arrived, he had turned over to the Governor and Council. This was all that Ethan owned up to. Not a word was mentioned about the clandestine dealings with Haldimand. Still, enough had been said to add to his jeopardy, and, according to a remark made later by Ethan himself, it was partly because of his conversation with Seth Warner that he decided to make an explanatory gesture to the outside world. With suspicion mounting about him on all sides, the time had arrived for him to disarm the doubtful by baring his breast. Obviously, however, he did not intend to bare very much of it.

Within a few days after Warner's visit, Ethan, with the approval of the Governor and Council, sent both of the Robinson letters to Congress in Philadelphia. "I shall make no comment on them," he remarked in an accompanying note. "They are the identical, and only letters, I ever have received from him, and to which I have never returned any manner of answer, nor have I ever had the least personal acquaintance with him directly or indirectly." And that was that. Of course, there were those several letters received from General Haldimand during the past few months, but why mention them? Ethan certainly did not intend to admit to any more than he had to. After all, this was something more than a child's game he was involved in.

Ethan ended his letter to Congress on a defiant note. This was typical of him. He had never been much given to humility or submission. In fact, the more exposed his own position, the more apt he was to strut haughtily before his adversaries, shake a threatening finger under their noses, and confound their councils with his aplomb. It was as natural for him to do this as it was for some men to cringe or hide. In this instance, he pointedly reminded the honorable members of Congress that through no fault of its own the Republic of Vermont was not a part of the American Union and therefore was in no way bound to dance to Congress' tune. In other words, Vermont was a free agent and would behave as it saw fit. In the past the Republic had made common cause with the American States against the British, but this did not mean that it felt under any obligation to continue to do so:

> I do not hesitate to say that Vermont has an indubitable right to agree on terms of cessation of hostilities with Great Britain, provided the United States persist in rejecting her application for a union with them, for Vermont, of all people, would be the most miserable, were she obliged to defend the independence of united claiming States, and they at the same time at full liberty to overturn and ruin the independence of Vermont.

Let it be clearly understood by all, Ethan stated in a final flourish of defiance, that he, Ethan Allen, was determined to see to it that Vermont's interests were upheld at any cost and by any means, and "rather than fail, I will retire with hardy Green Mountain Boys into the desolate caverns of the Mountains, and wage war with humanity at large."

It was in many ways an excellent letter, one of Ethan's more eloquent creations. Obviously designed as much for home consumption as for Congress, it was probably a good propaganda move on Ethan's part. If, however, it had been intended to lessen suspicion against him and his friends, then it was certainly at best a halfhearted effort. In fact, throughout the winter and spring of 1780–81, while rumors were mounting about secret meetings in the woods at Sunderland and other strange goings-on, Ethan and his co-conspirators were surprisingly casual about the whole affair. Perhaps because they still hoped to frighten Congress into recognition, the Vermont leaders made nothing but the most cursory attempts to deny or explain the ugly charges being made against them. Indeed, at times they appeared to go out of their way to behave so as to lend weight to reports of their burgeoning treason. Consider, for example, the junto's surprising cordiality at this time toward certain Americans known to be hostile to the Patriot cause.

Beginning in the late autumn of 1780, deserters from the Continental Army became a more or less common sight on the Grants, as did Loyalists from neighboring states. Furthermore, in open defiance of the law of the Republic, Ethan and his friends were now encouraging exiled Tories to return to Vermont and take up where they had left off. And return they did in considerable number. Some of them were even placed in high office by the Governor and Council—much to the consternation of patriotic Vermonters. As might have been suspected (and indeed was), all of this was done mainly to please General Haldimand, who had suggested to Ethan early in the negotiations that this would be one way for the Vermont leaders to ingratiate themselves with him and prove the sincerity of their intentions. At the same time, of course, by welcoming the Tories, Ethan and the others were strengthening their position within the Republic by bringing in persons who could be counted on for support when, if ever, the time came to turn Vermont over to the British.

Surveying the scene from afar, General Schuyler wrote to Governor Clinton in early May of 1781 that he could not help but wonder about the intentions of the Vermont leaders, "when I daily learn that the Tories are moving from all quarters to reside with them, where reports say they are well received." On at least one occasion, when the people of Bennington threatened to get out of control and manhandle a group of recently arrived Tories, Ethan himself appeared on the scene to offer the Tories protection. Strange behavior was this for a man who only two years before had spared no effort to rid the Grants of such "attrotious villains" and confiscate their property for the good of the Republic and the American Confederation.

In the mid-spring of 1781, the truce between the Republic of Vermont and the British was renewed. By this time there could no longer be any reasonable doubt that Ethan Allen and his Arlington friends were involved with the enemy in something more than a prisoner exchange, but it was still impossible to prove it. During the previous autumn, even before he had learned of the original cartel, Governor Clinton had grown so convinced of Ethan's complicity with the British that he began gathering a semi-official dossier of his doings. This was a job that the governor must have enjoyed thoroughly and given great attention to. Even so, by the late spring of the following year he had failed to come up with anything resembling conclusive evidence against Ethan or any of the others.

General Schuyler, who had been keeping a dossier of his own, could do no better. For months he had been poised, ready to swoop down on Ethan, but he continued to lack the necessary proof. It was infuriating, he wrote to Washington, to know virtually for a fact that the Vermont leaders were deeply involved in treason and yet be unable to take action against them. General Washington agreed. With rumors flying about in all directions, Washington was forced to conclude that "matters in a certain quarter carry a very suspicious face. . . . I do not believe that the people as a body have any evil intention, but I firmly believe that some of their leaders have, and that they will prevent us from deriving aid, though they may not be able to turn the Arms of their Countrymen against us."

The General ordered Schuyler to continue to keep a close watch on things, and be prepared to move in at any moment to seize Ethan and his papers "with the greatest secrecy." At the same time he made it clear that no action should be taken without "demonstrated proof," and this was something that would prove very difficult to come by. Ethan and his friends were obviously very clever in skirting the rim of the abyss, or very lucky—or both. They were also very devious. In midsummer of 1781, at a time when the Arlington conspirators were on the very verge of turning the Republic over to the British, Ethan wrote to General Schuyler that "the late reports or rather surmises of my corrisponding with the Enemy to the prejudice of the United States . . . is wholly without foundation." Schuyler immediately turned the letter over to Washington. Both were sure that Ethan was lying, but there was no way of proving it.

In spite of the strange and compromising doings of the Vermont leaders and the thick cloud of suspicion that long hovered over them, no serious attempt was ever made to bring a formal indictment against any of them—save for a single effort, abortive but nonetheless notable, that took place during the early stages of the Haldimand negotiations. Surprisingly enough, this was not the work of the Continental Congress or Governor Clinton, but of the Vermont Assembly, which Ethan and his friends had always more or less taken for granted as being safe ground. Apparently, however, it was not so safe as they had supposed. On this singular occasion the Assembly's behavior certainly represented no immediate threat to Ethan's plans or position. In fact, it was clear that most of the members were quite willing, as usual, to follow his lead without question. Still, the voice of dissent was sounded, and although feeble, it signaled the start of an important change in the character of Vermont politics: the Assembly was beginning to assert itself. Within three years' time it would succeed in getting the upper hand over the Governor and Council, and thereby put an end to government by oligarchy—or strong man.

In other words, the fortunes of the Arlington junto in general and their chief in particular began to decline on that day at the Bennington Meeting House in early November of 1780, less than a week after the news of the cartel had become known, when a small group of assembly-men dared to square off against their betters by bringing charges of misconduct against General Ethan Allen. Exactly what the charges were can not be ascertained from the records that remain, but they obviously carried the implication of treason to the Republic. Eleven in number, the charges were described by one assemblyman as "very heavy" and were considered serious enough to merit the introduction of two sep-arate impeachment resolutions against Ethan. Of course, neither of them carried or even came close. Still, it was a humiliating experience for Ethan—an aspersion upon his conduct and, what was worse, a question-ing of his authority. It was bad enough that the resolutions were intro-duced in the first place, but the Assembly's decision to consider them seriously and actually vote on them, instead of giving them the peremp-tory tabling they deserved, was more than Ethan could stand. Jumping up from his seat, he let out a torrent of awful profanity and threatened to cut off the heads of his tormentors. In the end, however, he merely withdrew from the hall, refusing to listen to "such scurrilous insinu-ations."

When he returned a few days later, he was naturally pleased to learn that the resolutions had been voted down by a heavy majority, and the whole business of impeachment had blown over. It was gratifying to know that the Assembly was still with him. Nevertheless, his dignity had been affronted by the affair and he wanted the members of the Assembly to understand that he had been hurt by their decision to "give ear to these false and ignominious aspersions." Since his conduct as a servant of the Republic had been called into question, and "there is a general uneasiness among some of the people on account of my command," he thought it best to resign his commission and return to private life. With surprising dispatch and few demurrers the Assembly proceeded to accept his resignation with thanks, and then, by way of putting some substance into its thanks, voted him a choice parcel of land in Easthaven.

There were those on hand who looked upon the Assembly's rapid acceptance of Ethan's resignation as a shattering blow to the great man's vanity and power. Governor Clinton's spies considered it so, and duly reported the happy event to their chief in Poughkeepsie. However, in view of Ethan's obvious control over the Assembly, it seems more likely that his resignation was accepted because he wanted it to be. And he wanted this because he believed that for reasons of strategy the time was right for him to resign his command. Being general of the Vermont Militia had been fun for awhile. He had enjoyed the glory of command and reveled in the public prominence that went with it. Still, the entire arrangement was nothing more than a superfluity. It was clear enough to Ethan, as it was to everyone else who understood the realities of the situation, that with or without gold braid and high-sounding title he was the boss, and this being the case, there was really no compelling reason for him to continue in command.

There was, however, good reason for him not to—namely, the fact that he would probably be considerably safer without his command than with it. Whatever else historians may say about the Haldimand intrigue, they all agree that Ethan's dealings with the British had much that was dark and devious about them, which, if brought into the open, could have placed him in a very embarrassing position. As a mere civilian, holding no office and acting in a private capacity, Ethan would doubtless have found the going rough enough if he had been exposed and brought to an accounting, but as commander of the Republic's militia he would certainly have fared much worse. In other words, given the work he was now involved in, his military command was clearly a liability, and a potentially dangerous one at that. Without it he could feel freer and less imperiled in his transactions with General Haldimand, and in view of the sensitive and high-powered nature of these transactions, it behooved Ethan to be as unencumbered as possible. In fact, some historians have even gone so far as to claim that Ethan deliberately staged the entire impeachment proceedings in order to provide himself with a convincing excuse for getting rid of the encumbrance of his command—all of which seems farfetched.

It is unlikely that Ethan actually created the impeachment fuss, such as it was. He merely exploited it to his own advantage. Or so at least it would seem. At any rate, as of November, 1780, Ethan was again a private citizen of the Republic. In April of the following year, the Assembly attempted to persuade him to resume his command but he declined, saying that although he would always stand ready to serve the people of Vermont to the best of his ability, he would accept no office, military or otherwise. And he remained true to his word. Never again would he hold official position of any sort.

To the outside world, save for the British who of course knew differently, Ethan attempted to give the impression that he was entirely out of power during the months immediately following his surrender of command, and implied that the machinery of government in Vermont was being run by others. Writing to a member of Congress in the spring of 1781, he made a special point of referring to himself as "a Private Gentleman." In order to strengthen the illusion of Allen impotence, he undertook from time to time to convince outsiders that he had been forced out of power against his will and was very angry at his fellow Vermonters for their shabby treatment of him: On one occasion he even went so far as to write to his old enemy, Governor Clinton, complaining of the ingratitude shown him by those he had served so selflessly and well, and (of all things!) offering to move away from Vermont and place himself and a small band of loyal followers at the service of the government of New York. "We would esteem it the greatest happiness of our lives," Ethan declared very seriously, as if he actually expected the governor to believe him, "to defend the State of New York against their cruel invaders."

Needless to say, Clinton did not snap up Ethan's offer. It was clear to the governor that all of this was nothing more than an awkward maneuver on the part of the Grants hoodlum-in-chief to turn suspicion away from himself and his sinister dealings with the British. In fact, despite Ethan's attempts to promote such an illusion, few people familiar with the man and the circumstances, least of all Governor Clinton—who was by now something of an expert on Ethan Allen—were naive enough to suppose for a moment that he had really dropped the reins of power or had had them wrested from him. This was especially true after it became known that he had been succeeded in militia command by his loyal and fawning friend, Samuel Spafford, a member in good standing of the Arlington junto. Indeed, it seems unlikely that Ethan himself seriously believed that he could convince the world of his fall from grace, or that he was willing to make much of an effort to do so. After all, at the very same time that he was so audibly complaining about his loss of power and offering his sword to the service of Governor Clinton, "Private Gentleman" Allen was busily and conspicuously engaged in stirring up secessionist agitation among the settlers of the Hudson strip. Not very convincing behavior for one who was supposed to have left the public arena.

Still, even though there had never been much chance that many people would actually believe him, Ethan's play at impotence might have been of some value for his purposes. At least, it had the effect of adding another element of confusion to the bewildering caldron of Vermont politics, and to Ethan and his friends, who counted confusion as an ally in their conspiratorial enterprises, this was all to the good.

# XIV. Vermont Stands Alone

ON MAY 1, 1781, his thirtieth birthday, Ira Allen left Sunderland and headed northward under a flag of truce into British-held territory. His destination was the Ile aux Noix, a desolate little speck in the Sorel River not far south of St. John's, where he would represent the Arlington junto before the councils of the enemy. Arriving at the island on May 8, he immediately began an extended series of meetings with Justus Sherwood and other agents of General Haldimand, ostensibly to make final arrangements for the long-deferred exchange of prisoners, but actually to further negotiations aimed at taking Vermont back into the British Empire.

Aside from his military escort of around twenty Vermont militiamen, Ira had come alone. As he himself put it, usually in affairs of this sort "one man is better than more." He was not, however, the best person in the world for the job at hand. Here was an exceedingly delicate enterprise that required plenty of faith and trust on the part of both sides, and Ira, with his strong odor of intrigue and duplicity, was hardly the man to inspire either. Justus Sherwood later said of him that he "sometimes induces contempt and always suspicion." Still, there was this much in Ira's favor: He was a quiet, self-effacing man who blended inconspicuously into the landscape. Furthermore, he could keep a secret. Add to this the fact that he was intensely loyal to his brother, and his presence on the island as sole negotiator for the Republic of Vermont does not seem so unreasonable. It would certainly have been unwise to send Ethan, who was temperamentally ill-suited for operating in the shadows, and, insofar as anyone knew, had never been able to keep a secret for very long.

For nearly three weeks Ira bargained with Sherwood and the others, even though the area for dickering was extremely limited. The British position was clearly stated in a letter from General Haldimand which arrived shortly after the meetings got underway. "The State of Vermont," Haldimand declared flatly, "must either be united in constituted liberty with Great Britain, or continue at enmity with it." There was, as far as the British were concerned, no middle ground. To this Ira replied that he personally would like to see reunion with the Empire and he knew that his brother felt the same. He assured Haldimand's agents that both he and Ethan had been working toward that end and would continue to do so. At the present time, however, neither the Vermont Assembly nor public opinion was ready to go beyond the point of neutrality. To bring Vermonters around to accepting reunion with Great Britain would be a perilous business and would require more time. How much time? Well, at least until after adjournment of the next session of the Assembly, scheduled to convene in mid-June. Meanwhile, the prisoner truce should be extended and all signs of hostility on the part of the British be avoided lest the public temper of the Vermonters be "inflamed" and the happy reunion of Vermont with the Empire thereby be rendered more difficult to effect.

After an exchange of notes with Haldimand, who was then in Quebec, the British emissaries agreed to extend the truce and give the Vermont leaders more time—until adjournment of the June session of the Assembly and "a reasonable period thereafter." Sherwood and friends were less than happy with this arrangement. They were inclined to think that the Vermonters had already used up their fair share of time, and then some. It seemed to them more than likely that Ira was stalling in an attempt to postpone the final irretrievable step for as long as possible. Still, all indications were that the Vermont leaders, although notably standoffish, were at least moving in the right direction, and in view of this, General Haldimand decided to wait a while longer. Actually, he had little alternative anyway. Although the Vermonters believed otherwise, his military position had seldom been weaker. In a sense, Haldimand was running a giant bluff and it would not do for him to force his own hand and thereby expose his hopeless lack of strength. Thus, as Ira later reported the affair in his *History,* the Ile aux Noix conference ended in a spirit of "high friendship," with Vermont still uncommitted to reunion, but somewhat closer to it than before.

And so the situation would stand throughout the spring and summer and into the autumn of 1781; with one side inching slowly, reluctantly, but certainly toward the precipice, apparently disposed toward reunion but determined to put off the grand decision for as long as possible, and the other side chafing and grumbling ill-naturedly over the delay but unable to do much to hurry the process. June arrived. The Vermont Assembly sat and rose, but the cause of reunion was not perceptibly advanced. The reason for this, Ethan explained in a letter to Haldimand, was that the Assembly was not considered safe. With representatives present in sizable number from the Eastern Union, probably no more than half of all the members could be counted on to support "the Governor's party." In fact, throughout the entire session the junto had experienced considerable difficulty because of these new members, many of whom insisted upon asking embarrassing questions about the truce. All of this would soon change, however, for the next Assembly, scheduled for October, would include representatives from the recently annexed Hudson strip and would be bound to be more friendly toward the Arlington leadership. Only a little more time was all that separated Vermont from the bosom of the Empire. Take Ethan Allen's word for that.

Naturally Haldimand was upset. He had recently received letters from General Clinton and Lord Germain telling of His Majesty's "utmost concern" over the progress of the negotiations with Vermont, which was another way of ordering Haldimand to get moving and produce something. And General Haldimand had generated a great deal of impatience of his own over the matter of Vermont's reunion, mainly perhaps because he had developed such high expectations. Only a short time before, he had been all but convinced that the reunion was about to be effected, and, of course, a triumph of this magnitude could conceivably determine the outcome of the American war. It could also do great things for his career.

But now, still another delay, and the general was far from satisfied that this latest postponement was necessary. In fact, it now seemed pretty clear to him that the Vermont leaders were determined to put off a final commitment for as long as possible. He liked to think that this was a result of caution on their part, rather than duplicity, but more and more he was beginning to wonder if he had perhaps permitted himself to be deluded by "the Allen people." Writing to Lord Germain in early July, Haldimand admitted that he was now somewhat inclined to question the faith he had recently come to have in Ethan Allen. It might be true after all, as he had originally suspected, that Allen and his subordinates were simply using the negotiations as a lever against the

American Congress. Still, after much soul-searching, the General notified the Vermont conspirators in mid-July that he would again prolong the truce. This he did partly because he still half-believed in the honest intentions of Ethan Allen, and partly because he had no reasonable alternative. It was to be understood, however, that his patience was wearing thin and that the truce would remain in effect only so long as progress was being made in arranging for the imminent return of Vermont to the Empire.

Actually, despite Haldimand's understandable doubts, it appears that Ethan and his friends were now acting in good faith. By this time they had almost certainly determined to deliver Vermont to the British. True, they moved slowly, but in view of the danger involved, they had to do so. Ethan, to be sure, was still the dominant political figure on the Grants, but his power was far from absolute. In the final reckoning he was only as strong as his popularity with the people, a fact that he was certainly wise enough to recognize. And up to this point the people of the Republic had shown themselves, as Ethan explained to Haldimand, "fully prepossessed in favor of Congress." There was no way of telling how they would react when confronted with the sudden prospect of rejoining the British Empire. Ethan was not even sure about the members of the governor's Council, some of whom were considered so unsafe that the real nature of the negotiations was carefully kept from them. The Vermont conspirators were involved in a perilous undertaking, a fact that Haldimand appears not to have fully appreciated, perhaps because for him the stakes were considerably less formidable. For Ethan and his friends there was more than a remote possibility of disaster if things should go wrong. It was unlikely that they would have a chance to second-guess. Their heads were on the block, and they were determined to move cautiously.

And cautiously they did move during the quiet summer of 1781, but with great effect nevertheless. Ira and Joseph Fay did most of the actual bargaining in a series of meetings with Haldimand's agents at which, for the sake of appearances, small groups of prisoners were exchanged. The guiding hand behind it all, though, was clearly Ethan's. It was he who made the major decisions, and it was mainly to him that Haldimand addressed his messages and, of course, his hopes of success. Occasionally, when matters of particular sensitivity arose, the general would send his couriers directly to Sunderland to seek out Ethan rather than deal with go-betweens. This brazen practice was discouraged by Ethan. The presence of British agents in his back yard frankly worried him. It was far safer to work through others. Of course, whenever it seemed advisable for him to communicate directly with Haldimand he did not hesitate to do so, but he preferred that on these occasions the traffic flow away from him rather than toward him. Consequently he arranged an elaborate system whereby he was able to get in touch with General Haldimand with a minimum of risk:

> That . . . he may not be at a loss to convey Intelligence when necessary [reported a British agent to Haldimand], he proposes the following Token by his messenger—viz—Three Smoaks on the Eastside the Lake opposite the Shipping, and at the middle Smoak a small white flag hoisted on a staff. He would propose to have the Commandant on the Lake instructed to receive such Messenger immediately on Board, and not interrogate him concerning his Business and send him to Canada. . . .

All very secretive and sinister—but also probably very conducive to Ethan's continued well-being.

By the time of the first frost in early September, the provisions governing Vermont's reentry into the Empire had been agreed upon by both sides. Obviously Ethan and his accomplices had done well for themselves and for those whom they intended to betray, for, to a people who had recently risen up in arms against him, His Majesty George III was now offering most generous terms of reconciliation:

> (1) All territory claimed by the Republic of Vermont, including the so-called Eastern and Western Unions, was to be incorporated into a British province controlled directly by the Crown.

It had really taken a good deal of persuasion by Ethan and the others to get Haldimand to agree to the inclusion of the Unions in the new Royal Province. The general was not at all sure that he had the authority to "guarantee parts of other Provinces" to Vermont. It was really, he supposed, a matter that Parliament should decide upon, but there was hardly time for that. To his superior, Sir Henry Clinton, he wrote of his misgivings and of his intention to move ahead nonetheless, because "if by Sacrificing a part of one province to the interest of the other, a Reunion of the most Valuable with the Mother Country can be effected, I think it my duty to make the attempt."

(2) Vermont was to be given the same liberal form of government as that formerly granted Connecticut, except that the governor of the new Province might from time to time be appointed by the Crown.

This provision, of course, reflects the fact that virtually all of the Vermont conspirators had come originally from Connecticut and still looked upon it as the closest thing to paradise on earth, even though most of them had found it next to impossible to make a decent living there.

(3) The new Royal Province was to raise two battalions of "properly officered" troops, to be paid for by the British and used for the defense of the Province. However, neither these nor any other Vermont troops would be called upon to fight in the American war unless Vermont were actually attacked. In the conflict between Great Britain and the so-called United States, Vermont would be permitted to remain neutral.

From the very beginning of the negotiations Ethan had insisted upon this provision as a *sine qua non*. Frequently in his letters to Haldimand and Sherwood he laid heavy emphasis upon the fact that, although Vermont would raise troops for the Empire, they were not to be used against the American States except in a clearly defensive manner. Specifically, they were to remain within the boundaries of "Greater Vermont" and fight only if attacked. This much can be said for Ethan: it was never any part of his plan to fight for the British against his former friends and comrades in arms, and he never gave anyone cause to believe differently.

(4) The Royal Province of Vermont was to be allowed free trade with Canada and "be protected therein."

The inclusion of this provision was mainly Ira's doing. With his merchant's mentality he was naturally sensitive to the economic advantages of an unencumbered trade relationship with Canada. He could visualize the day when a brisk traffic would pass along the waterways to and from Montreal and beyond, and the price of Onion River land would soar accordingly. As for Ethan, he was not especially interested in the matter. After all, this was not politics, but business, and at first he saw no reason for including it in the negotiations. But he was eventually persuaded by Ira, as he was in so many other things pertaining to profit and loss, that it would be of considerable benefit to Vermont and the Allen fortunes to have ready access to the St. Lawrence and the attractive Canadian markets. Even so, during the Haldimand negotiations Ethan left the unexciting matter of trading rights almost entirely up to Ira to settle as he saw fit. It was not in fact, until well after the negotiations had come to their inglorious end that Ethan finally grasped the full significance of what Ira had been after. By then, of course, it was too late.

Such were the terms of the "treaty" that was designed to take Vermont back into the Empire. There now remained only the question of how best to impose this new order of things upon the people who would have to live under it. The question was answered in September when a plan of execution was agreed upon by both parties. For the most part the plan was based upon suggestions made by the Vermont conspirators and submitted directly to General Haldimand in the form of a written proposal which, in view of the Vermonters' long trail of equivocation, delay, and ambiguity during the course of the negotiations, was remarkable for its directness and commitment. In fact, so specifically and completely were the details of execution spelled out that there now remained little question about the intent of the Vermont leaders. They were obviously going to do what they had long promised they would, and they were going to do it soon. General Haldimand was delighted when he saw the proposal. To General Clinton he wrote that he was now reassured and greatly encouraged. "My suspicions of Allen's Party have almost, if not entirely, been removed."

The plan was a simple but ingenious one that could hardly fail to provide Vermont with a safe and tranquil passage back into the Empire. It was to be put into operation during the second week of October, as soon as the new Assembly gathered for its fall meeting. With the Western Union about to have full representation in the Vermont Legislature for the first time, Ethan expected that the upcoming Assembly would be more favorably disposed towards the Arlington junto and less apt to cause trouble than the session of the preceding June. He estimated, immodestly but perhaps accurately, that this added west-side strength might mean that as many as two-thirds of the members of the new Assembly would be Allen men and follow obediently wherever he chose to lead them. Still, with his neck perilously close to the noose, he saw no sense in leaving anything to chance. Consequently, at the request of the Vermont leaders, the British were to step in and help force things a bit.

Immediately upon receipt of the word that the Assembly had convened, the British were to move up the lake with, as Haldimand described the plan to his superiors, "a force equal to support our friends . . . and awe those in opposition." The troops would disembark and bivouac at the upper narrows near Ticonderoga, from where, upon receiving the word from Ira, the officer in command would release a proclamation calling upon the settlers of the Grants to accept the generous terms of reconciliation being offered them by His Most Gracious and Forgiving Majesty, or suffer awful consequences. The proclamation, which would be drawn up by General Haldimand and issued in his name, would of course include the provisions agreed upon by the negotiators, and a brief but unspecified period of time would be allowed the people to make up their minds. Ethan could at this point reveal his complicity or not, just as he chose, but it would at any rate be incumbent upon him to persuade the Assembly to come to terms. Failing this, he and his friends were to dissolve the Assembly and accept the British ultimatum in the name of the Governor and Council. To further strengthen Ethan's hand, the British would accompany their proclamation with a campaign of conspicuous devastation against the frontier settlements of New York across the lake. "It is hoped this conduct," Haldimand explained to General Clinton, "will convince the people of Vermont that it is the intention of British Government to protect them, and will facilitate the Endeavors of the Leading Men in our favor to gain the populace."

Fortunately for subsequent generations of Vermonters, Ethan's great betrayal failed to come off as planned. Things went wrong almost from the very beginning. The British force under General Barry St. Leger was somewhat less than hoped for. In all, it numbered no more than two thousand troops, hardly the sort of military array that could be expected to "awe those in opposition," but probably the best that Haldimand could spare from his slender resources. Furthermore, St. Leger was late in getting underway and as a result did not arrive up-lake until more than a week after the Vermont Assembly had convened. There, near the abandoned ruins of Fort Ticonderoga his little army disembarked and, carefully watched by curious Vermonters from across the narrows, proceeded to wait. But for what purpose? For two days St. Leger fretted and fumed, with Haldimand's proclamation poised in readiness, waiting vainly for word from Ira to release it. Finally, his impatience got the better of him, and he did a very foolish thing.

If Ira would not get in touch with him, then he would get in touch with Ira and urge him to hurry things up. Reasoning that the safest and least suspicious way of doing this would be to make use of a Vermont courier, St. Leger dispatched a small raiding party over to the Vermont shore to capture one. Unfortunately for the general, his raiders overdid it. They brought back not one but six Vermonters, all of them militiamen whom the British party had happened upon, exchanged shots with, and ultimately overpowered. One of the Vermonters, Sergeant Archelaus Tupper, was dead on arrival, much to the General's consternation —shot through by a British ball. Here was a turn of events much to be deplored. Before leaving Canada, St. Leger had been lectured by Haldimand on the delicate nature of the assignment, and had been specifically warned that "every appearance of Hostility must be carefully avoided . . . that the Populace might not be exasperated." Obviously the death of Sergeant Tupper boded ill, and it was up to General St. Leger to make amends.

This he attempted with greater zeal than common sense. After wining and dining his Vermont prisoners, St. Leger had them escorted back to the opposite shore, where they were given a letter of apology to Governor Chittenden and then released. This letter was soon turned over to an officer in the Vermont militia and subsequently entrusted to a courier for delivery to the governor. By strange coincidence, the courier was Simon Hathaway, the very person who only a year before had introduced one of the impeachment resolutions against Ethan. Naturally he read the letter before he had gone very far, and the contents struck him as being extremely interesting; so much so that he shared them with persons he met along the way. And his way was a long one. The Governor and Council, together with the Assembly, were then in session in Charlestown, a river community on the far side of the Connecticut which prior to the recent establishment of the Eastern Union had belonged to New Hampshire. This meant that Hathaway traveled the entire width of the Republic, spreading the word as he went. By the time the letter reached Chittenden, probably half the people in Vermont knew its contents.

In view of the nature of General St. Leger's message and the widespread knowledge of it, it is not surprising that Hathaway was followed into the Assembly in Charlestown by an angry crowd demanding an explanation of these strange goings-on. There was indeed much to explain. In his letter St. Leger not only apologized for "the accidental death" of Sergeant Tupper, but also offered free passage through British lines to "your people . . . to see the last decencies paid to his corpse." The general then promised that the sergeant's clothes would be sent home to his widow. All of this was exceedingly considerate. It was also quite incomprehensible. Why, many people wondered, should an enemy commander show such remorse over the death of a Vermont militiaman? After all, Vermont and Great Britain were at war. The truce had ended more than a month before with the exchange of the last of the prisoners. Why this strange solicitude? Was there something that was being kept from the people, something that they should know? The crowd that had burst into the Charlestown meeting hall was in no mood to be trifled with. It wanted answers. So, for that matter, did the Vermont Assembly.

It took a great deal of doing, but with Ira at the helm the conspirators managed to weather the storm. This they did by a bold and imaginative bit of lying, cheating, and forgery. Never before had Ira's peculiar talents shone so brilliantly or to such great advantage. By his truly polished performance at Charlestown in the autumn of 1781 he proved himself to be without peer in his mastery of deceit. Several years later in his *History of Vermont* he proudly recorded the details of his triumphant duplicity, intimating in what was probably an accurate appraisal that his adroit handling of that crisis saved his brother, himself, and the rest of the Arlington junto from a great deal of unpleasantness at the hands of their neighbors. Even so, it was a near thing. In the end the crowd and a majority of the Assembly agreed to accept the junto's assurance that nothing was really amiss, but only because they could not prove anything different. It was obvious that suspicions continued to run high.

An ominous cloud now hung heavily over Ethan and his co-conspirators, and they knew it. On the evening following the worrisome scene in the Assembly, they sent off an urgent message to St. Leger, expressing their "highest consternation" over the furor caused by the Tupper affair, and begging the general to withhold Haldimand's proclamation until the public temper had subsided somewhat. In the opinion of the Vermont conspirators, now was hardly a propitious time to attempt the long leap back to the Empire.

Across the narrows in his quarters at Ticonderoga, General St. Leger agreed, and with great reluctance put away the proclamation. But not because of Sergeant Tupper. Earlier that same day, scarcely an hour after St. Leger had received the troubled dispatch from Charlestown, shattering intelligence arrived from the south: a week before, Lord Cornwallis and his entire army had surrendered to the Continentals and their French allies. Several weeks later when the news reached London, His Majesty's first minister, Lord North, overcome with despair, cried out again and again: "Oh, my God, my God! It is all over." General St. Leger, a less emotional man, said nothing. He merely began preparations for withdrawal, and on the following day, without waiting for orders from Haldimand, retired to Canada.

With the removal of British troops from the upper lake, the treasonous scheme to return Vermont to the British Empire was doomed. The execution of the great betrayal had been too long delayed, and now it could never come at all. Chittenden, a wise old man, recognized the fact clearly enough and soon turned his attention to other enterprises. So also did most of the other members of the conspiracy. But not Ethan. He absolutely refused to accept such a disappointing defeat. Nearly a year later he wrote to Haldimand: "I shall do anything in my power to render this State a British Province." And he was as good as his word. For months, even years, after Yorktown he would continue his efforts toward reunion. Even after the war had officially ended and his own public power had all but vanished, he was still corresponding with British officials in Quebec and London, declaring that "Vermont must either be annexed to Canada or become mistress of it." By this time, of course, he had become an embarrassment to the British, who, it appears, were doing their best to abide by that provision of the peace treaty of 1783 which had conceded the area of Vermont to the United States. For the most part his letters went unanswered, and what acknowledgments he did receive were curt and decidedly lacking in enthusiasm.

For several months immediately following Yorktown, however, Ethan's conspiracy was still taken seriously by a few of those more resolute Britishers who refused to recognize the realities of the military situation in America. Among them was the dogged Lord Germain who, in early 1782, instructed Haldimand to keep up the conversations with the Vermont leaders. The general did what he was told, and continued to conspire with Ethan through Sherwood and other Tories. In fact, it was not until the summer of 1783, in fact, only a couple of months shy of the official end of the war, that Haldimand received specific orders from the Home Government to terminate his attempts to win over the Vermonters.

then, he dutifully went through the motions of pushing the negotiations and pretending to share Ethan's hopeful expectations, even though he admitted to his intimates that Yorktown had made the entire business "an affair of Great Ridicule."

The general was right in concluding that, as he himself put it, "the happy moment has passed." The smashing success of Continental and French troops a thousand miles to the south had unleashed such a flurry of patriotism that there was now no longer even a remote possibility that the people of Vermont would submit quietly to betrayal by their leaders. Only by a major application of armed force could Vermont now be taken back into the Empire, and armed force had become a scarce commodity, not only with Haldimand, but with the rest of the British North American Command as well. The British military presence in America had, in fact, grown perilously weak, and all indications were that little would be done by the Home Government to strengthen it. The Revolution had already cost England two entire armies, one at Saratoga and another at Yorktown, and with British fortunes rapidly crumbling in Europe and elsewhere, His Majesty's Government was not inclined to sink more troops or materiel into the American quagmire. For all intents and purposes the War of the American Revolution was over, and so were the prospects for the successful betrayal of their neighbors by Ethan Allen and his Arlington friends. There was some comfort for Ethan and the others in the fact that they had not been exposed for what they were—not officially at least. They had lost without having had their complicity revealed, but they had lost nonetheless. Vermont, for better or for worse, was not to become a part of the British Empire.

Surveying the ruins from his headquarters in New York City, Sir Henry Clinton, commander in chief of England's forces in North America, could not resist speculating about what might have happened: "I have little doubt," he remarked with some bitterness, "that had Lord Cornwallis only remained where he was ordered, or even after his coming into Virginia had our operations there been covered by a superior fleet as I was promised, Vermont would probably have joined us."

Ironically enough, while the British were falling just short in their attempts to reclaim Vermont, they almost succeeded in getting it admitted into the Confederation of American States. By the summer of 1781, Congress had become thoroughly alarmed over the face of things on the northern frontier. If there had been doubts before about Britain's serious designs upon Vermont, all such doubts suddenly vanished on the last day of July when there turned up in Congress a highly interesting and revealing letter written by no less a person than Lord George Germain himself. This letter, intended for Sir Henry Clinton, had been captured at sea by the French some months before and had subsequently been handed over to Benjamin Franklin in Paris, who in turn sent it on to Congress. It told in clear and explicit terms of Vermont's importance to British strategy in the American war and of His Majesty's determination to "draw over these people." Here at last was official proof of what most people had strongly suspected for a long time: the British were making it a matter of major policy to entice Vermont back into the Empire. "The letter from Lord George Germain," remarked one member of Congress, "puts Vermont's connection with Great Britain out of doubt and renders our situation truly alarming"—so alarming, in fact, that Congress decided that the time had come to "put the Vermont question in a train of speedy decision." After years of stalling, the men at Philadelphia had finally been prodded into action by fear of the consequences of continuing to do nothing. Commented Ira at a later time:

> This letter had greater influence on the wisdom and virtue of Congress than all the exertions of Vermont in taking Ticonderoga, Crown Point, and the two divisions from General Burgoyne's Army, or their petition to be admitted as a state in the general confederation and offers to pay their proportions of the expenses of the war.

With almost unprecedented dispatch the Confederation Congress voted during the first week of August to deliberate immediately on the Vermont question with a view to final settlement. On the twentieth of the same month, Congress adopted a rather vaguely worded Resolution which, although not exactly saying so, clearly implied that Vermont would be recognized as an independent state and admitted into the Confederation if it would first agree to return to its former boundaries— that is, give up its Eastern and Western Unions. Naturally New York protested, but it protested alone, and without much hope of being listened to. "The doctrine that our jurisdiction over Vermont is to be

Until sacrificed for the Publick Tranquility is pretty fully established."
The Yorker delegation reported to Governor Clinton a week before the
adoption of the resolution. "Nothing remains . . . but the Formalities."

But Congress failed to reckon on Yankee obstinacy. When the Resolution reached the Grants in early September, it was received by the
people with something less than universal rejoicing. True, most of them
stood enthusiastically in favor of joining the American Confederation,
and under different circumstances would have jumped at the opportunity
to do so. There was, however, a mighty reluctance amongst them to give
up the recently established unions. In the following month, the Vermont
Assembly at its aforementioned Charlestown session, agonized over the
matter for several days before finally deciding that Congress was asking
too high a price. And so, at the very time that General St. Leger was
waiting vainly for Ira's go-ahead signal to reach him at Ticonderoga,
and Sergeant Tupper was getting himself so embarrassingly killed, the
Vermont Assembly resolved to "remain firm and hold the articles of
union inviolate." It was left up to Governor Chittenden to inform Congress, a task that the governor finally got around to doing some six
weeks later.

The Assembly's decision was fine with Ethan, of course. In fact, he
had used his considerable influence and energy to bring it about. On one
occasion private citizen Allen had even spoken from the floor of the
Assembly to argue against acceptance of the Congressional Resolution
on the grounds that it would be "immoral" to abandon the unions. This
was certainly a lofty attitude for Ethan to take. It seems likely, though,
that his opposition to the Resolution was prompted less by genuine
concern for the welfare of the Unions than by fear of what might happen
to his plans for treason if Vermont should decide to throw in its lot with
the American Confederation. It did not take much imagination to see
how even at this late date, with British troops poised in readiness at
Ticonderoga and the trap about to be sprung, a decision of this sort
could bode ill for his conspiracy and for himself.

Understandably, Vermont's refusal to relinquish the Unions did little
to improve its already frayed relations with New Hampshire and New
York. During the weeks immediately following the Assembly's decision,
tensions between the Republic and its despoiled neighbors mounted dangerously. There had been angry words before, but now, with victory

over the British all but assured, it seemed very probable that both New Hampshire and New York would actually attempt to do something about putting an end to Vermont's outrageous insolence. Reports had it that the two aggrieved states, their patience finally exhausted, were about to use military force to regain the territories recently taken from them by the Republic of Vermont, and, once this was accomplished, perhaps keep going and divide up all of Vermont between them.

As matters turned out, New Hampshire, for all of its fury, never did progress beyond the growling stage, but not so with New York. By mid-December of that year, 1781, an explosive situation had developed in the Western Union. While Governors Chittenden and Clinton were busy exchanging threats and insults, contingents of Vermont and Yorker militiamen took up positions on opposite banks of the Walloomsac River in the Hudson strip. There for several days more than four hundred Vermont troops, armed with a small iron cannon of which they appear to have been inordinately proud, proceeded to glower at the much weaker Yorker force across the narrow river, and the Yorkers glowered back.

During most of this time Ethan was comfortably lodged in a rented room back in Bennington, where he busied himself in dashing off another pamphlet, this one in support of Vermont's position in its latest crisis with New York and New Hampshire. The pamphlet, entitled *The Present State of the Controversy . . . ,* was to be the last of Ethan's long list of political treatises. It was also his least impressive—an awkward and uninspired treatment of an overworked theme: namely, why Vermont was, as usual, completely in the right while its adversaries were just as completely in the wrong. It was far from vintage Allen, but apparently Ethan thought well of it. As had become his custom in matters of this kind, he arranged to have the pamphlet printed at public expense and distributed as widely as possible among men in high places, including most of the members of Congress. He was even considerate enough to send along a copy to General Haldimand, who, Ethan was sure, would have a lively interest in political developments within the Hudson strip.

Eventually, the crisis at Walloomsac River ended without violence when in late December, after nearly a week of angry confrontation, the badly outnumbered Yorker force wisely decided to abandon the field to the Yankees. Once again Vermont had defied its powerful neighbor to the west, and got away with it. Once again, with no blood spilled, the Yorkers had been backed down. Temporarily at least, the Western Union had been cleansed of alien troops—but not until after Ethan had put in a brief but conspicuous appearance at what he afterward referred to as "the seige of Vallumcock." It was not exactly the thing for a private citizen to do, but the temptation became simply too powerful to resist, and so on an uncommonly fine day near the end of the year Ethan donned his uniform, fastened on his great sword, and rode over from Bennington to take his place at the head of the Vermont troops. That afternoon a review was held in his honor on the field at Walloomsac, and Ethan delivered a few words of cheer to "my brave men," after which, amidst much huzzaing, the little cannon was discharged. "General Allen was bound up in gold lace and felt himself grand as the Great Mogul," noted a Yorker observer who watched the proceedings from across the river. All in all, it turned out to be quite a day for a simple civilian. On the following morning Ethan returned to Bennington, leaving the field to lesser men after having clearly demonstrated that he was still the boss.

But Ethan's rule was rapidly drawing to an end. In late February, upon returning to the Grants after a few weeks of visiting in Connecticut, he received the almost unbelievable news that during his absence the Vermont Assembly, meeting in its winter session at Bennington, had done a complete about-face and agreed to accept Congress' terms for recognition and admission into the United States. Several explanations were given for this sudden change of heart, including concern on the part of the more conservative settlers over the increasing likelihood of violence in the Unions. The most telling factor, however, had been a recent letter to Governor Chittenden from the immensely respected Washington, urging Vermont to act favorably on Congress' Resolution and become a member of the new nation of states. "You have nothing to do but withdraw your jurisdiction to your old limits," General Washington assured the governor.

Thus, on February 23, 1782, the Vermont Assembly officially dissolved both the Eastern and Western Unions—over the outraged opposition of most of the inhabitants of those areas and their representatives in the Assembly. Especially upset by the dissolution were the people of the Eastern Union. Having been jilted once before by their neighbors across the river, on the occasion of their second merger they had demanded and received solemn assurance that this time the union would be forever inviolate. Now, only a year later, they were once again being cut adrift. "They took their leave," commented one observer, "with some expression of bitterness."

Ethan himself was certainly far from pleased by the Assembly's action, not only because it threatened to ruin his continuing plans for treason, but also (and perhaps even more important to him) because it represented an obvious and direct repudiation of his leadership. He had supported the Unions, and, as was his way, he had supported them loudly and wholeheartedly. He had even written a pamphlet on the subject, copies of which, embarrassingly enough, had been distributed among important people. He had put his influence on the line, and he had lost. For the first time since the summer of 1775, when the representatives of the towns had passed him by in favor of Seth Warner for command of the Green Mountain Regiment, Ethan had been publicly denied by his own people. This was indeed a highly disturbing turn of events, the significance of which could hardly have escaped him.

Scarcely had he been dealt this rebuff by the Assembly, however, when he received vindication of a sort from a most unexpected quarter —the United States Congress. By the time the delegates from the Grants reached Philadelphia in early March of 1782 to break the happy news to Congress that their state now stood ready to join the American Confederation, the attitude of most members of Congress toward Vermont had changed dramatically. Things were different now from what they had been six months earlier when Congress had made its offer of admission. Yorktown had been fought and won, and with victory over the British now assured and the peace negotiations already in progress, there remained little need to worry about what Vermont might or might not do. Certainly its leaders could no longer have any serious intention of defecting to the enemy—or so at least reasoned most congressmen, a large number of whom had only a few months before favored immediate admission of Vermont as the surest way of saving it for the Patriot cause.

Since there was now no compelling reason for taking action on the Vermont question, still an obviously painful subject as far as New York was concerned, why not do the politic thing and disregard it until a later time, preferably a much later time? And as for the promise of admission implicit in the Resolution of August 20, members of Congress need feel no moral qualms about failing to honor it. They had been released from all commitments by the recent perversity and arrogance of the Republic of Vermont. First, in a spirit of open defiance, Vermont had rejected Congress' generous offer by refusing to abandon its Unions. Then, nearly a half-year later, it suddenly announced that it had changed its mind and would condescend to join the American Confederation after all. This was hardly the sort of conduct calculated to win much support for Vermont among the men at Philadelphia, who, like politicians before and after, were particularly sensitive to affront. Even Connecticut's Roger Sherman, Vermont's most ardent champion in Congress, admitted to being more than a little put out with his Vermont friends for having behaved so badly.

Thus, long before its delegates arrived in Philadelphia, Vermont had ceased to occupy a very high place on the congressional calendar, and its position was obviously not likely to improve during the foreseeable future. "The affair of Vermont," noted one Congressman at about this time, "lies untouched and will not be stirred until it shall appear that some advantage will result from agitating it." On April 19, 1782, after more than a month of vain attempts to present their papers before Congress, the Vermont delegates finally concluded that they were wasting their time and left for home. A week later they submitted their report to the Governor and Council. The gist of it was that Congress, notwithstanding its Resolution of the previous summer, had no intention of admitting Vermont into the United States. In other words, Vermont had been hoodwinked, clear and simple.

Understandably, the people of the Grants were outraged, and none more so than Ethan, whose indignation was very real and very loud. At the same time, however, he would have been less than human if he had not derived some satisfaction from this new state of things. Perhaps he sensed that because of it his political stock, so recently sent plummeting, might rise again, although there is no real indication that it did. At any rate, he could enjoy the luxury—and he doubtless did on more than one occasion—of saying "I told you so" to those who had doubted his wisdom and voted to dismantle the Unions. Furthermore, Congress' rejection of Vermont had breathed new life into his plans for treason, or so at least Ethan himself chose to believe, and he proceeded to make the most of it.

During the months immediately following Vermont's rebuff by Congress, Ethan was untiring in his efforts to hand his neighbors over to the enemy. He was convinced, and he did his level best to convince others, that now was the perfect time for the British to make their move. The people of Vermont were disillusioned and angry with the American States: "The last refusal of Congress to admit this State into the Union," Ethan wrote to Haldimand in the late spring of 1782, "has done more to awaken the common people to a sense of . . . resentment of their [Congress'] conduct than all which they had done before. By their own account they declare that Vermont does not and shall not belong to their confederacy." This being the case, the people of Vermont, "except for a few hot heads," would now certainly be receptive, or at least non-resistant, to a return to British rule. All that was needed was for General Haldimand to make a token show of force. Let a small contingent of troops be sent up the lake, and the prize would drop into the general's hands. Within three weeks, Ethan assured Haldimand, Vermont could once again be part of the British Empire.

Throughout the spring and summer of 1782, Ethan continued to bombard Haldimand with urgent appeals to move against Vermont while time and conditions were still favorable. In fact, so great had become his enthusiasm for betrayal that he was often less insistent upon secrecy than he should have been. As a result, on more than one occasion he narrowly missed being exposed. Strangers, strongly suspected (usually with good cause) of being British agents, were a common sight in the Sunderland area. Once two of them attended a public dance in nearby Arlington—all of which was going a little too far, in Ethan's opinion, and he wrote a letter of complaint to Haldimand. One day in the early spring the principal courier between Ethan and Haldimand's headquarters, a half-breed named Crowfoot, was seized by Ethan's neighbors and nearly hung on the spot as a British spy. There was an anxious moment or two for Ethan, but Crowfoot kept a tight lip, and, finally saved from the noose by the personal intervention of Governor Chittenden, was ultimately exchanged as a prisoner of war.

These were risky days and risky deeds for Ethan, for the truth of the matter is that the temper of the Vermonters was not at all as he had represented it to Haldimand. In spite of their anger and disillusionment over the recent rejection by Congress, most Vermonters continued to identify strongly with the American States, and they held confidently to the hope that one day they would become a part of the Confederation.

In its June meeting at Windsor the Vermont Assembly, despite all that Ethan could do to the contrary, declared itself emphatically opposed to reestablishing the Unions. It was apparent that the people of Vermont meant to live up to their end of the bargain on this matter, and wait for Congress to change its mind about admission. In the meantime they could and did share with their American brethren an abounding pride in having brought the British down to defeat. And as for returning to the Empire, the very thought would have been laughable if it had not been so repugnant.

And yet, everyone who had stopped to think about it, must have come to accept the fact by this time that Ethan was doing his level best to turn Vermont over to the British. Why no serious action was taken against him, either by outsiders or by his own people, is not entirely clear. Surely it was not because evidence against him was still lacking, for in February of that year Governor Clinton had made public his completed dossier on Ethan Allen, which, even when viewed charitably, left little doubt about the extent and character of Ethan's involvement with Haldimand. The publication of this dossier in a Poughkeepsie newspaper was the end-result of a long and painstaking bit of detective work on the part of the governor, but he might just as well have spared himself the effort for no good came of it. What was meant to be a cannon turned out to be a popgun, and although its report was doubtless heard as far away as the Grants, it had little effect. Ethan continued his bold flirtations with the British; in fact, he stepped up their tempo, and no one came forward to challenge him.

In truth, there were probably very few people in Vermont or elsewhere who relished the idea of having to grapple with Ethan Allen. After all, it was generally understood that he continued to wield considerable influence over the militia which he had so thoughtfully staffed with officers of his own choosing, including the recently appointed Colonel Ira. It was also clear enough that even though his power over the Assembly had slipped rather dramatically of late, he still ranked high with the Governor and Council, as indeed he did with a great many of the settlers. In other words, an open confrontation with Ethan could prove to be a strenuous undertaking. Would-be challengers might do well to pause and reflect upon the power of the man before attempting to bring him down. Also conducing to Ethan's apparent immunity was the obviously chimerical nature of his conspiracy. Now that the war had been won, there was not the slightest chance that it could succeed. He was whipping a dead horse, and everybody knew it except Ethan himself. Why then bother to risk action against him? Despite the understandable temptation to bring him to an accounting, why undergo considerable unpleasantness, and perhaps danger, to battle an idle fancy? Better to let him play out his offensive but harmless little charade.

Thus Ethan was permitted to continue his dalliance with the British with little or no interference from either the American Confederation or the folks at home. From his headquarters in Quebec, General Haldimand kept the negotiations alive by listening and nodding politely to what Ethan had to say, but he offered little in the way of encouragement. Certainly at no time did he even intimate that he would make a renewed show of force up the lake or anywhere else. And yet Ethan remained hopeful. Buoyed up by his tremendous self-confidence and driven by his need to win, he continued to press hard for treason during the better part of 1782. Despite the obvious lack of enthusiasm on the part of his British friends, and the fact that peace between England and America was clearly imminent, he remained, as Haldimand himself put it, "as rapacious as a wolf" in his attempts to get Vermont back into the Empire.

And then suddenly Ethan's attention was diverted from conspiracy and directed toward a disturbing turn of events within the Republic itself. In the late summer word reached Governor Chittenden that trouble had again broken out on the east side of the mountains. This news could hardly have come as much of a surprise to anyone. Ethan's punitive campaign into that same area in the spring of 1779 had temporarily quieted things, but it had certainly not removed a deep-rooted Yorker sentiment shared by a goodly number of the east-side settlers. Hostility had continued to smolder, and now finally it had erupted once more into an act of open defiance against the Arlington regime. The seat of the disturbance in this instance was the Brattleboro area, located in the southeastern tip of the Republic, where Yorker sympathy had always been at its strongest. Here, emboldened perhaps by words of encouragement from Governor Clinton and the recent rebuff dealt the Republic by Congress, a Yorker mob had formed one day in late August and proceeded to prevent the county sheriff from performing the duties of his office.

Naturally, the Arlington government could not allow such an affront to pass unanswered. This was an act of rebellion, and who could be more aware than the leaders of young Vermont, itself the child of insurgency, that the best way to deal with rebellion was to nip it in the bud? Since the Assembly was not then in session, the governor took it upon himself to order a posse into the disturbed area to restore order and authority. Not surprisingly, command of the expedition was assigned to the governor's good friend Ethan Allen, who, after all, could claim considerable experience in dealing with troublemakers.

Early on the morning of September 7, 1782, mounted at the head of two hundred and fifty west-side militiamen, Ethan set out eastward from Bennington, following the same line of march he had taken three years before and bent upon the same purpose—putting the Yorkers in their place. He proceeded slowly, taking the better part of two days to cover the thirty-mile stretch across the narrowest part of the Republic. Word of his coming preceded him. Indeed, it was an important part of his strategy that it should. Terror had always been the weapon that Ethan understood best and used most effectively, and he was enough of a psychologist to know that anticipation is the essence of terror. He intended that the people of the east side should know, in advance of his coming, that certain retribution was on its way for those foolish enough to oppose him. Let them then dwell for a time upon the mighty potential for disaster, and fright would surely come forward to confound their councils and erode their power and will to resist. It had almost always worked out that way for Ethan in the past, and he supposed that it would on this occasion also.

By the time he had reached Guilford on the outskirts of Brattleboro, rumor had more than doubled the actual size of his army, and all signs of disturbance had disappeared. The Guilfordites appeared to be on their best behavior, and a casual passerby would have supposed that neither Ethan Allen nor the Republic of Vermont had an enemy in the lot. Ethan, of course, knew better. Even so, he allowed himself to get careless and failed to send out scouts. As a result, his advance guard marched headlong into a cleverly laid ambush just beyond the town. Fired upon by fifty or more Guilford residents, who were obviously more intent upon creating panic than casualties, Ethan's men broke ranks and raced to the rear, unscratched but badly shaken. There they were met by Ethan, who soon managed to rally them and persuade them to follow him back to the scene of action. According to a deposition later submitted by a Yorker witness, Ethan approached to within a few yards of the ambush area, halted his troops, and then from his position at the head of the column announced in a booming voice to the concealed enemy:

> I Ethan Allen do declare that I will give no quarter to the man woman or child who shall oppose me and unless the inhabitants of Guilford peacefully submit to the authority of Vermont I swear that I will lay it as desolate as Sodom and Gomorrah by God.

It was a typical bit of Allen bombast, delivered in typically dramatic Allen fashion, and the effect was about the same as usual. Once again Ethan succeeded in scaring his enemies half out of their wits, and after that nobody ventured to lift a hand against him. Marching unopposed into the center of Brattleboro an hour or so later, he seized about two dozen prominent Yorkers, thought to have been the instigators of the unrest, and hustled them up to Westminster to stand trial on charges of "enemical conduct." All but a few were either acquitted or let off with light fines. However, around a half-dozen of them, whose repeated misbehavior had stamped them as irreconcilable enemies of the Republic, were stripped of all their property and banished. It was, Ethan admitted, "a savage way to support government," but necessary and entirely justified. Eventually most of the exiles ended up in Poughkeepsie to recount their misadventures to Governor Clinton and seek redress. One of them, an intrepid Yorker named Charles Phelps, personally known to Ethan and Governor Chittenden and despised by them as "a notorious cheat and nuisance to mankind," ultimately made his way on foot to Philadelphia to lay his case before Congress. "Terribly distressed; without clothes fit for the season; without money or credit to pay his board," wrote New York Congressman James Duane to Clinton. But, in Duane's opinion, Phelps would make his presence felt in Philadelphia and perhaps even succeed in opening a few congressional eyes to the lawlessness and brutality of the Arlington bandits. "His singularity draws attention," noted Duane, "and he overflows in the plenitude of his communicative powers."

Ethan was not particularly concerned with what Phelps was up to, however. He had accomplished what he had set out to do, and that was that. And as for any attempts that Phelps or the others might make to cause further trouble by bringing in outside help, let them try. Certainly

New York held no terror for Ethan Allen. "He said that he could go to Albany and be head monarch if he had but orders in three weeks," one of Ethan's prisoners later reported, "and he had a good mind to do it, and further Allyn God damned Clinton over and over from time to time." Nor did Ethan expect much trouble from Congress. "You have called on your God Clinton till you are tired," he declared to one of those about to be banished. "Call now on your God Congress and they will answer you as Clinton has done."

# XV. The Oracles of Reason

GOVERNOR CLINTON and Congress naturally fumed over this latest outrage by the Vermonters, but Ethan had been right in supposing that neither would do anyting about it except unleash the customary torrents of hard words. Clinton, as usual, threatened to go to war against Vermont unless Congress took immediate action, and Congress, partly to register its own disapproval but mainly to console Clinton, responded by passing an angry Resolution which censured the Republic of Vermont and called upon it to make proper restitution to Phelps and the other Yorkers, "or the United States will take effectual measures to enforce a compliance." Governor Chittenden and his Council proceeded to denounce the Resolution as foolish and stupid, and in effect told Congress to mind its own business. There the matter ended.

Within a few months, in fact, the entire affair was all but forgotten, except by Clinton who persisted in his dogged but unsuccessful attempts to keep the embers aglow. Once again Ethan and the Republic of Vermont had not been called to an accounting for their insolent behavior, and the reasons are not very hard to find. Governor Clinton, who would of course have liked nothing better than to put Vermont out of business once and for all, had by this time come to realize that the Arlington regime could be eliminated only by the application of a considerable amount of military force. Such an undertaking would involve large expense and might well promote political difficulties at home from which the governor's enemies could profit. In short, Clinton did not intervene because he had concluded that it would be difficult and perhaps dangerous to do so. As for Congress, the less said and done about the Vermont situation, the better. Not only was there a notable lack of enthusiasm among the delegates for using force (despite the bold tone of their Resolution), but there was also a strong disinclination to become involved at all in the twisted affairs of the Republic of Vermont, for here was a matter that had by now become generally recognized as something of a political horror.

What had begun in 1777, when Vermont declared its independence, as just another problem among many Congress had to contend with, had developed into a hydra-headed monster. By the time of Ethan's expedition onto the east side in the late summer of 1782, the question of what to do about Vermont had become so intertwined with congressional politics, inter-state and inter-sectional rivalries, payment of the war debt, and the controversy over western lands, that a tacit agreement had been reached in Philadelphia not to meddle in the matter any more than was absolutely necessary. Thus, after its censure Resolution of December, 1782, the Confederation gave little serious attention to Vermont one way or the other. Indeed, it was not until 1791, after a new and more effective government had been set up under the Federal Constitution, that Congress ended its policy of calculated aloofness toward Vermont by accepting it into the American Union. Until then Vermonters would continue to press for admission, hopefully but vainly bombarding the Confederation with petitions and periodically holding elections to choose their would-be congressmen. Meanwhile they would manage to function well enough as an independent state, coining their own money, setting up tax systems and post offices, passing naturalization acts, and taking some comfort from the fact that they were at least not being called upon to share in the payment of the American war debt.

Ethan's campaign into the troublesome east-side area marked his last appearance of any consequence in a public role. For a year or so thereafter he would, it is true, emerge from time to time to strut briefly back onto the stage. In January of 1784 he returned to Guilford at the head of a small band of militia in response to a report that the Yorkers there were once more causing trouble. It was a needless errand, however. The seriousness of the disturbance had been greatly exaggerated, and the situation had been brought well under control by an east-side posse by the time of Ethan's arrival. Later that same year he campaigned actively for the reelection of his brother Ira and Governor Chittenden, and even wrote an open letter in defense of the government's foreign policy. Admittedly, remarked Ethan (who was certainly in a position to know), Vermont's relations with the outside world had at times perhaps seemed rather mysterious; still, "they have been demonstrated to be good in the final consequence of them."

These appearances and a few others like them were only momentary and minor, however, and did little to obscure a fact of some importance in the history of Vermont: by early 1783 Ethan's star had obviously set. The man who for nearly five years after his return from a British prison in 1778 had towered above all others in determining the course of things for the Republic of Vermont, had ceased to be of much consequence in affairs of state. The name of Ethan Allen no longer occupied a prominent place in the records of the Republic. His descent had on the whole been gradual and sometimes subtle enough to be all but indiscernible— but there it was, stretching back to those feeble impeachment attempts made against him in the autumn of 1780, and ending finally in public impotence, or something close to it.

There were, of course, good reasons for his fall from power, including the general knowledge that he had been involved (and still was) in shady dealings with the British. Granted, there were many Vermonters who saw Ethan as their champion. Traitor or not, he had saved them from the British—or so at least they believed—and because of it they were intensely loyal to him. For the greater part, however, his intrigue with Haldimand had offended his neighbors and seriously injured his standing among them. The fact that he insisted upon continuing the intrigue long after the threat of British invasion had passed was especially difficult to justify, even for Ethan's most devoted friends. Still, other leaders have backed a wrong horse on occasion and survived politically, and Ethan might have done so too had he not been afflicted with a more general malaise that ultimately could not fail to bring about his downfall. What really spelled his end was the erosion of his position by the passing of time and the changes wrought by it.

For one thing, time had made Ethan's special talents largely irrelevant; or worse, it had changed them from assets into liabilities for the Republic. Essentially he was an agitator, and the time for agitation had passed. With the war over, with the Yorker threat obviously less critical, and with the Republic safely through the perils of infancy, the need now was for constructive statesmanship rather than turbulence, and this was a role that Ethan was ill-equipped to fill. Admittedly, he had been a host in himself in his day and in his way. He had harassed, condemned, defended, and avenged. He had even judged. But he had never shown an aptitude or even an inclination for building, and building was what was now in order for the Republic of Vermont.

But time had done more than merely render Ethan's kind of leadership unfitting; it had also made it impossible by changing the very nature of the Republic itself. Slowly but persistently Vermont had become a democracy of sorts. It was no longer true, as it had been during the days of Ethan's hegemony, that Vermonters were willing to defer to their betters and allow government to be conducted by an oligarchy. Now it was the people themselves who intended to make the decisions that would determine the nature and direction of their lives. A great change had taken place in the political awareness and spirit of the people. This change was attributable partly to the easing of tensions that had plagued the Republic during its earliest years and had seemed to call for sudden and arbitrary decisions of the sort that Ethan Allen could and did make. It was also a natural consequence of the greater experience and confidence of the people. By the time of Ethan's expedition to the east side in 1782, the Republic was nearly five years old, and much had been learned about the process of self-government.

Most important, however, was the factor of growth. During the decade of the 1780's the population of Vermont jumped from forty-five thousand to nearly twice that number as waves of new people descended onto the Grants from nearby states, lured there by the prospect of cheap land and low taxes. These newcomers, many of them a generation younger than Ethan, held no special feelings of reverence or affection for the oligarchs of Arlington, and they were certainly not beholden in any way to private citizen Ethan Allen. It had not been their farms he had saved from the Yorker land-jobbers or their lives he had protected from the British. To them Ethan was simply a soldier of the Revolution, and a rather tainted one at that. They had no intention of allowing him to run their lives. They would make their own decisions by exercising the political rights given them by the Vermont Constitution.

Thus, the power of the Arlington junto tended to slip away more and more each month, and with it Ethan's position grew increasingly less imposing. In place of the old order of things the Assembly now came strongly forward to claim the prerogatives that rightfully belonged to it. Government was being taken over by the people, and in the process there were bound to be casualties. It would not be long before even the wily and adaptable Ira would be stripped bare of his power, but before then, indeed even before the official end of the war in April of 1783, Ethan himself had become for all intents and purposes a political has-been.

It appears, however, that Ethan was not particularly disturbed by all this. Certainly he showed no disposition to fight for his political survival. Perhaps he was merely making the best of a bad situation by pretending not to care. On the other hand, he may actually have welcomed the opportunity to quit the public arena and become once again, after so many years, a free agent. Certainly he had good reason to want to retire from public service. His efforts for the Republic had been long and arduous, and even for a man of Ethan's remarkable stamina they must have proved burdensome over the course of years. Furthermore, they had brought him considerable anxiety and not a little disillusionment. There can be no doubt, for instance, that the failure of the Haldimand negotiations came as a major disappointment to him and contributed in some measure to embittering his attitude towards Vermont politics.

But above and beyond all this were considerations of a more private nature which undoubtedly had much to do with making retirement more palatable for Ethan. Foremost among them was the fact that he was getting on in years. He was now in his mid-forties, old by frontier standards, and although his health remained excellent, he did not suppose that he could go on forever. Certainly there were reminders aplenty of his mortality. In the spring of 1782 his brother Heber died at the age of thirty-eight. "He was," Ethan remarked as he contemplated his loss, "the noblest work of God." Of the six Allen brothers, of whom Ethan was the oldest, only three now remained. First Zimri had gone, then Heman, and now Heber, at whose place in Poultney Ethan had lived from time to time during his early days on the Grants. In June of the following year Ethan's wife died of consumption, and a few months later his daughter Loraine went the same way. The loss of the girl, barely twenty years old, touched him deeply. He had never been especially close to her, but her passing had a sentimental sadness for him. After all, she had been the first-born.

As for Mary, his whining, scolding wife of more than two miserable decades, it was difficult for Ethan to feel much of anything except relief—and perhaps a small twinge of contrition. She had kept house for him and borne him five children, but she had been far from the ideal wife. Her ugly disposition was legend for miles around, and it is said that the gravedigger of Sunderland, an inordinately solemn man, was heard to whistle for the first time in his life as he prepared the final hole for Mary Allen. Still, she had in her own way contributed a great deal to making an important man of Ethan. Had she been of a different stripe,

Ethan might well have been less ready for adventure and more content to remain at home with his feet up to the fire. But this was not the way things had worked out for him. On a youthful impulse he had committed the awful error of marrying a dull, illiterate woman several years his elder, and in time he had learned to make the best of a bad situation by spending as little time with her as possible. Characteristically enough, he was away from home at the time of her death. Perhaps it was to ease his conscience that he wrote a brief poem to her memory and had it published in the *Bennington Gazette*. In his verse he spoke rather highly of her.

So the years were slipping by, and who could say how many of them remained for Ethan Allen? There were still many things he wanted to do, and he must have sensed that it would be unwise to put off doing them much longer. Among them, he dearly wished to devote himself once again to what he liked to call "matters of the mind." For one who had always thought of himself as being first and foremost a philosopher, he had wandered hopelessly far afield during the past few years. "I have," Ethan complained to a friend in the spring of 1782, "put aside my studies for too long." But now, with his services no longer in great demand by the Republic, he could return to the world of thought and letters that he professed to love so well. Most especially he was anxious to complete the exciting project that he and his good friend Thomas Young had begun in Salisbury nearly twenty years before.

When Dr. Thomas Young had left the Salisbury area in 1764, thereby terminating those lofty discussions on God and man that had so fired the imagination of his young friend from the ironworks, he had taken with him the manuscript that he and Ethan had been working on together for the better part of a year. After Salisbury, Young had moved about a great deal before eventually settling in Philadelphia. When the war broke out he attached himself fiercely to the Patriot cause and soon became a delegate to the Continental Congress. There, more than any other member, he championed the cause of independence for the people of the Grants—an unseemly bit of behavior that earned him the censure of his congressional colleagues. In the summer of 1777 he died suddenly, without ever having seen Ethan again. Not long thereafter his widow moved to Albany, and it was from her, probably early in 1782, that Ethan retrieved the precious manuscript, which had apparently been left untouched by Young during the intervening years.

Building upon this manuscript and drawing heavily from the many pages of rough notes that had been preserved along with it, Ethan proceeded during the months that followed to fashion his famous *Reason the Only Oracle of Man.* More familiarly known as *The Oracles of Reason,* or *Allen's Bible,* the book was published early in 1785 and was immediately recognized as a highly unusual piece of work. In fact, like so many other of Ethan's contributions, it was unique. Here for the first time in America was a full-length treatise aimed directly at the destruction of conventional Christianity, and, for that matter, all other forms of revealed religion. Written without fear or restraint, the book was a shocker from beginning to end. Nothing that Ethan Allen had done before or would do subsequently during his noisy, turbulent, event-packed life, save for his capture of Ticonderoga, would do more to insure him an abiding place in American history, and nothing else would contribute half so much to the controversy that still surrounds his name.

He would make no apology for anything he had to say, Ethan warned his readers in the introduction. Regardless of what might be thought of him and his book, he intended to speak his mind freely. And he proceeded to do just that. He began by doing his best to rip the Bible to shreds, using as his main weapon that special Allen brand of ridicule that had served him so well in the past. Commenting on Adam and Eve in the Garden of Eden, Ethan allowed as how he thought it very unfair that the devices of the Devil should have been turned loose upon this pair of nice young people "just out of the Mould . . . destitute of learning or instruction, having been formed at full size in the space of one day, and consequently void of experience. . . ." The least the Almighty could have done was to provide them with a "Guard of Angels."

For page after page he pushed his attack against the Old Testament, giving no quarter to anyone or anything he happened to pounce upon. He was particularly hard on Moses, whom Ethan considered the first of an unfortunately long line of priests. "It seems that God had the power, but Moses had the dictation of it." And like all priests since that time, Moses was obviously a colossal fraud—"the only historian in the circle of my reading, who has ever given the public a particular account of his own death." Nor did the New Testament fare much better. Concerning

Jesus' assurance that no harm could come to those that believed in Him ("They shall take up serpents, and if they drink any deadly thing it shall not hurt them"), Ethan suggested that he himself be permitted to prepare a concoction, "and if it does not 'hurt them,' I will subscribe to their divine authority and end the dispute."

It had never ceased to amaze Ethan that full-grown men and women could actually take all this Biblical nonsense seriously, but they obviously did, and Ethan thought he knew why. It was the priests, of course, who with their scheming ways were able to perpetrate and perpetuate this great fraud. Original sin, total depravity, etc., etc.—these were nothing more nor less than artful devices that had been invented and merchandised by a predatory priesthood in order to keep mankind forever in spiritual darkness and chains. From the days of the earliest Jews, it had been the aim of priests to enslave man, and to enable themselves to do this they had deliberately invalidated the laws of nature and reason. For years beyond number they had managed to have things pretty much their own way. In Ethan's judgment, however, their power was finally beginning to pass. Now that belief in witchcraft was on the wane, "priestcraft is being discredited at roughly the rate of 50% per annum." But the day of priestly demise could not come soon enough to suit Ethan. To his way of thinking, the world would be infinitely better off if all priests, ministers, and teachers of Christian doctrine were fired immediately from their positions. Society should then spend their salaries "in an economical manner which might better answer the purpose of our happiness, or lay it out in good wine or old spirits to make the heart glad, and laugh at the stupidity and cunning of those who would have made us mere machines."

As a substitute for the dreary, enshackling, priest-ridden way of things which "has little to do with our virtues or vices, or with our consciousness of righteousness or wickedness, happiness or misery, reward or blame," Ethan proposed what he called his "compenduous system of natural religion." This turned out to be something of a hodgepodge assortment of English Deism, Spinozan Naturalism, and rather liberal dashes of what would later become known as New England Transcendentalism. But in essence what Ethan was trying to say was that man is on his own. God is good, and God is all-powerful, "a cause uncaused and eternally self-existent," but He is not given to meddling in what goes on here below. He has created with His infinite might and wisdom a perfect system governed entirely by natural law, and He has no intention of tinkering with its wondrous operation.

Natural law—now here was indeed the heart and soul of things, just as Newton had said a hundred years earlier, natural law ordained by the Almighty Himself. For man to ask or expect God to interfere with the workings of this divine arrangement was, in Ethan's judgment, worse than vain; it was insulting. It was saying in effect that He had failed to do a satisfactory job in setting up His system, and that it had become necessary for Him to return and make adjustments. Prayer, therefore, was error, and insolent error at that. It was certainly not the sort of reverence that God expected from man. What God expected was that man, acting as a free agent, would keep himself in harmony with nature, for "nature is the medium or intermediate instrument, through which God dispenses his benignity to mankind. . . . Every enjoyment and support of life is from God, delivered to his creatures in and by the tendency, aptitude, disposition and operation of [natural] laws."

Thus, harmony with nature was, according to Ethan, the very essence of Godliness. It represented the real and the only meaning of morality in a mechanistic universe, and "is of more importance to us than any or all other attainments." As to exactly what constituted a harmonious relationship with nature, however, Ethan was rather vague, and it is at this point that his arguments begin to lose their ring and break down into a welter of diffusion and inconsistency. Although it had obviously occurred to him that even the most honest and well-intentioned men might have differing notions of what nature expected of them, he refused to permit himself to be drawn into the mire of relativism. Instead, as was his custom, he plunged boldly ahead to assure his readers that the true course of nature could always be recognized in the final instance because the Almighty had provided mankind with the precious gift of reason as a guide, and in case reason should ever fall short (which was unlikely), intuitive awareness would be bound to take over and show the way. Thus equipped, man could not possibly wander from the proper path because of confusion or insensitivity. Only through a deliberate act of defiance could he stray.

In most instances, Ethan believed, man would follow nature's way. If he should deviate, he would certainly be made to suffer—not from the intercession of an angry Deity, but from the inexorable workings of the system. Punishment, such as it was, would of course be confined entirely to this world. If there were a heaven, and Ethan was not at all convinced that there was, it would surely be open to all, and there on that high plain of eternal triumph even the most unseemly of men would be "reclaimed from viciousness and restored to virtue and happiness."

Thus spoke Ethan Allen, and in so doing revealed himself for what he truly was: not the atheist or infidel that history has so frequently represented him as being, but a devout believer in the omnipotence and omniscience of the Almighty and the perfection of His ineffable system. It was never any part of Ethan's intention to drive the Almighty from the minds of his neighbors. He wished instead to provide them with a clearer and truer vision of God which would enable them to "gain more exalted ideas of their obligations to Him and one another . . . , make better members of society, and acquire many powerful incentives to the practice of morality, which is the last and greatest perfection that human nature is capable of." And that this clearer and truer vision of God should reveal Him as cast in the role of an absentee landlord, content to leave man unattended here on earth, is not surprising.

Ethan's "compenduous system," with its emphasis upon man as a free agent operating within a framework prescribed by natural law, was a direct derivative of the sort of person he was and the sort of world he lived in. Always a free spirit who bridled at restraints, Ethan was, like so many of his frontier neighbors, not one to be held down or shoved around. His entire life was first and foremost an exercise in free will, carried at times to the point of turbulence. And as for nature, the only true delineator of human freedom, few men understood it better or enjoyed greater rapport with it than Ethan Allen. He was, after all, a child of the forest.

Ethan's book, when completed, turned out to be a rather long affair, totaling to somewhat more than one hundred thousand words. How many of these words were actually Ethan's, however, has been a matter of some conjecture for the last hundred years since the venerable Vermont historian Zadock Thompson, after a careful study of the book, charged that the *Oracles of Reason* was nothing more nor less than a high-handed job of plagiarism. Many scholars have been inclined to agree with Thompson that the book was largely the work of Thomas Young and that Ethan did little more than put its parts together. The evidence they cite is impressive enough to call into serious question the actual legitimacy of Ethan's claim to authorship. And yet, who among those familiar with Ethan's other writings can read the *Oracles* and doubt for a moment that, regardless of the source and structure of what the book has to say, the way in which it is said is pure Allen from beginning to end? If it is true, as some critics have contended, that Ethan failed to contribute a single significant idea to the *Oracles,* it is also true that it was the vigor and enthusiasm of his colorful prose that gave the book its engaging spirit. But above and beyond all else is the not inconsequential fact that had it not been for Ethan's efforts, the *Oracles of Reason* would have remained as nothing more than just another uncompleted manuscript, destined to vanish without trace in the ultimate dust of history.

All things considered, then, it is perhaps understandable that Ethan should feel justified in putting his name, and his name alone, on the title page of the *Oracles*. In fact, it would have been strange if he had decided to do otherwise, for Young was long dead, and no one believed more strongly than Ethan that the world belonged to the living. Still, it would have been more gracious of him if he had at least given his old friend and collaborator a passing nod of gratitude in the Preface, and perhaps he later regretted not having done so. During the two years following the book's publication, Ethan submitted three different petitions to the Vermont Assembly, requesting that a free grant of land in the north country be bestowed upon "the heirs of Thomas Young who are in low and indigent circumstances." These petitions, according to Ethan, represented a belated gesture of appreciation toward a man who had been a friend of the Republic when friends were few. They may also have represented an attempt on the part of a troubled author to soften the twinges of his conscience. At any rate, the petitions were all denied. The time had passed when Ethan Allen could expect much in the way of favors from the Vermont Assembly.

Getting the *Oracles* published proved to be no easy matter. It may be true, as some of Ethan's biographers have claimed, that the heretical nature of the book tended to frighten away prospective printers, some because they feared the wrath of God, and others because they feared the wrath of the Godly. It appears, however, that the main obstacle standing between Ethan and publication was cash—or lack of it. Unlike all of Ethan's other writings, including his *Narrative* which was not much more than pamphlet-size, the *Oracles of Reason* was a book-length project, abounding in italicized material and other fancy devices.

It would obviously be a costly and time-consuming item to publish, so much so that most printers preferred to shy away from it. Thus, Ethan's manuscript lay for some months on his desk while he searched without success for someone to make his message known to the world. Finally, in the autumn of 1784, the newly established Bennington press of Haswell and Russell agreed to take on the job—but only after Ethan had promised to pay for the book as work on it progressed.

Thus, belatedly and somewhat reluctantly, *Allen's Bible* began to be born. The process turned out to be a slow and rather painful one, however, for the simple reason that Ethan encountered great difficulty in raising enough money to keep the project moving. Although certainly far from poor, Ethan suffered from an affliction not uncommon among the prominent men of his time: his wealth was so heavily committed to investment that he was often hard-pressed to come up with any significant amount of cash when he needed it. Consequently, to meet the payments on the *Oracles* he was forced to exhaust his ready assets—and then some. In fact, even before the printing was half-finished, he found it necessary to borrow substantial sums of money. All of this was a great nuisance, of course, but really nothing to become overly concerned about. After all, as Ethan explained to one of his creditors, "I presume the book will turn to money."

But the book did not turn to money. Far from it. Whatever else it may or may not have been, the *Oracles of Reason,* which finally cleared the press in the spring of 1785, was a financial disaster. Out of fifteen hundred copies printed, probably not more than two hundred were sold. The rest remained tucked away in Anthony Haswell's attic until destroyed by fire several years later, an event regarded by the pious as a belated manifestation of Divine displeasure.

Critically, the book fared almost as badly. Although hailed enthusiastically by a few free spirits, it was generally given short shrift by those rare persons who bothered to read it (and by many who didn't) as "turgid and intensely tiresome," "brutal nonsense," "a pigmy in the field of literary contention," etc., etc. Commented that inflexible Calvinist sage, the Reverend Timothy Dwight, later to become President of Yale:

> When it came out, I read as much of it as I could summon patience to read, but the style was crude and vulgar, and the sentiments were coarser than the style. The arguments were flimsy and unmeaning, and the conclusions were fastened upon the premises by mere force.

Ethan, nonetheless, was far from despondent over the cool reception given the *Oracles*. It mattered little to him that sales were less than brisk. If need be, he could always sell off some of his acreage to cover the loss. Nor was he disturbed by the sour notes of criticism. This was to be expected. In fact, he would have had it no other way, for, as he pointed out to a friend, almost without exception those who denounced the book were clergymen, and he had never supposed or hoped that they would approve of what he had written, because it was "fatal to their Ministerial Damnation Salvation system and their merchandise thereof."

The important thing to Ethan was that his book managed to create something of a stir. Like most of Ethan's other enterprises, it did not pass unnoticed. Indeed, it very emphatically accomplished the main purpose for which it was intended, for although not widely read, the book certainly got itself widely discussed, and in so doing paraded the ideas (and of course the name) of Ethan Allen before the people. For the time being, this was about all that could reasonably be hoped for, but someday, Ethan knew, after the initial shock of so much truth and light had passed, the *Oracles of Reason* would come to be appreciated for the philosophical and literary marvel it actually was. And on the off-chance that he might hasten the day of recognition, he sent a copy of his book to an acquaintance in Paris with the request that it be brought to the attention of the Royal Academy of Arts and Sciences:

> I am not so vain as to imagine that my theology will afford any considerable entertainment to . . . any learned Gentlemen in France yet it is possible that . . . they may be somewhat diverted with the untutored logic and sallies of a mind nursed principally in the Mountainous wilds of America. And since it is the almost universal foible of mankind to aspire to something or other beyond their natural or acquired abilities, I feel the infection.

Since Ethan's time, generations of scholars have given much attention to the *Oracles,* and while it is true that they have never quite managed to share Ethan's exalted opinion of the book, they have nevertheless tended to think more highly of it than did its earliest critics. On the whole, they have been willing to concede that, although the *Oracles* failed to provide an acceptable substitute, it did succeed in delivering a few well-aimed and telling blows at Christian orthodoxy. Indeed, it was the first major work published in the Western Hemisphere to do so, and to Ethan Allen must go the credit or blame for its appearance—all of which has proved rather embarrassing to those filiopietistical historians, past and present, who have had occasion to deal with Ethan. Some of them, like Jared Sparks, Ethan's first biographer, have been forthright enough to denounce the *Oracles* as crude, offensive, and unworthy of General Allen, "a blight upon the life of an otherwise great man." Others have simply neglected to mention the fact that there ever was such a book, and have thus totally spared themselves the pain of having to handle the awkward subject of Ethan's heterodoxy. Of them all, however, none has handled the problem more artfully than the nineteenth-century historian and popular writer, B. J. Lossing, who had no difficulty at all in overcoming the inconvenience of writing about a hero who did not believe in God— at least not the conventional variety of God. Consider, for example, Lossing's treatment of the death of Ethan's daughter Loraine in the early 1780's:

> That Ethan's religious beliefs were not grounded in absolute conviction, the scene at the deathbed of his beloved daughter fully attests. She was a lovely, pious young woman, whose mother, then long in the spirit land, had instructed her in the truth of the Bible. When she was about to die, she called her father to her bedside, and, turning upon him her pale face, lighted by lustrous blue eyes, she said with a sweet voice, "Dear Father, I am about to cross the cold, dark river. Shall I trust to your opinions, or to the teachings of dear mother?" These words, like a keen arrow, pierced the recesses of his most truthful emotions. "Trust to your mother," said the champion of infidelity; and, covering his face with his hands, he wept like a child. Thus it is ever. There is a cell in the human soul in which lodges the germ of perennial faith in God and his revelations. When touched by the electric spark of conviction it springs forth into bloom and fruitfulness, defiant alike of the frosts of cold, unbelieving reason, and the scorching heat of human philosophy.

In other words, Ethan was not really an infidel; he just thought he was.

Today the *Oracles of Reason* remains a subject of interest and some controversy among students of American thought. Opinions continue to differ, as they did a century ago, on the nature and merits of the book, and on whether or not Ethan deserves the credit for authorship. But on one point there appears to be general agreement: the fact that such a book could and did arise out of the stark frontier conditions of eighteenth-century America is in itself truly remarkable. It is also, in a very special way, reassuring. In fact, for those who take humanity seriously, it is a highly gratifying thing to glance back upon a time and place that demanded a long price from man in exchange for mere survival, and to discover amidst the drab rigors of his life a lofty spirit of inquiry that neither hardship nor peril could subdue.

# XVI. Emeritus

THE last half-dozen years of Ethan's life were tranquil and apparently contented ones. Although no longer in a position of public power, he gave no sign of sensing the loss. For most of his life he seemed to have been driven by a compulsion to occupy the center of the stage and he had striven mightily to that end. He would strive no more, however. Stripped of his influence over the affairs of the Republic, he now directed his attention and energies along more personal lines, and he did so without any noticeable reluctance or desire to return to the good old days. It was almost as if he had lost his craving to be in the midst of things, and felt relieved to be relegated to the role of spectator. In his descent from Olympus he was not alone. By 1787 Ira no longer occupied a place of importance in Vermont councils, while Ethan's other cronies had either died or been shorn of most of their influence, save for the durable Chittenden who continued to serve term after term as governor, even though he too had seen his position eroded by the rising power of the Assembly. The old guard had, in effect, been relieved of duty after having made its considerable contribution to the welfare of the Republic.

Ethan's acceptance of the new order of things might well have been less gracious, however, had it not been for an extraordinarily happy development that gave new meaning and substance to his life. In February of 1784, less than a year after the death of his first wife, Ethan married again. His bride was a pretty young thing named Fanny, whom Ethan had met not long before on a visit to the east side. The courtship was brief and romantic, and their marriage was inevitable from the moment of their first meeting, for they were immediately smitten with one another. Fanny was young, only twenty-four, and generally thought to be quite beautiful. Furthermore, she was a highly polished and sophisticated young lady who, among her many other accomplishments, could play the guitar and sing prettily. Ironically enough, she was the step-daughter of the notorious Yorker and Tory, Crean Brush, who had managed before his death to accumulate 60,000 acres of Vermont land, one-third of which was ultimately bequeathed to Fanny. In fact, it was while she was up from New York City, visiting the east side to get an appraisal on her inheritance, that Ethan appeared upon the scene and claimed her.

The fact that Fanny's background was tainted by close family ties with Yorkers and Tories apparently did nothing to cool Ethan's ardor for her, nor was he bothered by the fact that virtually all of her acreage was New York issue. Perhaps in his bemused state it failed to occur to him that Fanny was one of those damned Yorker land-jobbers he had so vehemently browbeaten for the past dozen years or more. Or perhaps he was willing to make an exception in Fanny's case for the sake of winning her hand, and 20,000 acres of east-side land as well. As matters turned out, Fanny's land remained so long in litigation that it never did fall into Ethan's hands. But Fanny herself was prize enough. On the day following their wedding in Westminster, he bundled her up and carried her by sleigh across the mountains to Sunderland and a new life as General Ethan Allen's lady.

Ethan's second marriage was as happy and fulfilled as his first had been drab and empty. Fanny was expensive and flighty and sometimes given to sudden flurries of temper, but she was also young and gay and witty. In short, she was everything that Mary had not been. Ethan obviously adored her:

> Dear Fanny wise, the beautiful and young,
> The partner of my joys, my dearest self,
> My love, pride of my life, your sexes pride,
> And partner of Sincere politeness. . . .

In five years she bore him three children—a girl and two boys, one of whom was named after Ethan. Both of the boys eventually attended West Point and went on to serve with honor as officers in the regular army. As for the girl, not long after a dramatic teen-age conversion to Catholicism, she became a nun and entered the Hospitaliers of St. Joseph in Montreal. By this time, however, Ethan was long dead and thus mercifully spared the anguish of seeing his own daughter give herself over to the unspeakable forces of conjury and oppression.

Clearly Ethan's new marriage had a settling effect upon him. Only once, in fact, during these final years did he revert to his old adventurous ways, and then but briefly. This occurred in the summer of 1785 when he was approached by an agent of the Susquehannah Company of Connecticut with a proposition that could hardly have failed to stir his interest. The Susquehannah Company, composed almost entirely of Connecticut men, many of them prominent in the affairs of that state, had been organized in 1753 for the purpose of land speculation in the Wyoming Valley of Pennsylvania. This exceedingly fertile and attractive strip of land, in which the present-day city of Wilkes-Barre is situated, was the object of great expectations on the part of the Connecticut investors, but as was so often the case in colonial days, the Company soon ran afoul of conflicting jurisdictional claims which proved to be its undoing.

For the better part of a century prior to the founding of the company, the Wyoming Valley had been claimed by both Connecticut and Pennsylvania, which is not surprising in view of the fact that it had been granted to both by the British Crown. This was only one of many blunders committed by the Home Government in parceling out the New World among the Colonies, but it would prove to be among the most troublesome and persistent. In fact, the question of political jurisdiction over the Wyoming Valley was not finally settled until 1783 when Connecticut, acting under pressure from the Confederation Congress, agreed to abandon its claims. In the meantime the Susquehannah Company, operating under its Connecticut charter, had acquired a somewhat shadowy title to much of the land, spent a considerable sum of money in promoting the area for settlement, and actually sold several hundred proprietary rights to individual buyers. Indeed, despite considerable harassment from their Pennsylvania neighbors, by the early 1780's the Wyoming Valley had become home to more than six thousand Connecticut settlers, virtually all of them holders of Susquehannah titles.

It was generally supposed, or at least hoped, by the Connecticut proprietors that land titles in the valley would be unaffected by the political settlement between the two states, but this was not to be. Not long after Pennsylvania had been conceded jurisdiction over the area, it announced that all Susquehannah titles were to be considered invalid. Settlers were given one year in which to clear out, although special exception was made for widows of soldiers killed in the Revolution: they were given two years. Naturally the settlers refused to comply, and just as naturally attempts were made to oust them by force. Sporadic incidents of violence occurred, and open warfare might well have erupted at any time. As it turned out, a showdown battle was somehow avoided, but for several months the situation remained extremely volatile, and the beleaguered settlers of Wyoming Valley were forced to live from one day to the next, working their fields with their muskets at their side, while expecting the worst to befall them at any moment.

Such was the situation when the Susquehannah Company enlisted the services of Ethan Allen, in the hope that he could do for Wyoming what he had earlier done so successfully for the New Hampshire Grants. Exactly what was expected of him is uncertain, but it appears that the Susquehannah promoters shared the view of the actual settlers that a satisfactory solution could best be achieved by forming Wyoming and certain adjacent areas, including strips of New York, into an independent state. If not the only way, then surely this would be the safest way of guaranteeing the settlers their right of soil and, of course, protecting the interest of the Connecticut speculators.

Ethan was flattered and excited by his new assignment, and he accepted it almost at once. As he explained to a friend, he had always felt a strong affection for the Susquehannah Company because his father had been one of the original members. But more important, Ethan maintained, was the fact that his sense of fair play had been aroused by the brutal treatment given the Wyoming settlers. Once again the hated land-jobbers were at work. Here was the battle of the Grants all over again, and Ethan jumped at the opportunity to help see justice done. He might have added, but did not, that the enticement was made somewhat stronger by a retainer of twelve proprietary rights from the company, with the promise of more to come if he should succeed in making good the Susquehannah titles. For a man of Ethan's extensive holdings, this offer of land, handsome though it was, was probably not important enough to be the decisive factor in determining him to take up the Susquehannah cause, but 4,500 acres of lush Wyoming land was worth thinking about, nevertheless.

In August of 1785, Ethan wrote to the President of the Susquehannah Company to inform him that "I have agreed . . . to speedily repair to Wyoming with a small detachment of Green Mountain Boys to Vindicate (if it appears to me practicable) the right of soil to those proprietors of that territory." And repair he did, although not very speedily and not with a detachment of Green Mountain Boys. In April of the following year Ethan Allen, mounted, uniformed, and quite alone, appeared amidst the settlers of the Valley to take his place at their head and to encourage them to secede from Pennsylvania and erect their own independent state. Sounding and acting every bit as fearsome and confident as he had a dozen years ago in his war against the Yorkers, he assured the settlers that under his leadership they could win, if only they were strong enough and courageous enough to fight for their rights:

> If we have not fortitude enough to face danger, in a good cause, we are cowards indeed, and must in consequence of it be slaves. . . . Liberty and Property; or slavery and poverty are now before us, and our Wisdom and Fortitude, or Timidity or folly, must terminate the matter.

Keeping a careful watch on all this from far away in Philadelphia, Benjamin Franklin, then President of Pennsylvania's Executive Council, sent off an unexcited letter to Ethan's old adversary, Governor Clinton:

> Ethan Allen of Vermont . . . has lately been among the settlers in Wyoming, persuading them to join in erecting a new state to be composed of those settlements, those on the west branch of the Susquehannah, and a part of the State of New York. . . . Chimerical as it appears, and unlikely to succeed, we thought it nevertheless right to acquaint Your Excellency with it, that such inquiries may be made and measures taken as you may judge proper to prevent him from exciting disturbances that may divert the people's attention from their industry, and be attended with mischievous consequences.

Governor Clinton, never widely known for keeping a cool head, flew into one of his customary fits of rage when Franklin's letter reached him, and with good reason. His arch-enemy was up to his old tricks again. Not content with having stolen New York's eastern counties, this detestable hoodlum now obviously had it in mind to begin slicing away at the state's rich underbelly. Despite Dr. Franklin's apparent lack of concern, Clinton meant to keep a close watch on what was going on across the line in Pennsylvania.

Actually, however, there was little cause for concern. The whole affair was indeed, as Franklin had said, "chimerical," and nobody recognized this fact more clearly than Ethan himself, once he had sized up the situation. Two brief visits to the area, in the spring and autumn of 1786, were enough to convince him that the government of Pennsylvania meant business and it could, and would if necessary, match its determination with force. This being the case, conditions there seemed hopeless as far as the Susquehannah Company was concerned, and he so notified his employers. And then, in the spring of the following year, the government of Pennsylvania suddenly brought the entire matter to a close when, with an uncommon display of generosity and common sense, it agreed to recognize the soil rights of the actual settlers. This naturally spelled the doom of the speculators, for without the settlers to do battle for them, they obviously had no chance of making good their claim to the rest of the area. It also meant the end of any hope Ethan might have had of becoming a Wyoming land baron. This was a disappointment, to be sure, but he at least had the satisfaction of seeing justice done to the settlers, and it doubtless occurred to him that his appearance on the scene might possibly have had something to do with prompting the Pennsylvania authorities to change their mind and do the right thing by the people of Wyoming. It must also have occurred to him that if, during the early 1770's, the state of New York had acted with similar wisdom, there would almost certainly have been no Republic of Vermont, and consequently a much less prominent role for Ethan Allen in the affairs of his neighbors.

But the Wyoming venture, whatever else it may have been, was clearly an aberration from the normal tranquility of Ethan's final years. True, other opportunities for adventure presented themselves from time to time, but Ethan turned his back on all of them, including an interesting invitation from the rebel Daniel Shays of Massachusetts. Come down and lead us in our battle against the accursed exploiters of the poor, Shays told him in the autumn of 1786, and we shall crown you king of Massachusetts. But Ethan would have none of it. The thought of a crown for himself and a matching one for Fanny may have had some appeal for him, but he could muster little sympathy for Shays and his followers. He considered them a "damned bunch of rascals" whose main purpose was to get out of paying honest debts, and he would certainly have nothing to do with aiding defaulters. Besides, he found it increasingly difficult these days to work up much enthusiasm for slaying dragons. Fanny preferred that he stay at home, and so, it appears, did Ethan himself.

In the summer of 1784, Ethan sold the place in Sunderland and moved with Fanny to Bennington. There they took lodging at Timothy Follett's boardinghouse, with the idea in mind of staying only until the following summer when they would move into their new home in Burlington. Two years earlier Ethan had made a swap with Ira for a sizable parcel of partially cleared land near the mouth of the Onion River, and recently he had drawn up plans for building a house on it, "a two-story, 34 by 12 feet, which plan I will not depart from." He had even sent along instructions to Ira, who had just moved north and opened a mill in the Burlington area, to saw the "bords" so that building could begin that following spring. Things went much more slowly than Ethan had anticipated, however, and for one reason or another nearly three years passed before the house was ready for occupancy.

Meanwhile Ethan and Fanny stayed on in Bennington, which was all right with Fanny, for Bennington was an exciting town, a metropolis of sorts where people abounded and things happened. It was also an agreeable arrangement for Ethan because of the greater convenience in conducting his land business there. New settlers were pouring into the Republic by the thousands, and a great number of them passed through the town on their way northward. Consequently, during his stay in Bennington, Ethan found himself caught up in a flurry of selling, sometimes at prices in excess of fifteen Spanish dollars an acre. During the last half of 1784 he sold more than 4,000 acres, some of it Onion River Company land that had been reopened to settlement by the British defeat, but most of it his own, and in the following year he sold about equal that amount.

At the same time he was buying widely, and perhaps less wisely than he should have, with the result that his income was for the most part plowed back into the business. This was the cause of much embarrassment for Ethan, for if ever he had need of ready cash, it was at precisely this time. Fanny, for all her fine qualities, was a spendthrift who obviously placed something of a strain on his resources. Furthermore, there were other weighty expenses confronting him, including the printing costs of the *Oracles* and a bill owed to the doctor who had attended Mary and his daughter Loraine during their last days. Add to this his house-building expenses, which had begun to make themselves felt by 1786, and it is understandable why the matter of debts was an especially vexing one for him.

His situation was made even worse by an increasingly severe currency restriction within the Republic. With Vermont's population growing much more rapidly than its circulating medium, and with large sums leaving the Republic each year for the purchase of out-of-state goods, money had become critically scarce by the mid-1780's, so much so that business in many parts of the state had been reduced to a barter level. Conceivably the government could have alleviated conditions by authorizing a more liberal monetary policy, or by establishing a bank of issue. It did neither, however. Instead it tightened its laws against counterfeiting and urged Vermonters to manufacture more at home—all of which may have been sound reasoning, but certainly did not provide the people with much immediate relief. By the summer of 1786, Ethan was nearly frantic for want of cash: "I am drove almost to death for money," he wrote to Ira in the north country. "I have not a copper to save me from the devil." Ira, who was seldom found wanting where Ethan was concerned, sent his brother $15. It wasn't much, admitted Ira whose wealth at this time totaled to well over a $100,000, but it was all the cash he had on hand. Ethan was grateful but disappointed. Fifteen dollars was next to nothing. He owed his friends the Fays more than three times that amount for drinks he had consumed recently at the Catamount Tavern, which happened to be very conveniently located only a few steps up the hill from where he and Fanny were staying.

As his creditors proceeded to press in on him from all sides, Ethan did what he could to pay them off, or at least hold them at bay for a time longer. By calling in debts owed him, including a sum of nearly $1,000 from the Republic for services dating back to 1780, and by borrowing from old friends and from Dutch usurers in Albany, he managed to raise enough cash to settle up with most of his creditors—but not all. To those he could not pay he wrote urgent letters, promising that he would come up with every penny and then some, and pleading with them to give him more time. Most of them did, either because they trusted him or because they realized that they had little choice in the matter but to wait and hope for the best. On at least one occasion, however, Ethan was hauled into court and threatened with debtors' prison unless he paid up immediately, which he was clearly unable to do. Fortunately the judge saw fit to grant him an extension of time, not because he was Ethan Allen, but because judicial leniency in cases of this kind had become more or less mandatory in a land where money was in such short supply. Thus, what must have been a humiliating experience for Ethan ended harmlessly enough. Still, the problem of too little money and too many debts would continue to plague him for the rest of his days. A strange predicament was this for a man who, at the time of his death in 1789, held title to nearly 12,000 acres of land valued at just over $70,000—a handsome fortune indeed for that time and place. It is doubtful that many of his Vermont contemporaries could have come even close to matching it.

One good thing can be said for Ethan's financial distresses at this time: out of them came an interesting and highly unlikely friendship that would prove to be a source of great gratification and pride for him during his final years. In the late spring of 1785, Ethan journeyed to Congress, then sitting in New York City, in an attempt to collect the back military pay owed him. Actually he had a strong case. For nearly five years during the war he had held a brevet colonelcy in the Continental Army, but despite the fact that his commission was supposed to have paid him $75 a month, he had received virtually nothing during that entire period. Now he was asking for a settlement.

Of course, he must have realized that his chances of getting anything from Congress were pitifully slim. Even if the funds had been available (and they were not), Congress would hardly have seen fit to pay them over to that scoundrel Ethan Allen, long-time troublemaker and suspected traitor. Still, in his desperation for cash, Ethan had decided to do what he could to get what was owed him, even if it involved a futile trip to far-off New York—at best a long and arduous ride even for a young man, and Ethan was no longer young. Not surprisingly, his efforts before Congress proved to be a complete waste of time. But during his stay in the city, he had the good fortune to meet the distinguished French essayist and warm friend of America, Michel-Guillaume Jean de Crève-coeur, better known as Hector St. John, author of the charming and immensely popular *Letters from An American Farmer*.

Apparently Ethan and St. John got along famously with one another during their brief meeting; so much so that there developed out of it a lively correspondence. St. John, although a French aristocrat, had long been in love with America. In fact, as a young man mightily smitten by the Romantic writings of Rousseau, he had for several years lived the life of a frontier farmer in Orange County, New York. But the angry vicissitudes of the American Revolution had long since forced him to abandon his farm and take a place of preferment in the service of the

French King, and at the time of his meeting with Ethan in the mid-1780's, he held the exalted position of French Consul General to the United States. At heart, however, he remained a simple American farmer of the sort he had written about with so much reverence a few years earlier, and in Ethan he seemed to recognize a kindred spirit.

During the three years or so that were left for Ethan, the two men corresponded frequently. Since St. John had expressed an interest in the Republic of Vermont, Ethan proceeded to regale him with information about the soil ("It produces richly of every kind of groth in North America"), the flora and fauna ("more abundant and varied than in Urope"), the government ("the best and most regular and freed from debt of any part of America"), the projected State College ("Science increases very fast, and institutions of learning is much encouraged"), and anything else that came to mind. He also sent along several maps, a few native shrubs, and, of course, a copy of *The Oracles of Reason,* which was, after all, one of Vermont's most remarkable products.

St. John was much taken with Ethan's stories and descriptions of Vermont life, perhaps because they recalled for him those happy days on his farm in Orange County. After returning to France in late 1785, he wrote to Ethan of his intention to do something nice for the people of Vermont. It occurred to him that he might present them with a silver engraving of the Great Seal of their Republic, elegantly struck off by the King's own engraver. He would also do what he could to interest the French King in the affairs of Vermont, and perhaps thereby obtain royal favors for the Republic. Specifically, he would attempt to persuade the King to "bestow some bounty" upon the proposed college. Meanwhile, it would do no harm for the people of Vermont to give some outward indication of their feelings of friendship and appreciation toward France. St. John suggested to Ethan that one way of doing this would be for the Republic to name a few of its towns after distinguished Frenchmen who had aided the Americans in their War of Independence, and he sent along a list of around a dozen names. He also made it known to Ethan that he would be deeply honored if the Republic of Vermont would bestow citizenship upon himself and his three children. One day he might return to America, perhaps to farm again, and he could think of no place he would rather break soil than in the rich intervales that Ethan had so vividly described to him.

Naturally Ethan saw to it that all this was brought to the attention of the Vermont Assembly, which, probably more in spite of Ethan's involvement than because of it, proceeded to take the matter seriously. In the spring of 1787 the Assembly, after giving thanks to St. John for his gestures of friendship, conferred citizenship upon him and his three children. At the same time, two of the names on his list were given to Vermont towns (Danville and Vergennes), and it was further decreed that the east-side frontier town of Dunmore would thereafter be known as St. Johnsbury, a living memorial to the great Frenchman who had so generously befriended the Republic.

To Ethan, who had started it all, the Assembly's response must have been gratifying, but perhaps in a way it was also a little disappointing. The list of towns honoring the names of distinguished benefactors of the Republic continued to grow. Irasburgh, Starksboro, Chittenden, Warner's Gore, etc., had now been joined by Danville, Vergennes, and St. Johnsbury. Understandably it must have seemed inappropriate and rather unjust to Ethan that Vermont towns were now being named after men who had never so much as set foot in the Republic, while his own name had been passed by entirely. Without Ethan Allen and the great services he had rendered, there almost certainly would have been no Republic of Vermont. Who could deny that it had been he, more than any other man, who had stepped forward in times of great peril to save his neighbors from the Yorkers and British, and later stiffen their spines against the threatened encroachments of the American Confederation? And yet, where in all of Vermont was there an Ethanton, or even Allensville? Nowhere. Throughout the length and breadth of the state he had served with such uncommon ardor and sometimes brilliance, neither town nor village nor hamlet bore his name. So it was then, and so it has remained.

In the spring of 1787 Ethan moved to Burlington to get seed in the ground and help the builders put the finishing touches to his new house. In July he sent for Fanny and the children, and settled down at last to the quiet life of a north-country squire. His farm was an impressive spread, most of which had been acquired from Ira in exchange for several hundred acres of woodland adjacent to Ira's sawmill at the falls of the Onion River. For Ethan's purposes the swap was a good one.

"Fourteen hundred acres," he boasted to a friend, "in which are three hundred and fifty acres of choice river intervale, a quantity of Swaley and rich upland meadow interspersed with the finest wheat land and pasture land well watered and is by nature equal to any tract of land of the same number of acres I ever saw." The house itself was situated near the river, a few hundred yards below the falls.

Almost directly across the river on the Colchester side and set back a half-mile or so was Ira's place, in which the bachelor brother lived with his housekeeper and Heber's orphaned children. It was a rather pretentious affair, much more so than Ethan's, but then, Ira had more to be pretentious with. Even so, Ethan's new house was suitable to his needs. In it he lived with Fanny and the surviving children of his two marriages, five in all and soon to be six. Besides that, he provided lodging for two hired men, free Negroes who apparently did most of the hard work on the farm while Ethan supervised.

As a younger man, Ethan had never been particularly fond of farm life. He had found it dull and unrewarding and had resented its relentless routine. It appears, however, that this attitude had now changed, for he seems to have been genuinely contented with his new life in Burlington. Perhaps it was Fanny who made the difference, or perhaps his age had something to do with it. In January of 1788 he completed his fiftieth year, and although there is no indication that his health was failing, it is likely that the weight of his years alone was enough to slow him down and make him more receptive to the quiet life of his Onion River farm.

He could scarcely have chosen a setting better suited to his tastes. Burlington was a fine community. It was no longer the tiny frontier town it had been before the war. It had grown considerably, and now numbered nearly a hundred families. It had even taken on some of the amenities, including a tavern where, so the story goes, Ethan spent many happy days and nights during his final years. The town had not yet become congested, though, and to Ethan this was an important point. Throughout his life he had maintained a somewhat ambivalent attitude toward community life. As a man of curiosity and adventure, he found towns irresistible because of their excitement and conviviality, but as a child of the forest he resented being pressed in by them, and periodically fled from them to replenish his vigor, and most of all his freedom, in the northern wilderness he knew so well.

Thus, during Ethan's brief time there, the town of Burlington—where a man could mingle with neighbors and yet still shoot a deer from his front porch—was a good place to be; much better than Bennington where people had grown in on one another and there were laws against this and that. Still, there were moments when Ethan wished he were nearer the center of things, some place less off the beaten track where ideas were moving about and men sometimes talked of matters above and beyond the workaday world, as he and Jonas and the others had done so often in the long room of the Catamount Tavern. He felt the lack of intellectual companionship. "Little is said of Philosophy here," Ethan lamented to a friend in Westminster. "Here our talk is of Bullocks. . . . We mind earthly things."

While all this must have been disturbing to Ethan, he did not permit it to discourage him. He had long wished for the leisure to do more writing, and now here it was, and he intended to take advantage of it. Although very little of what he wrote during these final years has survived, he certainly wrote a great deal—much of it poetry, the quality of which is suggested by a mercifully brief sample from his "Monumental Lines on Capt. Elijah Golusha who was Killed by the Stroke of an Iron Bar while at Work in a Saw mill":

> Adieu Golusha! cruel fate employs
> The dreadful fury of its iron jaws,
> [Etc., etc.]

His major undertaking at this time was the completion of a manuscript he had sketched out in rough draft before leaving Bennington. Entitled *An Essay on the Universal Plenitude of Being,* this long and tedious effort was something of an afterthought. In fact, referred to by Ethan himself as an "appendix" to the *Oracles of Reason,* it was written primarily to clear up certain questions that the *Oracles* had left improperly answered, mainly questions relating to what Ethan called "the essence of the soul." In his essay Ethan reaffirmed his unflinching belief in the absolute perfection of God and His wondrous system. In contrast to the *Oracles,* however, he played down the role of reason and gave considerably more emphasis to the efficacy of intuition in bringing men into closer harmony with the ways of the Universe. As a result, critics have called the *Plenitude* less optimistic than the *Oracles,* but it would perhaps be fairer to say simply that it is less sure of man as a rational being. Lacking something of the arrogance and cocky defiance of the *Oracles,* it bespeaks a greater tranquility and acceptance of things.

Although Ethan probably would have denied it, he was now beginning to lean more discernibly toward the mystical. At any rate, his
*Plenitude* went some distance in the direction of Transcendentalism, and
it did so several years before the birth of Emerson and Alcott. Actually,
however, Ethan's essay would have little effect upon the subsequent rise
of the Transcendentalist movement. For some reason, probably lack of
money, it was not published until more than fifty years after his death,
and just as well, for it was a distinctly inferior piece of work. Compared
with the *Oracles,* it is second-rate at best, perhaps because this time
Ethan was forced to do the job alone, without the help of his one-time
collaborator Thomas Young. Still, *An Essay on the Universal Plenitude
of Being* is not without value. As an example of burgeoning Transcendentalism it has been and continues to be of considerable interest to
students of American thought.

During his first summer in Burlington, Ethan managed to bring forty
acres under cultivation. He also put cattle to grazing in the upland
meadows, although probably not very many. Since soon after the war,
Ira had been making occasional shipments of beef and lumber to the St.
John's–Montreal area, and Ethan, not long after his arrival in Burlington, was invited to throw in with Ira in what gave every indication of
becoming a very profitable venture. He jumped at the chance; so did
Levi, that atrocious Tory who by this time was back in the good graces
of his brothers, and soon a partnership was formed among the three
surviving Allen boys for the purpose of carrying on trade with the
Canadians.

Ethan and Ira were to provide the goods for export (cattle in Ethan's
case, and hopefully, an occasional shipment of masts for the Royal
Navy), and Levi, who had gone to St. John's to live because he could no
longer stand Americans, would act as general agent. It all seemed like a
wonderful opportunity for the Allen brothers and, incidentally, for the
Republic of Vermont. Ethan, perhaps with some coaching from Ira, was
now able to share his brother's vision of a day in the not-too-distant
future when a bustling two-way trade would be carried on with the
attractive Canadian markets to the north, and even beyond. If the St.
Lawrence were opened to the products of the Vermont farms and
forests, there need be no limit to the prosperity that would result.

As it happened, the British in Canada proved to be very accommodating—up to a point—mainly because they were as anxious to buy as

the Allens were to sell, especially beef. In the spring of 1787, at about the time of Ethan's arrival in Burlington, Governor Sir Guy Carleton (now Lord Dorchester) had ordered a temporary easement of trade restrictions along the lake route to Canada. Since the British feared that an agreement made specifically with the Republic of Vermont could not be effected without "infringing on the treaty of 1783," the arrangement had been thrown open to all who traded on the lake. It was the Vermonters, however, who were bound to be the major beneficiaries, and the Allens, because of their strategic position in the north country, stood in a fair way of becoming the biggest winners of all.

For Ethan, this was like old times, doing business again with the British. He had never really completely put aside his hopes for reannexation, although he was willing to concede now that the moment had long passed when it was possible to return to the Empire. Even if the people of Vermont would permit it (and they would not), it would surely bring on a disastrous war with the United States. It still might be possible, however, to effect a close working arrangement with the British, something short of reannexation. An alliance might do. This would permit Vermont to develop its potential in the way so clearly prescribed by nature—by attaching itself to the nation that controlled the water passage into and down the mighty St. Lawrence. Naturally Ethan was pleased with the easing of trade restrictions along the lake route, but he hoped for something more. In July of 1788 he wrote a long letter to Lord Dorchester, expressing fears of what might happen to Vermont if the new Federal Constitution were adopted by the American States, and calling for some kind of alliance—if not political, then economic. The governor sent the letter on to London as a matter of course, but nothing came of it.

Actually, what the British decided to do or not do would have little effect on Ethan one way or the other, except perhaps to excite his expectations. True, Canada wanted cattle, and it is probable that Ethan managed to send a few head northward. At the time, though, he was certainly in no position to take advantage of this promising opportunity except in a very small way. He was, after all, just getting started in his new business. Given a few years longer, he might have done quite well. Ira did. But for Ethan there was too little time left, and what remained was less than ideal for raising cattle or anything else.

It was a stroke of exceedingly poor luck that he chose about the worst possible time to get back into farming. The harvest his first year in Burlington was a bad one, due to a prolonged drought that parched the land. And then in early December the weather took a sudden turn. Snow fell heavily that winter, and during the following spring the rain came down relentlessly. Throughout much of Vermont, seeds rotted in the ground, or pushed their sickly shoots no higher than a man's hand. Hay mildewed in the fields. It was a terrible time, one of the worst in the history of the area, and the early months of the following year were the most desperate of all, as thousands of people took to grubbing for roots and beetles and anything else that might help them make it through to the next harvest. Travelers told of coming across families with ten or more children who had not eaten for several days. "A famine is now felt in the land," remarked a Congregational minister who happened to be passing through Vermont at this time. "The frowns of the Almighty are on this State for its Sins." At times Ethan was hard-put to come up with enough food for his table. So was Ira. Fortunately, though, unlike most of their neighbors they were able to get plenty of outside help, mainly from Levi whose generous shipments of flour from St. John's made life considerably more comfortable for his brothers than it would otherwise have been during this long period of privation.

In the late morning of February 11, 1789, Ira arrived back in Burlington from a trip south. He stopped by Ethan's place on a matter of business but missed his brother by a few hours. Not long after sunup, Ethan and one of his Negroes had set out on an ox-drawn hayrack to visit Cousin Ebenezer Allen, who a few years earlier had sold out his holdings in Poultney and moved to South Hero Island, about a dozen miles down-lake from the mouth of the Onion River. Although the grazing season was still several months off, Ethan's hay supply had become dangerously low, and if something were not done about the situation, he stood to lose his herd. Most of his neighbors were in a similar fix. Hay, like virtually everything else, was in short supply and almost impossible to come by in the Onion River area. It appears that Cousin Ebenezer was somewhat better off, however, for when he learned of Ethan's need, he invited him to come fill his rack. The trip down-lake over the ice was a slow one and cold, and with the lake wind whipping against them from the north, the going must have been a struggle all the way. They arrived at Ebenezer's in mid-afternoon and immediately began loading the rack in order to get the job done before dark.

Many colorful stories have been told and believed about what happened that night at Ebenezer's place. Most of them have it that Ethan and Ebenezer and a few of the neighbors thereabouts spent the night in a wild drinking spree, and that when the party broke up in the early hours of the following morning Ethan was so drunk that he had to be loaded onto the hayrack. These stories may be true, although there is not the slightest evidence that they are. About all that is known for sure is that Ethan spent the night at Ebenezer's and started for home on the morning of the next day. Then, as it was remembered many years later by an old man who had worked for Ethan on the Burlington farm as a chore-boy:

> The mulatto said that he [Ethan] was taken with a fit just as they entered the mouth of the Onion River. He said "It seems as if the trees are very thick here"—the last words he spoke. He then fell over back and struggled so that the mulatto man had to hold him on. He then became still and so remained until they arrived home where the man took him off the load on his shoulder and brought him into the house in an insensible state. Mrs. Allen fled into the other room, probably supposing him intoxicated.

Stories aplenty have also been told about the death scene in Ethan's front bedroom. One of these has Ethan recanting his sins and omissions in the presence of the local minister, and then begging for and receiving Communion with Christ. Another has him remaining defiant and unbelieving to the end. "The angels are waiting for you, General Allen," the minister is supposed to have said. Whereupon with his last ounce of strength Ethan raised himself up in bed and shouted: "They are, are they? Well, Goddam 'em, let 'em wait." Actually, he neither said nor did anything. He lingered in a coma until late that afternoon, when, after being bled and physicked, he died without ever having regained consciousness. That night they moved his body across the River to Ira's place where it was packed in ice and laid out for viewing.

> He was an honest man [recalled the hired boy]. He was very kind to his wife. She was a clever woman. He paid up well. . . . He always paid his men well but they had to stir about and tend to their business. He used to drink pretty hard at times. He was a tall man—pretty red face. I never heard that he had double teeth all around.

"It is with great regret, etc., etc.," announced the *Bennington Gazette* as soon as the word of Ethan's death reached the south. And then a tribute to his "exalted character," and his "indispensable service to the State," followed by expressions of condolence to Ethan's widow and children, "who, while they are deluged in tears for the loss of their best friend, have the consolation of being left with a handsome fortune."

On the whole the obituaries read rather well. Still, there is much to suggest that Ethan's passing was not a universally lamented event. There is no record, for instance, that New York's Governor Clinton, who would continue his stubborn war against Vermont for a year or so longer, was overwhelmed with grief. Nor did howls of sorrow arise from the ranks of America's clergy. In fact, in religious circles the news of Ethan's death appears to have been received with considerable gratification. Even that most charitable Congregational divine, the Reverend Ezra Stiles, President of Yale College, showed obvious satisfaction when the word reached him in New Haven on the final day of February. "Died in Vermont the profane and impious Deist Gen Ethan Allen," Stiles informed his diary. "And in Hell he lift up his eyes, being in Torments."

Many miles to the south, the Reverend Uzal Ogden of Newark saw things about the same way and said so publicly. "Allen was an ignorant and profane Deist," Ogden told his Episcopal flock, "who died with a mind replete with horror and despair." Quite right, agreed the learned Timothy Dwight, who would one day succeed to Stile's position at Yale. General Allen had been an awful man, "haughty," "licentious," "blunt," "coarse," "profane," and so on. He was "impatient of restraints either of government or religion, and not always submissive to those of common decency." Dwight did not say it in so many words, but he was glad Ethan Allen was dead, glad that the world was finally rid of his "peremptoriness and effrontery, rudeness and ribaldry." A terrible influence for evil had been removed. Here was a man who had exercised an extraordinary power over others. "The confidence which he seemed to possess in himself, naturally inspired confidence in others still less informed, and they readily believed that he, who asserted so positively, must be sure that his assertions were true."

And such unspeakable assertions they were! Not long after Ethan's death, the Reverend Nathan Perkins journeyed through Vermont on an errand for the Lord. Either to gloat or to shudder, he went out of his way to visit the General's grave. It was a soul-searing experience for the worthy cleric, and he was glad to get away from there as soon as he could. "One of the wickedest men that ever walked this guilty globe," he later remarked. "I stopped and looked at his grave with pious horror."

Whether Ethan actually went straight to Hell, as so many of his more respectable contemporaries supposed, is open to conjecture. Certainly in their eyes he was in most ways well-qualified for the trip. However, to believe, as a few rabid Allen-haters have, that Ethan was so excessively evil that he was gathered bodily into the nether regions, does seem a bit farfetched. And yet, how else can the mystery of his missing remains be explained?

On February 16, 1789, four days after Ethan's death, an elaborate ceremony was held at Burlington. Despite the bitter cold, a large number of people, mainly men in their middle years, came from all parts of the Republic of Vermont to pay final respects to a person who had, for better or worse, profoundly affected the lives of all of them. Among them were most of the high-ranking militia officers of the Republic, as well as several of its leading political figures, including President Tom Chittenden who had traveled the hundred-odd miles up from Arlington to bear pall for his old friend. But for the most part the crowd was made up of people of no special importance who had come there, some by foot or snowshoe over long distances, partly perhaps for reasons of curiosity or boredom but mainly out of gratitude to a man whom many of them had revered as their champion for a better part of a generation.

Since he had held high military office, Ethan was given a soldier's funeral with full honors. Drums rolled and cannons boomed as the procession, said to be "truly solemn and numerous," moved with slow cadence across the ice above the millpond dam on its way to the burial ground. At the grave, which had somehow been dug in the frozen earth, the coffin was opened for a final viewing before Ethan was lowered into the ground to the accompaniment of the musket salutes of six platoons of Vermont militia. "The whole was attended with greatest decorum," noted the *Bennington Gazette*. Some time later a stone plaque was placed upon the grave. It read:

> The Corporeal Part of Ethan Allen Rests Beneath
> this Stone, the 12th day of Feb. 1789, Aged 50
> Years [an error. He was 51]. His spirit tried the
> Mercies of his God
> In Whom he firmly Trusted.

The stone, with its words still legible, remained in place until the middle of the nineteenth century. And then, sometime during the early 1850's, it simply ceased to be. Most people, when confronted with the fact of the stone's mysterious disappearance, concluded that it had probably been chipped away by souvenir-hunters, but a few of the more devout preferred to believe that it had been blasted into oblivion by a lightning bolt as a dramatic reminder to all concerned that the great Jehovah was not one to forgive and forget. At any rate, in the late 1850's the Vermont Legislature voted to replace the plaque. By this time, though, Ethan's stature had grown mightily in the public fancy; so much so that he had come to stand high indeed among the nation's Revolutionary heroes. Obviously a common stone slab would no longer do. Thus, in a flurry of unaccustomed extravagance the Vermont Legislature appropriated $2,000 to provide something more suitable.

By 1858, the new monument was ready. It was a handsome piece from top to bottom—a column of native granite, forty-two feet high—and to help make sure that it was properly erected, a committee was assigned the job of determining the exact location of Ethan's grave. Despite a careful excavation of the site and much of the surrounding area, however, not even the faintest trace of General Ethan Allen could be found, a fact that explains why the inscription at the base of the column reads:

Vermont to Ethan Allen, born in Litchfield Ct.,
10th Jan AD 1737
Died in Burlington Vt 12th Feb 1789 and buried *near*
the site of this monument. (Italics mine.)

The mystery of Ethan Allen's missing remains continues unsolved. It doubtless always will, thereby giving rise to endless speculation among those who concern themselves with such matters. All of this, of course, would have pleased Ethan immensely, for he was a man inordinately fond of speculation, be it in politics, philosophy, or land. And as for his going to Hell—if indeed there were such a place—it is not likely that he would have been unduly upset by the thought of it. He was, after all, a person of rare parts who time and again during his lifetime had amply demonstrated that he could get by tolerably well under just about any conditions, and there would be no reason for him to suppose that he would not be able to do the same in the next world, regardless of the climate. In fact, given his uncommon enterprise and energy, and a powerful capacity for winning over the affection and support of others, he could very well end up in a position of high preferment there. In time he might even find himself in charge of things, just as he had been during those critical years on the New Hampshire Grants when, beset by great adversity and sometimes desperation, the State of Vermont was born.

# Notes on Sources

## I. APPRENTICESHIP IN LITCHFIELD COUNTY

There are two rather detailed works on Allen genealogy: Allen, O. P., *The Allen Memorial* (Palmer, Massachusetts: C. B. Fiske & Company, 1905); and Spargo, John, *Notes on the Ancestors and Immediate Descendants of Ethan and Ira Allen* (Bennington, Vermont: n.p., 1948). Neither is free of error, but both are accurate in the main. Much about life in Litchfield and Cornwall during Ethan Allen's youth can be found in the town records, especially the land records, in which the name of Allen is a frequent entry. For general background description of Litchfield County at this time, see: Cothren, William, *The History of Ancient Woodbury* (Waterbury, Connecticut: Bronson Brother, 1854); and Starr, Edward, *A History of Cornwall* (Cornwall, Connecticut: n.p., 1926).

Interesting information on frontier Connecticut can also be found in Volume I of: Beardsley, E. E., *A History of the Episcopal Church in Connecticut* (Cambridge, Massachusetts: Riverside Press, 1874). Occasional reference to Joseph Allen, Ethan, and Ethan's brothers and sisters during this early period is made in Ira Allen's autobiography which appears in Volume I of: Wilbur, James H., *Ira Allen, Founder of Vermont* (Boston: Houghton Mifflin, 1928). Unfortunately, the early chapters of this autobiography, "with an account of my brothers and sisters," was lost during the early nineteenth century.

For Ethan's brief service in the French and Indian War, see: *Connecticut Historical Society Collections,* IX (1903). Most of what is known of Ethan's life in Salisbury comes from the Salisbury Judicial Records, and from the land records of Salisbury and Cornwall. The story of the Lakeville Iron Works is told in: Rudd, Malcolm, *An Historical Sketch of Salisbury* (New York: n.p., 1899); and Smith, C. P., *The Housatonic: Puritan River* (New York: Rinehart, 1946). Ethan's own account of the inoculation incident and the subsequent blasphemy charges can be found in the Ethan Allen Papers. These papers, found in the office of the Secretary of State in Montpelier, are a hodgepodge assortment of various types of materials, including mainly transcripts of the badly charred Stevens Collection at the New York State Library in Albany, and the manuscript records of the Vermont Board of War. On the whole they are not very impressive, either in quality or quantity, but they represent the nearest thing there is to a significant body of Ethan Allen manuscripts. The best accounts of Ethan's relations with Thomas Young are in: Edes, Henry H., "Memoir of Dr. Thomas Young," in *Publications of the Colonial Society of Massachusetts,* XI (1906–1907); and Caldwell, Renwick K., "The Man Who Named Vermont," in *Vermont History,* XXVI (October, 1958).

## II. TROUBLE ON THE GRANTS

By far the best account of the evolution of the Grants controversy is: Jones, Matt, *Vermont in the Making* (Cambridge, Massachusetts: Harvard University Press, 1939). Many relevant documents are contained in the appendices of this excellent work. Also useful, especially for its Yorker point of view, is: Fox, Dixon Ryan, *Yankees and Yorkers* (New York: New York University Press, 1940). Most of the major documents pertaining to the early stages of the Grants controversy can be found in one or more of the following: Slade, William (ed.) *Vermont State Papers* (Middlebury: J. W. Copeland, 1823); Volume IV of O'Callaghan, E. B. (ed.) *Documentary History of the State of New York,* four volumes (Albany: Charles Van Benthuysen, 1851); Volume II of Labaree, Leonard (ed.) *Royal Instructions to the British Colonial Governors,* two volumes (New York: D. Appleton-Century Company, 1935)—See especially Volume II, 542, for specific instructions to New Hampshire on the granting of land; Volume III of *Laws of New Hampshire* (Bristol: Musgrave Printing House, 1915); and Volume I of *Vermont Historical Society Collections* (Montpelier: Vermont Historical Society, 1870), which contains much significant information on military grants, quit rents, and confirmation fees.

For an interesting view of the attitudes of one of the principal participants in the Grants controversy, see the letter book of Governor Colden in Volume IX of *New York Historical Association Collections.* This contains the best account of the Breakenridge affair. See also Volumes III and X of the same series for material in support of New York's position. Especially useful because of its information on the Wentworth proprietors' response to the Yorker threat are: Allen, Ira, *The Natural and Political History of the State of Vermont* (London: J. W. Myers, 1798); and Wilbur, *Ira Allen,* in which the author sees the controversy as stemming mainly from political rather than land-title differences.

Information on migration from Connecticut onto the Grants can be found in: Morrow, R. L., *Connecticut Influences in Western Massachusetts and Vermont* (New Haven: Yale University Press, 1934); and Goodrich, John E., "Immigration to Vermont," in *Vermont Historical Society Proceedings* (1908–1909). Descriptive material on the life and labor of the early settlers is given in: Wilson, Harold, *The Hill Country of Northern New England* (New York: Columbia University Press, 1936); Stillwell, L. D., "Migration from Vermont," in *Vermont Historical Society Proceedings,* V (June, 1937);

and Volume III of Dwight, Timothy, *Travels in New England and New York,* four volumes (London: William Baynes & Son, 1823). Also useful for its description of the early flora and fauna is the oldest and in some ways still the best history of Vermont: Williams, Samuel, *Natural and Civil History of Vermont* (Walpole, New Hampshire: Thomas & Carlisle, 1794).

For Ethan's whereabouts after the sale of the ironworks, see: Cothren, *Ancient Woodbury;* Tercentenary History Committee, *The Northampton Book* (Northampton, Massachusetts: Tercentenary Committee, 1954); and Clark, Solomon, *Antiquities, Historicals and Graduates of Northampton* (Northampton: Gazette Publishers, 1882). The exact time of Ethan's move to Sheffield cannot be determined because of a gap in the town records. As for his time of arrival on the Grants, in the summer of 1773 Ethan himself mentioned having been on the Grants "these seven years." (See below, notes for Chapter IV).

An interesting comment on Ethan's bent for leadership is given in: Thompson, Zadock, *History of the State of Vermont* (Burlington: Chauncey Goodrich, 1842). Some of Thompson's information came to him through interviews with persons who had known and associated with the Allens. On Ethan's trip to Portsmouth and New Haven, see mainly Ira's *History.*

Oddly enough, no mention is made of the ejectment trials in Lawrence Gipson's biography of Ingersoll. Information on the trial and the scene following in the tavern is included in Ira's *History* and in Ethan's pamphlet: *A Vindication of the Opposition of the Inhabitants of Vermont to the Government of New York* (Dresden, New Hampshire: Alden Spooner, 1779).

### III. YANKEES *vs.* YORKERS

On the Bennington Convention and the formation of the Green Mountain Boys, see Volume I of *Vermont Historical Society Collections,* and Ira's *History.* There is no adequate biographical treatment of either Remember Baker or Seth Warner, although creditable brief sketches of both have been done for the *Dictionary of American Biography* by Gilbert Doane and Edward Curtis respectively. Informative but incomplete and often suspect are: Baker, Ray Stannard. "Remember Baker," in *New England Quarterly,* IV (October, 1931); Harriman, W., "Seth Warner," in *Granite Monthly,* III (October, 1879); and, Chipman, Daniel, *Memoir of Colonel Seth Warner* (Middlebury, Vermont: L. W. Clark, 1848).

Many of those stories of Ethan's great strength and stamina were told by Ira to the historian Samuel Williams: See Ira Allen to S. Williams, June 6, 1795, in Ethan Allen Papers, Montpelier. Interesting comments on the bloodlessness of the Grants controversy appear in Dixon Ryan Fox' frequently biased *Yankees and Yorkers,* in which New York is given credit for "great humanity, good sense, and self-restraint."

On the conventions see: *Vermont Historical Society Collections,* I; and, Ira's *History.* Firsthand accounts of the Green Mountain Boys' harassment of Yorkers and their defense of James Breakenridge are given in affidavits in: O'Callaghan, *Documentary History of New York,* IV. See also: William Cockburn to James Duane, September 10 and 17, 1771, in Ethan Allen Papers, Montpelier; and Robert Yates to James Duane, July 20, 1771, in Duane Papers, New York Historical Society, New York City. The land records of Cornwall and Salisbury tell of Ethan's sale of property at this time in Litchfield County.

Information concerning his land dealings on the Grants comes largely from the painstaking work of John Pell who, in gathering material for his *Ethan Allen* (Boston: Houghton Mifflin, 1929), examined the land records of several of the west-side towns. His findings are of great value. They are far from complete, however, for many of the early town records are no longer extant, including most of those for Poultney. Some information on early Poultney can be found in: Joslin, J. (ed.), *A History of Poultney, Vermont* (Poultney: Journal Printing Office, 1875). Despite Pell's conclusion to the contrary, it appears that the Poultney house purchased by Ethan was bought for somebody else, probably Heber.

For Ethan's adventures and misadventures in the wilds, see Ira's account in Ethan Allen Papers. The story of the expulsion of the Yorkers from Rupert is told in affidavit in O'Callaghan, IV. For Munro's letter to Governor Tryon (November 6, 1771), and the governor's proclamation, see again O'Callaghan, IV.

## IV. A POSTURE OF DEFIANCE

For the New Year's celebration see the deposition of Benjamin Gardner before Justice Munro, undated, in Ethan Allen Papers. The Benjamin Buck affair is described by Buck himself in O'Callaghan, IV. Ethan's counter-reward may be found in the original in the Duane Papers, New York Historical Society. An account of Remember Baker's capture and recapture is given by Munro in his letter to Duane, March 28, 1772, in Ethan Allen Papers. Ethan's version appears in the *Connecticut Courant,* June 2 and 9, 1771.

Justice Munro's views on the Yankees are contained in letters to Duane, dated April 20, July 9, and August 17, 1772, all in Ethan Allen Papers. Benjamin Spencer's comments on harassment are given in his letters to Duane, April 11 and May 22, 1772, also in Ethan Allen Papers. The Warner–Munro confrontation is described in: Joslin (ed.), *Poultney.*

The story of Governor Tryon's "invasion" and Ira Allen's role in the affair is told by Ira himself in his *History.* For documents pertaining to the rise and fall of the Tryon truce, including the Cockburn affair and the ousting of the Jerseyites, see: Slade, *Vermont State Papers.*

An account of the formation of the Onion River Company is given in Ira's *History,* and more elaborately in Wilbur's *Ira Allen.* Copies of original documents pertaining to the Burling purchase, and also the important transaction with Thomas Chittenden and associates, can be found in the Ira Allen Papers, Burlington. A detailed account of Ethan's ousting of the Scots from New Haven is given in O'Callaghan, IV. For the assets of the Onion River Company at the time of the outbreak of the Revolution, see copies of company records in Wilbur's *Ira Allen,* II, Appendix.

### V. THE ENFORCER

A record of lands granted by New York at this time appears in: Nye, Mary (ed.), *New York Land Patents Covering Lands within the State of Vermont,* in *State Papers of Vermont,* VII (Montpelier: State of Vermont, 1947). See also: *Vermont Historical Society Collections,* I. An excellent account of New York's half-fee policy and the Wentworth response is given in Matt Jones' *Vermont in the Making.*

For the Green Mountain Boys' chastisement of Benjamin Spencer and the Durhamites, see the deposition of Charles Button, November 30, 1773, in Ethan Allen Papers; and, Ira's *History.* The story of Benjamin Hough is best told in a deposition by Hough himself, March 7, 1775, a copy of which is in the Ethan Allen Papers. The Andrew Graham incident is related in: Hoyt, Edward (ed.), *State Papers of Vermont,* VIII (Montpelier: State of Vermont, 1952).

Documents pertaining to the reward increase and the Outlawry Act appear in: O'Callaghan, IV; and Slade, (ed.) *Vermont State Papers.* Ethan's reaction can be found in the *Connecticut Courant,* June 8 and 21, 1774. Information on the Manchester conventions of April, 1774, and February, 1775, is available in: *Vermont Historical Society Collections,* I; Ira's *History;* and, Crockett, Walter H. (ed.), *State Papers of Vermont,* IV (Bellows Falls: Windham Press, 1932). For an account of the Sheffield meeting of the Onion River Company, see Pell, *Ethan Allen.*

Information concerning the Westminster riot and its effects on the Grants controversy can be found in Slade; Ira's *History;* and Governor Colden's Letter Book in Volume IX of *New York Historical Association Collections.* An account of the Westminster convention appears in: Walton, E. P., *Records of the Council of Safety and Governor and Council of the State of Vermont,* I (Montpelier: J. M. Poland, 1873). For Major Skene and his plans for a separate province, see Ira's *History,* and Pell's *Ethan Allen.*

## VI. A FORTRESS FALLS

Comments by Ethan on his decision to join the Patriot cause appear in his: *Narrative of Colonel Ethan Allen's Captivity . . .* , published in several editions from 1779 to the present; and, his previously cited *Vindication of the Opposition of the Inhabitants of Vermont to the Goverment of New York. . . .* For New York's earlier requests for regular troops to be used against the Grants, see Colden Letter Book in *New York Historical Association Collections,* IX.

Interesting accounts of the origins and strategic importance of Fort Ticonderoga appear in Francis Parkman's beautifully told *Montcalm and Wolfe,* two volumes (Boston: Little Brown, 1898); and Volume I of Justin Smith's not always reliable *Our Struggle for the Fourteenth Colony* (New York: G. P. Putnam's sons, 1907). Conditions at the fort and its dependencies on the eve of the Revolution are well described in: French, Allen, *The Taking of Ticonderoga in 1775: the British Story* (Cambridge: Harvard University Press, 1928), which contains the full report of Lieutenant Jocelyn Feltham; and Hamilton, Edward P., *Fort Ticonderoga: Key to a Continent* (Boston: Little Brown, 1964).

The meeting between Parsons and Arnold is given in Samuel Parson's letter to Joseph Trumbull, June 2, 1775, in *Connecticut Historical Society Collections,* I (Hartford: Connecticut Historical Society, 1860). Military events leading up to the attack on Ticonderoga are described in detail by two important participants in the journals of Edward Mott, *Connecticut Historical Society Collections,* I; and Epaphras Bull, *Bulletin of the Fort Ticonderoga Museum,* VII–2 (July, 1948).

Most of what is known about Ethan's planning and the capture of Ticonderoga comes from: the aforementioned Journals of Edward Mott and Epaphras Bull; the official report of Lieutenant Feltham to his superiors (see French, *Ticonderoga*); and Ethan's *Narrative*. The comments of another participant, Private Hinman, were apparently written down many years after the event and are somewhat suspect. A typescript copy of the Hinman manuscript can be found in the uncatalogued manuscript material at the Vermont Historical Society in Montpelier.

See also Benedict Arnold's Memorandum Book in *Pennsylvania Magazine of History and Biography,* VIII (1884). Although there is a considerable amount of conflict of fact and viewpoint among these accounts, the weight of evidence favors Ethan's version over Arnold's on the matters of command, troop behavior, etc.

## VII. ON TO CANADA!

The capture of Crown Point and Skenesboro is described in Volume I of Smith's *Struggle for our Fourteenth Colony,* and somewhat differently in:

Clinton, George, *Public Papers,* I (New York: State of New York, 1899). An accounting of the prisoners, cannons, etc., seized at Ticonderoga and Crown Point appears in Lieutenant Feltham's report, and in the detailed inventory by Benedict Arnold in his letter to the Massachusetts Committee of Safety, May 19, 1775, in: Clark, W. B. (ed.), *Naval Documents of the American Revolution,* I (Washington: U.S. Navy Department, 1964).

The behavior of the troops after the fort's capture is described in Feltham's report, Arnold's Memorandum Book, and Ethan's *Narrative.* For Arnold's reaction and treatment, see again his Memorandum Book; his letter to the Massachusetts Committee of Safety, May 11, 1775, in Force, Peter (ed.), *American Archives,* Fourth series, II (Washington: Clark & Force, 1839); and especially, Barnabas Deane to Silas Deane, June 1, 1775, in *Connecticut Historical Society Collections,* I.

Ethan's "commission" appears in Mott's Journal. His letters to Congress, the legislatures of the nearby colonies, and the Albany Committee of Correspondence may be found in one or both of the following: Force, Fourth series, II; and Clark (ed.), *Naval Documents,* I. For British military strength in Canada at this time, see: *A History of the Organization, Development and Services of the Military and Naval Forces of Canada* II. Edited by the Historical Section of the General Staff: (London, 1919–20).

Information on the campaign against St. John's is given in: Benedict Arnold's aforementioned letter to the Massachusetts Committee of Safety, May 19, 1775; Arnold's Memorandum Book; *Military and Naval Forces of Canada,* II; and, Ethan's letter to Noah Lee, May 21, 1775, in *The Historical Magazine,* III (November, 1859). See also: Bredenberg, Oscar E., "The American Champlain Fleet, 1775–1777," in *Bulletin of the Fort Ticonderoga Museum,* XII–4 (September, 1968).

On continuing difficulties over the question of command, see the following firsthand comments: Elisha Phelps to the Connecticut Assembly, May 16, 1775; and, Barnabas Deane to Silas Deane, June 1, 1775. Both these letters are in *Connecticut Historical Society Collections,* I. See also Ethan Allen to Noah Lee, May 25, 1775, in Miscellany, Houghton Library, Harvard University. Congressional reaction to the capture of Ticonderoga is given in: Burnett, Edmund C. (ed.), *Letters of the Members of the Continental Congress,* I (Washington: Carnegie Institute, 1921); and, also by Burnett, *The Continental Congress* (New York: Macmillan, 1941).

Ethan's reply to Congress is in the Ethan Allen Papers, while his enthusiasm for an invasion of Canada is clearly shown in his letters to the New York Provincial Assembly, June 2, 1775, and to the Massachusetts Congress, June 9, 1775, both of which appear in Force, Fourth series, II. Examples of Ethan's propaganda attempts to win over the habitants and the Indians are found in his letters written to: "the Merchants of Montreal," May 18, 1775; "the Canadians," June 4, 1775, both in Ethan Allen Papers; and, in his letter to the Northern Indians, May 24, 1775, in Trumbull Papers, Connecticut State Library, Hartford.

For Ethan and Warner before Congress, see: U.S. Continental Congress,

*Journals, 1774–1789,* I (Washington: Way & Gideon, 1821); and, *Secret Journals of the Acts and Proceedings of Congress,* I (Boston: Thomas B. Wait, 1821). Hancock's letter to the New York Provincial Congress, June 24, 1775, is in Burnett (ed.), *Letters of the Members of the Continental Congress,* I.

A copy of the resolution of the New York Congress is found in Ethan Allen Papers. For the New York interlude see also Ethan's letter to Jonathan Trumbull, July 6, 1775, in Trumbull Papers. In his letter of July 12, 1775, to Trumbull, Ethan reveals his impatience with Schuyler. His letter of appreciation to the New York Congress, July 20, 1775, is in the Ethan Allen Papers. For his rejection by the town committees see *State Papers of Vermont,* III (part 4), and *Vermont Historical Society Collections,* I.

### VIII. "DAY OF TROUBLE, IF NOT REBUKE"

Ethan's letter of August 3, 1775, informing Governor Trumbull of the action of the Dorset convention is in the Trumbull Papers, Connecticut State Library. For Ethan's offer of service and Schuyler's reaction, see Schuyler to John Hancock, October 5, 1775, in Ethan Allen Papers.

Primary material (mostly correspondence) pertaining to preparations for the invasion and to the move northward can be found in one or more of the following: Force, Fourth series, III; *Naval Documents of the Revolution,* I; and Sparks, Jared (ed.), *Correspondence of the American Revolution,* I (Boston: Little Brown, 1853). Also of value is "Benjamin Trumbull's Journal of 1775," in *Connecticut Historical Society Collections,* VII.

Baker's death is described in the "Journal of James Jeffry," in *Essex Institute Historical Proceedings* (April, 1914). On Ethan's visit among the Indians and the *habitants,* see Sparks (ed.), I (Appendix); and, Force, Fourth series, III.

For his attack on Montreal: Ethan's *Narrative;* Jeffry's Journal; *Military and Naval Forces of Canada,* II; and especially "A Letter from Montreal," September 25, 1775. A photostatic copy of the Montreal letter, with its detailed, eyewitness report of the skirmish and Ethan's capture, is in the Vermont Historical Society at Montpelier.

### IX. CAPTIVITY!

Reaction to Ethan's capture is given in: Seth Warner to Montgomery, September 26, 1775, and Schuyler to John Hancock, October 5, 1775, both in Ethan Allen Papers; also, Brook Watson to William Temple, October 19,

1775, in Sparks, I; and, the aforementioned Journal of Benjamin Trumbull. For Ethan's treatment after capture, see his letter to General Prescott, September 25, 1775, a copy of which is in the Ethan Allen Papers, and Jeffry's Journal in *Essex Institute Proceedings.*

From the time of his departure to England in November, 1775, until his parole in New York a year later, most of what is known, or thought to be known, about Ethan's adventures comes from his *Narrative,* which is not above suspicion. A brief reference to "Nathan" Allen's confinement in Pendennis Castle and attempts to have him "brought up by habeas corpus" appears in: *The Annual Register: A Review of Public Events at Home and Abroad* (London: J. Dodsley, XVIII, 1775).

British attitudes toward Ethan's prisoner status are reflected by remarks made in the House of Lords, March 5, 1776, especially those of the Duke of Richmond and the Earl of Suffolk, in Force, Fourth series, VI. See also Sparks, Jared. "Report on the Exchange of Prisoners during the American Revolution," in *Massachusetts Historical Society Proceedings,* V (1860–2).

The suggestion that Ethan might be purchased is found in Alexander Wedderburn's letter to William Eden, December 27, 1775, in Volume V of the very useful *Fascimiles of Manuscripts in European Archives Relating to America, 1773–1783,* prepared by B. F. Stevens and published in London in 1889–95.

Ethan's *Narrative* account of the Cork incident is more or less verified by "A Letter from Cork to a Gentleman in Philadelphia," January, 1776, a copy of which is in the Ethan Allen Papers. Ethan's "thank you" note appears in Force, Fourth series, IV. Conditions at Halifax are described in an angry letter from Ethan to Governor Trumbull, August 12, 1776, in Force, Fifth series, I.

For Ethan's brief stay as a parolee on Manhattan, see the sketchy but nonetheless valuable comments of another parolee in: Sabine, William (ed.), *The New York Diary of Lt. Jabez Fitch* (New York: Colburn & Tegg, 1954); also Ethan's letter to General Washington, November 2, 1776, in Ethan Allen Papers. Captain Alexander Graydon's comments on Ethan appear in Graydon's *Memoirs of His Own Time . . .* (Philadelphia: Lindsay & Blakiston, 1846).

Information on the long period of parole at New Lots, about which Ethan himself unaccountably says virtually nothing in his *Narrative,* may be found in Charles Huguenin's very useful article, "Ethan Allen, Parolee on Long Island," in *Vermont History,* XXV (April, 1957). Additional material is in Fitch's *Diary,* from which Huguenin draws heavily. The order of August 25, 1777, by Commissioner of Prisoners Joshua Loring, to seize Ethan for breaking parole may be found in the New York Historical Society. See also Fitch.

Congress' resolution, December 2, 1775, directing General Washington to work toward Ethan's exchange is in: *Journals of the Continental Congress,* I. Subsequent correspondence pertaining to Ethan's exchange may be found in

Force, Fourth series, IV—Fifth series, II; and Sparks (ed.), *Correspondence*, I and II.


## X. RETURN OF THE HERO

Information concerning Ethan's request for a commission is found in: Washington to President of Congress, May 12, 1778, in Fitzpatrick, John (ed.), *Writings of George Washington*, XI (Washington: U.S. Government Printing Office, 1934); *Journals of the Continental Congress*, II and III; and Ethan's letter to Washington, May 28, 1778, photostatic copy in Vermont Historical Society. See also Gouverneur Morris to George Clinton, September 28, 1778, in Burnett (ed.), *Letters of the Members of the Continental Congress*, III, in which Morris claims credit for blocking Ethan's attempts to obtain a regular commission.

The circumstances of Heman's illness and death and of Ethan's belated arrival in Salisbury are given in: Albert Wadhams to———, May 13, 1878, in Allen Family Miscellaneous Papers, Connecticut State Library, Hartford.

Documents pertaining to the formation of independent Vermont are plentiful and accessible. Especially useful are: *Journals of Continental Congress*, II; Burnett (ed.), *Letters*, III; and *Vermont Historical Society Collections*, I. Material of interest may also be found in the Ira Allen Papers, University of Vermont.

Ethan's homecoming is described by the hero himself in his *Narrative*. The extent of Ira's power in the government at this time is made clear by references in: Walton (ed.), *Records of the Governor and Council*, I, and Wilbur's *Ira Allen*. Interesting observations on Ethan's rapid ascendancy after his return from captivity are given in: Wardner, Henry, *The Birthplace of Vermont* (New York: Scribner's, 1927).

The story of the lost children is told in: Hemenway, Abby Maria (ed.), *Vermont Historical Gazeteer* (Burlington: A. M. Hemenway, 1867, I). For Ethan's part in the execution of Redding, see Walton (ed.), *Records,* and Slade (ed.), *Vermont State Papers.*

Material relating to confiscation and Ethan's part in it may be found in abundance in: Slade (ed.), *Vermont State Papers;* Walton (ed.), *Records of the Governor and Council,* I; and especially in: Nye, Mary (ed.), *Sequestration, Confiscation, and Sale of Estates,* in *State Papers of Vermont,* VI (Montpelier: State of Vermont, 1941). See also Ira's *History,* and Ethan's letter to "Oratio" Gates, July 15, 1778, in Duane Papers, New York Historical Society. For Clinton's reaction and his altercation with Stark, see: Clinton, *Public Papers,* III; and, Fitzpatrick (ed.), *Writings of Washington,* XII.

Information on Levi's alleged Toryism and his feud with Ethan is in:

Slade, Walton, I; and, Nye (ed.), *Sequestration.* See also *Connecticut Courant,* February–August, 1779, *passim;* and, Levi Allen to S. Hitchcock, April 29, 1800, in Ethan Allen Hitchcock Papers, Vermont Historical Society. Ethan's official complaint against Levi, dated January 9, 1779, is in Slade. The Salisbury Judicial Records and the Allen Family Miscellaneous Papers, Connecticut State Library, contain material on the settling of Heman's estate.

The angry exchange between Ethan and Governor Clinton is well documented in Walton, I. Andrew Elliott's report to his superiors, the original of which is in the Stevens Papers in the New York State Library, is quoted at length in Pell's *Ethan Allen.*

## XI. COURTSHIP WITH CONGRESS

Documents and correspondence pertaining to Vermont's persistent attempts at recognition and congressional reaction are conveniently accessible in the appropriate volumes of *Journals of the Continental Congress,* and Burnett (ed.), *Letters;* also, Clinton, *Papers,* especially IV and V.

For the establishment and dissolution of the Eastern Union, see: *Assembly Journals,* in *State Papers of Vermont,* III; Slade (ed.), *Vermont State Papers;* Walton (ed.), *Records of Governor and Council,* I; *New Hampshire State Papers,* X; and, Ira's *History.* Ethan's report to the Windsor Assembly and his vouchers for the trips to Philadelphia may be found in the Ethan Allen Papers. His letter to Weare is in Walton (ed.), I.

Chittenden's order to Ethan, along with a description of the unrest in Cumberland County, appears in Walton, I. Information on the east-side expedition and its aftermath abounds in letters to Governor Clinton from Eleazar Peterson (May 5, 1779), Samuel Minott (May 25), and Micah Townsend (June 9), all in Clinton, *Papers,* IV. See also Ira's *History,* and the interesting and useful article by John Alden, "Financing Ethan Allen," in *Vermont Historical Society Proceedings,* VI (March, 1938). Ethan's expense vouchers for the expedition are in the Ethan Allen Papers. His election to militia command is recorded in *Assembly Journals,* in *State Papers of Vermont,* III.

Clinton's reaction to the Cumberland County affair is revealed in his letters to President of Congress John Jay, May 29 and June 7, 1779, in Walton, I; and his letter to Washington, June 7, 1779, in Fitzpatrick, XV. For Congressional reaction to Ethan's east-side campaign, including the appointment of the investigation committee, and for Ethan and Jonas Fay in Philadelphia, see: *Journals of Continental Congress,* III; Burnett, IV; and Clinton, *Papers,* V.

## XII. FLIRTING WITH TREASON

Arguments favoring the reassertion of New Hampshire's claims to the Grants are given in the letters of William Whipple to Josiah Bartlett, June 21 and August 3, 1779, and Nathaniel Peabody to M. Weare, October 26, 1779, all in Burnett, IV. See also Ira's *History;* and, for Massachusetts' claims, Denio, Herbert, "Massachusetts Land Grants in Vermont," in *Colonial Society of Massachusetts Publications*, XXIV (1920–22). Congress' restraining resolution is in *Journals of the Continental Congress*, III. Vermont's response is best summarized by Ira in his *History*. The Manchester resolution appears in: Crockett, Walter (ed.), *Reports of Committees to the General Assembly*, in *State Papers of Vermont*, IV (1932).

For land grants and Ethan's involvement, see: Nye, Mary (ed.), *Petitions for Land Grants*, in *State Papers of Vermont*, V (1939); and *Index to the Papers of the Surveyor-General*, in *State Papers of Vermont*, I (1918). Information on Vermont's generous land policy toward important outsiders is contained in Walton, II. For Ethan's misadventure in Massachusetts, see: Clinton, *Papers*, V; and James Duane to Robert Livingston, January 24, 1780, in Duane Papers, New York Historical Society.

Many of the problems of frontier defense are referred to in the Records of the Board of War in Ethan Allen Papers. See also Slade and Walton, and Ira's *History*. During the twelve months following the close of the Bennington commissary, Vermont purchased two and a half tons of gunpowder from Connecticut alone. See especially Chittenden to Trumbull, November 23, 1780, in Trumbull Papers, Connecticut State Library.

Information on the origins of the Haldimand conspiracy appears in the following letters: Henry Clinton to William Eden, October 12 and December 24, 1778, in Stevens, *Facsimiles*, V; and George Germain to Clinton, March 3, 1779, in Van Doren, Carl, *The Secret History of the American Revolution* (Viking, 1941). Clinton's attempts to make contact with Ethan are revealed in his letters to Eden, October 10 and December 11, 1779, in Stevens, *Facsimiles*, X.

On Ethan's reported presence in New York, see Washington to James Mercereau, July 12, 1780, in Fitzpatrick, XIV. Schuyler's instructions to the investigators are contained in his letter to John Lansing, July 12, 1780, in the New York Historical Society. A copy of Beverly Robinson's letter to Ethan may be found in the Ethan Allen Papers.

For interesting comments on the nature of the Haldimand affair and how succeeding generations of Americans, and especially Vermonters, came to view it, see: Payne, J. L., "Curious Chapter in the History of Vermont," in *Magazine of American History*, XVII (1887). The standard interpretation of the Haldimand negotiations appears in *Vermont Historical Society Collections*, II. A decidedly anti-Allen version is contained in Henry Wardner's excellent article, "The Haldimand Negotiations," in *Vermont Historical Society Proceedings,* II, new series (1931).

### XIII. THE HALDIMAND AFFAIR

Most of the manuscripts pertaining to the Haldimand conspiracy are in the following collections: the Lord George Germain Papers and Sir Henry Clinton Papers, in the William L. Clements Library, University of Michigan; the Lord Dorchester (Sir Guy Carleton) Papers, in Public Record Office, London; and, series B and Q of the Public Archives of Canada, Ottawa. However, all of the more significant items, and many not so significant, have been extracted from these worked-over collections and made available in a multitude of primary and secondary published works.

The most useful of these are: *Vermont Historical Society Collections,* II; Stevens, *Facsimiles;* Wardner, H. S., "Journal of a Loyalist Spy Justus Sherwood," in *The Vermonter,* XXVIII (1923), and by the same author the aforementioned "Haldimand Negotiations," in *Vermont Historical Society Proceedings,* II, new series (1931); and Van Doren. *Secret History,* which draws heavily from the Germain and Clinton Papers. See also: Williamson, Chilton, *Vermont in Quandary,* 1763–1825 (Montpelier: Vermont Historical Society, 1949). This contains what is probably the best general treatment of the Haldimand conspiracy.

Chittenden's report of the cartel to the Vermont Assembly and the Assembly's response is given in: *Vermont Historical Society Collections,* II; *Assembly Journals,* III; and, Clinton, *Papers,* VI. For New York's near-recognition of Vermont, see again *Vermont Historical Society Collections,* II; and, Clinton, *Papers,* VI. Material on the establishment of "Greater Vermont" appears in Clinton, VI; *Assembly Journals,* III; and, Walton, II (especially Appendix H). See also Ira's *History,* which contains a particularly interesting account of the reestablishment of the Eastern Union.

A copy of the second Robinson letter is in Ethan Allen Papers. Ethan's letter to Congress (President Samuel Huntington), March 9, 1781, is in the Sir Henry Clinton Papers, Ann Arbor. His confrontation with Warner is described by John Williams in his undated letter to George Clinton, in Clinton, VI. The growing concern of Washington and Schuyler over Vermont's behavior is revealed in the interesting correspondence between the two men in: *Vermont Historical Society Collections,* II. On the return of the Tories to Vermont, see especially Schuyler to Clinton, May 4, 1781, in Clinton, VI.

There is a wide scattering of material on the impeachment attempts against Ethan and his resignation of command, but none of it sheds much light on what actually happened. See mainly: *Assembly Journals,* III; Walton (ed.), *Records of the Governor and Council,* I; and, *Vermont Historical*

*Society Collections,* II. Ethan's strange offer of service to New York appears in his letter to George Clinton, April 14, 1781, in Clinton, VI.

## XIV. VERMONT STANDS ALONE

Material on the negotiations at Ile aux Noix and the subsequent extension of the truce, can be found in: Ira's *History;* Sherwood's "Journal"; *Vermont Historical Society Collections,* II; and, Ira Allen Papers, Burlington. Ethan's concern for his own safety and the need for greater caution is reported by a British agent in a letter to Major Lernault, May 22, 1781, in Ethan Allen Papers.

The best discussion of the terms of reannexation is in A. J. H. Richardson's useful article, "Chief Justice William Smith and the Haldimand Negotiations," in *Vermont Historical Proceedings,* IX (June, 1941). See the same article for a description of the plan of execution, especially Haldimand's letter to Henry Clinton, October 1, 1781, the original of which is in the British Museum.

The Sergeant Tupper affair is best told in Wardner, "The Haldimand Negotiations," and somewhat differently by Ira in his *History.* Ethan's continuing attempts at reannexation are dealt with in Walton (ed.), *Records of Governor and Council,* III; Richardson, "Chief Justice Smith"; Williamson, *Vermont in Quandary;* and Bemis, S. F., "Relations between the Vermont Separatists and Great Britain," in *American Historical Review,* XXI (1916).

The effect of the captured Germain letter on Congress can be seen in Burnett, *Letters,* VI, especially the report of the New York delegation to Governor Clinton, August 7, 1781; also Ira's *History.* Yorker reaction to Congress' August Resolution is revealed in James Duane's letter to Robert Livingston, August 11, 1781, in Burnett, VI. For Governor Chittenden's explanation of Vermont's refusal to come to terms with Congress, see his letter to Washington, November 14, 1781, in Sparks, *Correspondence,* III. There is much firsthand material, mainly correspondence, on the Walloomsac episode in Walton, II, and in Clinton, VII. Washington's letter to Chittenden, January 1, 1782, is in Fitzpatrick, XXIII.

The following letters tell much about Congress' change of heart on the matter of recognizing Vermont: Rhode Island delegation to Governor William Greene, May 7, 1782, and William Floyd to Governor Clinton, May 22, 1782, both in Burnett, VI; also, Jonas Fay, Ira Allen, and Abel Curtis to John Hanson (President of Congress), February 21, 1782, in Ira Allen Papers.

For Governor Clinton's dossier on Ethan, see especially Richardson, "Chief Justice Smith." Detailed accounts of Ethan's east-side expedition appear in the depositions of Joel Bigelow, September 15, 1782, and Thomas Baker and David Lamb, September 9, 1782, all in Ethan Allen Papers. The story of Charles Phelps' appearance before Congress is in Duane's letter to Governor Clinton, October 9, 1782, in Burnett, VI.

## XV. *THE ORACLES OF REASON*

Congress' censure resolution and Chittenden's response are most conveniently found in Slade (ed.), *Vermont State Papers*. The best edition of the *Oracle* is John Pell's (New York: Scholars' Facsimiles and Reprints, 1940).

For comments on the *Oracle*, Ethan's claim to authorship, its reception and impact, see especially the following: Riley, Isaac W., *American Philosophy: The Early Schools* (New York: Dodd, Mead & Co., 1907); Koch, G. A., *Republican Religion: the American Revolution and the Cult of Reason* (New York: Henry Holt, 1933); Morais, H. M., *Deism in Eighteenth Century America* (New York: Columbia University Press, 1934); Schantz, B. T., "Ethan Allen's Religious Ideas," in *Journal of Religion*, XVIII (April, 1938); Doten, D., "Ethan Allen's Original Something," in *New England Quarterly*, XI (June, 1938); Anderson, G. P., "Who Wrote Ethan Allen's Bible?" in *New England Quarterly*, X (December, 1937).

Ethan's problems in financing the book are referred to in Koch and in Ethan's letter to James Caldwell, February 7, 1785, in Miscellaneous Collection, Vermont Historical Society. Ethan's letter to his friend St. John in Paris, March 2, 1786, is in Ethan Allen Papers.

## XVI. EMERITUS

Reference to Fanny Allen's interest in Vermont lands can be found in *Sequestration. . . .*, in *State Papers of Vermont*, VI. Good background material on the Wyoming controversy is provided by: Nevins, Allan, *The American States during and after the Revolution* (New York: Macmillan, 1927).

For Ethan's involvement, see his letters to: W. S. Johnson, August 15, 1785, in Oliver Wolcott, Sr., Papers, Connecticut Historical Society; Zebulon Butler, October 27, 1785, in Pickering Papers, Massachusetts Historical Society; Governor Griswold of Connecticut, April 30, 1786, in Cabell Gwathmey Papers, University of Virginia; and, Stephen Bradley, June 21, 1786, in New York Historical Society. Also, Joseph Hamilton to Z. Butler, April 19, 1786, extract in Pickering Papers; and "An Address From the Inhabitants of Wyoming and others, etc. to the People at Large of the Commonwealth of Pennsylvania," broadside signed by Ethan and others in the Pickering Papers.

Information on the Shays affair can be found in the recently opened Royall Tyler Papers, Vermont Historical Society, and in Walton, *Records of Governor and Council*, III.

For Ethan's land dealings at this time, see Wilbur, *Ira Allen,* I. His financial problems are discussed by Ethan himself in his letters to:————, December 3, 1784, in Fort Ticonderoga Museum; Van Schack, August 5, 1784, in Ethan Allen Miscellany, Vermont Historical Society (copy); and Ira, August 18, 1786, in Ira Allen Papers. See also Ledger of the Catamount Tavern, April to December, 1785, in Bennington Museum; and *Assembly Journals,* III–3.

Copies of Ethan's correspondence with St. John are in Ethan Allen Papers. The action of the Assembly is recorded in *Journals,* III–3.

For descriptive material on Ethan's farm and the Onion River area at this time see the various bills of sale, deeds, etc., in the Ira Allen Papers. The details of the exchange of land between the two brothers are given in a paper dated May 1, 1787. See also Ethan's letter to Stephen Bradley, November 6, 1787, in Ethan Allen Papers.

The *Plenitude,* one of Ethan's less widely published works, appears in its entirety in Pell's edition of the *Oracle.* Information on the brothers' trade with Canada can be found in Williamson, *Quandary;* Bemis, "Vermont Separatists"; and Wilbur, *Ira Allen,* I. Ethan's letter to Lord Dorchester is in the Bemis article. For the effects of the weather upon Ethan's fortunes, see especially his letters to Levi, July 3, 1787, in the Vermont Historical Society, and November 28, 1787, in the New York Historical Society.

The hired man's account of Ethan's death and funeral appeared in the *Burlington Free Press,* March 26, 1943. The story of Ethan's disappearing gravestone is entertainingly told by Stewart Holbrook in his racy and somewhat fictionalized *Ethan Allen* (New York: Macmillan, 1940).

# Index

*Adamant:* 161ff.

Adams, Samuel: 52–53

Alamance, Battle of: 49

Albany ejectment suits: *See* Ejectment suits

Albany, New York: 15, 34ff., 54–55

Allen & Baker Company: *See* Onion River Company

Allen Ebenezer: 56, 329–30

Allen, Ethan: birth of, 2: influence of father, 4; early education, 5; death of father, 5; scholarly inclination, 6, 13ff.; militia service, 7; buys share in ironworks, 7; marries Mary Brownson, 7; operates Lakeville Ironworks, 8–10; land speculation, 9; fracas with Tousley brothers, 10–11; fights with Caldwell, 11; smallpox inoculation, 12; blasphemy charge, 12; drinking habits, 12–13; and Thomas Young, 15–17; works on *Oracles,* 16–17; sells ironworks, 30; at Northampton, 30; settles in Sheffield, 31; visits Grants, 31; organizes Wentworth defense, 31ff.; character traits, 32; visits Portsmouth and New Haven, 32–33; early Grants land purchases, 33–34; comments on ejectment trials, 34, 36; rebukes Duane, 37–38; commandant of Green Mountain Boys, 41; description of, 41–44; strategy against Yorkers, 44–45; use of violence, 45–46; writes for *Connecticut Courant,* 45; defends against Yorkers, 51–52; punishes Dr. Adams, 52–53; drives off Cockburn, 53–54; comments on Breakenridge defense, 56; at Poultney, 56ff.; land purchases, 57–58; drives off Rupert settlers, 58–59; declared outlaw, 59–60; abuses Buck, 61–62; issues counter-reward, 62–63; and Baker's kidnapping, 66; responds to invasion reports, 67ff.; writes to Tryon, 70–71; releases Cockburn, 72; dominates Manchester Convention, 73; replies to Tryon, 73; visits Onion River, 76; joins Onion River Company, 76ff.; visits White Plains, 77; advertizes Onion River land, 78; destroys New Haven settlement, 80–81; punishes Clarendon and Spencer, 86–88; punishes Hough, 88–90; popularity with settlers, 90–91; and "Bloody Act," 92–93; writes *Brief Narrative,* 94–95; at Westminster Convention, 99ff.; and Philip Skene, 100–101; attitude toward Revolution, 103; muster at Castleton, 110; named commandment, 110; controversy with Arnold, 113–14; attacks Fort Ticonderoga, 115ff.; and the Great Jehovah, 118–19; commissioned by Committee of War, 125; informs Congress, 126; and St. John's campaign, 129ff.; surrenders command, 132; urges retention of Fort, 133–34; letters to Canadians and Indians, 135–37; visits Congress, 138; before New York Assembly, 139–40; chafes at Schuyler's slowness, 140ff.; letter to New York Assembly, 142; rejected for command, 142ff.; complains to Trumbull, 143; reasons for rejection, 144ff.; description of, 145ff.; named civilian scout, 146–47; recruits for Montgomery,

Allen, Ethan (*continued*)
150ff.; at St. John's, 151; reports to Montgomery, 152; attacks Montreal, 156; captured, 158–60; on *Adamant,* 161ff.; confinement in England, 162; returned to America, 164ff.; at Cork, 165–66; aboard *Mercury,* 166ff.; at Halifax, 167–68; aboard *Lark,* 169–70; paroled, 170; description of, 171; attempts by British to bribe, 172–73; at New Lots, 173ff.; death of son, 174; violates parole, 174–75; in Provost Jail, 175ff.; exchanged, 176; visits Valley Forge, 177ff.; awarded brevet commission, 179; description of, 180; returns to Grants, 186ff.; assumes leadership, 189ff.; description of, 191–92; and lost children, 192; moves to Bennington, 192; welcomed by Assembly, 194; and Redding hanging, 195–96; oversees confiscation, 197ff.; escorts Tories, 198; feud with Levi, 200–203; inherits land from Heman and Zimri, 204; writes *Animadversory Address,* 205ff.; visits Congress, 212; helps dissolve Union with New Hampshire towns, 211ff.; returns to Congress, 215; writes *Narrative of Captivity,* 216ff.; invades Cumberland County, 221–25; elected General of Militia, 225; final visit to Congress, 227–29; writes *Vindication,* 232; persuades Assembly to defy Congress, 233; and land grants, 233–34; visits Massachusetts General Court, 236; writes *Concise Refutation,* 236–37; compensation from Republic, 237; writes Washington for troops, 238–39; and militia activity, 238; British attempts to win over, 242; reported in New York City, 244; investigated, 245; receives Robinson letter, 246; involvement in conspiracy with British, 247ff.; and Haldimand affair, 253ff.; writes Washington for prisoner exchange, 254; confers with Sherwood, 255ff.; furloughs militia, 258; favors annexing towns, 262ff.; active in Hudson Strip, 264; receives

second Robinson letter, 267; confronted by Warner, 267; letter to Congress, 268; protects Tories, 269; denies misbehavior to Schuyler, 270; impeachment attempts against, 217ff.; resigns militia command, 272; granted land in Easthaven, 272; offers aid to G. Clinton, 273; communicates with Haldimand, 279; pursues conspiracy, 285ff.; favors preservation of Unions, 288; writes *The Present State . . . ,* 289; at Walloomsac, 290; continues Haldimand conspiracy, 293; east-side campaign (1782), 295ff.; returns to Guilford, 300; campaigns for Ira and Chittenden, 300; power declines, 300ff.; writes *Oracles of Reason,* 305ff.; difficulty financing *Oracles'* publication, 310; marries Fanny, 315; children by Fanny, 315; and Wyoming Valley controversy, 317ff.; rejects Shays' offer, 319; moves to Bennington, 320; financial condition, 320–22; friendship with St. John, 322ff.; at Burlington, 324; completes *Essay on Plenitude,* 326; death of, 329; grave and monument, 332–33

Allen, Fanny: 314–15, 320, 325ff.

Allen, Heber: 3, 56, 303

Allen, Heman: description of, 3; role in early Vermont, 3; partner in ironworks, 9–10; fight with Tousley brothers, 9–10; opens store, 30; and Onion River Company, 76ff.; visits White Plains, 77; death of, 180; estate, 203–204

Allen, Ira: description of, 3; chosen to spy on Yorkers, 68; description of, 68–69; early land speculation, 68–69; reports on Cockburn, 72; surveys north country, 75–76; and Onion River Company, 76ff.; visits White Plains, 77; builds road and store, 79–80; and New Haven settlement, 80–81; and founding of Republic of Vermont, 186–87; prospers during war, 188; political offices, 189; urges confiscation, 196; inherits land, 204; land granted to, 234; surveyor-general, 239; and Robinson letter, 246–47; involvement in conspiracy with British, 247ff.; and Haldimand Affair, 253; prisoner exchange, 258–59; annexation of towns, 262; negotiates with British, 275ff.; seeks Canadian trade, 280–81; and Haldimand proclamation, 282–83; obscures Tupper affair, 284; loss of power, 301, 314; sends Ethan money, 321; land transaction with Ethan, 324; at Burlington, 325; trades with Canada, 327ff.; mentioned, 39, 53, 56–58, 95, 225, 232–33, 258, 265, 294

Allen, Joseph (father): 4–5
Allen, Joseph (son): 174
Allen, Levi: 3, 201–203, 327
Allen, Loraine: 8, 303, 312
Allen, Lucy: 3
Allen, Lucy Caroline: 31
Allen, Lydia: 3
Allen, Mary (mother): 2–3
Allen, Mary (wife): 7–8, 31, 181, 188, 221, 303–304
Allen, Mary Ann: 31
Allen, Matthew: 1
Allen, Samuel: 1
Allen, Thomas: 1
Allen, Zimri: 3, 31, 76–78, 180
*Allen's Bible: See, Oracles of Reason*
Ashley, Thomas: 28–29


Baker, Desire: 40
Baker, Ozzie: 40
Baker, Remember: settles on Grants, 30; elected captain, 39; description of, 40; at Rupert, 58–59; declared outlaw, 59–60; kidnapped, 63–64; helps seize Cockburn, 72; drives off Panton settlers, 72; and Onion River Company, 76ff.; visits White Plains, 77; builds store and road, 79–80; and New Haven settlement, 80–81; punishes Spencer, 87; helps seize Crown Point, 122; death of, 150; mentioned, 51, 138, 180, 204
Bancker, Abraham: 244

Banishment: *See* Confiscation
Banishment Act: 197
Bartlett, Josiah: 213
Belknap, Jeremy: 219
Bennington: 22, 26, 29, 31, 36, 67, 109, 181, 193–95, 221, 240, 266
Bennington, Battle of: 145, 265
Bennington Conventions: *See* New Hampshire Grants; *also* Vermont, Republic of
Bennington County: 187, 198ff.
*Bennington Gazette:* 304, 331
Bloody Act: *See* Outlawry Act
Board of War: 238
Bolton, Vermont: 72
Boston, Massachusetts: 236–37
Bradley, Stephen: 224
Braintree, England: 1
Brattleboro, Vermont, 222, 295ff.
Breakenridge, James: 26, 54–55
*A Brief Narrative . . . :* 94–96
British North American Command: *See* Howe, William, *and* Clinton, Henry
Brown, John: 152ff., 157
Brownson, Israel: 30
Brush, Crean: 314
Buck, Benjamin: 61–62
Burgoyne, John: 175
Burlington, Vermont: 72, 79, 325–26

Caldwell, George: 11
Cambridge, Massachusetts: 231
Canaan, Connecticut: 26
Canada: poses military threat, 127; invasion of urged by Ethan, 134; invasion authorized, 139; invasion, 149ff.; proposed Vermont trade with, 280–81; trade with Vermont, 327–28
Canadians: courted by Ethan, 135ff.; attitude toward Revolution, 135ff.; recruited by Ethan, 150ff.; desert Ethan, 157; effects upon of Ethan's capture, 160
Canfield, Thomas: 266
Carillon: 105. *See also* Fort Ticonderoga
Carleton, Guy: 137, 151, 155, 157, 252, 328
Carpenter, Isaiah: 36

Castleton, Vermont: Ethan's land interests, 33; muster of troops, 109–10; defense line, 204, 238; Ethan confers with Sherwood, 255ff.; mentioned, 72, 79

Catamount Tavern: description of, 41; Adams' punishment, 53; Parsons confers with Ethan, 109; mentioned, 38, 56, 61, 67, 94, 140, 187, 194, 321

Caughnawaga Indians: 136ff.

Charlestown, New Hampshire: 283–84

Charlestown Convention: See Vermont, Republic of

Chittenden, Thomas: purchases Grants lands, 78; description of, 78–79, 189ff.; driven from Burlington, 193; orders Ethan to Cumberland County, 222; warned by Congress, 231; involved in conspiracy, 247ff., 253ff.; announces cartel, 258; writes conciliatory letter, 260; receives St. Leger's apology, 283; letter from Washington, 290; dispatches Ethan to east-side, 295; intervenes to save Crowfoot, 293; at Ethan's funeral, 332

Chittenden, Vermont: 324

Clarendon, Vermont: 67, 86–88

Clinton, George: reaction to Vermont independence, 182–83; and Tory banishment, 199–200; recognized Wentworth titles, 205; reacts to Ethan's pamphlet, 206–207; opposes Congress' recognition of Vermont, 208ff.; reaction to Cumberland County disturbance, 226–27; letter to Washington, 227; considers seizing Ethan, 228; blocks recognition, 260–61; dossier on Ethan, 269–70; receives aid offer from Ethan, 273; releases dossier, 294; and Charles Phelps, 299; warned by Franklin, 319

Clinton, Henry: 242–45, 250, 258, 279, 281, 286–87

Cochran, Robert: 54–55, 60–61, 71, 87, 99

Cockburn, William: 53–54, 72

Colden, Cadwallader: 36, 39, 48, 85, 92, 95, 99

Committee of Safety (Vermont): 50, 53, 196. See also New Hampshire Grants

Committee of War (Connecticut): 173

Committee of War (Vermont): 110ff., 125–127

A Concise Refutation of the Claims . . . : 236–37

Confederation Congress: See Congress

Confirmation: 23–25, 51, 84–85

Confiscation: 196ff., 233

Congress: Second Continental Congress opens, 116; informed of seizure of Ticonderoga, 126; reaction to seizure, 132–33; authorizes Vermont regiment, 138–39; authorizes invasion of Canada, 139; efforts for Ethan's exchange, 175ff.; awards Ethan brevet commission, 179; refuses Vermont recognition, 183–208; Ethan visits, 213ff.; committee visits Grants, 227, 230; Ethan and Jonas Fay visit, 227–29; restraining order, 231ff.; defied by Vermont, 233ff.; infected by Vermont land grants, 235; defer action on Vermont controversy, 240; receives intercepted Germain letter, 287; August 20th (1781) resolution, 287–88; withdraws offer of recognition, 291; censures Vermont, 299; remains inactive on Vermont controversy, 300

Connecticut: 27, 208, 16

Connecticut Courant: 14, 15, 66, 78, 188, 202

Connecticut River Valley: 21, 29, 211, 262

Continental Army: 178–79, 182, 235, 238–39

Continental Commissary: See Continental Army

Continental Congress: See Congress

Conventions: See New Hampshire Grants; also Vermont, Republic of

Cork, Ireland: 165–66, 221

Cornwall, Connecticut: 2–8, 29

Cornwallis, Lord: 165, 189, 285

Crèvecoeur, M-G. Jean de: See St. John, Hector

Crowfoot: 293
Crown Point: 121ff., 183
Cumberland County: 98–99, 221ff. *See also* Westminster Massacre

Danville, Vermont: 324
Dartmouth, Lord: 106–107, 120, 151
Decree of 1764: 35, 41, 85
Decree of 1767: 21–25
Deism: 16
Delaplace, William: 117ff., 123–24
Dorchester, Lord: *See* Carleton, Guy
Dorset Convention: *See* New Hampshire Grants
Douglas, Asa: 111
Dresden, New Hampshire: 231
Duane, James, description of, 34–36; role in ejectment trials, 36; visits Ethan, 37–38; mentioned, 46, 53, 63, 65, 95, 235–36, 297
Duke's Charter: 19ff.
Dunmore, Earl of: 48–49
Durham, Vermont: *See* Clarendon
Dwight, Timothy: 310, 331

Eastern Union: established, 210ff.; dissolved, 214; re-established, 262ff.; dissolved, 290; mentioned, 277
Easthaven, Vermont: 272
Easton, James: 108
"Edward Burling and Associates," 77
Ejectment suits: 26–34
Elliott, Andrew: 207
England: *See* Home Government
*An Essay on Universal Plenitude,* 326
Essex, Vermont: 77

Falmouth, England: 162–63
Fay, Jonas: 41, 70–71, 194, 227–29, 236
Fay, Joseph: 41, 194, 198, 258, 278
Fay, Stephen: 39, 41, 70–71, 194
Fay's tavern: *See* Catamount Tavern
Feltham, Jocelyn: 118ff., 124
Fort Ticonderoga: Abercrombie's attack on, 40; description of, 104–106; strategic importance, 107–10; seizure of, 114ff.; spoils, 122ff.; plundered, 124; Congress' reaction to seizure,

133–34; Schuyler makes headquarters, 140ff.; British withdraw from, 183; St. Leger occupies, 282; mentioned, 6, 103
Fort William Henry: 6
Franklin, Benjamin: 287, 318
French and Indian War: 6–7, 27, 40

Gage, Thomas: 117
*Gaspée:* 155, 159ff.
Gates, Horatio: 180, 183, 200, 235
George III: 164, 243, 277
Germain, George: 86, 164–65, 243ff., 250, 257–58, 277, 285–87
Glover, John: 235
Golusha, Elijah: 326
Governor and Council (Vermont): 193, 221, 236, 240–41, 267, 278, 283–84, 302. *See also* Chittenden, Thomas
Graham, Andrew: 90
Grants: *See* New Hampshire Grants
Graydon, Alexander: 171
"Greater Vermont": 268, 280
Green Mountains: 236
Green Mountain Boys: formation of, 39; drive off Cockburn, 53–54; defend Breakenridge farm, 54; drive settlers from Rupert, 58–59; Bennington muster, 61; prepare for Yorker invasion, 68–69; seize Cockburn, 72; drive off Panton settlers, 72; destroy New Haven, 80–81; punish Clarendon, 86–88; punish Hough, 88–90; offer to help Westminster, 99; muster at Castleton, 110; react to Arnold, 110–11; seize Fort Ticonderoga, 115ff.; join in plunder, 124; at St. John's, 129ff.; disband, 131–32; Cumberland County Campaign, 223ff.; mentioned, 268, 317
Green Mountain Regiment, 138–40, 142, 148. *See also* Warner's Regiment
Guilford, Vermont: 222, 296–97

Habitants: *See* Canadians
Haldimand Affair: nature of, 253ff.; Sherwood proposal to Ethan, 255ff.;

Haldimand Affair (*continued*)
truce renewed, 269; Ile aux Noix negotiations, 275–76; terms agreed on, 279ff.; plan of execution, 281; St. Leger moves up lake, 282; after Yorktown, 282ff., 286. *See also* Haldimand, Frederick; *and* Sherwood, Justus

Haldimand, Frederick: opinion on Fort Ticonderoga, 107; description of, 252; strength of command, 255; and Ethan, 256–60; extends truce, 276–78; intended proclamation, 282; reports to Clinton, 279, 281–82; continues conspiracy after Yorktown, 286; lacks enthusiasm for conspiracy, 295

Haldimand negotiations: *See* Haldimand Affair

Halifax, Nova Scotia: 168ff

Halifax, Vermont: 20

Hancock, John: 139, 146, 161

Hand's Cove: 110ff. *See also* Shoreham

Hartford, Connecticut: 96, 240

Hartford Committee of Correspondence: 108–109

Haswell and Russell, Printers: 310

Haswell, Anthony: 310

Hathaway, Simon: 283

Herrick, Sam: 111, 122, 186, 234

Hinsdale, Vermont: 222

Home Government (England): instructions for granting land, 18–19; Duke's Charter, 19; Decree of 1764, 21; Decree of 1767, 24ff.; fails to resolve Grants problem, 44; petitioned by Westminster Convention, 99–100; protects Grants settlers, 102; troops requested by New York, 104; neglects Fort Ticonderoga, 106; attitudes towards Ethan's captivity, 163ff.; plans to win over American leaders, 242ff.; opposed to continuing war, 286; conflicting grants to Wyoming Valley, 316

Hooker, Thomas: 1

Hoosic River: 29

Hough, Benjamin: 88–90

Housatonic River: 7, 29

Howe, William: 170, 172

Hubbardton, Battle of: 265

Hudson Strip: 257, 262ff., 289

Hutcheson, Charles: 59

Ile Aux Noix: 150, 275

Impeachment: *See* Vermont, Republic of; *also* Allen, Ethan

Indians: 136, 150–52. *See also* Caughnawaga Indians

Ingersoll, Jared: 33, 36

Irasburg, Vermont: 324

Jay, John: 232

Jericho, Vermont: 77

Kempe, John Tabor: 37–38, 95, 167

Knickerbocker, John: 204

Lake Champlain: 76, 105, 128ff.

Lake George: 6, 105

Lake Wononscopomuc (Connecticut): 9

Lakeville, Connecticut: 8

Lakeville Ironworks: 7–9

La Prairie: 153

*Lark:* 169–70

Laurens, Henry: 213–14

Lee, Jonathan: 5

*Letters from an American Farmer:* 322

Litchfield, Connecticut: 2

Litchfield County: 6, 15, 29–31, 33, 78

Livingston, Robert: 36

Locke, John: 15, 103

Long Island, Battle of: 170

Longueil Parish: 154

Lossing, B. J.: 312

Lotbinière, Sieur de: 105

Lyon, Matthew: 193

Manchester, Vermont: 67, 73

Manchester Conventions: *See* New Hampshire Grants; *also* Vermont, Republic of

Massachusetts: 132–33, 230–31, 236, 240

Massachusetts Committee of Safety: 112

*Mercury:* 166ff.
Militia: *See* Vermont, Republic of
Montague, James: 167ff.
Montgomery, Richard: 149ff., 160, 265
Montreal: 106, 153ff., 157–58, 164
Mott, Edward: 110, 113, 125
Mount Mansfield, Vermont: 75
Munro, John: 59–66, 87
Murray, John: *See* Dunmore, Earl of

*Narrative of . . . Captivity:* 166ff., 216ff.
Newbury, Vermont: 238
New England: 182, 210
New Hampshire: opposes Union of towns, 211ff.; reasserts claims to Grants, 230–31; presses claims, 240; reaction to Eastern Union, 264. *See also* Wentworth, Benning
New Hampshire claimants: *See* Wentworth Proprietors
New Hampshire Grants: early stages of controversy, 20ff.; early settlement, 28–29; convention of towns, 39–40; population of (1763), 40; condition of settlers, 47; resolutions passed, 50–51; town committees accept truce, 70–71; Manchester Convention supports Ethan, 73; Manchester Convention (1774), 93ff.; Manchester Convention, (1775), 96–97; Westminster Convention, 98–99; attitude toward Revolution, 102; population (1775), 103; Dorset Convention rejects Ethan, 142
New Hampshire towns: *See* Eastern Union
New Haven, Vermont: 80–81
New Huntington, Vermont: 77
New Lots, Long Island: 173ff.
New York City: 34, 70, 88–89, 138–40, 244–45, 322
New York land grants: 22, 24ff., 34, 36, 46, 48–49
New York Province: reacts to Wentworth grants, 19, 21; orders confirmation, 23–24; reacts to Decree of 1767, 25; ejectment suits, 26, 31, 34–36; options for ending Grants controversy, 46–48; land grants, 22, 24ff., 34, 36, 46, 48–49; quality of leadership, 48–50; passes Outlawry Act, 91–92; reacts to seizure of Fort Ticonderoga, 132–33; approves Green Mountain Regiment, 139–40. *See also* Colden, Dunmore; *and* Tryon, William
New York State: threatens to withhold taxes, 240; Hudson Strip included in cartel, 257; Senate recognizes Vermont, 260; reaction to Western Union, 264-65; threatens force against Vermont, 289–90. *See also* Clinton, George
Newton, Isaac: 15, 16, 307
Newtowne, Massachusetts: 1
Northampton, Massachusetts: 30
Northern Department: *See* Continental Army
North, Lord: 285

Ogden, Uzal: 331
Onion River: 75–76, 79–80
Onion River Company: formation of, 76ff.; Burling purchase, 77; land advertized, 78; construction of road and fort, 79–80; extent of holdings, 82; business meeting, 82–83; lands occupied by British, 204; diffusion of ownership, 204; mentioned, 234, 250
*The Oracles of Reason:* 305–11
Otter Creek: 80
Outlawry Act: 91ff.

Paine, Thomas: 216
Panton, Vermont: 72, 80
Parsons, Samuel: 108–109
Peace of Paris (1763): 121
Pendennis Castle: 162–63
Pennsylvania: 316ff.
*Pennsylvania Packet:* 219
Perkins, Nathan: 331
Phelps, Charles: 297–98
Phelps, Noah: 110
Philadelphia: 116, 212–13, 227–29, 291
Pittsfield, Massachusetts: 109
Pittsford, Vermont: 53

Portsmouth, New Hampshire: 18, 32–33
Poughkeepsie, New York: 182, 277, 294
Poultney, Vermont: 29, 33, 54, 56, 66, 76, 303
Prescott, Richard: 158, 164
*The Present State of the Controversy. . . :* 289
Provost Jail: 170
Putney, Vermont: 222

Quit-rent: 21–22

*Reason the Only Oracle of Man: See, The Oracles of Reason*
Redding, David: 195–96
Regulators: 49
Reid, John (Panton): 80–81
Reid, John (Rupert): 59
Rhode Island: 236
Richelieu River: *See* Sorel River
Richmond, Duke of: 163
Richmond, Vermont: 77
Robinson, Beverly: 245ff., 254, 267
Rowley, Thomas: 38
Roxbury, Connecticut: 2, 8, 30, 40
Royalton, Vermont: 255
Rupert, Vermont: 58
Rutland, Vermont: 239

St. John, Hector: 322–24
St. John's: 127ff., 151ff., 241, 257, 259, 275
St. Johnsbury, Vermont: 324
St. Lawrence River: 151
St. Leger, Barry: 282–85
Salisbury, Connecticut: 3, 5, 10ff., 29, 98, 180, 193, 203–204. *See also* Lakeville Ironworks
Saratoga, Battle of: 175, 188, 286
Schuyler, Philip: command of Northern Department, 138n; headquarters at Fort Ticonderoga, 140; slowness of action, 140ff.; reacts to Ethan's rejection, 146; description of, 147–48; delays, 148ff.; illness, 149; on Ethan's capture, 161; investigates Ethan's movements, 244–45; com-

plains of Tories, 269; writes Washington about Vermont leaders, 270
Scotch Highlanders: *See* Rupert
Scurvy: 168
Seven Years' War: 106
Shaftsbury, Vermont: 22, 36, 63, 65, 67
Sharon, Connecticut: 26
Shays, Daniel: 319
Sheffield, Massachusetts: 33, 66, 83, 96, 140
Sherman, Roger: 213, 292
Sherwood, Justus: 255ff., 275ff., 285
Shoreham, Vermont: 110–11
Skene, Philip: 100–101
Skenesboro: 100, 111, 122, 127
Small *vs.* Carpenter: 36. *See also* Ejectment suits
Small, John: 36
*Solebay:* 165–66
Sorel River: 105, 130, 151, 275
South Hero Island: 329
Spafford, Samuel: 273
Sparks, Jared: 92, 312
Spencer, Benjamin: 67, 86–88
Spooner, Alden: 231–32
Stark, John: 198–99, 265–66
Starksboro, Vermont: 324
Staten Island, New York: 176
Stephen Day Press: 231
Sunderland, Vermont: 11, 89, 192, 259, 267, 278–79, 319, 331
Susquehannah Company: 316ff.

Taylor, Eldad: 192
Ten Eyck, Henry: 54–55
Thompson, Daniel Pierce: 42
Thompson, Zadock: 308
Tinmouth, Vermont: 204
Tories (Vermont): 196ff., 233, 269
Tousley, John: 10–11
Tousley, Samuel: 10–11
Town conventions: *See* New Hampshire Grants
Trevelyan, George: 132
Trumbull, Benjamin: 160
Trumbull, Jonathan: 141, 143
Tryon, William: description of, 49–50; named New York governor, 49; com-

ments on Grants unrest, 54; declares Ethan outlaw, 60; proclamation, 61; truce offer, 69–70; withdraws truce offer, 72–75; issues New York patents, 84–85; Outlawry Act, 92; aboard *Mercury*, 167

Tupper, Archelaus: 283–84, 288

Two Heroes Grant: 234

U.S. Congress: *See* Congress

Valley Forge: 177

Vauban, Sebastien: 105

Vergennes, Vermont: 324

Vermont, Republic of: establishment of, 181ff.; military peril, 183; economic hardships, 183–84; internal dissensions, 184–86; Assembly, Bennington session (1778), 193ff.; passes Banishment Act, 197; currency shortage, 196ff.; confiscation of Tory property, 196–97; attempts to obtain recognition, 208ff.; annexes New Hampshire towns, 210ff.; Assembly, Windsor session (1778), 213–14; dissolves union with New Hampshire towns, 214; passes blue laws, 220; puts down Cumberland County disturbance, 221–25; Assembly, Windsor session (1779), 225–26; names Ethan militia general, 225; Congress' restraining order, 231ff.; Assembly, Manchester session (1779), 233ff.; defies Congress, 233ff.; land grants, 233ff.; passes Militia Act, 238; Assembly, Westminster session (1780), 239–40; growing dissension within, 240–41; object of King's interest, 243–44; Treason Act, 249; disbands militia, 258; re-establishes Eastern Union, 262; Assembly, Windsor session (1781), 262; annexes Hudson Strip, 263ff.; Assembly impeachment resolutions against Ethan, 271ff.; Assembly, Bennington session (1781), 271; Assembly, Charlestown session (1781), 283ff.; rejects Congress' conditions for recognition, 288; Assembly, Bennington session (1782), 290–91; dissolves Unions, 290–91; Assembly, Windsor session (1782), 294; puts down east-side disturbance, 295ff.; population growth, 302; increase of Assembly's power, 302; rejects aid to Thomas Young's family, 309; confers citizenship upon Hector St. John, 324; names towns after French leaders, 324; and trade with Canada, 327–28

*Vindication of the Opposition . . . :* 232

Walloomsac River: 289

Walloomsac Tract: 54

Warner, Seth: elected captain, 39; description of, 40–41; at Breakenridge farm, 55; with Ethan at Rupert, 58–59; assaults Munro, 65–66; declared outlaw, 66; helps seize Cockburn, 72; drives off Panton settlers, 72; helps punish Spencer, 87; and Benjamin Hough, 89–90; captures Crown Point, 122; visits Congress, 138; before New York Assembly, 139–40; chosen for command, 142ff.; description of, 145–46; comments on Ethan's capture, 160; record of service, 265–66; wounded, 266; confronts Ethan, 266; death of, 266; mentioned, 30, 183, 212, 238, 249

Warner's Gore, Vermont: 324

Washington, George: siege at Boston, 122; comments on Ethan's capture, 161; efforts for Ethan's exchange, 175–76; receives Ethan, 177; recommends Ethan's commission, 178; orders Tories confined, 200; letter from Clinton, 227; fears corrupting influence of Vermont land grants, 235; orders Schuyler to investigate Ethan, 244; refuses prisoner exchange, 254; comments on Vermont, 270; urges Vermont accept Congress' resolution, 290

Warner's Regiment: 183, 265–66

Weare, Meshech: 211–12, 231

Webster, Alexander: 258

Wentworth, Benning: 18ff., 21

Wentworth, John: 32–33
Wentworth Grants: issued, 18ff.; protested by New York, 21; threatened by Decree of 1764, 21ff.; effect of Decree of 1767, 24ff.; overlapped by Yorker grants, 22, 26; extent of, 46
Wentworth Proprietors: titles threatened, 22ff.; petition King, 24; organize legal defense, 31; determine to resist, 39; petition London, 44; seek support of neighboring colonies, 44–45; granted Tryon truce, 71; resistance weakens, 84ff.
Wentworth titles: 33–34, 205. *See also* Confirmation; *and* Wentworth Proprietors
Western Union: 263ff., 281, 289, 290–91

Westminster, Vermont: 97–99, 315
Westminster Convention: *See* New Hampshire Grants
Westminster Massacre: 98–99
Whipple, William: 215
White Plains, New York: 77, 200
Wilkes-Barre, Pennsylvania: 316
Williams, Samuel: 92
Willow Point: 115
Windsor Conventions: *See* Vermont, Republic of
Woodbury, Connecticut: 150, 266
Wyoming Valley, Pennsylvania: 316ff.

Yale College: 5
Yorktown, Battle of: 189, 285–86
Young, Thomas: 15–17, 304, 308–309, 327